The Fir
King Henry the Fourth

Texts and Contexts

William Shakespeare, *The Taming
of the Shrew: Texts and Contexts*
(The Bedford Shakespeare Series)
EDITED BY FRANCES E. DOLAN,
MIAMI UNIVERSITY

*The Bedford Companion to Shakespeare:
An Introduction with Documents*
BY RUSS MCDONALD,
UNIVERSITY OF NORTH CAROLINA AT GREENSBORO

William Shakespeare, *Hamlet*
(Case Studies in Contemporary Criticism)
EDITED BY SUSANNE L. WOFFORD,
UNIVERSITY OF WISCONSIN-MADISON

The First Part of
King Henry the Fourth

Texts and Contexts

—⟩⟨—

BARBARA HODGDON

Drake University

Bedford Books

BOSTON ≋ NEW YORK

For Bedford Books
President and Publisher: Charles H. Christensen
General Manager and Associate Publisher: Joan E. Feinberg
Managing Editor: Elizabeth M. Schaaf
Developmental Editor: Karen S. Henry
Editorial Assistant: Rebecca Jerman
Production Editor: Maureen Murray
Production Assistant: Deborah Baker
Copyeditor: Jane Zanichkowsky
Text Design: Claire Seng-Niemoeller
Cover Design: Donna Lee Dennison
Cover Art: Costumes from the time of James I, #8d cardplaying scene; details from John
Speed, *Theatre of the Empire of Great Britain,* frontispiece of Coats of Arms; and de-
tail from Coat of Arms of Elizabeth I. All courtesy of the Folger Shakespeare Li-
brary.

Library of Congress Catalog Card Number: 96–86771

1   0   9   8
f   e   d   c   b

For information, write: Bedford Books, 75 Arlington Street, Boston, MA 02116
(617–426–7440)

ISBN: 0–312–13402–9 (paperback)
ISBN: 0–312–16377–0 (hardcover)

Published and distributed outside North America by:

MACMILLAN PRESS LTD.
Houndmills, Basingstoke, Hampshire RG21 2XS and London
Companies and representatives throughout the world.

ISBN: 0–333–69098–2

For Dodge and Jack
History is what you can remember,
And it depends on who tells the story

About the Series

><

Shakespeare wrote his plays in a culture unlike, though related to, the culture of the emerging twenty-first century. The Bedford Shakespeare Series resituates Shakespeare within the sometimes alien context of the sixteenth and seventeenth centuries while inviting students to explore ways in which Shakespeare, as text and as cultural icon, continues to be part of contemporary life. Each volume frames a Shakespearean play with a wide range of written and visual material from the early modern period, such as homilies, polemical literature, emblem books, facsimiles of early modern documents, maps, woodcut prints, court records, other plays, medical tracts, ballads, chronicle histories, and travel narratives. Selected to reveal the many ways in which Shakespeare's plays were connected to the events, discourses, and social structures of his time, these documents and illustrations also show the contradictions and the social divisions in Shakespeare's culture and in the plays he wrote. Engaging critical introductions and headnotes to the primary materials help students identify some of the issues they can explore by reading these texts with and against one another, setting up a two-way traffic between the Shakespearean text and the social world these documents help to construct.

Jean E. Howard
Columbia University
Series Editor

About This Volume

> ✦

The First Part of King Henry the Fourth: Texts and Contexts represents an attempt to put Shakespeare's play in cultural perspective. Recently an increased historical awareness has sharpened our sense that understanding Shakespeare's plays depends on some familiarity with multiple contexts, and this book invites readers to consider Shakespeare's *Henry IV, Part 1* in relation to other texts with similar cultural status and value. Such an approach — which views the play not just as a literary work of art belonging to a unique or special category but as a document marked by the specific historical and cultural conditions prevailing at the time it was written — refuses to make simple distinctions between literature and history, text and context. One aim of this volume is to invite a parallel, or intertextual, reading which decenters the play. This type of reading does not mean, however, that the play disappears; instead, it reappears, looking even richer and more complex than before.

What distinguishes this volume is its collection of a broad range of primary materials: facsimile title pages from a Shakespearean quarto and a chronicle history; selections from chronicle histories, chorographies, political and military treatises, and a conduct book on marriage; maps; drawings; scenes from several non-Shakespearean plays; commentaries on the theatre and the language of London's underworld; excerpts from a popular marty-rology; a portrait of the Earl of Essex as well as photographs of actors who have played Hal, Henry IV, Falstaff, Mistress Quickly, and Doll Tearsheet. These selections offer a partial introduction to the cultures and subcultures of early modern England, and those interested in further exploring a partic-ular text or passage can find complementary or contradictory materials in modern editions, facsimiles, or microfilm versions of the originals.

To a large extent, the choice to reproduce particular documents derives from and is determined by the play: its mixture of official and popular his-tories; its various geographical locales and lines of action, each commenting on the other; its diverse characters, clowns as well as kings and nobles; and its status as a product of an early modern entertainment industry. This choice is also influenced by the issues the play raises, among them the rela-tions between centralized royal authority and several dissident "rebel" fac-tions — including a Northern feudal culture and an equally vital London tavern subculture. Just as these documents help to extend our understanding of *Henry IV, Part 1*'s cultural contexts, they are also tied to the reading and performance histories of Shakespeare's play. The book's six chapters, for in-stance, reflect both traditional and emergent critical perspectives on the play, and the Introduction traces some of the trends in literary study and cultural history that have shaped the critical and cultural destinies of *Henry IV, Part 1* as well as Shakespeare's English history plays. Although it is usual for editions of Shakespeare's plays to include a brief account of its theatrical history from its earliest to its most recent performances, I have chosen in-stead to refer to moments in particular performances both in the Introduc-tion and in subsequent headnotes. For one thing, I want to counter the illusion that performance constitutes a discrete or separate history; for an-other, I want to call attention to performances that are readily available on film or video.

Most chapters offer several kinds of documents, and many are well known to specialist readers, though not as immediately accessible to stu-dents. Examples include the excerpts from Edward Hall's and Raphael Holinshed's chronicles, which are important sources for the histories. Oth-ers, such as the selections from Sir William Segar's *Honor Military and Civil* and the illustrations from *The Beauchamp Pageants,* have rarely been reprinted. In deciding what to include, I not only consulted colleagues but listened to, and usually took, advice offered by readers of a preliminary pro-posal. Certain documents — such as those included in Chapter 1, "Histori-ography and the Uses of History" — were obvious choices. Others, such as the excerpts from William Harrison's *Description of England* and Thomas Dekker's *Of Lantern and Candlelight,* point to areas that Shakespeare's play takes for granted as part of what we would call cultural literacy. Still others, especially the selections from John Dod and Robert Cleaver's *A Godly Form of Household Government* and Joseph Swetnam's *Arraignment,* which document notions about women's position in early modern culture, provide perspectives that Shakespeare's text, with particular ideological consequences, rigorously excludes.

In some cases, I have chosen one text over another for particular reasons. Rather than reprinting excerpts from Erasmus's *Education of a Christian Prince,* for instance, I chose Roger Ascham's *Schoolmaster,* primarily because Ascham was Queen Elizabeth's tutor. I have also included excerpts from a modern prompt copy, for I thought it important to provide an idea of how performance interprets the stage direction "the lady speaks in Welsh" (3.1) and of what the Welsh language looks and might sound like. While some readers will find gaps in these materials, others will think that there are too many; it is probably impossible to agree on an ideal selection of documents, and this collection represents one teacher's idea of what might be useful to readers of this play as well as Shakespeare's other histories.

Although the documents are organized into six chapters, these represent artificial boundaries, and readers may elect to mix and match introductory materials, headnotes, and documents in several ways. Cross-references call attention to relations between chapters and documents, and references to texts other than those reprinted here direct readers, on occasion, to additional materials. Although many readers may wish simply to read these documents, or a particular selection of them, in conjunction with *Henry IV, Part I,* others may wish to make the documents themselves the center of further investigations into historiography or chorography, women's history, the circumstances and practices of the early modern playhouses, or the many faces of chivalry. In either case, the bibliography at the back of this volume provides a list of primary and secondary sources for further study.

EDITORIAL POLICY

In transcribing and editing the texts in this volume, I have used the earliest editions available either on microfilm or in facsimile and have checked one against the other. The one exception involves the selections from Edward Hall's *Union* and Raphael Holinshed's *Chronicles,* which have been set from 1809 and 1807–08 editions respectively, all printed in London by J. Johnson and others. The 1807 and 1808 printings of Holinshed rely on the 1587 edition and restore material "castrated" by early modern censors. For Machiavelli's *Prince,* I have used Edward Dacres's 1640 translation. Since most documents represent selections from longer texts, I have summarized omitted sections in square brackets; in general, the material summarized bears little or no relation to the points in question and consists primarily of classical or biblical authorities and anecdotes cited to support the writer's argument.

Since it seemed desirable to offer readers some experience of an early modern printed text, the short selections from Holinshed's *Chronicles* and William Harrison's *Description of England* ("Of Degrees of People in the Commonwealth of England" and "Of Their Apparell and Attire," published as part of the first volume of Holinshed's *Chronicles*) have not been modernized, except to regularize the letters *u* and *v*. In the case of Holinshed, marginal notations have been preserved. In order to make the rest of the documents, including the longer sections from Holinshed's *Chronicles*, more easily available to readers, the texts have been modernized according to the following principles:

1. Spelling has been modernized and regularized, though with some exceptions. For instance, archaic verb endings (e.g., *-eth*) and plurals have been retained; and while the names of some persons and places mentioned have been changed to reflect modern spellings, others (particularly names not found in the *Dictionary of National Biography* [*DNB*]) appear as in the originals. In the case of obsolete words, I have used the preferred spelling in the *Oxford English Dictionary* (*OED*) wherever possible.

2. Punctuation has been lightly modernized. Because the original texts do not always conform to strict rules of sentence structure, alterations in punctuation attempt to clarify meanings rather than to conform precisely with grammatical technicalities. At times, too, I have created paragraphs in order to break up long sections of text and to emphasize points. Rather than attempting to achieve overall consistency, I have considered each text on its own terms and tried to minimize interfering with its particular conventions. Although no quotation marks appear in the originals to identify what speakers say, I have followed modern conventions in this respect.

3. Italics have been retained as in the original texts.

4. With some few exceptions, capitalization follows that of the original texts. Since the capitalization of words in early modern texts represented one form of emphasis, retaining the old capitalization (as well as italics) helps to preserve traces of the original texts without affecting their clarity. The only changes made involve capitalizing proper nouns or titles (such as *King, Sir,* or *Saint*) and initial words when punctuation changes have created new sentences.

5. Titles of early modern texts have been modernized according to the above principles in both the Introduction and in headnotes. The bibliogra-

phy of primary sources, however, lists titles in their original form, together with printers' names and *Short-Title Catalogue* numbers. (The *Short-Title Catalogue* records all "English" books printed before the close of the year 1640 of which copies exist, either in major libraries or in private collections.) Where modern editions of early modern texts or compilations of official documents, such as Bowen's *Statutes of Wales* and Hughes and Larkin's *Tudor Royal Proclamations,* have been consulted, these also appear under primary sources. In citing sixteenth- and seventeenth-century texts, I have used signature rather than page numbers where appropriate. Signature numbers, a now-obsolete method of pagination, indicate how large pages were folded (into four to create *quarto* volumes, eight to create *octavo* volumes, etc.) and then stitched or "gathered" together to form a book. They include a letter, which identifies all of the pages printed on a single sheet, a number, and in the case of the reverse side of a given page, a *v* for *verso*. To find C4v, you would turn to the C gathering, then count only the right (or recto) pages in each opening until you get to C4 (which might not be marked as such). The back of that page would be C4v.

6. Quotations from other early modern printed texts have also been modernized according to these principles, except for citations from well-known literary works, where the editorial policy of the edition cited has been used. Act, scene, and line references to *Henry IV, Part 1* are from David Bevington's edition, reprinted in this volume. References to other plays by Shakespeare are to *William Shakespeare: The Complete Works,* ed. Stanley Wells and Gary Taylor (Oxford University Press, 1986).

7. In dramatic texts, I have expanded speech prefixes to ensure that readers will recognize who is speaking.

A word about dates. In this period, the year (still reckoned according to the Julian calendar) began not on 1 January but on 25 March (the Feast of the Annunciation, or "Lady Day"). The Gregorian calendar, which makes 1 January the official first day of the year, was not adopted until 1752. Apparent inconsistencies in dates sometimes arise from this feature of the early modern calendar; diaries, letters, and legal documents can be particularly confusing. For example, the date of the Lord Mayor's letter to John Whitgift, the Archbishop of Canterbury, given as 25 February 1591, was actually the year we call 1592. When a document printed here contains such a date, the inconsistency is noted with a slash mark — 1591/92. The date for John Speed's *Theatre of the Empire of Great Britain* and his *History of Great Britain* is also listed as 1611/12, but for a different reason. In this case, although publication information lists 1611, the volumes did not appear until 1612.

I have annotated all the documents in the volume, explaining archaic or obsolete words or word usages in accordance with the *OED*. Foreign words, phrases, and citations not already translated in the original have been translated and, for the most part, identified. In clarifying references to particular persons, events, and place names, I have consulted the *DNB* as well as other standard sources. A few notes point to errors of fact, as in the chroniclers' conflation of two Earls of Mortimer; a few others gloss puns. Since I believe that copious or lengthy notes interrupt a reader's encounter with a text, these notes do not represent a complete scholarly apparatus but are designed to help readers understand and enjoy these documents.

ACKNOWLEDGMENTS

In many ways, a book like this is a collaborative project, and I want to thank those who have helped with this one, to whom I owe deep gratitude.

Staff members at a number of libraries have responded helpfully to my requests at all stages of the process: Cowles Library at Drake University, especially Liege Briedis and Karl Schaefer; the Folger Shakespeare Library, particularly Jean Miller, Elizabeth Walsh, and Laetitia Yaendle; the Shakespeare Centre Library, notably Sylvia Morris and James Shaw; the Shakespeare Institute; the British Library; and the Guildhall Library. The College of Arts and Sciences, the Humanities Center, and the Department of English at Drake University have enabled me to have course release over the past year, for which I thank Dean Ronald Troyer, Jon Torgerson, Joseph M. Lenz, and my colleagues.

Jean Howard read the entire manuscript and made extremely valuable suggestions about downsizing a much larger collection of documents, adjusting emphases, and improving organization. I have also profited immensely from the suggestions of readers, both those who commented on a prospectus and those who provided advice in revising the manuscript. For guidance in choosing materials, I am indebted to all these readers, as well as to Lynda Boose, Albert Braunmuller, Frances Dolan, Miriam Gilbert, David Scott Kastan, Leah Marcus, Russ McDonald, and Phyllis Rackin. I am especially grateful to Carol Rutter, who sought out photocopies of primary documents at a crucial moment; and I also want to thank Barbara Fitton of the Shakespeare Centre Library for translating the Welsh passages and Hywel B. Evans, Terence Hawkes, and Robert Smallwood for clarifications.

My students at Drake University have also helped to shape this volume: some chapters of this book derive from cultural studies seminars, and it gives me pleasure to thank Mark Franciscus, Shari Stenberg, and Jonathan

Shectman especially for teaching me how to help them work with these, and similar, materials.

Throughout, it has been a distinctive pleasure to work with Karen Henry of Bedford Books, who knows how to encourage an author into producing the kind of book she wants. Sensitive to the needs of student readers as well as their mentors, she has not only guided my selections of documents but given meticulous attention to all the details involved in making this book. My thanks also to others at Bedford Books, especially to Maureen Murray, a talented and expert production editor, to Rebecca Jerman for research assistance, to Deborah Baker for production assistance, and to Charles Christensen, the publisher, for supporting the Bedford Shakespeare Series from the beginning. Thanks also to Jane Zanichkowsky for copyediting assistance, to Gail Segal, whose persistence in locating and securing the illustrations made all the difference, and to Lorna Notsch, who helped secure permissions.

The greatest debt I owe, again and once again, is to my partner, Richard Abel, who has read and reread this collection more than twice o'er, dealing kindly and firmly with every word and calling my attention to what I could not see. This book is his as much as it is mine. He knows just how important he is to me, but as Pooh would say, I just want to make sure of that. And so, this time, in public and right there in print: *Je t'aime.*

Barbara Hodgdon
Drake University

Contents

→ 4. The "Education" of a Prince 275

→ 5. Honor and Arms: Elizabethan Neochivalric Culture and the Military Trades 318

Illustrations

The First Part of
King Henry the Fourth

Texts and Contexts

———————————————— ›‹ ————————————————

Introduction

—>*<—

In 1987 a group of actors, dressed not in Elizabethan doublet and hose but in rehearsal gear, walked onto a stage cluttered with an oversized couch and armchair, a standing microphone, and coatracks on which hung medieval armor, Victorian frock coats, Edwardian military tunics, and camouflage fatigues to perform *Henry IV, Parts 1 and 2* and *Henry V* (McMillin 106). Instead of beginning, as the first play does, with Henry IV addressing his court — "So shaken as we are, so wan with care" — they joined together, led by the actor who would play Ned Poins, in song:

> Come all you good people, who would hear a song:
> Of men brave and men bold, of men weak and men strong,
> Of a king who was mighty, but wild as a boy,
> And list to the ballad of Harry le Roy.

"Looking back at now" was how one critic described this English Shakespeare Company staging, which used three of Shakespeare's plays about England's monarchical past to highlight parallels between the conflicts separating London and the provinces — south from north — in Henry IV's era and similar political and socioeconomic conditions in Margaret Thatcher's Britain. "Looking back at now" might also describe Shakespeare's play, for *Henry IV, Part 1* brings forward a past to speak to the

Elizabethan present, weaving together an account of early-fifteenth-century political and military conflicts with scenes drawn from early modern contemporary life to tell a double history.

The great sixteenth-century prose chronicles standing behind all of Shakespeare's histories make England's story that of its monarchs, an emphasis reflected in the titles of his plays. In Shakespeare's earlier English history plays, the deeds — and misdeeds — of the monarch and his nobles are the focal point of the action. But with *Henry IV, Part 1*, the history play embraces a much wider range of characters and takes on a different shape. As the English Shakespeare Company's ballad suggests, it is a coming-of-age story, that of "a king who was mighty, but wild as a boy." Yet in telling that story the play mixes kings and princes with the denizens of a London tavern where the wily, witty Falstaff rules over a community of thieves and pickpockets and where Prince Hal, the heir to Henry IV's throne, drinks, carouses, and even takes part in a robbery. No longer exclusively confined to scenes at court and on English and French battlefields, the play's locales include a castle in Wales, the home of the Percies and Owen Glendower; a roadside inn; and the haunts of London's underworld. Moving back and forth among these varied locations, languages, and communities, the play unfolds several lines of action simultaneously, each commenting on the others. Overall, this strategy creates the illusion of an England that is not identified exclusively with the king's name; far from being a unified entity, it is instead a country made up of discrete geographical territories inhabited by people who speak diverse languages and dialects and who belong to distinctive local cultures and subcultures. *Henry IV, Part 1* tells the story of an emerging nation (Humphreys xxi–xxii; Helgerson).

Shakespeare's historical writing occurs in a transitional period between medieval and modern times and coincides with a widespread interest in recovering the nation's past (see Holderness; Rackin, *Stages*). At a time of rapid social, economic, and political change, the study of recent English history was of particular concern for subjects as well as monarchs, who looked to the past for models that could stabilize and legitimate their status in an emergent nation-state. Following the Wars of the Roses, the new Tudor dynasty commissioned official histories that authorized its reign; one of these, Edward Hall's *Union of the Two Noble and Illustrious Families of Lancaster and York* (1548), does so by linking monarchs' reigns to an overarching design. With Henry Bolingbroke's deposition of Richard II, a ruler with superior statesmanship replaces one with personal and political faults; however, Henry IV's guilt for having deposed a legitimate king (the last to hold office by divine right) contributes to his downfall. His son, the Prince Hal of *Henry IV, Parts 1 and 2*, becomes a model ruler who manages to erase that guilt; but after winning France back for England, Henry V is cut off in his prime, and the "curse" extends to his son, Henry VI, who not only loses France but incurs civil war, raising once again issues of royal legitimacy and succession. Henry VI is replaced by yet another insufficient king, the York-ist Edward IV, whose infamous successor, Richard III, dies at the hand of the Earl of Richmond, the future Henry VII. By marrying the Yorkist princess Elizabeth, Henry VII unites the warring houses of Lancaster and York, bringing the Wars of the Roses to an end and heralding the beginning of the Tudor age. As Hall reaches his own present time, with the reign of Edward VI, his history takes shape as a providential biblical plot, much like the medieval cycle plays that, in dramatizing world history, began with a myth of the Fall, worked through a long process of suffering and penance, and ended with Christ's redemption of mankind. Viewed through this lens, *Henry IV, Part I* takes place in a fallen world, where the monarch and his son must struggle to regain the ideal order and its accompanying sense of legitimacy, which were lost when Henry IV usurped Richard II's throne (Rackin, *Stages* 59–60).

Although this narrative is the dominant one Shakespeare found in sixteenth-century historiography, it is not the only version he could have drawn from Tudor writings, nor is it the only one critics have found in the plays. Moreover, the order in which Shakespeare composed the plays, be-ginning with *Henry VI* and ending with *Henry V,* constructs a more compli-cated story than that of the officially moralized historical record (Kelly 304). In the later plays, *Henry IV, Part I* among them, Shakespeare demonstrates an increasingly self-conscious and skeptical attitude — shaped in part by humanist principles and also by the emergent study of political science — not only toward history's major actors but also toward the processes of his-torical mythmaking (Rackin, *Stages* 34–35, 61). Hall's story of the House of Lancaster differs from that in Raphael Holinshed's *Chronicles* (1587), and Samuel Daniel's *The Civil Wars Between the Two Houses of Lancaster and York* (1595) and *A Mirror for Magistrates* (1559) offer additional, sometimes com-peting, points of view. In *Henry IV, Part I,* Shakespeare draws selectively on all of these texts and, like their authors, chooses to include some materials and exclude others. Whose version is more reliable? There is no answer to that question. Defending his exaggerated tale of dispatching many men at Gadshill, Falstaff asks, "Is not the truth the truth?" It all depends on who is telling the story.

Just as Shakespeare's plays contributed to late-sixteenth-century debates over the idea of history and the interpretive nature of history writing, simi-lar debates have marked their critical history. Writing just after World War II, E. M. W. Tillyard saw Shakespeare's histories as reflecting a universally accepted historical scheme, a Tudor myth of moral order that mimicked an underlying cosmic design. Not only did the plays take England, or *Respublica,* as their central theme, but in them Shakespeare expressed orthodox views shared by everyone in the culture (319). By the late 1960s, however, critics were disputing Tillyard's ideas. Some denied ideology (of any kind) altogether, preferring to see Shakespeare as primarily concerned with universal qualities of human nature and experience. More recent critics, among them Stephen Greenblatt and others belonging to the school of criticism known as new historicism, have argued that Shakespeare's histories did not merely reflect the hierarchical views of his age but that they helped to produce and sustain dominant political theory and practice. For these critics, the plays do not simply mirror ideology but aid in creating it.

New historicism and its British cousin, cultural materialism, have markedly affected critical response to Shakespeare's history plays (see Dollimore and Sinfield; Holderness). For one thing, both schools begin with the assumption that since all written language is rooted in its own time and place, understanding any text, whether a chronicle, a religious tract, a poem, or a play, requires an awareness of the cultural milieu that produced it. For another, both summarily reject the notion that one system of thought prevailed during the period in which Shakespeare and his contemporaries wrote. Whereas such a system might express the culture's dominant *ideology,* and so serve those in positions of power, it could not adequately account for the circumstances of lived experience, nor was it wholeheartedly accepted by everyone. Who, these critics asked, was permitted to speak? And who was silenced? Those who read printed books obviously differed from those who were illiterate; class, occupation, and gender were equally important factors in determining how individuals perceived themselves as cultural subjects. To address these questions as well as others, critics turned to a wide range of social, economic, and political documents — manuals on marriage and courtiership, records of scientific discoveries, treatises on sexuality, ballads about strange marvels, letters and travel diaries, accounts of gardening, cookery books, proclamations governing wages and prices, court records and proceedings, to name a few — in order to reread dramatic and literary texts within a broader cultural context.

Reading a culture's past also, of course, entails the conditions of another culture, that of the critic. Each generation makes or remakes "Shakespeare" in its own image, and the sense readers as well as theatregoers make of his texts depends on the range of interpretive strategies available at any one historical moment. Today, it is easy to see Tillyard as projecting a nostalgic desire for postwar order back into the plays, reading them as antithetic to his own confusing modern cultural milieu. It is perhaps more difficult to see how new historicist critics, living within a postmodern capitalist economy, have turned to an early modern moment of protocapitalism for an explanation of their disillusionment and projected fantasies of (male) power back onto Shakespeare's histories. Similarly, critics subscribing to cultural materialism, feminisms, and queer studies approach early modern texts from oppositional positions: rereading them so as to amplify the voices of the ruled, the exploited, the oppressed, and the excluded, these critics also make use of Shakespeare's plays to rethink and rewrite their own histories. There is, in other words, no "authentic" Shakespeare, no authoritative approach to his plays. Is *Henry IV, Part 1* a record of English history? a pre-text for theatrical performance? a chorography (the art of mapping or describing a region or district)? a document of political theory? a portrait of tavern life in London? a depiction of masculinist codes? It is all of these. Every reader will address the play differently, just as each will read the documents included in this volume differently. This book is designed to supply information as well as contextual material that will enable such differences to appear. By inviting readers to encounter Shakespeare's play in relation to other texts, considered not merely as background or source materials but as having similar cultural status and value, this book also aligns more with the agendas of cultural poetics than with Tillyard's views. The six chapters of this volume, however, reflect both traditional and emergent critical perspectives. And since more recent modes of criticism sustain and reframe those of the past, this introduction points to some of the ways in which readers and performers have configured *Henry IV, Part 1* and, in seeking to explore its contexts, have claimed it as part of a wider cultural territory.

Chapter 1 of this volume, "Historiography and the Uses of History," focuses on how history was conceptualized and written in the early modern period. The British scholar Geoffrey Bullough has collected excerpts from these writings and labeled them either as sources, possible sources, probable sources, or analogues, and such excerpts often appear in modern editions of the play. The selections here — from Edward Hall's *Union of the Two Noble and Illustrious Families of Lancaster and York* (1548), Raphael Holinshed's *Chronicles of England, Scotland, and Ireland* (1587), and Samuel Daniel's *The Civil Wars Between the Two Houses of Lancaster and York* (1595) — represent texts that Shakespeare used in one way or another, borrowing an overall emphasis here, a particular detail there. And because the selections here are longer than those usually reprinted, readers can not only trace Shakespeare's skill at weaving together historical "fact" with poetic invention but also explore these texts in their own right, for what they reveal about history writing in the period.

Significantly, the chroniclers were convinced that what we today call literature was an indispensable part of the cultural record, both that of the individual careers of "great men" and that of the nation and its institutions. A number of literary techniques and genres were available to them, and these enliven and intensify the accounts they constructed from extremely diverse materials. Many of the strategies Shakespeare uses — inventing scenes and speeches attributed to particular historical actors, accounts of their personal and domestic lives, details of character — fit perfectly within the historiographical protocols of the time. Reading these texts can raise questions about the distinctions between fact and fiction or between documents and stories (Patterson, *Reading* 55); it can also enable us to see Shakespeare's history writing as taking shape within a wide field of possibility.

In Shakespeare's time, written history was available only to those who could read (a small percentage of English subjects), but Shakespeare's plays were accessible to all who had the price of admission to the public playhouses, where history was not only made but remade. Documents from the period suggest the immense popularity of these plays. According to Philip Henslowe's *Diary* (1591–92), *Henry VI, Part 1* (1592) brought in some of the largest box-office receipts on record, and the appearance of seven quarto editions of *Henry IV, Part 1* (two in 1598 and one each in 1599, 1604, 1608, 1613, and 1622) before its inclusion in the First Folio attests to its appeal, which has endured over the centuries. Especially in twentieth-century Britain, *Henry IV, Part 1* has been used to celebrate connections between the theater and national history. The Royal Shakespeare Company, for instance, has repeatedly staged the play, usually together with *Henry IV, Part 2* (1597) or as part of an entire cycle of histories, as a way of marking particular occasions, such as the 1951 Festival of Britain or the 1982 opening of London's Barbican Theatre (see McMillin; Hodgdon, *Henry IV, Part 2*). Each of these stagings reflected contemporary critical visions of the play: Tillyard's cosmic scheme, with Hal as its epic hero, lay behind the 1951 cycle, and a highly detailed social milieu aligned the 1982 *Henrys* with the emergent critical emphasis on material culture.

Film and video texts reveal a similar traffic between literary and theatrical cultures. The 1979 BBC video, designed to reach a global audience and to fix the play for all time, not only adopted Tillyard's moral view but also attempted to convey a degree of historical accuracy that Shakespeare never specifies. Researching chronicle records, the producers discovered that Henry IV's illness may have been leprosy or syphilis, which accounts for Jon Finch's obsessive hand-rubbing; David Gwillim's Hal has a scar on his cheek from the arrow wound reported by chroniclers. By contrast, Orson Welles's earlier *Chimes at Midnight, or Falstaff* (1965–66) replaces Tillyard's

Tudor myth with a nostalgic lament for a lost past and, most especially, for Falstaff's place in the story (Crowl; Andrew). In the film the last voice we hear speaks a passage from Holinshed's *Chronicles*. More recently, the English Shakespeare Company's video, based on their 1986–89 stagings, which toured worldwide, appropriates the *Henrys* for the last two hundred years of British (or Western imperialist) history: in addition to those already mentioned, costumes included punk gear and motorcycle leathers; properties ranged from broadswords to machine guns, parchment scrolls to personal computers. To justify their eclectic approach, the directors recalled Henry Peacham's famous drawing of a scene from *Titus Andronicus* showing the central figure in a form of Roman dress resembling a toga, while the men flanking him are dressed as Elizabethan soldiers (Bogdanov and Pennington 28–29). In its own way, each of these interpretations reads Shakespeare's play in conjunction with other historical records.

In dramatizing a moment when an alliance among Northern feudal families challenged the Crown's legitimacy and its central authority, *Henry IV, Part 1* concerns the problem of rule in an emergent nation-state deeply divided by geographical as well as political faultlines. Age-old distinctions still pertained between the south of England, including London's seat of government, and the ancient British kingdoms of Wales and Scotland, considered in the period as "foreign" countries. Henry IV faces the difficult task of unifying a country fractured by discontented voices: the Percies and the Archbishop of York in the North and, closer to home, his son. The play raises questions about the nature of royal authority and its limits, the extent of subjects' obedience to a sovereign, and the conditions that justify rebellion. In Chapter 2, "Civic Order and Rebellion," two documents — *An Homily Against Disobedience and Willful Rebellion* (1571) and selections from John Ponet's *Short Treatise of Politic Power* (1556) — offer contradictory perspectives on these questions. Basing his views primarily on documents such as the *Homily*, Tillyard read *Henry IV, Part 1* as Elizabethan propaganda endorsing absolute obedience to sovereign rule. Recent critics, however, have turned to the writings of political theorists such as Ponet and George Buchanan, who offer dissenting opinions (Bushnell; Strier). When read in conjunction with state-authorized political doctrine *and* Ponet's views, not only do the issues of obedience and rebellion look more equivocal than Tillyard supposed, but the play can be seen as raising questions about the relations between subjects and sovereigns that have no easy resolution within the culture.

However strongly recent criticism has taken issue with Tillyard's views, his notion, shared by many others, that *Henry IV, Part 1* exemplifies the very nature of England has shown remarkable resilience. Present-day critics and cultural historians have reconfigured Tillyard's idea of the play as an epic morality in terms of nation building (see Helgerson). Chapter 3, "Cultural Territories," collects a series of documents that offer snapshots of national life, and, of all the chapters in this book, responds the most to recent work in early modern cultural studies. The extended chapter introduction (replacing explanatory headnotes for each selection) is organized around ideas of place — as geographical, institutional, or commercial site as well as indicator of social and gender status — and language. Here the real estate broker's stress on "location, location, location" takes on particular resonance, both in John Speed's maps from his *Theatre of the Empire of Great Britain* (1611/12) and two selections from William Harrison's *Description of England* (1587), one of which ("Of Degrees of People in the Commonwealth of England") "maps" the hierarchical divisions of class, while the other ("Of Their Apparell and Attire") lets us overhear what he thought of fashionable "newfangledness." Speed's *Theatre* was a major contribution to early modern chorography — the mapping of England's terrain, its shires, cities, towns, and villages. John Stow's *Survey of London* (1603) was another, represented here by his descriptions of locations pertinent to the play: "Candlewick Street Ward," the site of Eastcheap's tavern; and the "Borough of Southwark and Bridge Ward Without," an area outside the City's walls and jurisdiction, known as the "Liberties," which contained prisons, hospitals, taverns, and playhouses as well as other entertainment venues such as gambling houses, brothels (the "stews"), and the arena for bearbaiting, called the Bear Garden.

Shakespeare's play seems to collapse the topographical and cultural ambiguities of both these neighborhoods — the one within the City, the other in its suburbs — into Eastcheap's tavern, a place for eating and drinking which is also the site of a theatrical performance in which Falstaff and Hal play Henry IV as well as various versions of themselves. Both tavern and theatre were places where people from all classes, women and men, gathered, and as such both were seen by some social critics as contributing to a dangerous blurring of class boundaries and to a generalized moral decline. Offering cheap food and drink to the urban poor, alehouses were associated with criminals, drifters (known as "masterless men"), prostitutes, and all who eked out an existence at the margins of the culture. In the more upscale taverns, aristocrats (like Hal) might not only indulge their tastes for slumming but sample one of the newest commodities, tobacco, brought to England by New World travelers.

Thomas Dekker's *Of Lantern and Candlelight* (1609), which offers a guide to wary travelers, depicts London as filled with temptations and crime, but the theatres, at least according to the Puritan antitheatrical commentators, were even worse. From the 1570s forward, virulent attacks on the stage began to appear in print, drawing responses from those who defended both its practices and its morality. In large part, this debate over the theatre's place in the culture was a function of the professionalization of the theatre, the construction of permanent playhouses, and the widespread popularity of theatregoing. Chapter 3 reprints a 1592 letter from London's Lord Mayor to the Archbishop of Canterbury imploring him to ask the Master of the Revels, who licensed the theatre under the Queen's authority, to find a means for the Queen to "be served with these recreations" in *private* and to prevent *public* playing, which encourages disorder and corrupts religion. Two further excerpts — one from Stephen Gosson's *School of Abuse* (1579) and the other from Thomas Heywood's *Apology for Actors* (1612) — focus on some of the arguments in that debate, which also included the Protestant distaste for ceremony and spectacle and a suspicion of representation of any sort, especially those that erased distinctions of class and gender. While Heywood views the theatre as an institution that gives the nation international status, Gosson depicts it as a highly eroticized terrain where lewd behaviors flourish. Warning London's gentlewomen to avoid the theatre's "Market of Bawdry" and stay safely enclosed within doors, Gosson appeals to the widely held view that a woman's place was in the home.

That idea, strongly urged by moralists and social theorists, helped to ensure a status quo in which women occupied a position subordinate to men. Even though England was ruled by a learned woman with brilliant political skills, the normal occupation for women was marriage and motherhood; wives were expected to put their duty to their husbands and their domestic responsibilities at the center of their lives. Obviously, however, women did work, and not only in terms of household management and child-rearing. They kept shops and ran alehouses and taverns, sometimes (like Mistress Quickly) alone but often with their husbands; they participated as much as men did in London's growing commercial milieu. And, in spite of Gosson's warnings, gentlewomen, along with those lower down on the social scale, attended the theatre. *Henry IV, Part 1,* however, tells us very little about women's lives and histories. Taking patriarchal history as its ground and focusing on the heroic deeds of fathers and sons, the play marginalizes women's roles and voices. When women do appear, they almost invariably threaten to disrupt a relentlessly masculine narrative. To say that is to describe the critical history of these plays, for only within the last several decades have feminist literary critics and cultural historians begun to explore the means by which women's voices have been either repressed or erased from the record and to offer alternative readings.

Two texts in Chapter 3 offer very different perspectives on gender roles, marriage, and the regulation of women's bodies. Although it outlines a wife's duties and prescribes her behaviors, John Dod and Robert Cleaver's *Godly Form of Household Government* (1621), a popular handbook on marriage, also points to ideals of mutual love and companionship, suggesting that marriage is a two-way street. But if they recognize, and seem to approve of, a need for something like equality within marriage, there were those who perceived women's (relative) freedom, independence, and increased access to education as potentially disruptive to the social order. One response to such social changes came from Joseph Swetnam, whose *Arraignment of Lewd, Idle, Froward, and Unconstant Women* (1615) represents one entry in a misogynistic, polemical controversy over womankind. In this backlash against early modern feminism, the free-thinking woman was associated with free speech, and her loose tongue, especially when it spoke against her husband or defied his rule, signified a loose body (Boose). Swetnam surely would condemn the outspoken Quickly, but he might also consider Kate Percy and Lady Mortimer monstrous, if only for inciting desire.

Swetnam's notion of women as dangerous "others" appears, though not in the form of angry polemic, in *Henry IV, Part 1*'s representation of Wales. In this "foreign" borderland, women take on greater importance than in Eastcheap's tavern community. Significantly, Shakespeare seems uninterested in the political implications of the Percy and Mortimer marriages or in noticing that it is only through marriage that Mortimer can lay claim to the throne. Rather, the play stresses the affections and desires of the rebel husbands and their wives, using its women characters to reveal the potential threat such passions were thought to represent to the exclusively masculine pursuits of politics and, especially, war. The historical record provides evidence of Welsh women brutally mutilating corpses following a battle; although the play mentions this practice only in passing, the selection from Holinshed's *Chronicles* provides a more specific account. In connecting them with sexual desire, sexualized violence, and rebellion, the play marks the Welsh women irrevocably.

The play also identifies Wales through its language. As with Mistress Quickly's malapropisms, this "strange tongue" is spoken by a woman. The Welsh language, represented in Shakespeare's text only by stage directions, was outlawed early in the century by Henry VIII's royal proclamation. It was (and still is), however, spoken on the stage, and an excerpt from a 1964 Royal Shakespeare Company prompt copy (Shakespeare's text as prepared for performance) fills in what the play leaves unrecorded. As perhaps the most significant marker of cultural — and class — distinctions, language is important to *Henry IV, Part 1* in other ways. In Eastcheap, Hal tells Ned Poins that, having learned the terms of drinking from the tavern's tapsters, he can "drink with any tinker in his own language during my life." If his boast points to one profession's idiom, there were many such "gross terms" and dialects to be heard in London's streets, among them one of the argots of its criminal subculture, recorded in Thomas Dekker's "Of Canting." Could Hal also rob with thieves and pickpockets in their own language? Even though the play does not say so, it seems likely. What seems indisputable, however, is that Hal knows that learning to speak, or to put on, others' languages enhances his power. Perhaps the most potent illustration of this effect occurs not in this play but in *Henry V*, where the former Hal, now King Henry, woos Princess Katherine of France, using English to tell her his history and accomplishments and French, her own language, to flatter her.

The idea that *Henry IV, Part 1* dramatizes one stage of Hal's preparation for kingship has been a perennial concern of its critics. In bringing together documents that include Roger Ascham's views on education (1570), *The Famous Victories of Henry V* (the anonymous play based on popular stories of Hal's youthful escapades and published in 1598), selections from a fifteenth-century chronicle, *The Brut*, and from Machiavelli's *The Prince* ([1513], trans. 1640), Chapter 4, "The 'Education' of a Prince," offers several perspectives on Hal's various guises: aristocratic courtier, holiday player, rebellious son and heir, and political actor. Once again, Tillyard's vision of the prince as resembling T. H. White's "once and future king" set a pattern that later critics have modified. Tillyard's Hal, in training for office, typifies a golden mean, a perfectly balanced figure who does precisely what history requires of him. Like the heroes of medieval romances, he undergoes various tests of virtue in which he invariably does the right thing, choosing Chivalry (Hotspur) over Sloth and Vanity (Falstaff), Order and Justice (Henry IV) over Disorder and Misrule (again, Falstaff). In this morality scheme, Hal draws meaning from other characters and from the values they stand for. More recently, criticism as well as theatrical practice have emphasized the psychological contours of Hal's character and have viewed him as a son trapped between two fathers, turning to Falstaff for the affection denied him by a stern father who represents discipline and duty. Welles's film, for instance, brilliantly conveys the appeal of Eastcheap's tavern kingdom, setting its bustling energies against Henry IV's ascetic presence, his desire to maintain distance from his subjects and his son and to go on a penitential crusade. Yet that film also suggests that Hal is a Machiavellian schemer: skilled at concealing his true nature beneath a holiday humor, he uses his tavern companions for his own political ends.

The notion of an ironic Hal gained favor in the 1960s, coinciding with a widespread mistrust of political rhetoric and politicians' behavior. Focusing on Hal as a political actor, critics saw him as a performer, an imitator of others who forges his own identity through role-playing. Like psychoanalysis, this metatheatrical approach tends to dislodge the play from its historical contexts, and its most recent critics, drawing on early modern conceptions of selfhood, see the drama as contributing to an emergent sense of the fluidity of the self and, ultimately, to the formation of the modern individual (see Belsey; Stallybrass, "Shakespeare"; Sinfield). For critics interested in the relations between authority and subversion, Hal's Machiavellian performance takes on slightly different contours. Stephen Greenblatt, for instance, claims that Hal incites the crimes that he will afterwards condemn in order to reinforce his own authority (254). Recently, too, critics have highlighted the play's homosocial and homoerotic dimensions, pointing to the heavily eroticized relationship between Hal and Hotspur and to suggestions that Falstaff — as father, mother, and riotous mentor — may also be his lover (Goldberg, *Sodometries*). However they configure the prince, critics of *Henry IV, Part 1* align themselves with Hal. Whether praising his moral nature, identifying with his oedipal conflict, alternately admiring and deploring his manipulative political skills, or taking pleasure in his (ambiguous) sexuality, readers and playgoers subject themselves to precisely the same questions of loyalty and systems of value that are under discussion in the play.

Prominent among these issues is honor. As the play opens, Henry IV speaks of wanting to exchange Hal for Hotspur, "the theme of honor's tongue," and it is through Hal's actions at Shrewsbury's battle that he becomes like Hotspur, redeeming himself in his father's eyes. As the epitome of a chivalric code of honor, Hotspur has been considered the play's "true" hero, and a long-standing critical tradition has, like Henry IV, measured both Hal and Falstaff against him. Teasing out topical references, scholars have noted his resemblance to Robert Devereux, the Earl of Essex, one of Queen Elizabeth's favored courtiers. Like Hotspur, Essex stood for the ancient ideals of England's feudal aristocracy; also like Hotspur, he was associated with a circle of political dissidents. In 1601, he led an unsuccessful rising against Elizabeth's government and was tried and executed for treason (see James; Barroll; Smith). Although that event lies beyond the time frame of Shakespeare's histories, Essex's career as a military commander and his aggressive, self-assertive behavior at court made him prominent enough for playgoers to connect him with a figure like Hotspur (see Cartelli). Certainly Shakespeare associated Essex with Elizabethan ideals of heroic masculinity: in *Henry V* he aligns Essex's return from the Irish Wars with Henry's triumphant entry into London after his successful French campaign.

Recent critical interest in gender ideologies has called attention to how the history play invoked cultural memories of an ancient heroic past, making it present and giving renewed immortality to the deeds of great men (see Howard, *Stage;* Rackin, *Stages;* Hodgdon, *End*). In defending plays against the objections of antitheatrical commentators, Thomas Nashe writes:

> Nay, what if I prove Plays to be no extreme; but a rare exercise of virtue? First, for the subject of them (for the most part) it is borrowed out of our English Chronicles, wherein our forefathers' valiant acts (that have lain long buried in rusty brass and worm-eaten books) are revived, and they themselves raised from the Grave of Oblivion, and brought to plead their aged Honors in open presence: than which, what can be a sharper reproof to these degenerate effeminate days of ours? (*Pierce Penniless his Supplication to the Devil* [1592], qtd. in Chambers 4: 238)

Likewise, Thomas Heywood speaks of the "bewitching" power of "lively and well spirited action" to "new mold the hearts of the spectators and fashion them to the shape of any noble and notable attempt" (*Apology for Actors* [1612] Book 1, B4r).

Much like today's action films, the history play circulated warrior ideals and codes of violence that both reflected and helped to shape cultural constructions of masculinity. The documents in Chapter 5, "Honor and Arms," sample a wide range of handbooks devoted to these subjects, which informed the ideals as well as the practice of Elizabethan heroic courtiership. Sir William Segar's *Honor Military and Civil* (1602), for instance, codifies the honor ideals lying behind such valor, and George Silver's *Paradoxes of Defense* (1599) offers more practical advice on the rules governing combat with particular weapons, even to mentioning those Hotspur associates with Hal, "that sword-and-buckler Prince of Wales." Drawings of a tilt and sword play and a portrait of Essex as Queen Elizabeth's knight point to an equally important context for this kind of masculine display: the ceremonial Accession Day Tilts staged yearly on 17 November at Elizabeth's court, through which the Queen sought to appease and mediate the factional and personal conflicts of her courtiers (see McCoy).

While some recent critics have been especially interested in the relations among these highly symbolic chivalric performances, the drama, and royal authority, others, particularly just after World War II, focused on Shakespeare's depictions of warfare and the connections between the plays and treatises on the theory and practice of soldiership (Webb; Boynton). Here, selections from Barnaby Rich's *Path-Way to Military Practice* (1587) and Matthew Sutcliffe's *Right Practice, Proceedings, and Laws of Arms* (1593) are especially germane contexts for examining Falstaff's abuses of his office and of military rules and regulations. Aptly enough, some historians of early modern warfare have claimed that Shakespeare's knowledge of the late-sixteenth-century military profession came not from the extensive treatises published during the period but from casual conversations with soldiers in London's inns and taverns. That the plays may in part depend on such ephemeral traces suggests the tenuous nature of present-day attempts to recover, and to overhear, the voices of a culture's past.

Recovering Falstaff's historical identity as the Protestant martyr Sir John Oldcastle, however, rests on much firmer ground. The final chapter of this volume, "The Oldcastle Controversy," which includes selections from John Foxe's popular *Acts and Monuments* (1563), Holinshed's *Chronicles* (1587), and Michael Drayton's play *The True and Honorable History of Sir John Oldcastle* (1600), explores that history (see Scoufos; Taylor). Whereas scholars have long known of the connection between Falstaff and Oldcastle, that association has usually been mentioned only in passing.

With the exception of Hamlet, more has been written about Falstaff than about any of Shakespeare's characters, and just as a theatrical production of *Hamlet* depends on casting its central role, any staging of *Henry IV, Part 1* (and *Henry IV, Part 2*, as well as *The Merry Wives of Windsor* [1597]) takes life from its Falstaff. In advertising "the humorous conceits of Sir John Falstaff" as one reason for buying the play, the title page of the 1598 first Quarto (see Figure 1, p. 18) almost seems to prophesy the delight his figure has brought to generations of critics and theatregoers. Morality vice, epitome of the seven deadly sins, *miles gloriosus* (braggart warrior), cowardly adventurer, eternal child, symbol of ribaldry and lawlessness, the voice of the belly, unregenerate man, the first major joke of the English against their own class system: criticism has attributed all these labels to Falstaff, who seems capable of absorbing a wealth of allusions. Perhaps most famously, especially as a point of departure for later-twentieth-century readings, sympathetic critics have looked backward from the end of *Henry IV, Part 2* to take Falstaff's part and to condemn Hal for rejecting the fat knight. Traditionally, critics have thought of Falstaff primarily as an ahistorical figure who constructs himself out of theatrical conventions, with the willing cooperation of a complicit audience — a view that has somewhat dismembered him by splitting his historical from his theatrical antecedents and disempowering him as a political, religious, and military figure. Recently, however, critics have attempted to put Shakespeare's great Humpty-Dumpty back together again.

One strand of thinking locates him in relation to the material conditions of the early modern playhouse and to particular traditions of playing associated with Will Kempe, the actor who originally performed the role (Wiles).

Scholars interested in reconstructing Elizabethan performances call attention to the clown's radical potential; his ability to address the audience, often from a downstage position, and to comment on and question what he saw and heard could alert playgoers to alternative perspectives (Weimann). As a lord of misrule who displaces legitimate authority, Falstaff represents just such an interruptive presence, one associated with traditions of carnivalesque, which turned proper authority upside down and inside out, and with popular rather than elitist culture (Bristol; Laroque). Such investigations, which call attention to how a character's "identity" or position may shift from scene to scene, have had an impact on rethinking Falstaff's character, a concern of theatregoers as well as critics.

In one way, the issue of identity plays into a recent attempt to reconsider Falstaff's history, even to restore his "original" name. A fairly recent edition of Shakespeare's plays (1986) substitutes "Oldcastle," the name first given to the character and changed at the request of Oldcastle's descendants, the Cobham family, to "Falstaff" (Wells and Taylor). The editors' decision has provoked controversy, particularly about issues of censorship, and has brought renewed attention to other changes. Peto once bore the name of Harvey, who was the stepfather of the Earl of Southampton, one of Shakespeare's patrons; Bardolph was originally called Russell, the name of the Earls of Bedford. It may be that objections from those families prompted Shakespeare to rename them too. Moreover, the name Shakespeare chose for Falstaff connects him with another historical figure. Chroniclers report that a Sir John Fastolf (1378?–1459), who served in France under Henry VI, was a coward, and since Shakespeare had already used his name as well as his reputation in *Henry VI, Part 1* with no objections, he apparently did so again. Whatever the case, bringing forward such local identities has revitalized the study of topicality, inviting scholars to reread Oldcastle/Falstaff through Elizabethan anti-Puritan tracts and burlesques and to give Shakespeare's grandly grotesque figure of superabundance yet another history (Poole).

"Yet another history" might describe this book, which attempts to map *Henry IV, Part 1*'s cultural terrains, but it might also describe all of Shakespeare's plays. Although they are called tragedies, *Hamlet, King Lear, Macbeth, Julius Caesar, Antony and Cleopatra,* and *Coriolanus* also draw on, and reshape, historical materials; and when, in *The Taming of the Shrew,* Christopher Sly asks what a comedy is, he is told it is "a kind of history." The English history play, of course, tells a very specific kind of history. Rising to assured prominence in the last two decades of the sixteenth century, coincident with the final years of Elizabeth's reign, the genre (if it can be called that) practically disappeared after 1600, the date of *Henry V,* or was reconfigured, most notably in *Henry VIII, or All Is True* (1613), which Shakespeare wrote in collaboration with John Fletcher, and John Ford's *Perkin Warbeck* (1634) (see Bevington, *Tudor Drama;* Ribner). As much if not more than any of the categories *Hamlet*'s Polonius includes in his comprehensive catalogue, the English history plays made a particular imprint of, and on, early modern culture.

PART ONE

✦

WILLIAM SHAKESPEARE

The First Part of
King Henry the Fourth

Edited by David Bevington

THE
HISTORY OF
HENRIE THE
FOVRTH;

With the battell at Shrewsburie,
betweene the King and Lord
Henry Percy, ſurnamed
Henrie Hotſpur of
the North.

With the humorous conceits of Sir
Iohn Falſtalffe.

AT LONDON,

Printed by *P. S.* for *Andrew Wiſe*, dwelling
in Paules Churchyard, at the ſigne of
the Angell. **1598.**

FIGURE 1 *Title page for the first Quarto of* Henry IV, Part 1 *(1598). The subtitles
function as an advertisement for the play's most memorable events.*

The First Part of
King Henry the Fourth

>‹

LADY PERCY, *Hotspur's wife and Mortimer's sister*
LADY MORTIMER, *Mortimer's wife and Glendower's daughter*

SIR JOHN FALSTAFF
NED POINS
BARDOLPH
PETO
GADSHILL, *arranger of the highway robbery*
HOSTESS *of the tavern, Mistress Quickly*
FRANCIS, *a drawer, or tapster*
VINTNER, *or tavern keeper*

FIRST CARRIER
SECOND CARRIER
HOSTLER
CHAMBERLAIN
FIRST TRAVELER
SHERIFF
SERVANT *to Hotspur*
MESSENGER
SECOND MESSENGER

Soldiers, Travelers, Lords, Attendants

SCENE: *England and Wales*]

ACT I, SCENE I°

Enter the King, Lord John of Lancaster, [the] Earl of Westmorland, [Sir Walter Blunt,] with others.

KING:
So shaken as we are, so wan with care,
Find we° a time for frighted° peace to pant,
And breathe short-winded accents° of new broils°
To be commenced in strands afar remote.°
No more the thirsty entrance° of this soil   5
Shall daub° her lips with her own children's blood;

ACT I, SCENE I. Location: The royal court.   2. **Find we:** let us find.   **frighted:** frightened.   3. **breathe short-winded accents:** speak, even though we are out of breath.   **accents:** words.   **broils:** battles.   4. **strands afar remote:** far-off shores; i.e., of the Holy Land (to which, at the end of *Richard II*, Henry has pledged himself to a crusade).   5. **thirsty entrance:** i.e., parched mouth.   6. **daub:** coat, smear.

No more shall trenching° war channel her fields
Nor bruise her flowerets with the armèd hoofs
Of hostile paces.° Those opposèd eyes,
Which, like the meteors of a troubled heaven,   10
All of one nature, of one substance bred,
Did lately meet in the intestine° shock
And furious close° of civil° butchery,
Shall now in mutual well-beseeming ranks
March all one way and be no more opposed   15
Against acquaintance, kindred, and allies.
The edge of war, like an ill-sheathèd knife,
No more shall cut his° master. Therefore, friends,
As far as to the sepulcher of Christ —
Whose soldier now, under whose blessèd cross   20
We are impressèd° and engaged to fight —
Forthwith a power° of English shall we levy,
Whose arms were molded in their mother's° womb
To chase these pagans in those holy fields
Over whose acres walked those blessèd feet   25
Which fourteen hundred years ago were nailed
For our advantage on the bitter cross.
But this our purpose now is twelve month old,
And bootless° 'tis to tell you we will go.
Therefore we meet not now. Then let me hear   30
Of° you, my gentle cousin° Westmorland,
What yesternight our council did decree
In forwarding this dear expedience.°

WESTMORLAND:
My liege, this haste was hot in question,°
And many limits of the charge° set down   35
But yesternight, when all athwart° there came
A post° from Wales loaden° with heavy news,
Whose worst was that the noble Mortimer,
Leading the men of Herefordshire to fight
Against the irregular and wild Glendower,   40

---

7. **trenching:** cutting. 9. **paces:** horses' tread. 12. **intestine:** internal. 13. **close:** hand-to-hand encounter. **civil:** (as in "civil war"). 18. **his:** its. 21. **impressèd:** conscripted. 22. **power:** army. 23. **their mother's:** i.e., England's, but also suggesting *their mothers'*. 29. **bootless:** useless. 31. **Of:** from. **gentle cousin:** noble kinsman. 33. **dear expedience:** urgent expedition. 34. **hot in question:** being hotly debated. 35. **limits . . . charge:** particulars of military responsibility. 36. **athwart:** at cross purposes, contrarily. 37. **post:** messenger. **loaden:** heavily laden.

Was by the rude hands of that Welshman taken,
A thousand of his people butcherèd —
Upon whose dead corpse° there was such misuse,
Such beastly shameless transformation,°
By those Welshwomen done as may not be   45
Without much shame retold or spoken of.

KING:
It seems then that the tidings of this broil
Brake off our business for the Holy Land.

WESTMORLAND:
This matched with other° did, my gracious lord;
For more uneven° and unwelcome news   50
Came from the north, and thus it did import:
On Holy Rood Day,° the gallant Hotspur there,
Young Harry Percy, and brave Archibald,
That ever-valiant and approvèd° Scot,
At Holmedon° met, where they did spend   55
A sad and bloody hour,
As by° discharge of their artillery
And shape of likelihood° the news was told;
For he that brought them,° in the very heat
And pride° of their contention did take horse,   60
Uncertain of the issue any way.

KING:
Here is a dear, a true industrious friend,
Sir Walter Blunt, new lighted from his horse,
Stained with the variation of each soil
Betwixt that Holmedon and this seat of ours;   65
And he hath brought us smooth° and welcome news.
The Earl of Douglas is discomfited;°
Ten thousand bold Scots, two-and-twenty knights,
Balked° in their own blood, did Sir Walter see
On Holmedon's plains. Of prisoners, Hotspur took   70
Mordake,° Earl of Fife and eldest son
To beaten Douglas, and the Earl of Atholl,

---

43. **corpse:** corpses. 44. **transformation:** mutilation. 49. **other:** i.e., other news. 50. **uneven:** disconcerting, distressing. 52. **Holy Rood Day:** September 14. 54. **approvèd:** proved by experience. 55. **Holmedon:** Humbleton in Northumberland. 57. **by:** i.e., judging from. 58. **shape of likelihood:** likely outcome. 59. **them:** i.e., the news. 60. **pride:** height. 66. **smooth:** pleasant. 67. **discomfited:** defeated. 69. **Balked:** heaped up in balks, or ridges. 71. **Mordake:** i.e., Murdoch, son of the Earl of Albany.

Of Murray, Angus, and Menteith.
And is not this an honorable spoil?
A gallant prize? Ha, cousin, is it not?   75

WESTMORLAND:
In faith, it is a conquest for a prince to boast of.

KING:
Yea, there thou mak'st me sad, and mak'st me sin
In envy that my lord Northumberland
Should be the father to so blest a son —
A son who is the theme of honor's tongue,   80
Amongst a grove the very straightest plant,°
Who is sweet Fortune's minion° and her pride,
Whilst I, by looking on the praise of him,
See riot° and dishonor stain the brow
Of my young Harry. O, that it could be proved   85
That some night-tripping° fairy had exchanged
In cradle clothes our children where they lay,
And called mine Percy, his Plantagenet!°
Then would I have his Harry, and he mine.
But let him° from my thoughts. What think you, coz,°   90
Of this young Percy's pride? The prisoners
Which he in this adventure hath surprised°
To his own use° he keeps, and sends me word
I shall have none but Mordake,° Earl of Fife.

WESTMORLAND:
This is his uncle's teaching. This is Worcester,   95
Malevolent° to you in all aspects,°
Which makes him prune himself° and bristle up
The crest of youth against your dignity.

KING:
But I have sent for him to answer this;
And for this cause awhile we must neglect   100
Our holy purpose to Jerusalem.
Cousin, on Wednesday next our council we

---

81. **plant:** i.e., young tree.   82. **minion:** favorite.   84. **riot:** debauchery.   86. **night-tripping:** i.e., moving nimbly in the night.   88. **Plantagenet:** (Family name of English royalty since Henry II.)   90. **let him:** let him go.   **coz:** cousin, i.e., kinsman.   92. **surprised:** ambushed, captured.   93. **To ... use:** i.e., to collect ransom for them.   94. **none but Mordake:** (Since Mordake was of royal blood, being grandson to Robert II of Scotland, Hotspur could not claim him as his prisoner according to the law of arms.)   96. **Malevolent, aspects:** (Astrological terms.)   97. **Which ... himself:** i.e., which teaching makes Hotspur preen himself (as a falcon preens its feathers).

Will hold at Windsor. So inform the lords.
But come yourself with speed to us again,
For more is to be said and to be done   105
Than out of anger can be utterèd.
WESTMORLAND: I will, my liege.   *Exeunt.*

ACT I, SCENE II°

Enter Prince of Wales and Sir John Falstaff.

FALSTAFF: Now, Hal, what time of day is it, lad?

PRINCE: Thou art so fat-witted with drinking of old sack,° and unbutton-
ing thee after supper, and sleeping upon benches after noon, that thou
hast forgotten° to demand that truly which thou wouldst truly know.
What a devil° hast thou to do with the time of the day? Unless hours   5
were cups of sack, and minutes capons, and clocks the tongues of bawds,
and dials° the signs of leaping houses,° and the blessed sun himself a fair
hot wench in flame-colored taffeta,° I see no reason why thou shouldst be
so superfluous° to demand the time of the day.

FALSTAFF: Indeed, you come near me now,° Hal, for we that take purses go   10
by° the moon and the seven stars,° and not by Phoebus, "he, that wandering knight so fair."° And I prithee, sweet wag, when thou art king, as,
God save Thy Grace° — Majesty I should say, for grace thou wilt have
none —

PRINCE: What, none?   15

FALSTAFF: No, by my troth,° not so much as will serve to be prologue to an
egg and butter.°

PRINCE: Well, how then? Come, roundly, roundly.°

FALSTAFF: Marry,° then, sweet wag,° when thou art king, let not us that are
squires of the night's body be called thieves of the day's beauty.° Let us be   20

ACT I, SCENE II. **Location:** London, perhaps in an apartment of the Prince's.   **2. sack:** a
Spanish white wine.   **4. forgotten:** forgotten how.   **5. a devil:** in the devil.   **7. dials:**
clocks.   **leaping houses:** houses of prostitution.   **8. taffeta:** (Commonly worn by prostitutes.)   **9. superfluous:** (1) unnecessarily concerned (2) self-indulgent.   **10. you . . . now:** i.e.,
you've scored a point on me.   **10–11. go by:** (1) travel by the light of (2) tell time by.   **11. the
seven stars:** the Pleiades.   **11–12. Phoebus . . . fair:** (Phoebus, god of the sun, is here equated
with the wandering knight of a ballad or popular romance.)   **13. Grace:** royal highness (with
pun on spiritual *grace* and also on the *grace* or blessing before a meal).   **16. troth:**
faith.   **16–17. prologue . . . butter:** i.e., grace before a brief meal.   **18. roundly:** i.e., out with
it.   **19. Marry:** indeed. (Literally, "by the Virgin Mary.")   **wag:** joker.   **19–20. let . . .
beauty:** i.e., let not us who are attendants on the goddess of night, members of her household,
be blamed for stealing daylight by sleeping in the daytime.

Diana's foresters,° gentlemen of the shade, minions° of the moon; and let men say we be men of good government,° being governed, as the sea is, by our noble and chaste mistress the moon, under whose countenance° we steal.°

PRINCE: Thou sayest well, and it holds well° too, for the fortune of us that are the moon's men doth ebb and flow like the sea, being governed, as the sea is, by the moon. As, for proof, now: a purse of gold most resolutely snatched on Monday night and most dissolutely spent on Tuesday morning, got with swearing "Lay by"° and spent with crying "Bring in,"° now in as low an ebb as the foot of the ladder° and by and by in as high a flow as the ridge° of the gallows.

FALSTAFF: By the Lord, thou sayst true, lad. And is not my hostess of the tavern a most sweet wench?

PRINCE: As the honey of Hybla,° my old lad of the castle.° And is not a buff jerkin° a most sweet robe of durance?°

FALSTAFF: How now, how now, mad wag, what, in thy quips and thy quiddities?° What a plague have I to do with a buff jerkin?

PRINCE: Why, what a pox° have I to do with my hostess of the tavern?

FALSTAFF: Well, thou hast called her to a reckoning° many a time and oft.

PRINCE: Did I ever call for thee to pay thy part?

FALSTAFF: No, I'll give thee thy due, thou hast paid all there.

PRINCE: Yea, and elsewhere, so far as my coin would stretch, and where it would not I have used my credit.

FALSTAFF: Yea, and so used it that, were it not here apparent that thou art heir apparent — But I prithee, sweet wag, shall there be gallows standing in England when thou art king? And resolution° thus fubbed° as it is with the rusty curb of old father Antic° the law? Do not thou, when thou art king, hang a thief.

PRINCE: No, thou shalt.

FALSTAFF: Shall I? O rare! By the Lord, I'll be a brave° judge.

21. **Diana's foresters:** (An elegant name for thieves by night; Diana is goddess of the moon and the hunt.) **minions:** favorites. 22. **government:** (1) conduct (2) commonwealth. 23. **countenance:** (1) face (2) patronage, approval. 24. **steal:** (1) move stealthily (2) rob. 25. **it holds well:** the comparison is apt. 29. **Lay by:** (A cry of highwaymen, like "Hands up!") **Bring in:** (An order given to a waiter in a tavern.) 30. **ladder:** (1) pier ladder (2) gallows ladder. 31. **ridge:** crossbar. 34. **Hybla:** (A town, famed for its honey, in Sicily near Syracuse.) **old . . . castle:** (1) a roisterer (2) the name, Sir John Oldcastle, borne by Falstaff in the earlier version of the Henry IV plays. 35. **buff jerkin:** (A leather jacket worn by officers of the law.) **durance:** (1) imprisonment (2) durability, durable cloth. 37. **quiddities:** subtleties of speech. 38. **pox:** syphilis. (Here, *what a pox* is used as an expletive, like "what the devil.") 39. **reckoning:** settlement of the bill (with bawdy suggestion that is continued in *pay thy part* and *my coin would stretch*). 46. **resolution:** courage (of a highwayman). **fubbed:** cheated. 47. **Antic:** buffoon. 50. **brave:** excellent.

PRINCE: Thou judgest false already. I mean, thou shalt have the hanging of
the thieves,° and so become a rare° hangman.

FALSTAFF: Well, Hal, well; and in some sort it jumps with my humor° as
well as waiting in the court,° I can tell you.

PRINCE: For obtaining of suits?° 55

FALSTAFF: Yea, for obtaining of suits, whereof the hangman hath no lean
wardrobe. 'Sblood,° I am as melancholy as a gib cat° or a lugged bear.°

PRINCE: Or an old lion, or a lover's lute.

FALSTAFF: Yea, or the drone of a Lincolnshire bagpipe.

PRINCE: What sayest thou to a hare,° or the melancholy of Moorditch?° 60

FALSTAFF: Thou hast the most unsavory similes, and art indeed the most
comparative,° rascalliest, sweet young prince. But Hal, I prithee, trouble
me no more with vanity.° I would to God thou and I knew where a com-
modity° of good names° were to be bought. An old lord of the council
rated° me the other day in the street about you, sir, but I marked him not; 65
and yet he talked very wisely, but I regarded him not; and yet he talked
wisely, and in the street too.

PRINCE: Thou didst well, for wisdom cries out in the streets and no man
regards it.°

FALSTAFF: O, thou hast damnable iteration,° and art indeed able to cor- 70
rupt a saint. Thou hast done much harm upon me, Hal, God forgive thee
for it. Before I knew thee, Hal, I knew nothing;° and now am I, if a man
should speak truly, little better than one of the wicked. I must give over
this life, and I will give it over. By the Lord, an° I do not I am a villain.
I'll be damned for never a king's son in Christendom. 75

PRINCE: Where shall we take a purse tomorrow, Jack?

FALSTAFF: Zounds,° where thou wilt, lad, I'll make one.° An I do not, call
me villain and baffle° me.

PRINCE: I see a good amendment of life in thee — from praying to purse
taking. 80

51–52. have . . . thieves: (1) be in charge of hanging thieves (or protecting them from
hanging) (2) hang like other thieves.   52. rare: (1) rarely used (2) excellent.   53. jumps . . .
humor: suits my temperament.   54. waiting in the court: being in attendance at the
royal court.   55. suits: petitions. (But Falstaff uses the word to mean suits of clothes;
clothes belonging to an executed man were given to the executioner.)   57. 'Sblood: by his
(Christ's) blood.   gib cat: tomcat.   lugged bear: bear led by a chain and baited by
dogs.   60. hare: (A proverbially melancholy animal.)   Moorditch: (A foul ditch draining
Moorfields, outside London walls.)   62. comparative: given to abusive comparisons.
63. vanity: worldliness.   63–64. commodity: supply.   64. names: reputations.   65. rated:
chastised.   68–69. wisdom . . . it: (An allusion to Proverbs 1:20–24.)   70. iteration: repeti-
tion (of biblical texts, with a neat twist).   72. nothing: i.e., no evil.   74. an: if.   77. Zounds:
by his (Christ's) wounds.   make one: be one of the party.   78. baffle: publicly disgrace.

FALSTAFF: Why, Hal, 'tis my vocation, Hal. 'Tis no sin for a man to labor in his vocation.

Enter Poins.

Poins! Now shall we know if Gadshill° have set a match.° O, if men were to be saved by merit,° what hole in hell were hot enough for him? This is the most omnipotent° villain that ever cried "Stand!" to a true° man.   85

PRINCE: Good morrow, Ned.

POINS: Good morrow, sweet Hal. — What says Monsieur Remorse? What says Sir John, Sack-and-Sugar Jack? How agrees the devil and thee about thy soul that thou soldest him on Good Friday last for a cup of Madeira and a cold capon's leg?   90

PRINCE: Sir John stands to° his word; the devil shall have his bargain, for he was never yet a breaker of proverbs. He will give the devil his due.

POINS: Then art thou damned for keeping thy word with the devil.

PRINCE [*to Falstaff*]:   Else° he had been damned for cozening° the devil.

POINS: But my lads, my lads, tomorrow morning, by four o'clock early, at   95
Gad's Hill,° there are pilgrims going to Canterbury with rich offerings and traders riding to London with fat purses. I have vizards° for you all; you have horses for yourselves. Gadshill lies° tonight in Rochester. I have bespoke° supper tomorrow night in Eastcheap. We may do it as secure as sleep. If you will go, I will stuff your purses full of crowns; if you will not,   100
tarry at home and be hanged.

FALSTAFF: Hear ye, Yedward,° if I tarry at home and go not, I'll hang you° for going.

POINS: You will, chops?°

FALSTAFF: Hal, wilt thou make one?   105

PRINCE: Who, I rob? I a thief? Not I, by my faith.

FALSTAFF: There's neither honesty, manhood, nor good fellowship in thee, nor thou cam'st not of the blood royal, if thou darest not stand for ten shillings.°

PRINCE: Well then, once in my days I'll be a madcap.   110

FALSTAFF: Why, that's well said.

PRINCE: Well, come what will, I'll tarry at home.

---

83. **Gadshill:** (The name of one of the highwaymen.)   **set a match:** arranged a robbery.   84. **by merit:** i.e., according to their deservings rather than by God's grace.   85. **omnipotent:** unparalleled, utter.   **true:** honest.   91. **stands to:** keeps.   94. **Else:** otherwise.   **cozening:** cheating.   96. **Gad's Hill:** (Location near Rochester on the road from London to Canterbury; one of the highwaymen is called Gadshill.)   97. **vizards:** masks.   98. **lies:** lodges.   99. **bespoke:** ordered.   102. **Yedward:** (Nickname for *Edward*, Poins's first name.)   **hang you:** have you hanged.   104. **chops:** i.e., fat jaws or cheeks.   108–09. **stand . . . shillings:** (1) stand up and fight for money (2) be worth ten shillings, the value of the *royal*, the gold coin alluded to in *blood royal* (line 108).

FALSTAFF: By the Lord, I'll be a traitor then, when thou art king.

PRINCE: I care not.

POINS: Sir John, I prithee leave the Prince and me alone. I will lay him   115
down such reasons for this adventure that he shall go.

FALSTAFF: Well, God give thee the spirit of persuasion and him the ears of
profiting, that what thou speakest may move and what he hears may be
believed, that the true prince may, for recreation's sake, prove a false thief;
for the poor abuses of the time want countenance.° Farewell. You shall   120
find me in Eastcheap.

PRINCE: Farewell, thou latter spring! Farewell, All-hallown summer!°

[*Exit Falstaff.*]

POINS: Now, my good sweet honey lord, ride with us tomorrow. I have a
jest to execute that I cannot manage alone. Falstaff, Peto, Bardolph, and
Gadshill shall rob those men that we have already waylaid° — yourself   125
and I will not be there — and when they have the booty, if you and I do
not rob them, cut this head off from my shoulders.

PRINCE: How shall we part with them in setting forth?

POINS: Why, we will set forth before or after them and appoint them a
place of meeting, wherein it is at our pleasure° to fail; and then will they   130
adventure upon the exploit themselves, which they shall have no sooner
achieved but we'll set upon them.

PRINCE: Yea, but 'tis like° that they will know us by our horses, by our
habits,° and by every other appointment,° to be ourselves.

POINS: Tut, our horses they shall not see — I'll tie them in the wood; our   135
vizards we will change after we leave them; and, sirrah,° I have cases of
buckram for the nonce,° to immask° our noted° outward garments.

PRINCE: Yea, but I doubt° they will be too hard° for us.

POINS: Well, for two of them, I know them to be as true-bred cowards as
ever turned back;° and for the third, if he fight longer than he sees   140
reason, I'll forswear arms. The virtue of this jest will be the incompre-
hensible° lies that this same fat rogue will tell us when we meet at
supper — how thirty at least he fought with, what wards,° what blows,
what extremities he endured; and in the reproof° of this lives the jest.

---

120. **want countenance:** lack encouragement and protection (from men of rank).   122. **All-hallown summer:** (Compare with "Indian summer." Falstaff's summer or *latter spring*, i.e., his youth, has lasted to All Saints' Day, November 1.)   125. **waylaid:** set an ambush for.   130. **pleasure:** choice, discretion.   133. **like:** likely.   134. **habits:** garments. **appointment:** accoutrement.   136. **sirrah:** (Usually addressed to an inferior; here, a sign of intimacy.)   136–37. **cases . . . nonce:** suits of buckram, a stiff-finished heavily sized fabric, for the purpose.   137. **immask:** hide, disguise. **noted:** known.   138. **doubt:** fear. **too hard:** too formidable.   140. **turned back:** turned their backs and ran away.   141–42. **incomprehensible:** boundless.   143. **wards:** parries.   144. **reproof:** disproof.

PRINCE: Well, I'll go with thee. Provide us all things necessary and meet me   145
tomorrow night in Eastcheap. There I'll sup. Farewell.

POINS: Farewell, my lord.   *Exit Poins.*

PRINCE:

    I know you all, and will awhile uphold
    The unyoked humor of your idleness.°
    Yet herein will I imitate the sun,   150
    Who doth permit the base contagious° clouds
    To smother up his beauty from the world,
    That° when he please again to be himself,
    Being wanted° he may be more wondered at
    By breaking through the foul and ugly mists   155
    Of vapors that did seem to strangle him.
    If all the year were playing holidays,
    To sport would be as tedious as to work;
    But when they seldom come, they wished-for come,
    And nothing pleaseth but rare accidents.°   160
    So when this loose behavior I throw off
    And pay the debt I never promisèd,
    By how much better than my word I am,
    By so much shall I falsify men's hopes;°
    And like bright metal on a sullen ground,°   165
    My reformation, glittering o'er my fault,
    Shall show more goodly and attract more eyes
    Than that which hath no foil° to set it off.
    I'll so offend to° make offense a skill,°
    Redeeming time° when men think least I will.   *Exit.*   170

Act i, Scene iii°

Enter the King, Northumberland, Worcester, Hotspur, Sir Walter Blunt, with others.

KING:

    My blood hath been too cold and temperate,
    Unapt to stir at these indignities,

---

149. unyoked . . . idleness: unbridled inclinations of your frivolity.   **151. contagious:** noxious.
153. That: so that.   **154. wanted:** missed, lacked.   **160. accidents:** events.   **164. hopes:** expectations.   **165. sullen ground:** dark background, like a *foil*. (See line 168.)   **168. foil:** metal
sheet laid contrastingly behind a jewel to set off its luster.   **169. to:** as to.   **skill:** i.e., clever tactic, piece of good policy.   **170. Redeeming time:** i.e., making amends for lost time.   **Act i,
Scene iii. Location:** London. The court (historically at Windsor).

And you have found me,° for accordingly
You tread upon my patience. But be sure
I will from henceforth rather be myself,°   5
Mighty and to be feared, than my condition,°
Which hath been smooth as oil, soft as young down,
And therefore lost that title of respect
Which the proud soul ne'er pays but to the proud.

WORCESTER:
Our house,° my sovereign liege, little deserves   10
The scourge of greatness to be used on it —
And that same greatness too which our own hands
Have holp° to make so portly.°

NORTHUMBERLAND [to the King]: My lord —

KING:
Worcester, get thee gone, for I do see   15
Danger and disobedience in thine eye.
O sir, your presence is too bold and peremptory,
And majesty might never yet endure
The moody frontier° of a servant brow.
You have good leave° to leave us. When we need   20
Your use and counsel, we shall send for you.   Exit Worcester.
[To Northumberland.] You were about to speak.

NORTHUMBERLAND: Yea, my good lord.
Those prisoners in Your Highness' name demanded,
Which Harry Percy here at Holmedon took,
Were, as he says, not with such strength denied   25
As is delivered° to Your Majesty.
Either envy,° therefore, or misprision°
Is guilty of this fault, and not my son.

HOTSPUR [to the King]:
My liege, I did deny no prisoners.
But I remember when the fight was done,   30
When I was dry with rage and extreme toil,
Breathless and faint, leaning upon my sword,
Came there a certain lord, neat and trimly dressed,

---

3. **found me:** found me so.   5. **myself:** i.e., my royal self.   6. **my condition:** my natural (mild) disposition.   10. **Our house:** i.e., the Percy family.   13. **holp:** helped.   **portly:** majestic, prosperous.   19. **moody frontier:** i.e., angry brow, frown. (*Frontier* literally means "outwork" or "fortification.")   20. **good leave:** full permission.   26. **delivered:** reported.   27. **envy:** malice.   **misprision:** misunderstanding.

Fresh as a bridegroom, and his chin new reaped°
Showed° like a stubble land at harvest home.°   35
He was perfumèd like a milliner,°
And twixt his finger and his thumb he held
A pouncet° box, which ever and anon
He gave his nose and took 't away again,
Who° therewith angry, when it next came there,   40
Took it in snuff;° and still° he smiled and talked,
And as the soldiers bore dead bodies by
He called them untaught knaves, unmannerly,
To bring a slovenly unhandsome corpse
Betwixt the wind and his nobility.   45
With many holiday and lady° terms
He questioned° me, amongst the rest demanded
My prisoners in Your Majesty's behalf.
I then, all smarting with my wounds being cold,
To be so pestered with a popinjay,°   50
Out of my grief° and my impatience
Answered neglectingly I know not what,
He should, or he should not; for he made me mad
To see him shine so brisk, and smell so sweet,
And talk so like a waiting-gentlewoman   55
Of guns and drums and wounds — God save the mark!° —
And telling me the sovereignest° thing on earth
Was parmacety° for an inward bruise,
And that it was great pity, so it was,
This villainous saltpeter° should be digged   60
Out of the bowels of the harmless earth,
Which many a good tall° fellow had destroyed
So cowardly, and but for these vile guns
He would himself have been a soldier.

---

34. chin new reaped: i.e., with beard freshly barbered according to the latest fashion, not like a soldier's beard. **35. Showed:** looked. **harvest home:** end of harvest, fields being neat and bare. **36. milliner:** man dealing in fancy articles, such as gloves and hats. **38. pouncet box:** perfume box with perforated lid. **40. Who:** i.e., his nose. **41. Took it in snuff:** (1) inhaled it (2) took offense. **still:** continually. **46. holiday and lady:** dainty and effeminate. **47. questioned:** (1) conversed with (2) put questions to. **50. popinjay:** parrot. **51. grief:** pain. **56. God . . . mark:** (Probably originally a formula to avert evil omen; here, an expression of impatience.) **57. sovereignest:** most efficacious. **58. parmacety:** spermaceti, a fatty substance taken from the head of the sperm whale, used as a medicinal ointment. **60. saltpeter:** potassium nitrate, used to make gunpowder and also used medicinally. **62. tall:** brave.

This bald° unjointed chat of his, my lord,   65
I answered indirectly,° as I said,
And I beseech you, let not his report
Come current° for an accusation
Betwixt my love and your high majesty.

BLUNT [*to the King*]:
The circumstance considered, good my lord,   70
Whate'er Lord Harry Percy then had said
To such a person and in such a place,
At such a time, with all the rest retold,
May reasonably die, and never rise
To do him wrong or any way impeach°   75
What then he said, so° he unsay it now.

KING:
Why, yet° he doth deny° his prisoners,
But with proviso and exception°
That we at our own charge shall ransom straight°
His brother-in-law, the foolish Mortimer,°   80
Who, on my soul, hath willfully betrayed
The lives of those that he did lead to fight
Against that great magician, damned Glendower,
Whose daughter, as we hear, that Earl of March°
Hath lately married. Shall our coffers then   85
Be emptied to redeem a traitor home?
Shall we buy treason and indent with fears°
When they have lost and forfeited themselves?
No, on the barren mountains let him starve!
For I shall never hold that man my friend   90
Whose tongue shall ask me for one penny cost
To ransom home revolted° Mortimer.

---

65. **bald:** trivial. 66. **indirectly:** inattentively, offhandedly. 68. **Come current:** (1) be taken at face value (2) come rushing in. 75. **impeach:** discredit. 76. **so:** provided that. 77. **yet:** (emphatic) i.e., even now. **deny:** refuse to surrender. 78. **proviso and exception:** (synonymous terms). 79. **straight:** straightway, at once. 80, 84. **Mortimer, Earl of March:** (There were two Edmund Mortimers; Shakespeare confuses them and combines their stories. It was the uncle [1376–1409?] who was captured by Glendower and married Glendower's daughter; it was the nephew [1391–1425], fifth Earl of March, who was proclaimed heir presumptive to King Richard II after the death of his father, the fourth earl, whom Richard had named as his heir. The uncle was brother to the fourth earl and to Hotspur's wife, Elizabeth, called Kate in this play.) 87. **indent with fears:** i.e., make a bargain or come to terms with traitors whom we have reason to fear. 92. **revolted:** rebellious.

HOTSPUR: Revolted Mortimer?
He never did fall off,° my sovereign liege,
But by the chance of war. To prove that true   95
Needs no more but one tongue for all those wounds,
Those mouthèd° wounds, which valiantly he took,
When on the gentle Severn's° sedgy° bank,
In single opposition, hand to hand,
He did confound° the best part of an hour   100
In changing hardiment° with great Glendower.
Three times they breathed,° and three times did they drink,
Upon agreement, of swift Severn's flood,°
Who° then, affrighted with their bloody looks,
Ran fearfully among the trembling reeds   105
And hid his crisp° head in the hollow bank,
Bloodstainèd with these valiant combatants.
Never did bare° and rotten policy°
Color° her working with such deadly wounds,
Nor never could the noble Mortimer   110
Receive so many, and all willingly.
Then let not him be slandered with revolt.°

KING:
Thou dost belie him, Percy, thou dost belie him.
He never did encounter with Glendower.
I tell thee,   115
He durst as well have met the devil alone
As Owen Glendower for an enemy.
Art thou not ashamed? But, sirrah, henceforth
Let me not hear you speak of Mortimer.
Send me your prisoners with the speediest means,   120
Or you shall hear in such a kind° from me
As will displease you. — My lord Northumberland,
We license your departure with your son.
Send us your prisoners, or you will hear of it.

Exit King [with Blunt, and train].

---

94. **fall off:** abandon his loyalty.   97. **mouthèd:** gaping and eloquent.   98. **Severn's:** (The Severn River flows from northern Wales and western England into the Bristol Channel.)   **sedgy:** bordered with reeds.   100. **confound:** consume.   101. **changing hardiment:** exchanging blows, matching valor.   102. **breathed:** paused for breath.   103. **flood:** river.   104. **Who:** i.e., the river.   106. **crisp:** curly, i.e., rippled.   108. **bare:** paltry.   **policy:** cunning.   109. **Color:** disguise.   112. **revolt:** i.e., the accusation of rebellion.   121. **kind:** manner.

HOTSPUR:
An if° the devil come and roar for them   125
I will not send them. I will after straight°
And tell him so, for I will ease my heart,
Albeit I make a hazard of my head.

NORTHUMBERLAND:
What, drunk with choler?° Stay and pause awhile.
Here comes your uncle.

Enter Worcester.

HOTSPUR: Speak of Mortimer?   130
Zounds, I will speak of him, and let my soul
Want mercy° if I do not join with him!
Yea, on his part° I'll empty all these veins,
And shed my dear blood drop by drop in the dust,
But I will lift the downtrod Mortimer   135
As high in the air as this unthankful king,
As this ingrate and cankered° Bolingbroke.°

NORTHUMBERLAND:
Brother, the King hath made your nephew mad.

WORCESTER:
Who struck this heat up after I was gone?

HOTSPUR:
He will forsooth have all my prisoners;   140
And when I urged the ransom once again
Of my wife's brother, then his cheek looked pale,
And on my face he turned an eye of death,°
Trembling even at the name of Mortimer.

WORCESTER:
I cannot blame him. Was not he° proclaimed   145
By Richard, that dead is, the next of blood?°

NORTHUMBERLAND:
He was; I heard the proclamation.
And then it was when the unhappy° king —
Whose wrongs in us° God pardon! — did set forth

---

125. **An if:** if.   126. **will after straight:** will go after immediately.   129. **choler:** anger.   132. **Want mercy:** lack mercy, be damned.   133. **on his part:** i.e., fighting on Mortimer's side.   137. **cankered:** spoiled, malignant.   **Bolingbroke:** i.e., King Henry IV; Hotspur pointedly refuses to acknowledge his royalty.   143. **an eye of death:** a fearful look.   145. **he:** i.e., Mortimer.   146. **next of blood:** heir to the throne.   148. **unhappy:** unfortunate.   149. **in us:** caused by our doings.

Upon his Irish expedition;° 150
From whence he, intercepted,° did return
To be deposed and shortly murderèd.

WORCESTER:
And for whose death we in the world's wide mouth
Live scandalized and foully spoken of.

HOTSPUR:
But, soft,° I pray you, did King Richard then 155
Proclaim my brother° Edmund Mortimer
Heir to the crown?

NORTHUMBERLAND: He did; myself did hear it.

HOTSPUR:
Nay, then I cannot blame his cousin° king,
That wished him on the barren mountains starve.
But shall it be that you that set the crown 160
Upon the head of this forgetful man,
And for his sake wear the detested blot
Of murderous subornation° — shall it be
That you a world of curses undergo,
Being the agents, or base second means,° 165
The cords, the ladder, or the hangman rather?
O, pardon me that I descend so low
To show the line° and the predicament°
Wherein you range° under this subtle king!
Shall it for shame be spoken in these days, 170
Or fill up chronicles in time to come,
That men of your nobility and power
Did gage them° both in an unjust behalf,
As both of you — God pardon it! — have done,
To put down Richard, that sweet lovely rose, 175
And plant this thorn, this canker,° Bolingbroke?
And shall it in more shame be further spoken
That you are fooled, discarded, and shook off

---

150. **Irish expedition:** (Richard was putting down a rebellion in Ireland when Bolingbroke returned to England from exile.) 151. **intercepted:** interrupted. 155. **soft:** i.e., wait a minute. 156. **brother:** i.e., brother-in-law. 158. **cousin:** (with a pun on *cozen*, "cheat"). 163. **murderous subornation:** the suborning of, or inciting to, murder. 165. **second means:** agents. 168. **line:** station, rank; also, hangman's rope. **predicament:** category; also, dangerous situation. 169. **range:** i.e., are classified. 173. **gage them:** engage, pledge themselves. 176. **canker:** (1) canker rose or dog rose, wild and unfragrant (2) ulcer.

By him for whom these shames ye underwent?
No! Yet° time serves wherein you may redeem   180
Your banished honors and restore yourselves
Into the good thoughts of the world again;
Revenge° the jeering and disdained° contempt
Of this proud king, who studies day and night
To answer° all the debt he owes to you   185
Even with the bloody payment of your deaths.
Therefore, I say —

WORCESTER: Peace, cousin, say no more.
And now I will unclasp a secret book,
And to your quick-conceiving° discontents
I'll read you matter deep and dangerous,   190
As full of peril and adventurous spirit
As to o'erwalk a current roaring loud
On the unsteadfast footing of a spear.°

HOTSPUR:
If he fall in, good night, or sink or swim!°
Send danger from the east unto the west,   195
So° honor cross it from the north to south,
And let them grapple. O, the blood more stirs
To rouse a lion than to start a hare!

NORTHUMBERLAND [to Worcester]:
Imagination of some great exploit
Drives him beyond the bounds of patience.   200

HOTSPUR:
By heaven, methinks it were an easy leap
To pluck bright honor from the pale-faced moon,
Or dive into the bottom of the deep,
Where fathom line° could never touch the ground,
And pluck up drownèd honor by the locks,   205
So he that doth redeem her thence might wear
Without corrival° all her dignities;
But out upon this half-faced fellowship!°

---

180. Yet: still.   183. Revenge: i.e., wherein you may revenge yourself against. **disdained:** disdainful.   185. answer: satisfy, discharge.   189. quick-conceiving: comprehending quickly. 193. spear: i.e., spear laid across a stream as a narrow bridge.   194. If . . . swim: i.e., such a man will face a life-or-death challenge if he falls in.   196. So: provided that. (Also at line 206.)   204. fathom line: a weighted line marked at fathom intervals (six feet), used for measuring the depth of water.   207. corrival: rival, competitor.   208. out . . . fellowship: down with this paltry business of sharing glory with others.

WORCESTER [*to Northumberland*]:
  He apprehends° a world of figures° here,
  But not the form° of what he should attend.° —
  Good cousin, give me audience for a while.

HOTSPUR:
  I cry you mercy.°

WORCESTER: Those same noble Scots
  That are your prisoners —

HOTSPUR: I'll keep them all.
  By God, he shall not have a Scot of them,
  No, if a scot° would save his soul, he shall not!
  I'll keep them, by this hand.

WORCESTER: You start away
  And lend no ear unto my purposes.
  Those prisoners you shall keep.

HOTSPUR: Nay, I will, that's flat.°
  He said he would not ransom Mortimer,
  Forbade my tongue to speak of Mortimer,
  But I will find him when he lies asleep,
  And in his ear I'll holler "Mortimer!"
  Nay, I'll have a starling shall be taught to speak
  Nothing but "Mortimer," and give it him
  To keep his anger still° in motion.

WORCESTER: Hear you, cousin, a word.

HOTSPUR:
  All studies° here I solemnly defy,°
  Save how to gall and pinch this Bolingbroke.
  And that same sword-and-buckler° Prince of Wales —
  But that I think his father loves him not
  And would be glad he met with some mischance —
  I would have him poisoned with a pot of ale.

WORCESTER:
  Farewell, kinsman. I'll talk to you
  When you are better tempered to attend.

210

215

220

225

230

---

209. **apprehends:** snatches at. **figures:** figures of the imagination, or figures of speech. 210. **form:** essential nature. **attend:** give attention to. 212. **cry you mercy:** beg your pardon. 214–15. **Scot . . . scot:** Scotsman . . . trifling amount. 218. **that's flat:** that's for sure. 225. **still:** continually. 227. **studies:** pursuits. **defy:** renounce. 229. **sword-and-buckler:** (Arms improper for a prince, who should carry rapier and dagger.)

NORTHUMBERLAND [*to Hotspur*]:

    Why, what a wasp-stung and impatient fool   235

    Art thou to break into this woman's mood,

    Tying thine ear to no tongue but thine own!

HOTSPUR:

    Why, look you, I am whipped and scourged with rods,

    Nettled and stung with pismires,° when I hear

    Of this vile politician,° Bolingbroke.   240

    In Richard's time — what do you call the place? —

    A plague upon it, it is in Gloucestershire;

    'Twas where the madcap duke his uncle kept,°

    His uncle York; where I first bowed my knee

    Unto this king of smiles, this Bolingbroke —   245

    'Sblood, when you and he came back from Ravenspurgh.°

NORTHUMBERLAND: At Berkeley Castle.°

HOTSPUR: You say true.

    Why, what a candy° deal of courtesy

    This fawning greyhound then did proffer me!   250

    "Look when° his infant fortune came to age,"

    And "gentle Harry Percy," and "kind cousin" —

    O, the devil take such cozeners!° — God forgive me!

    Good uncle, tell your tale; I have done.

WORCESTER:

    Nay, if you have not, to it again;   255

    We will stay° your leisure.

HOTSPUR: I have done, i' faith.

WORCESTER:

    Then once more to your Scottish prisoners.

    Deliver them up° without their ransom straight,

    And make the Douglas' son° your only means°

    For powers° in Scotland, which, for divers reasons   260

    Which I shall send you written, be assured

    Will easily be granted. [*To Northumberland.*] You, my lord,

    Your son in Scotland being thus employed,

---

239. **pismires:** ants. (From the urinous smell of an anthill.) **240. politician:** deceitful schemer. **243. kept:** dwelled. **246. Ravenspurgh:** (A port at the mouth of the River Humber in Yorkshire, now covered by the sea, where Bolingbroke landed on his return from exile.) **247. Berkeley Castle:** castle near Bristol. **249. candy:** sugared, flattering. **251. Look when:** when, as soon as. **253. cozeners:** cheats (with pun on *cousins*). **256. stay:** await. **258. Deliver them up:** free them. **259. the Douglas' son:** i.e., Mordake. (See 1.1.71 and note.) **means:** i.e., agent. **260. For powers:** for raising an army.

Shall secretly into the bosom creep°
Of that same noble prelate well beloved,   265
The Archbishop.
HOTSPUR: Of York, is it not?
WORCESTER: True, who bears hard°
    His brother's death at Bristol, the Lord Scroop.
    I speak not this in estimation,°   270
    As what I think might be, but what I know
    Is ruminated, plotted, and set down,
    And only stays but to behold the face
    Of that occasion that shall bring it on.
HOTSPUR:
    I smell it. Upon my life, it will do well.   275
NORTHUMBERLAND:
    Before the game is afoot thou still lett'st slip.°
HOTSPUR:
    Why, it cannot choose but be° a noble plot.
    And then the power° of Scotland and of York,
    To join with Mortimer, ha?
WORCESTER: And so they shall.
HOTSPUR:
    In faith, it is exceedingly well aimed.°   280
WORCESTER:
    And 'tis no little reason bids us speed,
    To save our heads by raising of a head;°
    For, bear ourselves as even° as we can,
    The King will always think him° in our debt,
    And think we think ourselves unsatisfied   285
    Till he hath found a time to pay us home.°
    And see already how he doth begin
    To make us strangers to his looks of love.
HOTSPUR:
    He does, he does. We'll be revenged on him.
WORCESTER:
    Cousin, farewell. No further go in this   290
    Than I by letters shall direct your course.

---

264. **secretly . . . creep:** win the confidence. 268. **bears hard:** resents. 270. **estimation:** guesswork. 276. **still lett'st slip:** always let loose the dogs. 277. **cannot choose but be:** cannot help being. 278. **power:** army. 280. **aimed:** designed. 282. **head:** army. 283. **even:** carefully. 284. **him:** himself. 286. **home:** (1) fully (2) with a thrust to the heart.

When time is ripe, which will be suddenly,°
I'll steal to Glendower and Lord Mortimer,
Where you and Douglas and our powers at once,°
As I will fashion it, shall happily° meet   295
To bear our fortunes in our own strong arms,°
Which now we hold at much uncertainty.

NORTHUMBERLAND:
Farewell, good brother. We shall thrive, I trust.

HOTSPUR:
Uncle, adieu. O, let the hours be short
Till fields° and blows and groans applaud our sport!   300

Exeunt [in separate groups].

ACT II, SCENE I°

Enter a Carrier with a lantern in his hand.

FIRST CARRIER: Heigh-ho! An° it be not four by the day,° I'll be hanged.
Charles's Wain° is over the new chimney, and yet our horse° not packed.
What, hostler!°

HOSTLER [*within*]:   Anon, anon.°

FIRST CARRIER: I prithee, Tom, beat° Cut's saddle,° put a few flocks° in the   5
point.° Poor jade° is wrung in the withers° out of all cess.°

Enter another Carrier.

SECOND CARRIER: Peas and beans° are as dank here as a dog,° and that is
the next° way to give poor jades the bots.° This house° is turned upside
down since Robin Hostler died.

FIRST CARRIER: Poor fellow never joyed since the price of oats rose. It was   10
the death of him.

---

292. **suddenly:** soon.   294. **at once:** all together.   295. **happily:** fortunately.   296. **arms:**
(1) limbs (2) military might.   300. **fields:** battlefields.   **ACT II, SCENE I.** Location: An inn-
yard on the London-Canterbury Road.   s.d. **Carrier:** one whose trade was conveying goods,
usually by pack-horses.   1. **An:** if.   **by the day:** in the morning.   2. **Charles's Wain:** i.e.,
Charlemagne's wagon; the constellation Ursa Major (the Big Dipper).   **horse:**
horses.   3. **hostler:** groom.   4. **Anon:** right away, coming.   5. **beat:** soften.   **Cut's saddle:**
packsaddle of the horse named *Cut*, meaning "bobtailed."   **flocks:** tufts of wool.   6. **point:**
pommel of the saddle.   **jade:** nag.   **wrung . . . withers:** chafed (by his saddle) on the ridge
between his shoulder-blades.   **cess:** measure, estimate.   7. **Peas and beans:** i.e., horse fodder.   **dank . . . dog:** i.e., damp as can be.   8. **next:** nearest, quickest.   **bots:** intestinal mag-
gots.   **house:** inn.

SECOND CARRIER: I think this be the most villainous house in all London road for fleas. I am stung like a tench.°

FIRST CARRIER: Like a tench? By the Mass, there is ne'er a king Christian° could be better bit than I have been since the first cock.°   15

SECOND CARRIER: Why, they will allow us ne'er a jordan,° and then we leak in your chimney,° and your chamber-lye° breeds fleas like a loach.°

FIRST CARRIER: What, Hostler! Come away° and be hanged! Come away.

SECOND CARRIER: I have a gammon of bacon° and two races° of ginger, to be delivered as far as Charing Cross.°   20

FIRST CARRIER: God's body, the turkeys in my pannier° are quite starved. What, hostler! A plague on thee! Hast thou never an eye in thy head? Canst not hear? An° 'twere not as good deed as drink to break the pate on thee,° I am a very° villain. Come, and be hanged! Hast no faith° in thee?   25

Enter Gadshill.

GADSHILL: Good morrow, carriers. What's o'clock?

FIRST CARRIER: I think it be two o'clock.

GADSHILL: I prithee, lend me thy lantern to see my gelding in the stable.

FIRST CARRIER: Nay, by God, soft,° I know a trick worth two of that, i' faith.   30

GADSHILL: I pray thee, lend me thine.

SECOND CARRIER: Ay, when, canst tell?° Lend me thy lantern, quoth he! Marry, I'll see thee hanged first.

GADSHILL: Sirrah carrier, what time do you mean to come to London?

SECOND CARRIER: Time enough to go to bed with a candle, I warrant thee. 35 Come, neighbor Mugs, we'll call up the gentlemen. They will along with company, for they have great charge.°   *Exeunt [Carriers].*

GADSHILL: What, ho! Chamberlain!°

Enter Chamberlain.

---

13. **tench:** a spotted fish, whose spots may have been likened to flea bites.   14. **king Christian:** Christian king, accustomed to have the best of everything.   15. **first cock:** i.e., midnight.   16. **jordan:** chamberpot.   17. **chimney:** fireplace.   **chamber-lye:** urine.   **loach:** a small freshwater fish, thought to harbor parasites.   18. **Come away:** come along.   19. **gammon of bacon:** ham.   **races:** roots.   20. **Charing Cross:** a market town lying between London and Westminster.   21. **pannier:** basket.   23. **An:** if.   23–24. **to break . . . thee:** to give you a blow on the head.   24. **very:** true.   **faith:** trustworthiness.   29. **soft:** i.e., wait a minute.   32. **Ay . . . tell:** i.e., you must be joking.   36–37. **They . . . charge:** i.e., they wish to travel in company, because they have lots of valuable cargo.   38. **Chamberlain:** (Male equivalent of a chambermaid. His entrance in the Quarto at line 37 may suggest that he is visible before Gadshill calls for him, giving point to his remark about being "At hand.")

CHAMBERLAIN: At hand, quoth pickpurse.°

GADSHILL: That's even as fair° as — at hand, quoth the chamberlain; for 40
thou variest no more from picking of purses than giving direction doth
from laboring; thou layest the plot how.°

CHAMBERLAIN: Good morrow, Master Gadshill. It holds current that° I
told you yesternight: there's a franklin° in the Weald° of Kent hath
brought three hundred marks° with him in gold. I heard him tell it to one 45
of his company last night at supper — a kind of auditor, one that hath
abundance of charge too, God knows what. They are up already, and call
for eggs and butter. They will away presently.°

GADSHILL: Sirrah, if they meet not with Saint Nicholas' clerks,° I'll give
thee this neck. 50

CHAMBERLAIN: No, I'll none° of it. I pray thee, keep that for the hangman,
for I know thou worshipest Saint Nicholas as truly as a man of falsehood
may.

GADSHILL: What° talkest thou to me of the hangman? If I hang, I'll make
a fat pair of gallows; for if I hang, old Sir John hangs with me, and thou 55
knowest he is no starveling. Tut, there are other Trojans° that thou
dream'st not of, the which for sport's sake are content to do the profes-
sion° some grace,° that would, if matters should be looked into, for their
own credit's sake make all whole. I am joined° with no foot-landrakers,°
no long-staff sixpenny strikers,° none of these mad mustachio purple- 60
hued malt-worms,° but with nobility and tranquillity,° burgomasters and
great oneyers,° such as can hold in,° such as will strike sooner than speak,
and speak sooner than drink, and drink sooner than pray. And yet,
zounds, I lie, for they pray continually to their saint, the commonwealth,
or rather not pray to her but prey on her, for they ride up and down on 65
her and make her their boots.°

---

39. **At . . . pickpurse:** i.e., I am right beside you, as the pickpurse said.   40. **fair:** good,
apt.   41–42. **thou variest . . . how:** i.e., you don't actually do the stealing, but you give directions, like a master workman to his apprentices.   43. **holds current that:** holds true
what.   44. **a franklin:** a farmer owning his own land.   **Weald:** wooded region.   45. **marks:**
coins of the value of thirteen shillings four pence.   48. **presently:** immediately.   49. **Saint
Nicholas' clerks:** highwaymen. (Saint Nicholas was popularly supposed the patron of
thieves.)   51. **I'll none:** I want none.   54. **What:** Why.   56. **Trojans:** i.e., slang for "sports" or
"roisterers."   57–58. **profession:** i.e., robbery.   58. **grace:** credit, favor.   59. **joined:** associated.   **foot-landrakers:** thieves who travel on foot.   60. **long-staff sixpenny strikers:** robbers
with long staves who would knock down their victims for sixpence.   60–61. **mustachio purple-
hued malt-worms:** purple-faced drunkards with huge mustaches.   61. **tranquillity:** those who
lead easy lives.   62. **oneyers:** ones (?).   **hold in:** keep a secret; hold fast.   66. **boots:** booty
(with pun on *boots*, "shoes").

CHAMBERLAIN: What, the commonwealth their boots? Will she hold out water in foul way?°

GADSHILL: She will, she will. Justice hath liquored° her. We steal as in a castle,° cocksure. We have the receipt° of fern seed;° we walk invisible. 70

CHAMBERLAIN: Nay, by my faith, I think you are more beholding° to the night than to fern seed for your walking invisible.

GADSHILL: Give me thy hand. Thou shalt have a share in our purchase,° as I am a true man.

CHAMBERLAIN: Nay, rather let me have it as you are a false thief. 75

GADSHILL: Go to; *homo* is a common name to all men.° Bid the hostler bring my gelding out of the stable. Farewell, you muddy° knave.

[*Exeunt separately.*]

Act ii, Scene ii°

Enter Prince, Poins, Peto, [and Bardolph].

POINS: Come, shelter, shelter! I have removed Falstaff's horse, and he frets° like a gummed velvet.

PRINCE: Stand close.°   [*They step aside.*]

Enter Falstaff.

FALSTAFF: Poins! Poins, and be hanged! Poins!

PRINCE [*coming forward*]: Peace, ye fat-kidneyed rascal! What a brawling dost 5 thou keep!°

FALSTAFF: Where's Poins, Hal?

PRINCE: He is walked up to the top of the hill. I'll go seek him.

[*He steps aside.*]

FALSTAFF: I am accursed to rob in that thief's company. The rascal hath re-moved my horse and tied him I know not where. If I travel but four foot 10 by the square° further afoot, I shall break my wind. Well, I doubt not but to die a fair° death for all° this, if I scape hanging for killing that rogue. I have forsworn his company hourly any time this two-and-twenty years,

---

67–68. **Will . . . way:** will she let you go dry in muddy roads, i.e., will she protect you in tight places.   69. **liquored:** (1) made waterproof by oiling (2) bribed (3) made drunk.   69–70. **as in a castle:** i.e., in complete security.   70. **receipt:** recipe, formula.   **of fern seed:** i.e., of becom-ing invisible (since fern seed, almost invisible itself, was popularly supposed to render its pos-sessor invisible).   71. **beholding:** beholden.   73. **purchase:** booty.   76. **homo . . . men:** i.e., the Latin name for man applies to all types.   77. **muddy:** stupid.   **Act ii, Scene ii. Loca-tion:** The highway, near Gad's Hill.   2. **frets:** chafes (with pun on another meaning of the word, applying to *gummed velvet*, velvet stiffened with gum and therefore liable to *fret*, or "wear").   3. **close:** concealed.   6. **keep:** keep up.   11. **square:** a measuring tool.   12. **fair:** exemplary.   **for all:** despite all.

and yet I am bewitched with the rogue's company. If the rascal have not given me medicines° to make me love him, I'll be hanged; it could not be else — I have drunk medicines. Poins! Hal! A plague upon you both! Bardolph! Peto! I'll starve ere I'll rob a foot further. An 'twere not as good a deed as drink to turn true man° and to leave these rogues, I am the veriest varlet that ever chewed with a tooth. Eight yards of uneven ground is three-score-and-ten miles afoot with me, and the stony-hearted villains know it well enough. A plague upon it when thieves cannot be true one to another! (*They whistle.*) Whew!° A plague upon you all! Give me my horse, you rogues, give me my horse, and be hanged!

PRINCE [*coming forward*]: Peace, ye fat-guts! Lie down. Lay thine ear close to the ground and list° if thou canst hear the tread of travelers.

FALSTAFF: Have you any levers to lift me up again, being down? 'Sblood, I'll not bear mine own flesh so far afoot again for all the coin in thy father's Exchequer. What a plague mean ye to colt° me thus?

PRINCE: Thou liest. Thou art not colted, thou art uncolted.

FALSTAFF: I prithee, good Prince Hal, help me to my horse,° good king's son.

PRINCE: Out, ye rogue! Shall I be your hostler?

FALSTAFF: Go hang thyself in thine own heir-apparent garters! If I be ta'en, I'll peach° for this. An° I have not ballads made on you all and sung to filthy tunes, let a cup of sack be my poison. When a jest is so forward,° and afoot° too! I hate it.

Enter Gadshill.

GADSHILL: Stand.°

FALSTAFF: So I do, against my will.

POINS [*coming forward with Bardolph and Peto*]: O, 'tis our setter.° I know his voice.

BARDOLPH: What news?

GADSHILL: Case ye,° case ye, on with your vizards! There's money of the King's coming down the hill; 'tis going to the King's Exchequer.

---

15. **medicines:** love potions.   18. **turn true man:** turn honest; turn informer.   22. **Whew:** (Perhaps Falstaff tries to answer the whistling he hears or mocks it.)   25. **list:** listen.   28. **colt:** trick, cheat. (In line 29, Prince Hal puns on the common meaning.)   30. **help . . . horse:** help me to find my horse. (But in line 32, the Prince comically retorts as though having been asked to hold the stirrup while Falstaff mounted, as a hostler would do.)   34. **peach:** inform on you.   **An:** if.   35. **so forward:** (1) so far advanced (referring to the robbery plot) (2) so presumptuous (referring to the joke played on him).   36. **afoot:** (1) in progress (2) on foot, i.e., not on horseback.   37. **Stand:** don't move. (But Falstaff answers in the sense of "stand on one's feet.")   39. **setter:** arranger of the robbery. (See 1.2 83 and note.)   42. **Case ye:** put on your masks.

FALSTAFF: You lie, ye rogue, 'tis going to the King's Tavern.

GADSHILL: There's enough to make us all.°   45

FALSTAFF: To be hanged.

PRINCE: Sirs, you four shall front° them in the narrow lane; Ned Poins and
   I will walk lower. If they scape from your encounter, then they light
   on us.

PETO: How many be there of them?   50

GADSHILL: Some eight or ten.

FALSTAFF: Zounds, will they not rob us?

PRINCE: What, a coward, Sir John Paunch?

FALSTAFF: Indeed, I am not John of Gaunt,° your grandfather, but yet no
   coward, Hal.   55

PRINCE: Well, we leave that to the proof.°

POINS: Sirrah Jack, thy horse stands behind the hedge. When thou need'st
   him, there thou shalt find him. Farewell, and stand fast.

FALSTAFF: Now cannot I strike him, if I should be hanged.°

PRINCE [*to Poins*]:   Ned, where are our disguises?   60

POINS [*to Prince*]:   Here, hard by. Stand close.   [*Exeunt Prince and Poins.*]

FALSTAFF: Now, my masters, happy man be his dole,° say I. Every man to
   his business.   [*They stand aside.*]

Enter the Travelers.

FIRST TRAVELER: Come, neighbor. The boy shall lead our horses down the
   hill; we'll walk afoot awhile, and ease our legs.   65

THIEVES [*coming forward*]:   Stand!

TRAVELERS: Jesus bless us!

FALSTAFF: Strike! Down with them! Cut the villains' throats! Ah, whore-
   son° caterpillars,° bacon-fed° knaves! They hate us youth. Down with
   them, fleece them!   70

TRAVELERS: O, we are undone, both we and ours forever!

FALSTAFF: Hang ye, gorbellied° knaves, are ye undone? No, ye fat chuffs;°
   I would your store° were here. On, bacons,° on! What, ye knaves, young
   men must live. You are grandjurors,° are ye? We'll jure ye, 'faith.

Here they rob them and bind them. Exeunt.

---

45. **make us all:** make our fortunes (or, as Falstaff sees it, make us be hanged).   47. **front:** con-
front.   54. **Gaunt:** i.e., Ghent (but punning on *gaunt,* "thin").   56. **proof:** test.   59. **Now
. . . hanged:** (Falstaff wishes he could hit Poins, who is too quick for him.)   62. **happy . . .
dole:** may happiness be every man's portion or lot.   68–69. **whoreson:** i.e., scurvy, abominable.   69. **caterpillars:** i.e., parasites.   **bacon-fed:** i.e., well-fed.   72. **gorbellied:** big-
bellied.   **chuffs:** churls, rich but miserly.   73. **store:** total wealth.   **bacons:** fat
men.   74. **grandjurors:** i.e., men of wealth, able to serve on juries.

Enter the Prince and Poins [in buckram].

PRINCE: The thieves have bound the true men. Now could thou and I rob 75
the thieves and go merrily to London, it would be argument° for a week,
laughter for a month, and a good jest forever.

POINS: Stand close. I hear them coming.   *[They stand aside.]*

Enter the thieves again.

FALSTAFF: Come, my masters, let us share, and then to horse before day.
An the Prince and Poins be not two arrant° cowards, there's no equity° 80
stirring. There's no more valor in that Poins than in a wild duck.
        [The thieves begin to share the booty.]

PRINCE: Your money!

POINS: Villains!

*As they are sharing, the Prince and Poins set upon
them. They all run away, and Falstaff, after a blow
or two, runs away too, leaving the booty behind
them.*

PRINCE:
Got with much ease. Now merrily to horse.
The thieves are all scattered and possessed with fear 85
So strongly that they dare not meet each other;
Each takes his fellow for an officer.
Away, good Ned. Falstaff sweats to death
And lards° the lean earth as he walks along.
Were't not for laughing, I should pity him. 90

POINS: How the fat rogue roared!   *Exeunt.*

ACT II, SCENE III°

Enter Hotspur, solus,° reading a letter.

HOTSPUR: "But, for mine own part, my lord, I could be well contented to
be there, in respect of the love I bear your house."° He could be contented; why is he not, then? In respect of the love he bears our house! He
shows in this he loves his own barn° better than he loves our house. Let

---

76. **argument:** a subject for conversation. 80. **arrant:** notorious, unmitigated. **equity:**
judgment, discernment. 89. **lards:** drips fat, bastes. ACT II, SCENE III. Location: Hotspur's estate (identified historically as Warkworth Castle in Northumberland). s.d. *solus:*
alone. 2. **house:** family. 4. **barn:** (Hotspur refers derisively to the writer's residence, taking
house, line 2, in its literal sense.)

me see some more. "The purpose you undertake is dangerous" — why, 5
that's certain. 'Tis dangerous to take a cold, to sleep, to drink; but I tell
you, my lord fool, out of this nettle, danger, we pluck this flower, safety.
"The purpose you undertake is dangerous, the friends you have named
uncertain, the time itself unsorted,° and your whole plot too light for the
counterpoise of° so great an opposition." Say you so, say you so? I say 10
unto you again, you are a shallow, cowardly hind,° and you lie. What a
lack-brain is this! By the Lord, our plot is a good plot as ever was laid,
our friends true and constant; a good plot, good friends, and full of expectation;° an excellent plot, very good friends. What a frosty-spirited
rogue is this! Why, my lord of York° commends the plot and the general 15
course of the action. Zounds, an° I were now by this rascal, I could brain
him with his lady's fan. Is there not my father, my uncle, and myself?
Lord Edmund Mortimer, my lord of York, and Owen Glendower? Is
there not besides the Douglas? Have I not all their letters to meet me in
arms by the ninth of the next month, and are they not some of them set 20
forward already? What a pagan° rascal is this, an infidel! Ha, you shall see
now in very sincerity of fear and cold heart will he to the King and lay
open all our proceedings. O, I could divide myself and go to buffets° for
moving° such a dish of skim milk with so honorable an action! Hang
him, let him tell the King, we are prepared. I will set forward tonight. 25

Enter his Lady.

How now, Kate? I must leave you within these two hours.
LADY PERCY:
O my good lord, why are you thus alone?
For what offense have I this fortnight been
A banished woman from my Harry's bed?
Tell me, sweet lord, what is't that takes from thee 30
Thy stomach,° pleasure, and thy golden sleep?
Why dost thou bend thine eyes upon the earth
And start so often when thou sitt'st alone?
Why hast thou lost the fresh blood in thy cheeks
And given my treasures and my rights of thee° 35
To thick-eyed° musing and curst° melancholy?

---

9. **unsorted:** unsuitable.   9–10. **for . . . of:** to counterbalance.   11. **hind:** menial, peas-
ant.   13–14. **expectation:** promise.   15. **lord of York:** i.e., Archbishop Scroop. (Also in line
18.)   16. **an:** if.   21. **pagan:** unbelieving.   23. **divide . . . buffets:** i.e., fight with myself.   24. **moving:** urging.   31. **stomach:** appetite.   35. **And . . . thee:** i.e., and given what I
treasure in you and have a right, as wife, to share.   36. **thick-eyed:** dull-sighted, vacant, ab-
stracted.   **curst:** ill-tempered.

In thy faint° slumbers I by thee have watched°
And heard thee murmur tales of iron wars,
Speak terms of manage° to thy bounding steed,
Cry, "Courage! To the field!" And thou hast talked   40
Of sallies and retires,° of trenches, tents,
Of palisadoes,° frontiers,° parapets,
Of basilisks,° of cannon, culverin,°
Of prisoners' ransom, and of soldiers slain,
And all the currents of a heady° fight.   45
Thy spirit within thee hath been so at war,
And thus hath so bestirred thee in thy sleep,
That beads of sweat have stood upon thy brow
Like bubbles in a late-disturbèd° stream,
And in thy face strange motions have appeared,   50
Such as we see when men restrain their breath
On some great sudden hest.° O, what portents are these?
Some heavy° business hath my lord in hand,
And I must know it, else he loves me not.

HOTSPUR:
What, ho!

[*Enter a Servant.*]

       Is Gilliams with the packet gone?   55
SERVANT: He is, my lord, an hour ago.
HOTSPUR:
Hath Butler brought those horses from the sheriff?
SERVANT:
One horse, my lord, he brought even° now.
HOTSPUR:
What horse? A roan, a crop-ear, is it not?
SERVANT:
It is, my lord.
HOTSPUR: That roan shall be my throne.   60
Well, I will back° him straight. O, *Esperance!*°
Bid Butler lead him forth into the park.   [*Exit Servant.*]

---

37. **faint:** restless. **watched:** lain awake. 39. **manage:** horsemanship. 41. **retires:** retreats. 42. **palisadoes:** stakes set in the ground for defense. **frontiers:** outworks, ramparts. 43. **basilisks:** large cannon. **culverin:** long cannon. 45. **heady:** headlong. 49. **late-disturbèd:** recently stirred up. 52. **hest:** command. 53. **heavy:** weighty; sorrowful. 58. **even:** just. 61. **back:** mount. *Esperance:* hope. (The motto of the Percy family.)

LADY PERCY: But hear you, my lord.

HOTSPUR: What sayst thou, my lady?

LADY PERCY: What is it carries you away?°   65

HOTSPUR: Why, my horse, my love, my horse.

LADY PERCY: Out, you mad-headed ape!
   A weasel hath not such a deal of spleen°
   As you are tossed° with. In faith,
   I'll know your business, Harry, that I will.   70
   I fear my brother Mortimer doth stir
   About his title,° and hath sent for you
   To line° his enterprise; but if you go —

HOTSPUR:
   So far afoot, I shall be weary, love.

LADY PERCY:
   Come, come, you paraquito,° answer me   75
   Directly unto this question that I ask.
   In faith, I'll break thy little finger, Harry,
   An if° thou wilt not tell me all things true.

HOTSPUR: Away,
   Away, you trifler! Love? I love thee not;   80
   I care not for thee, Kate. This is no world
   To play with mammets° and to tilt with lips.
   We must have bloody noses and cracked crowns,°
   And pass them current too. Gods me,° my horse!
   What sayst thou, Kate? What wouldst thou have with me?   85

LADY PERCY:
   Do you not love me? Do you not, indeed?
   Well, do not, then, for since you love me not
   I will not love myself. Do you not love me?
   Nay, tell me if you speak in jest or no.

HOTSPUR: Come, wilt thou see me ride?   90
   And when I am a-horseback I will swear
   I love thee infinitely. But hark you, Kate,
   I must not have you henceforth question me
   Whither I go, nor reason whereabout.°

---

65. carries you away: separates you from your judgment. (But Hotspur puns on the literal meaning.)   **68. spleen:** (The spleen was thought to be the source of impulsive and irritable behavior.)   **69. tossed:** tossed about, agitated.   **72. title:** claim to the throne.   **73. line:** strengthen.   **75. paraquito:** little parrot. (A term of endearment.)   **78. An if:** if.   **82. mammets:** dolls (with a quibble on the Latin *mamma* meaning "breast").   **83. crowns:** (1) heads (2) coins worth five shillings. (Cracked coins would not "pass current," as Hotspur jokes in the next line.)   **84. Gods me:** God save me.   **94. reason whereabout:** discuss about what.

Whither I must, I must; and, to conclude,   95
This evening must I leave you, gentle Kate.
I know you wise, but yet no farther wise
Than Harry Percy's wife; constant you are,
But yet a woman; and for secrecy,
No lady closer,° for I well believe   100
Thou wilt not utter what thou dost not know,
And so far will I trust thee, gentle Kate.

LADY PERCY: How, so far?

HOTSPUR:
Not an inch further. But hark you, Kate:
Whither I go, thither shall you go too.   105
Today will I set forth, tomorrow you.
Will this content you, Kate?

LADY PERCY: It must, of force.°   *Exeunt.*

ACT II, SCENE IV°

Enter Prince and Poins.

PRINCE: Ned, prithee, come out of that fat° room, and lend me thy hand
to laugh a little.

POINS: Where hast been, Hal?

PRINCE: With three or four loggerheads° amongst three or four score
hogsheads.° I have sounded the very bass° string of humility. Sirrah, I am   5
sworn brother to a leash of drawers,° and can call them all by their Christian names, as Tom, Dick, and Francis. They take it already upon their
salvation° that, though I be but Prince of Wales, yet I am the king of
courtesy, and tell me flatly I am no proud Jack° like Falstaff, but a
Corinthian,° a lad of mettle, a good boy — by the Lord, so they call   10
me! — and when I am King of England I shall command all the good
lads in Eastcheap. They call drinking deep "dyeing scarlet";° and when
you breathe in your watering° they cry "hem!" and bid you "play it off."°

---

100. **closer:** more close-mouthed.   107. **of force:** perforce, of necessity.   ACT II, SCENE IV. Location: A tavern in Eastcheap, London, usually identified as the Boar's Head. Some tavern furniture, including stools, is provided onstage.   1. **fat:** stuffy, or, a vat room.   4. **loggerheads:**
blockheads.   5. **hogsheads:** wine barrels.   **bass:** (With a pun on *base.*)   6. **leash of drawers:**
i.e., three waiters.   7–8. **take . . . salvation:** already maintain it as they hope to be saved.
9. **Jack:** (1) Jack Falstaff (2) fellow.   10. **Corinthian:** i.e., gay blade, good sport. (Corinth was reputed to be licentious.)   12. **They . . . scarlet:** (Either because excessive drinking causes a red
complexion or because urine, produced by *drinking deep,* was sometimes used for fixing
dyes.)   13. **breathe . . . watering:** pause for breath in your drinking.   **play it off:** drink it up.

To conclude, I am so good a proficient in one quarter of an hour that I
can drink with any tinker in his own language during my life. I tell thee,   15
Ned, thou hast lost much honor that thou wert not with me in this action. But, sweet Ned — to sweeten which name of Ned, I give thee this
pennyworth of sugar,° clapped even now into my hand by an underskinker,° one that never spake other English in his life than "Eight
shillings and sixpence," and "You are welcome," with this shrill addition,   20
"Anon,° anon, sir! Score° a pint of bastard° in the Half-Moon,"° or so.
But, Ned, to drive away the time till Falstaff come, I prithee do thou
stand in some by-room° while I question my puny° drawer° to what end
he gave me the sugar; and do thou never leave calling "Francis," that his
tale to me may be nothing but "Anon." Step aside, and I'll show thee a   25
precedent.°   [*Exit Poins.*]

POINS [*within*]:   Francis!
PRINCE: Thou art perfect.
POINS [*within*]:   Francis!

Enter [*Francis, a*] *drawer.*

FRANCIS: Anon, anon, sir. — Look down into the Pomgarnet,° Ralph.   30
PRINCE: Come hither, Francis.
FRANCIS: My lord?
PRINCE: How long hast thou to serve,° Francis?
FRANCIS: Forsooth, five years, and as much as to —
POINS [*within*]:   Francis!   35
FRANCIS: Anon, anon, sir.
PRINCE: Five year! By 'r Lady,° a long lease for the clinking of pewter. But
Francis, darest thou be so valiant as to play the coward with thy inden-
ture° and show it a fair pair of heels and run from it?
FRANCIS: O Lord, sir, I'll be sworn upon all the books° in England, I could   40
find in my heart —
POINS [*within*]:   Francis!
FRANCIS: Anon, sir.
PRINCE: How old art thou, Francis?
FRANCIS: Let me see, about Michaelmas° next I shall be —   45
POINS [*within*]:   Francis!

18. sugar: (Used to sweeten wine.) 18–19. underskinker: assistant to a waiter or
bartender. 21. Anon: right away, coming. Score: charge. bastard: (A sweet Spanish
wine.) Half-Moon: (The name of a room in the inn.) 23. by-room: side-room. puny:
inexperienced, raw. drawer: tapster, one who draws liquor. 26. precedent:
example. 30. Pomgarnet: Pomegranate. (Another room in the inn.) 33. serve: i.e., serve
out your apprenticeship. 37. By 'r Lady: by Our Lady. 38–39. indenture: contract of apprenticeship. 40. books: i.e., Bibles. 45. Michaelmas: September 29.

FRANCIS: Anon, sir. Pray, stay a little, my lord.

PRINCE: Nay, but hark you, Francis: for the sugar thou gavest me, 'twas a pennyworth, was 't not?

FRANCIS: O Lord, I would it had been two! 50

PRINCE: I will give thee for it a thousand pound. Ask me when thou wilt, and thou shalt have it.

POINS [*within*]: Francis!

FRANCIS: Anon, anon.

PRINCE: Anon, Francis? No, Francis; but tomorrow, Francis, or, Francis, o' 55 Thursday, or indeed, Francis, when thou wilt. But, Francis —

FRANCIS: My lord?

PRINCE: Wilt thou rob this leathern-jerkin, crystal-button, not-pated, agate-ring, puke-stocking, caddis-garter, smooth-tongue, Spanish-pouch° — 60

FRANCIS: O Lord, sir, who do you mean?

PRINCE: Why, then, your brown bastard is your only drink; for look you, Francis, your white canvas doublet will sully. In Barbary, sir, it° cannot come to so much.°

FRANCIS: What, sir? 65

POINS [*within*]: Francis!

PRINCE: Away, you rogue! Dost thou not hear them call?

> *Here they both call him; the drawer stands amazed, not knowing which way to go.*

Enter Vintner.

VINTNER: What° stand'st thou still and hear'st such a calling? Look to the guests within. [*Exit Francis.*] My lord, old Sir John, with half a dozen more, are at the door. Shall I let them in? 70

PRINCE: Let them alone awhile, and then open the door. [*Exit Vintner.*] Poins!

Enter Poins.

POINS: Anon, anon, sir.

PRINCE: Sirrah, Falstaff and the rest of the thieves are at the door. Shall we be merry? 75

58–60. Wilt . . . Spanish-pouch: i.e., will you rob your master of your services by running away, he who is characterized by a leather jacket, transparent buttons, cropped hair, a ring with small figures in an agate stone for a seal, dark woolen stockings, worsted garters, an ingratiating flattering manner of speech, wallet of Spanish leather. **62–64. Why . . . much:** (The Prince talks seeming nonsense in order to bewilder Francis, but he also implies that Francis should stick to his trade, since he will not cut much of a figure in the world.) **63. it:** i.e., sugar. **68. What:** why.

POINS: As merry as crickets, my lad. But hark ye, what cunning match°
have you made with this jest of the drawer? Come, what's the issue?°

PRINCE: I am now of all humors that have showed themselves humors
since the old days of Goodman° Adam to the pupil° age of this present
twelve o'clock at midnight.°   80

[*Enter Francis, hurrying across the stage with wine.*]

What's o'clock, Francis?

FRANCIS: Anon, anon, sir.   [*Exit.*]

PRINCE: That ever this fellow should have fewer words than a parrot, and
yet the son of a woman! His industry is upstairs and downstairs, his eloquence the parcel of a reckoning.° I am not yet of Percy's mind, the Hot-   85
spur of the north, he that kills me° some six or seven dozen of Scots at a
breakfast, washes his hands, and says to his wife, "Fie upon this quiet life!
I want work." "O my sweet Harry," says she, "how many hast thou killed
today?" "Give my roan horse a drench,"° says he,° and answers, "Some
fourteen," an hour after, "a trifle, a trifle." I prithee, call in Falstaff. I'll   90
play Percy, and that damned brawn° shall play Dame Mortimer his wife.
"Rivo!"° says the drunkard. Call in ribs,° call in tallow.°

Enter Falstaff [*Gadshill, Bardolph and Peto; Francis following with wine*].

POINS: Welcome, Jack. Where hast thou been?

FALSTAFF: A plague of° all cowards, I say, and a vengeance too! Marry and
amen! Give me a cup of sack, boy. Ere I lead this life long, I'll sew nether-   95
stocks,° and mend them and foot° them too. A plague of all cowards!
Give me a cup of sack, rogue. Is there no virtue extant?   *He drinketh.*

PRINCE: Didst thou never see Titan° kiss a dish of butter, pitiful-hearted
Titan, that° melted at the sweet tale of the sun's? If thou didst, then behold that compound.°   100

FALSTAFF: You rogue, here's lime in this sack° too. There is nothing but
roguery to be found in villainous man, yet a coward is worse than a cup
of sack with lime in it. A villainous coward! Go thy ways, old Jack, die

---

76. **match:** game, contest.   77. **issue:** outcome, point.   78–80. **I . . . midnight:** i.e., I'm now
in a mood for anything that has happened in the whole history of the world.   79. **Goodman:**
(Title for a farmer.)   **pupil:** youthful.   85. **parcel . . . reckoning:** items of a bill.   86. **kills
me:** i.e., kills. (*Me* is used colloquially.)   89. **drench:** draft (sometimes of medicine).   **says he:**
i.e., he tells a servant.   91. **brawn:** fat boar.   92. **Rivo:** (An exclamation of uncertain meaning, but related to drinking.)   **ribs:** rib roast.   **tallow:** fat drippings.   94. **of:**
on.   95–96. **netherstocks:** stockings (the sewing or mending of which is a menial occupation).   96. **foot:** make a new foot for.   98. **Titan:** i.e., the sun.   99. **that:** i.e., the butter.   100. **compound:** melting butter, i.e., Falstaff.   101. **lime in this sack:** i.e., lime added to
make the wine sparkle.

when thou wilt. If manhood, good manhood, be not forgot upon the face of the earth, then am I a shotten herring.° There lives not three good men 105 unhanged in England, and one of them is fat and grows old, God help the while!° A bad world, I say. I would I were a weaver;° I could sing psalms or anything. A plague of all cowards, I say still.

PRINCE: How now, woolsack,° what mutter you?

FALSTAFF: A king's son! If I do not beat thee out of thy kingdom with a 110 dagger of lath,° and drive all thy subjects afore thee like a flock of wild geese, I'll never wear hair on my face more. You, Prince of Wales!

PRINCE: Why, you whoreson round man, what's the matter?

FALSTAFF: Are not you a coward? Answer me to that. And Poins there?

POINS: Zounds, ye fat paunch, an° ye call me coward, by the Lord, I'll stab 115 thee.

FALSTAFF: I call thee coward? I'll see thee damned ere I call thee coward, but I would give a thousand pound I could run as fast as thou canst. You are straight enough in the shoulders; you care not who sees your back. Call you that backing of your friends? A plague upon such backing! Give 120 me them that will face me. Give me a cup of sack. I am a rogue if I drunk today.

PRINCE: O villain, thy lips are scarce wiped since thou drunk'st last.

FALSTAFF: All is one for that.° (*He drinketh.*) A plague of all cowards, still say I. 125

PRINCE: What's the matter?

FALSTAFF: What's the matter? There be four of us here have ta'en a thousand pound this day morning.°

PRINCE: Where is it, Jack, where is it?

FALSTAFF: Where is it? Taken from us it is. A hundred upon poor four 130 of us.

PRINCE: What, a hundred, man?

FALSTAFF: I am a rogue if I were not at half-sword° with a dozen of them two hours together. I have scaped° by miracle. I am eight times thrust through the doublet,° four through the hose,° my buckler° cut through 135 and through, my sword hacked like a handsaw — *ecce signum!*° I never

105. **a shotten herring:** a herring that has cast its roe and is consequently thin. 107. **the while:** i.e., in these bad times. **weaver:** (Many psalm-singing Protestant immigrants from the Low Countries were weavers.) 109. **woolsack:** bale of wool. 111. **dagger of lath:** (The Vice, a stock comic figure in morality plays, was so armed.) 115. **an:** if. 124. **All . . . that:** i.e., no matter. 128. **this day morning:** this morning. 133. **at half-sword:** fighting at close quarters. 134. **scaped:** escaped. 135. **doublet:** Elizabethan upper garment like a jacket. **hose:** close-fitting breeches. **buckler:** shield. 136. *ecce signum:* behold the proof. (Familiar words from the Mass.)

dealt better since I was a man. All would not do.° A plague of all cowards! Let them speak. If they speak more or less than truth, they are villains and the sons of darkness.

PRINCE: Speak, sirs, how was it?   140

GADSHILL: We four set upon some dozen —

FALSTAFF: Sixteen at least, my lord.

GADSHILL: And bound them.

PETO: No, no, they were not bound.

FALSTAFF: You rogue, they were bound, every man of them, or I am a Jew   145
else, an Hebrew Jew.

GADSHILL: As we were sharing, some six or seven fresh men set upon
us —

FALSTAFF: And unbound the rest, and then come in the other.°

PRINCE: What, fought you with them all?   150

FALSTAFF: All? I know not what you call all, but if I fought not with fifty
of them, I am a bunch of radish. If there were not two- or three-and-fifty
upon poor old Jack, then am I no two-legged creature.

PRINCE: Pray God you have not murdered some of them.

FALSTAFF: Nay, that's past praying for. I have peppered° two of them. Two   155
I am sure I have paid, two rogues in buckram suits. I tell thee what, Hal,
if I tell thee a lie, spit in my face, call me horse. Thou knowest my old
ward.° Here I lay,° and thus I bore my point. [*He demonstrates his stance.*]
Four rogues in buckram let drive at me —

PRINCE: What, four? Thou saidst but two even° now.   160

FALSTAFF: Four, Hal, I told thee four.

POINS: Ay, ay, he said four.

FALSTAFF: These four came all afront,° and mainly° thrust at me. I made
me° no more ado but took all their seven points in my target,° thus.

PRINCE: Seven? Why, there were but four even now.   165

FALSTAFF: In buckram?

POINS: Ay, four, in buckram suits.

FALSTAFF: Seven, by these hilts,° or I am a villain° else.

PRINCE [*aside to Poins*]: Prithee, let him alone. We shall have more anon.

FALSTAFF: Dost thou hear me, Hal?   170

PRINCE: Ay, and mark° thee too, Jack.

---

137. **All . . . do:** i.e., all that I did was of no use.   149. **other:** others.   155. **peppered:** i.e., killed.   158. **ward:** defensive stance, parry.   **lay:** stood.   160. **even:** just.   163. **afront:** abreast.   **mainly:** powerfully.   163–64. **made me:** made. (*Me* is used colloquially.)   164. **target:** shield.   168. **by these hilts:** by my sword hilt.   **villain:** i.e., no gentleman.   171. **mark:** (1) pay heed (2) keep count.

FALSTAFF: Do so, for it is worth the listening to. These nine in buckram that I told thee of —

PRINCE: So, two more already.

FALSTAFF: Their points° being broken — 175

POINS: Down fell their hose.

FALSTAFF: Began to give me ground; but I followed me° close, came in foot and hand; and with a thought° seven of the eleven I paid.

PRINCE: O monstrous! Eleven buckram men grown out of two!

FALSTAFF: But, as the devil would have it, three misbegotten knaves in 180 Kendal° green came at my back and let drive at me; for it was so dark, Hal, that thou couldst not see thy hand.

PRINCE: These lies are like their father that begets them, gross as a mountain, open, palpable. Why, thou claybrained guts, thou knotty-pated° fool, thou whoreson, obscene, greasy tallow-keech° — 185

FALSTAFF: What, art thou mad? Art thou mad? Is not the truth the truth?

PRINCE: Why, how couldst thou know these men in Kendal green when it was so dark thou couldst not see thy hand? Come, tell us your reason. What sayest thou to this?

POINS: Come, your reason, Jack, your reason. 190

FALSTAFF: What, upon compulsion? Zounds, an I were at the strappado,° or all the racks in the world, I would not tell you on compulsion. Give you a reason on compulsion? If reasons were as plentiful as blackberries,° I would give no man a reason upon compulsion, I.

PRINCE: I'll be no longer guilty of this sin. This sanguine° coward, this 195 bed-presser, this horse-backbreaker, this huge hill of flesh —

FALSTAFF: 'Sblood, you starveling, you eel-skin, you dried neat's° tongue, you bull's pizzle,° you stockfish!° O, for breath to utter what is like thee! You tailor's yard,° you sheath, you bowcase, you vile standing tuck° —

PRINCE: Well, breathe awhile, and then to it again, and when thou hast 200 tired thyself in base comparisons, hear me speak but this.

POINS: Mark, Jack.

PRINCE: We two saw you four set on four and bound them, and were masters of their wealth. Mark now how a plain tale shall put you down. Then did we two set on you four, and, with a word,° outfaced° you from your 205

---

175. **points:** sword points. (But Poins puns on the sense of laces, by which the hose were attached to the doublet.) 177. **followed me:** followed. 178. **with a thought:** quick as a thought. 181. **Kendal:** a town known for its textiles. 184. **knotty-pated:** thickheaded. 185. **tallow-keech:** lump of tallow. 191. **strappado:** a kind of torture. 193. **reasons ... blackberries:** (Falstaff puns on *raisins,* pronounced nearly like *reasons.*) 195. **sanguine:** ruddy. 197. **neat's:** ox's. 198. **pizzle:** penis. **stockfish:** dried cod. 199. **yard:** yardstick. **standing tuck:** rapier standing on its point, or no longer pliant. 205. **with a word:** (1) in a word (2) with a minimum of speech. **outfaced:** frightened.

prize, and have it, yea, and can show it you here in the house. And, Falstaff, you carried your guts away as nimbly, with as quick dexterity, and roared for mercy, and still run and roared, as ever I heard bull calf. What a slave art thou, to hack thy sword as thou hast done, and then say it was in fight! What trick, what device, what starting-hole° canst thou now find out to hide thee from this open and apparent shame? 210

POINS: Come, let's hear, Jack. What trick hast thou now?

FALSTAFF: By the Lord, I knew ye as well as he that made ye. Why, hear you, my masters, was it for me to kill the heir apparent? Should I turn upon the true prince? Why, thou knowest I am as valiant as Hercules, but 215 beware instinct. The lion will not touch the true prince. Instinct is a great matter; I was now a coward on instinct. I shall think the better of myself and thee during my life — I for a valiant lion, and thou for a true prince. But by the Lord, lads, I am glad you have the money. Hostess, clap to the doors! Watch° tonight, pray° tomorrow. Gallants, lads, boys, hearts of 220 gold, all the titles of good fellowship come to you! What, shall we be merry? Shall we have a play extempore?

PRINCE: Content; and the argument° shall be thy running away.

FALSTAFF: Ah, no more of that, Hal, an thou lovest me!

Enter Hostess.

HOSTESS: O Jesu, my lord the Prince! 225

PRINCE: How now, my lady the hostess, what sayst thou to me?

HOSTESS: Marry, my lord, there is a nobleman of the court at door would speak with you. He says he comes from your father.

PRINCE: Give him as much as will make him a royal man,° and send him back again to my mother. 230

FALSTAFF: What manner of man is he?

HOSTESS: An old man.

FALSTAFF: What doth° Gravity out of his bed at midnight? Shall I give him his answer?

PRINCE: Prithee, do, Jack. 235

FALSTAFF: Faith, and I'll send him packing. *Exit.*

PRINCE: Now, sirs. By 'r Lady, you fought fair; so did you, Peto; so did you, Bardolph. You are lions too, you ran away upon instinct, you will not touch the true prince; no, fie!

---

210. **starting-hole:** point of shelter (like a rabbit's hole). 220. **Watch:** (1) keep watchful vigil. (See Matthew 26:41.) (2) carouse. **pray:** (1) pray to God (2) prey. 223. **argument:** plot of the play. 229. **Give . . . man:** (Prince Hal puns on the value of coins: a *noble* was worth six shillings eight pence; a *royal* was worth ten shillings.) 233. **What doth:** why is.

BARDOLPH: Faith, I ran when I saw others run.   240

PRINCE: Faith, tell me now in earnest, how came Falstaff's sword so hacked?

PETO: Why, he hacked it with his dagger, and said he would swear truth out of England but he would° make you believe it was done in fight, and persuaded us to do the like.   245

BARDOLPH: Yea, and to tickle our noses with spear grass to make them bleed, and then to beslubber° our garments with it and swear it was the blood of true men. I did that° I did not this seven year before: I blushed to hear his monstrous devices.

PRINCE: O villain, thou stolest a cup of sack eighteen years ago and wert   250
taken with the manner,° and ever since thou hast blushed extempore.° Thou hadst fire° and sword on thy side, and yet thou rann'st away. What instinct hadst thou for it?

BARDOLPH: My lord, do you see these meteors?° Do you behold these exhalations?°   [Pointing to his own face.]   255

PRINCE: I do.

BARDOLPH: What think you they portend?°

PRINCE: Hot livers and cold purses.°

BARDOLPH: Choler,° my lord, if rightly taken.°

PRINCE: No, if rightly taken, halter.°   260

Enter Falstaff.°

Here comes lean Jack, here comes bare-bone. How now, my sweet creature of bombast?° How long is 't ago, Jack, since thou sawest thine own knee?

FALSTAFF: My own knee? When I was about thy years, Hal, I was not an eagle's talon in the waist; I could have crept into any alderman's thumb   265
ring. A plague of sighing and grief! It blows a man up like a bladder. There's villainous news abroad. Here was Sir John Bracy from your father. You must to the court in the morning. That same mad fellow of the

---

244. but he would: if he did not. **247. beslubber:** smear, cover. **248. that:** something. **251. taken . . . manner:** caught with the goods. **extempore:** without needing any occasion. (Bardolph is red-faced whether he blushes or not.) **252. fire:** i.e., a red nose and complexion caused by heavy drinking. **254, 255. meteors, exhalations:** i.e., the red blotches on Bardolph's face. **257. portend:** signify. (Continues the metaphor of astrological influence begun in *meteors* and *exhalations*.) **258. Hot . . . purses:** i.e., livers inflamed by drink and purses made empty by spending. **259. Choler:** a choleric or combative temperament. **taken:** understood. (But the Prince, in his next speech, uses the word to mean "arrested.") **260. halter:** hangman's noose. (The Prince plays on Bardolph's *choler,* which he takes as *collar.*) **s.d.** (Falstaff's entry in the Quarto after line 259 suggests he is visible to the audience while the Prince talks of a hangman's halter.) **262. bombast:** (1) cotton padding (2) fustian speech.

north, Percy, and he of Wales that gave Amamon° the bastinado° and
made Lucifer cuckold° and swore the devil his true liegeman° upon the   270
cross of a Welsh hook° — what a plague call you him?

POINS: Owen Glendower.

FALSTAFF: Owen, Owen, the same; and his son-in-law Mortimer, and old
Northumberland, and that sprightly Scot of Scots, Douglas, that runs
a-horseback up a hill perpendicular —   275

PRINCE: He that rides at high speed, and with his pistol kills a sparrow flying.

FALSTAFF: You have hit it.°

PRINCE: So did he never the sparrow.

FALSTAFF: Well, that rascal hath good mettle in him; he will not run.°   280

PRINCE: Why, what a rascal art thou then to praise him so for running!

FALSTAFF: A-horseback, ye cuckoo; but afoot he will not budge a foot.

PRINCE: Yes, Jack, upon instinct.

FALSTAFF: I grant ye, upon instinct. Well, he is there too, and one Mordake, and a thousand blue-caps° more. Worcester is stolen away tonight.   285
Thy father's beard is turned white with the news. You may buy land now
as cheap as stinking mackerel.

PRINCE: Why, then, it is like,° if there come a hot June and this civil buf-
feting hold,° we shall buy maidenheads as they buy hobnails, by the hun-
dreds.   290

FALSTAFF: By the mass, lad, thou sayest true; it is like we shall have good
trading that way. But tell me, Hal, art not thou horrible afeard? Thou being heir apparent, could the world pick thee out three such enemies again
as that fiend Douglas, that spirit Percy, and that devil Glendower? Art
thou not horribly afraid? Doth not thy blood thrill at it?   295

PRINCE: Not a whit, i' faith. I lack some of thy instinct.

FALSTAFF: Well, thou wilt be horribly chid° tomorrow when thou comest
to thy father. If thou love me, practice an answer.

PRINCE: Do thou stand for my father, and examine me upon the particulars of my life.   300

FALSTAFF: Shall I? Content. This chair shall be my state,° this dagger my
scepter, and this cushion my crown.

---

269. Amamon: (The name of a demon.) **bastinado:** beating on the soles of the
feet. **270. made . . . cuckold:** i.e., gave Lucifer his horns, the sign of cuckoldry. **and swore
. . . liegeman:** and made the devil take an oath of allegiance as a true subject. **271. Welsh
hook:** curved-bladed pike lacking the cross shape of the sword on which such oaths were usually sworn. **278. hit it:** described it exactly. (But the Prince takes *hit* literally in the next
line.) **280. run:** flee. (But the Prince answers punningly in the sense of "ride at high
speed.") **285. blue-caps:** Scottish soldiers. **288. like:** likely. **289. hold:** continues.
297. chid: chided. **301. state:** chair of state, throne.

[Falstaff establishes himself on his "throne."]

PRINCE: Thy state is taken for a joint stool,° thy golden scepter for a leaden° dagger, and thy precious rich crown for a pitiful bald crown.

FALSTAFF: Well, an° the fire of grace be not quite out of thee, now shalt thou be moved. Give me a cup of sack to make my eyes look red, that it may be thought I have wept; for I must speak in passion, and I will do it in King Cambyses' vein.° 305

PRINCE: Well, here is my leg. *[He bows.]*

FALSTAFF: And here is my speech. Stand aside, nobility. 310

HOSTESS: O Jesu, this is excellent sport, i' faith!

FALSTAFF:

Weep not, sweet queen, for trickling tears are vain.

HOSTESS: O, the Father,° how he holds his countenance!°

FALSTAFF:

For God's sake, lords, convey° my tristful° queen,
For tears do stop° the floodgates of her eyes. 315

HOSTESS: O Jesu, he doth it as like one of these harlotry° players° as ever I see!

FALSTAFF:

Peace, good pint pot; peace, good tickle-brain.° — Harry, I do not only marvel where thou spendest thy time, but also how thou art accompanied; for though the camomile, the more it is trodden on the faster it grows, yet youth, the more it is wasted the sooner it wears.° That thou art my son I have partly thy mother's word, partly my own opinion, but chiefly a villainous trick° of thine eye and a foolish hanging of thy nether lip that doth warrant° me. If then thou be son to me, here lies the point: why, being son to me, art thou so pointed at? Shall the blessed sun of heaven prove a micher° and eat blackberries? A question not to be asked. Shall the son of England prove a thief and take purses? A question to be asked. There is a thing, Harry, which thou hast often heard of, and it is known to many in our land by the name of pitch. This pitch, as ancient writers do report, doth 320 325

---

303. **joint stool:** a stool made by a joiner or furniture maker. (To "take someone for a joint stool" is to offer an intentionally silly apology for overlooking that person, as in *King Lear,* 3.6.52. Prince Hal suggests that Falstaff's *state* is ridiculous [punning on *state,* "throne"].) 304. **leaden** of soft metal, hence inferior. 305. **an:** if. 308. **in . . . vein:** i.e., in the ranting and (by Shakespeare's time) old-fashioned style of Thomas Preston's *Cambyses,* an early Elizabethan tragedy. 313. **the Father:** i.e., in God's name. **holds his countenance:** keeps a straight face. 314. **convey:** escort away. **tristful:** sorrowing. 315. **stop:** fill. 316. **harlotry:** scurvy, vagabond. **players:** actors. 318. **tickle-brain:** (A slang term for strong liquor, here applied as a nickname for the tavern hostess.) 320–21. **camomile . . . wears:** (This parodies the style of Lyly's *Euphues* and exaggerates the balance and alliteration of the style.) **camomile:** an aromatic creeping herb whose flowers and leaves are used medicinally. 323. **trick:** trait. 324. **warrant:** assure. 326. **micher:** truant.

defile;° so doth the company thou keepest. For, Harry, now I do not speak   330
to thee in drink but in tears, not in pleasure but in passion, not in words
only but in woes also. And yet there is a virtuous man whom I have often
noted in thy company, but I know not his name.

PRINCE: What manner of man, an it like° Your Majesty?

FALSTAFF: A goodly portly° man, i' faith, and a corpulent; of a cheerful   335
look, a pleasing eye, and a most noble carriage; and, as I think, his age
some fifty, or, by 'r Lady, inclining to threescore; and now I remember
me, his name is Falstaff. If that man should be lewdly° given, he deceiveth me; for, Harry, I see virtue in his looks. If then the tree may be
known by the fruit,° as the fruit by the tree, then peremptorily° I speak it,   340
there is virtue in that Falstaff. Him keep with, the rest banish. And tell
me now, thou naughty varlet, tell me, where hast thou been this month?

PRINCE: Dost thou speak like a king? Do thou stand for me, and I'll play
my father.

FALSTAFF: Depose me? If thou dost it half so gravely, so majestically, both   345
in word and matter, hang me up by the heels for a rabbit-sucker° or a
poulter's° hare.

[*Hal takes Falstaff's place on the "throne."*]

PRINCE: Well, here I am set.°

FALSTAFF: And here I stand. Judge, my masters.

PRINCE: Now, Harry, whence come you?   350

FALSTAFF: My noble lord, from Eastcheap.

PRINCE: The complaints I hear of thee are grievous.

FALSTAFF: 'Sblood,° my lord, they are false. — Nay, I'll tickle ye for° a
young prince, i' faith.

PRINCE: Swearest thou, ungracious boy? Henceforth ne'er look on me.   355
Thou art violently carried away from grace. There is a devil haunts thee
in the likeness of an old fat man; a tun° of man is thy companion. Why
dost thou converse° with that trunk of humors,° that bolting-hutch° of
beastliness, that swollen parcel of dropsies, that huge bombard° of sack,
that stuffed cloak-bag° of guts, that roasted Manningtree ox° with the   360

329–30. This . . . defile: (An allusion to the familiar proverb from Ecclesiasticus 13:1 about the defilement of touching pitch.)   **pitch:** a sticky, black residue from the distillation of tar, used to seal wood from moisture.   **334. an it like:** if it please.   **335. portly:** (1) stately (2) corpulent.   **338. lewdly:** wickedly.   **339–40. If . . . by the fruit:** (See Matthew 12:33.)   **340. peremptorily:** decisively.   **346. rabbit-sucker:** unweaned rabbit.   **347. poulter's:** poulterer's.   **348. set:** seated.   **353. 'Sblood:** i.e., by Christ's blood.   **tickle ye for:** amuse you in the role of.   **357. tun:** (1) large barrel (2) ton.   **358. converse:** associate.   **humors:** body fluids, diseases.   **bolting-hutch:** large bin.   **359. bombard:** leathern drinking vessel.   **360. cloak-bag:** portmanteau.   **Manningtree ox:** (Manningtree, a town in Essex, had noted fairs where, no doubt, oxen were roasted whole.)

pudding° in his belly, that reverend Vice,° that gray Iniquity,° that father ruffian, that vanity° in years? Wherein is he good but to taste sack and drink it? Wherein neat and cleanly° but to carve a capon and eat it? Wherein cunning° but in craft? Wherein crafty but in villainy? Wherein villainous but in all things? Wherein worthy but in nothing? 365

FALSTAFF: I would Your Grace would take me with you.° Whom means Your Grace?

PRINCE: That villainous abominable misleader of youth, Falstaff, that old white-bearded Satan.

FALSTAFF: My lord, the man I know. 370

PRINCE: I know thou dost.

FALSTAFF: But to say I know more harm in him than in myself were to say more than I know. That he is old, the more the pity, his white hairs do witness it; but that he is, saving your reverence,° a whoremaster, that I utterly deny. If sack and sugar be a fault, God help the wicked! If to be old 375 and merry be a sin, then many an old host° that I know is damned. If to be fat be to be hated, then Pharaoh's lean kine° are to be loved. No, my good lord, banish Peto, banish Bardolph, banish Poins; but for sweet Jack Falstaff, kind Jack Falstaff, true Jack Falstaff, valiant Jack Falstaff, and therefore more valiant being as he is old Jack Falstaff, banish not him thy 380 Harry's company, banish not him thy Harry's company — banish plump Jack, and banish all the world.

PRINCE: I do, I will. *[A knocking.*
Exeunt Hostess, Francis, and Bardolph.]

Enter Bardolph, running.

BARDOLPH: O, my lord, my lord! The sheriff with a most monstrous watch° is at the door. 385

FALSTAFF: Out, ye rogue! Play out the play. I have much to say in the behalf of that Falstaff.

Enter the Hostess.

HOSTESS: O Jesu, my lord, my lord!

PRINCE: Heigh, heigh! The devil rides upon a fiddlestick.° What's the matter? 390

---

361. **pudding:** sausage.   **Vice, Iniquity:** (Allegorical names for the chief comic character and tempter in morality plays.)   362. **vanity:** person given to worldly desires.   363. **cleanly:** (1) pure (2) deft.   364. **cunning:** (1) skillful (2) crafty.   366. **take me with you:** let me catch up with your meaning.   374. **saving your reverence:** i.e., with my apology for using offensive language.   376. **host:** innkeeper.   377. **Pharaoh's lean kine:** (See Genesis 41:3–4, 8–21.)   385. **watch:** posse of constables.   389. **The . . . fiddlestick:** i.e., here's much ado about nothing.

HOSTESS: The sheriff and all the watch are at the door. They are come to search the house. Shall I let them in?

FALSTAFF: Dost thou hear, Hal? Never call a true piece of gold a counterfeit. Thou art essentially made without seeming so.°

PRINCE: And thou a natural coward without instinct. 395

FALSTAFF: I deny your major.° If you will deny the° sheriff, so; if not, let him enter. If I become° not a cart° as well as another man, a plague on my bringing up!° I hope I shall as soon be strangled with a halter as another.

PRINCE: Go hide thee behind the arras.° The rest walk up above.° Now, my masters, for a true face and good conscience. 400

FALSTAFF: Both which I have had, but their date is out,° and therefore I'll hide me. [*He hides behind the arras.*]

PRINCE: Call in the sheriff. [*Exeunt all except the Prince and Peto.*]

Enter Sheriff and the Carrier.

Now, Master Sheriff, what is your will with me?

SHERIFF:
First, pardon me, my lord. A hue and cry° 405
Hath followed certain men unto this house.

PRINCE: What men?

SHERIFF:
One of them is well known, my gracious lord,
A gross, fat man.

CARRIER: As fat as butter.

PRINCE:
The man, I do assure you, is not here, 410
For I myself, at this time have employed him.
And, Sheriff, I will engage° my word to thee
That I will, by tomorrow dinnertime,°
Send him to answer thee, or any man,
For anything he shall be charged withal; 415
And so let me entreat you leave the house.

393–94. Dost . . . seeming so: (In this difficult passage, Falstaff seems to suggest that he is true gold, not counterfeit, and so should not be betrayed to the watch by the Prince, who, he hopes, is not merely playacting at the tavern but is truly one of its madcap members.) **396. deny your major:** reject your major premise. **deny the:** refuse entrance to. **397. become:** befit, adorn. **cart:** i.e., hangman's cart. **398. bringing up:** (1) upbringing (2) being brought before the authorities to be hanged. **399. arras:** wall hanging of tapestry. **up above:** upstairs. **401. date is out:** lease has run out. **405. hue and cry:** outcry calling for the pursuit of a felon. **412. engage:** pledge. **413. dinnertime:** i.e., about noon.

SHERIFF:

I will, my lord. There are two gentlemen
Have in this robbery lost three hundred marks.

PRINCE:

It may be so. If he have robbed these men,
He shall be answerable; and so farewell.   420

SHERIFF: Good night, my noble lord.

PRINCE:

I think it is good morrow,° is it not?

SHERIFF:

Indeed, my lord, I think it be two o'clock.   *Exit [with Carrier].*

PRINCE: This oily rascal is known as well as Paul's.° Go call him forth.

PETO [*discovering Falstaff*]: Falstaff! — Fast asleep behind the arras, and   425
snorting like a horse.

PRINCE: Hark, how hard he fetches breath. Search his pockets. (*He
searcheth his pockets, and findeth certain papers.*) What hast thou found?

PETO: Nothing but papers, my lord.

PRINCE: Let's see what they be. Read them.   430

PETO [*reads*]:

Item, A capon, ...2s. 2d.
Item, Sauce, ... 4d.
Item, Sack, two gallons, ... 5s. 8d.
Item, Anchovies and sack after supper, ...2s. 6d.
Item, Bread, ... ob.°   435

PRINCE: O, monstrous! But one halfpennyworth of bread to this intoler-
able deal of sack? What there is else, keep close;° we'll read it at more advantage.° There let him sleep till day. I'll to the court in the morning. We
must all to the wars, and thy place shall be honorable. I'll procure this fat
rogue a charge of foot,° and I know his death will be a march of twelve   440
score.° The money shall be paid back again with advantage.° Be with me
betimes° in the morning; and so, good morrow, Peto.

PETO: Good morrow, good my lord.

Exeunt [separately. Falstaff is concealed
once more behind the arras.]

---

422. **morrow:** morning.   424. **Paul's:** Saint Paul's Cathedral.   435. **ob.:** obolus, i.e., halfpenny.   437. **close:** hidden.   437–38. **advantage:** favorable opportunity.   440. **charge of foot:**
command of a company of infantry.   440–41. **twelve score:** i.e., two hundred and forty
yards.   441. **advantage:** interest.   442. **betimes:** early.   **s.d.** *Exeunt . . . arras:* (Onstage, the
arras is evidently arranged so that Falstaff can exit behind it once the scene is over.)

ACT III, SCENE I°

Enter Hotspur, Worcester, Lord Mortimer, [and] Owen Glendower.

MORTIMER:
  These promises are fair, the parties sure,
  And our induction° full of prosperous hope.°
HOTSPUR:
  Lord Mortimer, and cousin Glendower,
  Will you sit down? And uncle Worcester —   [*They sit.*]
  A plague upon it, I have forgot the map.   5
GLENDOWER [*producing a map*]:
  No, here it is. Sit, cousin Percy,
  Sit, good cousin Hotspur — for by that name
  As oft as Lancaster° doth speak of you
  His cheek looks pale, and with a rising sigh
  He wisheth you in heaven.
HOTSPUR: And you in hell,   10
  As oft as he hears Owen Glendower spoke of.
GLENDOWER:
  I cannot blame him. At my nativity
  The front° of heaven was full of fiery shapes,
  Of burning cressets,° and at my birth
  The frame and huge foundation of the earth   15
  Shaked like a coward.
HOTSPUR: Why, so it would have done
  At the same season, if your mother's cat
  Had but kittened, though yourself had never been born.
GLENDOWER:
  I say the earth did shake when I was born.
HOTSPUR:
  And I say the earth was not of my mind,   20
  If you suppose as fearing you it shook.
GLENDOWER:
  The heavens were all on fire; the earth did tremble.

ACT III, SCENE I. **Location:** Wales. Glendower's residence. (Holinshed places a meeting of the rebel deputies at Bangor in the archdeacon's house, but in this present "unhistorical" scene, as invented by Shakespeare, Glendower is host throughout.) Seats are provided onstage.   2. **induction:** beginning.   **prosperous hope:** hope of prospering.   8. **Lancaster:** i.e., King Henry, here demoted to Duke of Lancaster.   13. **front:** brow, face (as also at line 36).   14. **cressets:** lights burning in metal baskets at the end of long poles or suspended; hence, meteors.

HOTSPUR:

O, then the earth shook to see the heavens on fire,
And not in fear of your nativity.
Diseasèd nature oftentimes breaks forth   25
In strange eruptions; oft the teeming earth
Is with a kind of colic pinched and vexed
By the imprisoning of unruly wind
Within her womb, which, for enlargement° striving,
Shakes the old beldam° earth and topples down   30
Steeples and moss-grown towers. At your birth
Our grandam earth, having this distemp'rature,°
In passion° shook.

GLENDOWER: Cousin, of° many men
I do not bear these crossings.° Give me leave
To tell you once again that at my birth   35
The front of heaven was full of fiery shapes,
The goats ran from the mountains, and the herds
Were strangely clamorous° to the frighted fields.
These signs have marked me extraordinary,
And all the courses of my life do show   40
I am not in the roll of common men.
Where is he° living, clipped in with° the sea
That chides the banks of England, Scotland, Wales,
Which° calls me pupil or hath read to° me?
And bring him out° that is but woman's son   45
Can trace me in the tedious ways of art°
And hold me pace° in deep° experiments.

HOTSPUR:

I think there's no man speaks better Welsh.°
I'll to dinner.

MORTIMER:

Peace, cousin Percy; you will make him mad.   50

GLENDOWER:

I can call° spirits from the vasty deep.°

---

29. **enlargement:** release. 30. **beldam:** grandmother. 32. **distemp'rature:** disorder. 33.
passion: suffering. **of:** from. 34. **crossings:** contradictions. 38. **clamorous:** noisy. 42. **he:**
anyone. **clipped in with:** enclosed by. 44. **Which:** who. **read to:** instructed. 45. **bring
him out:** produce any man. 46. **Can . . . art:** who can follow me in the laborious ways of
magic. 47. **hold me pace:** keep up with me. **deep:** occult. 48. **speaks better Welsh:** (Hotspur hides an insult behind the literal meaning, since "to speak Welsh" meant colloquially both
"to boast" and "to speak nonsense.") 51. **call:** summon. (But Hotspur sardonically replies in
the sense of "call out to," whether or not there is any response.) **vasty deep:** lower world.

HOTSPUR:

Why, so can I, or so can any man;
But will they come when you do call for them?

GLENDOWER:

Why, I can teach you, cousin, to command the devil.

HOTSPUR:

And I can teach thee, coz, to shame the devil   55
By telling truth. Tell truth and shame the devil.
If thou have power to raise him, bring him hither,
And I'll be sworn I have power to shame him hence.
O, while you live, tell truth and shame the devil!

MORTIMER:

Come, come, no more of this unprofitable chat.   60

GLENDOWER:

Three times hath Henry Bolingbroke made head°
Against my power;° thrice from the banks of Wye
And sandy-bottomed Severn have I sent him
Bootless° home and weather-beaten back.

HOTSPUR:

Home without boots, and in foul weather too!   65
How scapes he agues,° in the devil's name?

GLENDOWER:

Come, here is the map. Shall we divide our right
According to our threefold order ta'en?°

MORTIMER:

The Archdeacon° hath divided it
Into three limits° very equally: 70
England, from Trent and Severn hitherto,°
By south and east is to my part assigned;
All westward, Wales beyond the Severn shore,
And all the fertile land within that bound,
To Owen Glendower; and, dear coz, to you   75
The remnant northward, lying off from Trent.

---

61. **made head:** raised a force. 62. **power:** army. 64. **Bootless:** without advantage. (But Hotspur quibbles on the sense of "barefoot.") 66. **agues:** fevers. 68. **order ta'en:** arrangements made. 69. **Archdeacon:** i.e., the Archdeacon of Bangor, in whose house, according to Holinshed, a meeting took place between deputies of the rebel leaders. 70. **limits:** regions. 71. **hitherto:** to this point.

And our indentures tripartite° are drawn,°
Which being sealèd interchangeably —
A business that this night may execute° —
Tomorrow, cousin Percy, you and I   80
And my good lord of Worcester will set forth
To meet your father and the Scottish power,
As is appointed us, at Shrewsbury.
My father° Glendower is not ready yet,
Nor shall we need his help these fourteen days.   85
[*To Glendower.*] Within that space you may° have drawn together
Your tenants, friends, and neighboring gentlemen.

GLENDOWER:
A shorter time shall send me to you, lords;
And in my conduct° shall your ladies come,
From whom you now must steal and take no leave,   90
For there will be a world of water shed
Upon the parting of your wives and you.

HOTSPUR [*consulting the map*]:
Methinks my moiety,° north from Burton here,
In quantity equals not one of yours.
See how this river comes me cranking in°   95
And cuts me from the best of all my land
A huge half-moon, a monstrous cantle,° out.
I'll have the current in this place dammed up,
And here the smug° and silver Trent shall run
In a new channel, fair and evenly.   100
It shall not wind with such a deep indent
To rob me of so rich a bottom° here.

GLENDOWER:
Not wind? It shall, it must. You see it doth.

MORTIMER:
Yea, but mark how he bears his course and runs me° up
With like advantage on the other side,   105

---

77. **tripartite:** i.e., drawn up in triplicate, each document sealed *interchangeably* (line 78) with the seal of all signatories. **drawn:** drawn up. 79. **this night may execute:** may be carried out tonight. 84. **father:** i.e., father-in-law. 86. **may:** will be able to. 89. **conduct:** escort. 93. **moiety:** share. 95. **comes me cranking in:** comes bending in on my share. (The Trent, by turning northward instead of continuing eastward into the Wash, cuts Hotspur off from rich land in Lincolnshire and its vicinity.) 97. **cantle:** piece. 99. **smug:** smooth. 102. **bottom:** valley. 104. **runs me:** runs. (*Me* is used colloquially.)

Gelding the opposèd continent° as much
As on the other side it takes from you.

WORCESTER:

Yea, but a little charge° will trench° him here
And on this north side win this cape of land;
And then he runs straight and even.   110

HOTSPUR:

I'll have it so. A little charge will do it.

GLENDOWER: I'll not have it altered.

HOTSPUR: Will not you?

GLENDOWER: No, nor you shall not.

HOTSPUR: Who shall say me nay?   115

GLENDOWER: Why, that will I.

HOTSPUR:

Let me not understand you, then; speak it in Welsh.

GLENDOWER:

I can speak English, lord, as well as you;
For I was trained up in the English court,
Where, being but young, I framèd to the harp°   120
Many an English ditty lovely well,
And gave the tongue a helpful ornament° —
A virtue that was never seen in you.

HOTSPUR:

Marry, and I am glad of it with all my heart!
I had rather be a kitten and cry "mew"   125
Than one of these same meter balladmongers.
I had rather hear a brazen can'stick turned°
Or a dry wheel grate on the axletree,°
And that would set my teeth nothing° on edge,
Nothing so much as mincing poetry.   130
'Tis like the forced gait of a shuffling° nag.

GLENDOWER: Come, you shall have Trent turned.

HOTSPUR:

I do not care. I'll give thrice so much land
To any well-deserving friend;

---

106. **Gelding . . . continent:** cutting off from the land which it bounds on the opposite side. (The Trent's southerly loop from Stoke to Burton deprives Mortimer of a piece of land, just as its later northerly course deprives Hotspur.) 108. **charge:** expenditure. **trench:** provide a new channel. 120. **framèd to the harp:** set to harp accompaniment. 122. **gave . . . ornament:** i.e., added to the words a pleasing ornament of music; also, gave to the English tongue the ornament of music and poetry. 127. **can'stick turned:** candlestick turned on a lathe. 128. **axletree:** axle. 129. **nothing:** not at all. 131. **shuffling:** hobbled.

But in the way of bargain, mark ye me,   135
I'll cavil on the ninth part of a hair.°
Are the indentures drawn?° Shall we be gone?

GLENDOWER:
The moon shines fair; you may away by night.
I'll haste the writer° and withal°
Break with° your wives of your departure hence.   140
I am afraid my daughter will run mad,
So much she doteth on her Mortimer.   *Exit.*

MORTIMER:
Fie, cousin Percy, how you cross my father!

HOTSPUR:
I cannot choose. Sometimes he angers me
With telling me of the moldwarp° and the ant,   145
Of the dreamer Merlin° and his prophecies,
And of a dragon and a finless fish,
A clip-winged griffin° and a moulten° raven,
A couching° lion and a ramping° cat,
And such a deal of skimble-skamble° stuff   150
As puts me from my faith.° I tell you what:
He held me last night at least nine hours
In reckoning up the several° devils' names
That were his lackeys. I cried "Hum," and "Well, go to,"°
But marked him not a word. O, he is as tedious   155
As a tirèd horse, a railing wife,
Worse than a smoky house. I had rather live
With cheese and garlic in a windmill, far,
Than feed on cates° and have him talk to me
In any summer house in Christendom.   160

MORTIMER:
In faith, he is a worthy gentleman,
Exceedingly well read, and profited°

---

136. **cavil . . . hair:** i.e., argue about the most trivial detail. 137. **drawn:** drawn up. 139. **writer:** i.e., scrivener who would be drawing the indentures. **withal:** also. 140. **Break with:** inform. 145. **moldwarp:** mole. (Holinshed tells us that the division was arranged because of a prophecy that represented King Henry as the mole and the others as the dragon, the lion, and the wolf, who should divide the land among them.) 146. **Merlin:** the bard, prophet, and magician of Arthurian story, Welsh in origin. 148. **griffin:** a fabulous beast, half lion, half eagle. **moulten:** having molted. 149. **couching:** couchant, crouching. (Heraldic term.) **ramping:** rampant, advancing on its hind legs. (Hotspur is ridiculing the heraldic emblems that Glendower holds so dear.) 150. **skimble-skamble:** foolish, nonsensical. 151. **puts . . . faith:** drives me from my (Christian) faith. 153. **several:** various. 154. **go to:** i.e., you don't say. 159. **cates:** delicacies. 162. **profited:** proficient.

In strange concealments,° valiant as a lion
And wondrous affable, and as bountiful
As mines of India. Shall I tell you, cousin?   165
He holds your temper° in a high respect
And curbs himself even of his natural scope°
When you come 'cross° his humor. Faith, he does.
I warrant you that man is not alive
Might° so have tempted him as you have done   170
Without the taste of danger and reproof.
But do not use it oft, let me entreat you.

WORCESTER [*to Hotspur*]:
    In faith, my lord, you are too willful-blame,°
    And since your coming hither have done enough
    To put him quite beside° his patience.   175
    You must needs learn, lord, to amend this fault.
    Though sometimes it show greatness, courage, blood° —
    And that's the dearest grace° it renders you —
    Yet oftentimes it doth present° harsh rage,
    Defect of manners, want of government,°   180
    Pride, haughtiness, opinion,° and disdain,
    The least of which haunting a nobleman
    Loseth men's hearts and leaves behind a stain
    Upon the beauty of all parts besides,°
    Beguiling° them of commendation.   185

HOTSPUR:
    Well, I am schooled. Good manners be your speed!°
    Here come our wives, and let us take our leave.

Enter Glendower with the ladies.

MORTIMER:
    This is the deadly spite° that angers me:
    My wife can speak no English, I no Welsh.

GLENDOWER:
    My daughter weeps she'll not part with you;   190
    She'll be a soldier too, she'll to the wars.

---

163. **concealments:** occult practices. 166. **temper:** temperament. 167. **scope:** freedom of
speech. 168. **come 'cross:** contradict. 170. **Might:** who could. 173. **too willful-blame:**
blameworthy for too much self-will. 175. **beside:** out of. 177. **blood:** spirit. 178. **dearest
grace:** best (and costliest) credit. 179. **present:** represent. 180. **want of government:** lack of
self-control. 181. **opinion:** vanity, arrogance. 184. **all parts besides:** all other abili-
ties. 185. **Beguiling:** depriving. 186. **be your speed:** give you good fortune. 188. **spite:**
vexation.

MORTIMER:
　Good Father, tell her that she and my aunt° Percy
　Shall follow in your conduct speedily.

Glendower speaks to her in Welsh,
and she answers him in the same.

GLENDOWER:
　She is desperate here;° a peevish self-willed harlotry,°
　One that no persuasion can do good upon.　　　　　　　　195

The lady speaks in Welsh.

MORTIMER:
　I understand thy looks. That pretty Welsh°
　Which thou pourest down from these swelling heavens°
　I am too perfect° in; and, but for shame,
　In such a parley° should I answer thee.

The lady again in Welsh.

　I understand thy kisses and thou mine,　　　　　　　　200
　And that's a feeling disputation.°
　But I will never be a truant, love,
　Till I have learned thy language; for thy tongue
　Makes Welsh as sweet as ditties highly° penned,
　Sung by a fair queen in a summer's bower,　　　　　　　205
　With ravishing division,° to her lute.

GLENDOWER:
　Nay, if you melt,° then will she run mad.

The lady speaks again in Welsh.

MORTIMER:
　O, I am ignorance itself in this!

GLENDOWER:
　She bids you on the wanton° rushes° lay you down
　And rest your gentle head upon her lap,　　　　　　　210
　And she will sing the song that pleaseth you
　And on your eyelids crown° the god of sleep,
　Charming your blood with pleasing heaviness,°

---

192. **aunt:** (Percy's wife, here called Kate, was aunt of Edmund Mortimer, the fifth Earl of March, but was sister-in-law to the Sir Edward Mortimer who married Glendower's daughter.) 194. **desperate here:** adamant on this point (i.e., her decision to accompany Mortimer). **peevish self-willed harlotry:** childish, willful, silly wench. 196. **That pretty Welsh:** i.e., your eloquent tears. 197. **heavens:** i.e., eyes. 198. **perfect:** proficient. 199. **such a parley:** i.e., the same language (of weeping). 201. **disputation:** conversation, debate. 204. **highly:** eloquently, nobly. 206. **division:** variation, passage in which rapid short notes vary a theme. 207. **melt:** i.e., weep. 209. **wanton:** soft, luxurious. **rushes:** (Used as floor covering.) 212. **crown:** give sway to. 213. **heaviness:** drowsiness.

Making such difference twixt wake and sleep
As is the difference betwixt day and night   215
The hour before the heavenly-harnessed team°
Begins his golden progress in the east.

MORTIMER:
With all my heart I'll sit and hear her sing.
By that time will our book,° I think, be drawn.

GLENDOWER: Do so;   220
And those musicians that shall play to you
Hang in the air a thousand leagues from hence,
And straight they shall be here. Sit, and attend.

                                        [*Mortimer reclines with his head
                                                        in his wife's lap.*]

HOTSPUR: Come, Kate, thou art perfect in lying down; come, quick, quick,
that I may lay my head in thy lap.   225

LADY PERCY: Go, ye giddy goose.

                                        [*Hotspur lies with his head
                                        in Kate's lap.*] *The music plays.*

HOTSPUR:
Now I perceive the devil understands Welsh;
And 'tis no marvel he is so humorous.°
By 'r Lady, he is a good musician.

LADY PERCY: Then should you be nothing but musical, for you are alto-   230
gether governed by humors. Lie still, ye thief, and hear the lady sing in
Welsh.

HOTSPUR: I had rather hear Lady, my brach,° howl in Irish.

LADY PERCY: Wouldst thou have thy head broken?°

HOTSPUR: No.   235

LADY PERCY: Then be still.

HOTSPUR: Neither, 'tis a woman's fault.°

LADY PERCY: Now God help° thee!

HOTSPUR: To the Welsh lady's bed.

LADY PERCY: What's that?   240

HOTSPUR: Peace, she sings.

                                        Here the lady sings a Welsh song.

HOTSPUR: Come, Kate, I'll have your song too.

---

216. **the heavenly-harnessed team:** i.e., the team of horses drawing the chariot of the sun.   219. **book:** document, indentures.   228. **humorous:** whimsical, capricious.   233. **brach:** bitch hound.   234. **broken:** i.e., struck so as to break the skin.   237. **Neither . . . fault:** i.e., I won't do that either; it's womanish to be submissive.   238. **help:** amend. (But Hotspur answers in the sense of "assist with an amour.")

LADY PERCY: Not mine, in good sooth.

HOTSPUR: Not yours, in good sooth! Heart,° you swear like a comfit
maker's° wife. "Not you, in good sooth," and "as true as I live," and "as 245
God shall mend me," and "as sure as day,"
And givest such sarcenet° surety for thy oaths
As if thou never walk'st further than Finsbury.°
Swear me, Kate, like a lady as thou art,
A good mouth-filling oath, and leave "in sooth," 250
And such protest of pepper-gingerbread,°
To velvet-guards° and Sunday citizens.
Come, sing.

LADY PERCY: I will not sing.

HOTSPUR: 'Tis the next° way to turn tailor,° or be redbreast teacher.° An 255
the indentures be drawn, I'll away within these two hours; and so, come
in when you will.   *Exit.*

GLENDOWER:
Come, come, Lord Mortimer. You are as slow
As hot Lord Percy is on fire to go.
By this° our book is drawn; we'll but° seal, 260
And then to horse immediately.

MORTIMER: With all my heart.   *Exeunt.*

ACT III, SCENE II°

Enter the King, Prince of Wales, and others.

KING:
Lords, give us leave. The Prince of Wales and I
Must have some private conference; but be near at hand,
For we shall presently have need of you.   *Exeunt Lords.*
I know not whether God will have it so
For some displeasing service I have done 5
That in his secret doom° out of my blood°

---

244. **Heart:** i.e., by Christ's heart. 244–45. **comfit maker's:** confectioner's. 247. **sarcenet:**
soft, flimsy (from the soft silken material known as *sarcenet*). 248. **Finsbury:** a field just outside London frequented by the London citizenry. (Hotspur jokes with Kate as though she were
a citizen's wife, using the pious and modest oaths of such people.) 251. **protest . . . ginger-
bread:** i.e., mealy-mouthed protestations. 252. **velvet-guards:** i.e., wives who wear velvet
trimming. 255. **next:** nearest, quickest. **turn tailor:** (Tailors were noted for singing and ef-
feminacy.) **be redbreast teacher:** i.e., teach birds to sing. (Hotspur is expressing his contempt
for music.) 260. **By this:** by this time. **but:** just. ACT III, SCENE II. **Location:** The royal
court (historically, Westminster). 6. **doom:** judgment. **blood:** offspring.

He'll breed revengement and a scourge for me;
But thou dost in thy passages° of life
Make me believe that thou art only marked
For the hot vengeance and the rod of heaven   10
To punish my mistreadings.° Tell me else,°
Could such inordinate° and low desires,
Such poor, such bare, such lewd,° such mean attempts,°
Such barren pleasures, rude society,
As thou art matched withal° and grafted to,   15
Accompany the greatness of thy blood
And hold their level° with thy princely heart?

PRINCE:
So please Your Majesty, I would I could
Quit° all offenses with as clear excuse
As well as I am doubtless° I can purge   20
Myself of many I am charged withal.
Yet such extenuation let me beg
As, in reproof° of many tales devised,
Which oft the ear of greatness needs must hear
By° smiling pickthanks° and base newsmongers,°   25
I may, for some things true, wherein my youth
Hath faulty wandered and irregular,
Find pardon on my true submission.

KING:
God pardon thee! Yet let me wonder, Harry,
At thy affections,° which do hold a wing°   30
Quite from° the flight of all thy ancestors.
Thy place in Council thou hast rudely° lost,
Which by thy younger brother is supplied,
And art almost an alien to the hearts
Of all the court and princes of my blood.   35
The hope and expectation of thy time°

---

8. passages: course, conduct.   9–11. thou . . . mistreadings: (1) you are marked as the means of heaven's vengeance against me, or (2) you are marked to suffer heaven's vengeance because of my sins.   11. else: how otherwise.   12. inordinate: (1) immoderate (2) unworthy of your rank.   13. lewd: low, base.   attempts: undertakings.   15. withal: with.   17. hold their level: claim equality.   19. Quit: acquit myself of.   20. doubtless: certain.   23. in reproof: upon disproof.   25. By: from.   pickthanks: flatterers.   newsmongers: talebearers.   30. affections: inclinations.   hold a wing: fly a course.   31. from: at variance with.   32. rudely: by violence. (According to an apocryphal story, Prince Hal boxed the ears of the Lord Chief Justice and was sent to prison for it; see *Henry IV, Part 2*, 1.2.54–55, 192, and 5.2.70–71.)   36. time: time of life, youth.

Is ruined, and the soul of every man
Prophetically do forethink thy fall.
Had I so lavish of my presence been,
So common-hackneyed° in the eyes of men,   40
So stale and cheap to vulgar company,.
Opinion,° that did help me to the crown,
Had still kept loyal to possession°
And left me in reputeless banishment,
A fellow of no mark° nor likelihood.°   45
By being seldom seen, I could not stir
But like a comet I was wondered at,
That men would tell their children, "This is he!"
Others would say, "Where, which is Bolingbroke?"
And then I stole all courtesy from heaven,°   50
And dressed myself in such humility
That I did pluck allegiance from men's hearts,
Loud shouts and salutations from their mouths,
Even in the presence of the crownèd King.
Thus did I keep my person fresh and new,   55
My presence, like a robe pontifical,°
Ne'er seen but wondered at; and so my state,°
Seldom° but sumptuous, showed like a feast
And won by rareness such solemnity.°
The skipping King, he ambled up and down   60
With shallow jeeters and rash bavin° wits,
Soon kindled and soon burnt; carded° his state,°
Mingled his royalty with capering fools,
Had his great name profanèd with their scorns,°
And gave his countenance, against his name,°   65
To laugh at gibing boys and stand the push°
Of every beardless vain comparative;°
Grew a companion to the common streets,

---

40. **common-hackneyed:** cheapened, vulgarized.   42. **Opinion:** public opinion.   43. **to possession:** i.e., to Richard II's sovereignty.   45. **mark:** importance. **likelihood:** likelihood of success.   50. **I . . . heaven:** i.e., I assumed a bearing of the utmost graciousness.   56. **pontifical:** like that of a pope or archbishop.   57. **state:** magnificence in public appearances.   58. **Seldom:** infrequent.   59. **such solemnity:** i.e., the solemnity appropriate to a festival.   61. **bavin:** brushwood, soon burnt out.   62. **carded:** debased. (A term applied to the adulteration or combing of wool.) **state:** royal status.   64. **with their scorns:** by the scornful opinion people had of these favorites.   65. **gave . . . name:** lent his authority, to the detriment of his royal dignity and reputation.   66. **stand the push:** put up with the impudence.   67. **comparative:** maker of comparisons, wisecracker.

Enfeoffed himself° to popularity,
That, being daily swallowed by men's eyes,   70
They surfeited with honey and began
To loathe the taste of sweetness, whereof a little
More than a little is by much too much.
So when he had occasion to be seen,
He was but as the cuckoo is in June,   75
Heard, not regarded — seen, but with such eyes
As, sick and blunted with community,°
Afford no extraordinary gaze,
Such as is bent on sunlike majesty
When it shines seldom in admiring eyes;   80
But rather drowsed and hung their eyelids down,
Slept in his face,° and rendered such aspect°
As cloudy° men use to their adversaries,
Being with his presence glutted, gorged, and full.
And in that very line, Harry, standest thou;   85
For thou hast lost thy princely privilege
With vile participation.° Not an eye
But is aweary of thy common sight,
Save mine, which hath desired to see thee more —
Which now doth that° I would not have it do,   90
Make blind itself with foolish tenderness.°

PRINCE:
I shall hereafter, my thrice gracious lord,
Be more myself.

KING: For all the world°
As thou art to this hour was Richard then
When I from France set foot at Ravenspurgh,   95
And even as I was then is Percy now.
Now, by my scepter, and my soul to boot,°
He hath more worthy interest to the state
Than thou the shadow of succession.°
For of no right, nor color like to right,°   100

---

69. **Enfeoffed himself:** gave himself up.   77. **community:** commonness.   82. **in his face:**
right before his eyes.   **aspect:** look.   83. **cloudy:** sullen. (Also refers to the image of the
sun.)   87. **vile participation:** base   association   or   companionship.   90. **that:** that
which.   91. **tenderness:** i.e., tears.   93. **For all the world:** in every way.   97. **to boot:** in addition.   98–99. **He ... succession:** i.e., even this rebel Hotspur has a better claim to the
throne than you, the mere shadow of an heir.   100. **of ... to right:** having no rightful claim or
even the pretext of one.

He doth fill fields with harness° in the realm,
Turns head° against the lion's° armèd jaws,
And, being no more in debt to years than thou,°
Leads ancient lords and reverend bishops on
To bloody battles and to bruising arms.   105
What never-dying honor hath he got
Against renownèd Douglas! Whose° high deeds,
Whose hot incursions and great name in arms
Holds from all soldiers chief majority°
And military title capital°   110
Through all the kingdoms that acknowledge Christ.
Thrice hath this Hotspur, Mars in swaddling clothes,
This infant warrior, in his enterprises
Discomfited° great Douglas, ta'en him once,
Enlargèd° him and made a friend of him,   115
To fill the mouth of deep defiance up°
And shake the peace and safety of our throne.
And what say you to this? Percy, Northumberland,
The Archbishop's Grace° of York, Douglas, Mortimer,
Capitulate° against us and are up.°   120
But wherefore do I tell these news to thee?
Why, Harry, do I tell thee of my foes,
Which art my nearest and dearest° enemy?
Thou that art like° enough, through vassal° fear,
Base inclination,° and the start of spleen,°   125
To fight against me under Percy's pay,
To dog his heels and curtsy at his frowns,
To show how much thou art degenerate.

PRINCE:
Do not think so. You shall not find it so.
And God forgive them that so much have swayed   130
Your Majesty's good thoughts away from me!
I will redeem all this on Percy's head

---

101. **harness:** armor, i.e., men in armor.   102. **Turns head:** leads an armed insurrection.   **lion's:** i.e., King's.   103. **being . . . thou:** i.e., being no older than you (though historically Hotspur was twenty-three years older than the Prince).   107. **Whose:** i.e., Hotspur's.   109. **majority:** preeminence.   110. **capital:** chief, principal.   114. **Discomfited:** defeated.   115. **Enlargèd:** freed.   116. **To . . . up:** to swell the roar of deep defiance.   119. **The Archbishop's Grace:** His Grace the Archbishop.   120. **Capitulate:** form a league, draw up articles.   **up:** up in arms.   123. **dearest:** (1) most precious (2) direst.   124. **like:** likely.   **vassal:** slavish.   125. **Base inclination:** inclination for baseness.   **start of spleen:** fit of ill temper.

And in the closing of some glorious day
Be bold to tell you that I am your son,
When I will wear a garment all of blood   135
And stain my favors° in a bloody mask,
Which, washed away, shall scour my shame with it.
And that shall be the day, whene'er it lights,°
That this same child of honor and renown,
This gallant Hotspur, this all-praisèd knight,   140
And your unthought-of° Harry chance to meet.
For every honor sitting on his helm,
Would they were multitudes, and on my head
My shames redoubled! For the time will come
That I shall make this northern youth exchange   145
His glorious deeds for my indignities.
Percy is but my factor,° good my lord,
To engross up° glorious deeds on my behalf;
And I will call him to so strict account
That he shall render every glory up,   150
Yea, even the slightest worship of his time,°
Or I will tear the reckoning from his heart.
This in the name of God I promise here,
The which if He be pleased I shall perform,
I do beseech Your Majesty may salve°   155
The long-grown wounds of my intemperance.°
If not, the end of life cancels all bonds,
And I will die a hundred thousand deaths
Ere break the smallest parcel of this vow.

KING:
A hundred thousand rebels die in this!   160
Thou shalt have charge° and sovereign trust herein.

Enter Blunt.

How now, good Blunt? Thy looks are full of speed.

BLUNT:
So hath the business that I come to speak of.
Lord Mortimer of Scotland° hath sent word

---

136. **favors:** features. 138. **lights:** dawns. 141. **unthought-of:** ignored, disregarded.
147. **factor:** agent. 148. **engross up:** amass, buy up. 151. **worship of his time:** honor of his
youthful lifetime. 155. **salve:** soothe, heal. 156. **intemperance:** dissolute living, sickness.
161. **charge:** command (of troops). 164. **Lord Mortimer of Scotland:** (A Scottish nobleman,
unrelated to Glendower's son-in-law.)

That Douglas and the English rebels met   165
The eleventh of this month at Shrewsbury.
A mighty and a fearful head° they are,
If promises be kept on every hand,
As ever offered foul play in a state.

KING:
The Earl of Westmorland set forth today,   170
With him my son, Lord John of Lancaster;
For this advertisement° is five days old.
On Wednesday next, Harry, you shall set forward;
On Thursday we ourselves will march. Our meeting°
Is Bridgnorth.° And, Harry, you shall march .   175
Through Gloucestershire; by which account,
Our business valuèd,° some twelve days hence
Our general forces at Bridgnorth shall meet.
Our hands are full of business. Let's away!
Advantage feeds him fat° while men delay.   *Exeunt.*   180

Act iii, Scene iii°

Enter Falstaff and Bardolph.

FALSTAFF: Bardolph, am I not fallen away° vilely since this last action?° Do
I not bate?° Do I not dwindle? Why, my skin hangs about me like an old
lady's loose gown; I am withered like an old applejohn.° Well, I'll repent,
and that suddenly, while I am in some liking.° I shall be out of heart°
shortly, and then I shall have no strength to repent. An° I have not for-   5
gotten what the inside of a church is made of, I am a peppercorn,° a
brewer's horse.° The inside of a church! Company, villainous company,
hath been the spoil of me.
BARDOLPH: Sir John, you are so fretful° you cannot live long.

---

167. **head:** armed force.   172. **advertisement:** tidings, news.   174. **meeting:** place of rendezvous.   175. **Bridgnorth:** a town near Shrewsbury.   177. **Our business valuèd:** estimating
how long our business will take.   180. **Advantage . . . fat:** opportunity (for rebellion) pros-
pers.   **him:** himself.   ACT III, SCENE III. **Location:** A tavern in Eastcheap, as in 2.4.
1. **fallen away:** shrunk.   **action:** i.e., the robbery at Gad's Hill.   2. **bate:** lose weight.   3. **applejohn:** a kind of apple still in good eating condition when shriveled.   4. **liking:** (1) good
bodily condition (2) inclination.   **out of heart:** (1) disinclined, disheartened (2) out of condition.   5. **An:** if.   6. **peppercorn:** unground dried pepper berry.   7. **brewer's horse:** i.e., one
that is old, withered, and decrepit.   9. **fretful:** (1) anxious (2) fretted, frayed.

FALSTAFF: Why, there is it. Come sing me a bawdy song; make me merry. 10
I was as virtuously given° as a gentleman need to be, virtuous enough:
swore little, diced not above seven times — a week, went to a bawdy
house not above once in a quarter — of an hour, paid money that I borrowed — three or four times, lived well and in good compass;° and now
I live out of all order, out of all compass. 15

BARDOLPH: Why, you are so fat, Sir John, that you must needs be out of all
compass, out of all reasonable compass, Sir John.

FALSTAFF: Do thou amend thy face, and I'll amend my life. Thou art our
admiral,° thou bearest the lantern° in the poop, but 'tis in the nose of
thee. Thou art the Knight of the Burning Lamp. 20

BARDOLPH: Why, Sir John, my face does you no harm.

FALSTAFF: No, I'll be sworn, I make as good use of it as many a man doth
of a death's-head or a *memento mori*.° I never see thy face but I think upon
hellfire and Dives° that lived in purple; for there he is in his robes, burning, burning. If thou wert any way given to virtue, I would swear by thy 25
face; my oath should be "By this fire, that's God's angel."° But thou art altogether given over,° and wert indeed, but for the light in thy face, the
son of utter darkness. When thou rann'st up Gad's Hill in the night to
catch my horse, if I did not think thou hadst been an *ignis fatuus*° or a ball
of wildfire,° there's no purchase in money. O, thou art a perpetual tri- 30
umph,° an everlasting bonfire light! Thou hast saved me a thousand
marks in links° and torches, walking with thee in the night betwixt tavern and tavern; but the sack that thou hast drunk me would have bought
me lights as good cheap° at the dearest° chandler's° in Europe. I have
maintained that salamander° of yours with fire any time this two-and- 35
thirty years. God reward me for it!

BARDOLPH: 'Sblood, I would my face were in your belly!°

FALSTAFF: God-a-mercy! So should I be sure to be heartburned.

Enter Hostess.

---

11. **given:** inclined.   14. **good compass:** reasonable limits; also, in Bardolph's speech, girth,
circumference.   19. **admiral:** flagship.   **lantern:** i.e., a light for the rest of the fleet to follow:
here applied to Bardolph's inflamed nose, red from overdrinking.   23. *memento mori:* reminder of death, such as a death's head or a skull engraved on a seal ring.   24. **Dives:** the rich
man who went to hell, referred to in Luke 16:19–31.   26. **By . . . angel:** (A biblical echo, perhaps to Psalms 104:4, Hebrews 1:7, or Exodus 3:2.)   27. **given over:** abandoned to wickedness.   29. *ignis fatuus:* will-o'-the-wisp.   30. **wildfire:** fireworks; lightning; will-o'-the-wisp.
30–31. **triumph:** procession led by torches.   32. **links:** torches, flares.   34. **good cheap:**
cheap.   **dearest:** most expensive.   **chandler's:** candle maker's.   35. **salamander:** lizard reputed to be able to live in fire.   37. **I . . . belly:** (A proverb meaning "I wish I were rid of this
irritation"; stock response to an insult based on physical deformity.)

How now, Dame Partlet° the hen? Have you inquired yet who picked my
pocket? 40

HOSTESS: Why, Sir John, what do you think, Sir John? Do you think I
keep thieves in my house? I have searched, I have inquired, so has my
husband, man by man, boy by boy, servant by servant. The tithe° of a hair
was never lost in my house before.

FALSTAFF: Ye lie, hostess. Bardolph was shaved° and lost many a hair;° and 45
I'll be sworn my pocket was picked. Go to, you are a woman, go.

HOSTESS: Who, I? No, I defy thee! God's light,° I was never called so in
mine own house before.

FALSTAFF: Go to, I know you well enough.

HOSTESS: No, Sir John, you do not know me, Sir John. I know you, Sir 50
John. You owe me money, Sir John, and now you pick a quarrel to beguile
me of it. I bought you a dozen of shirts to your back.

FALSTAFF: Dowlas,° filthy dowlas. I have given them away to bakers'
wives; they have made bolters° of them.

HOSTESS: Now, as I am a true woman, holland° of eight shillings an ell.° 55
You owe money here besides, Sir John, for your diet° and by-drinkings,°
and money lent you, four-and-twenty pound.

FALSTAFF: He° had his part of it. Let him pay.

HOSTESS: He? Alas, he is poor, he hath nothing.

FALSTAFF: How, poor? Look upon his face. What call you rich? Let them 60
coin his nose, let them coin his cheeks. I'll not pay a denier.° What, will
you make a younker° of me? Shall I not take mine ease in mine inn but I
shall have my pocket picked? I have lost a seal ring of my grandfather's
worth forty mark.

HOSTESS: O Jesu, I have heard the Prince tell him, I know not how oft, 65
that that ring was copper.

FALSTAFF: How? The Prince is a Jack,° a sneak-up.° 'Sblood, an he were
here, I would cudgel him like a dog if he would say so.

*Enter the Prince [with Peto], marching, and Falstaff meets him playing upon his
truncheon° like a fife.*

How now, lad, is the wind in that door,° i' faith? Must we all march?

---

39. **Partlet:** (Traditional name of a hen.)   43. **tithe:** tenth part.   45. **was shaved:** (1) had his
beard cut (2) was cheated and robbed.   **lost many a hair:** (1) was shaved (2) was made bald by
syphilis.   47. **God's light:** (A mild oath.)   53. **Dowlas:** a coarse kind of linen.   54. **bolters:**
cloths for sifting flour.   55. **holland:** fine linen.   **an ell:** a measure of forty-five
inches.   56. **diet:** meals.   **by-drinkings:** drinks between meals.   58. **He:** i.e., Bardolph.   61. **denier:** one-twelfth of a French sou; type of very small coin.   62. **younker:**
greenhorn.   67. **Jack:** knave, rascal.   **sneak-up:** sneak.   s.d. *truncheon:* officer's staff.
69. **is . . . door:** i.e., is that the way the wind is blowing.

BARDOLPH: Yea, two and two, Newgate° fashion.   70

HOSTESS: My lord, I pray you, hear me.

PRINCE: What sayst thou, Mistress Quickly? How doth thy husband? I love him well; he is an honest man.

HOSTESS: Good my lord, hear me.

FALSTAFF: Prithee, let her alone and list to me.   75

PRINCE: What sayst thou, Jack?

FALSTAFF: The other night I fell asleep here behind the arras and had my pocket picked. This house is turned bawdy house; they pick pockets.

PRINCE: What didst thou lose, Jack?

FALSTAFF: Wilt thou believe me, Hal? Three or four bonds of forty pound   80
apiece and a seal ring of my grandfather's.

PRINCE: A trifle, some eightpenny matter.

HOSTESS: So I told him, my lord, and I said I heard Your Grace say so; and, my lord, he speaks most vilely of you, like a foulmouthed man as he is, and said he would cudgel you.   85

PRINCE: What, he did not!

HOSTESS: There's neither faith, truth, nor womanhood in me else.

FALSTAFF: There's no more faith in thee than in a stewed prune,° nor no more truth in thee than in a drawn fox;° and for womanhood, Maid Marian may be the deputy's wife of the ward to thee.° Go, you thing, go.   90

HOSTESS: Say, what thing, what thing?

FALSTAFF: What thing?° Why, a thing to thank God on.

HOSTESS: I am no thing to thank God on, I would thou shouldst know it! I am an honest man's wife, and, setting thy knighthood aside,° thou art a knave to call me so.   95

FALSTAFF: Setting thy womanhood aside, thou art a beast to say otherwise.

HOSTESS: Say, what beast, thou knave, thou?

FALSTAFF: What beast? Why, an otter.

PRINCE: An otter, Sir John! Why an otter?   100

FALSTAFF: Why? She's neither fish nor flesh; a man knows not where to have° her.

---

70. **Newgate:** (A famous city prison in London. Prisoners marched two by two.)   88. **stewed prune:** (Customarily associated with bawdy houses.)   89. **drawn fox:** fox driven from cover and wily in getting back.   89–90. **Maid . . . thee:** i.e., Maid Marian, a disreputable woman in Robin Hood ballads, morris dances, and the like, was a model of respectability compared with you.   92, 93. **What thing . . . no thing:** (With sexual quibbles.)   94, 96. **setting . . . aside:** (Mistress Quickly means, "without wishing to offend your rank of knighthood," but Falstaff replies in line 96 with the meaning, "setting aside your womanhood as of no value or pertinence.")   102. **have:** understand (with suggestion of enjoying sexually).

HOSTESS: Thou art an unjust man in saying so. Thou or any man knows
where to have me, thou knave, thou.

PRINCE: Thou sayst true, hostess, and he slanders thee most grossly.   105

HOSTESS: So he doth you, my lord, and said this other day you owed him
a thousand pound.

PRINCE: Sirrah, do I owe you a thousand pound?

FALSTAFF: A thousand pound, Hal? A million. Thy love is worth a million; thou owest me thy love.   110

HOSTESS: Nay, my lord, he called you Jack and said he would cudgel you.

FALSTAFF: Did I, Bardolph?

BARDOLPH: Indeed, Sir John, you said so.

FALSTAFF: Yea, if he said my ring was copper.

PRINCE: I say 'tis copper. Darest thou be as good as thy word now?   115

FALSTAFF: Why, Hal, thou knowest, as thou art but man, I dare; but as
thou art prince, I fear thee as I fear the roaring of the lion's whelp.°

PRINCE: And why not as the lion?

FALSTAFF: The King himself is to be feared as the lion. Dost thou think
I'll fear thee as I fear thy father? Nay, an I do, I pray God my girdle break.   120

PRINCE: O, if it should, how would thy guts fall about thy knees! But, sirrah, there's no room for faith, truth, nor honesty in this bosom of thine;
it is all filled up with guts and midriff. Charge an honest woman with
picking thy pocket? Why, thou whoreson, impudent, embossed° rascal,°
if there were anything in thy pocket but tavern reckonings, memoran-   125
dums° of bawdy houses, and one poor pennyworth of sugar candy to
make thee long-winded, if thy pocket were enriched with any other in-
juries° but these, I am a villain. And yet you will stand to it;° you will not
pocket up° wrong! Art thou not ashamed?

FALSTAFF: Dost thou hear, Hal? Thou knowest in the state of innocency   130
Adam fell; and what should poor Jack Falstaff do in the days of villainy?
Thou seest I have more flesh than another man, and therefore more
frailty. You confess then you picked my pocket.

PRINCE: It appears so by° the story.

FALSTAFF: Hostess, I forgive thee. Go make ready breakfast. Love thy   135
husband, look to thy servants, cherish thy guests. Thou shalt find me
tractable to any honest reason; thou seest I am pacified still.° Nay,

---

117. **whelp:** cub.   124. **embossed:** (1) swollen with fat (2) foaming at the mouth and ex-
hausted, like a hunted animal.   **rascal:** (1) scoundrel (2) immature and inferior
deer.   125–26. **memorandums:** souvenirs.   127–28. **injuries:** i.e., those things you claim to
have lost, thereby suffering harm.   128. **stand to it:** make a stand, insist on your supposed
rights.   129. **pocket up:** endure silently.   134. **by:** according to.   137. **still:** always.

prithee, begone. (*Exit Hostess.*) Now, Hal, to the news at court: for the robbery, lad, how is that answered?

PRINCE: O my sweet beef, I must still be good angel to thee. The money is 140
paid back again.

FALSTAFF: O, I do not like that paying back. 'Tis a double labor.°

PRINCE: I am good friends with my father and may do anything.

FALSTAFF: Rob me the exchequer the first thing thou dost, and do it with
unwashed hands too.° 145

BARDOLPH: Do, my lord.

PRINCE: I have procured thee, Jack, a charge of foot.°

FALSTAFF: I would it had been of horse. Where shall I find one° that can
steal well? O, for a fine thief, of the age of two-and-twenty or thereabouts! I am heinously unprovided.° Well, God be thanked for these 150
rebels; they offend none but the virtuous.° I laud them, I praise them.

PRINCE: Bardolph!

BARDOLPH: My lord?

PRINCE [*giving letters*]:
Go bear this letter to Lord John of Lancaster,
To my brother John; this to my lord of Westmorland. 155

[*Exit Bardolph.*]

Go, Peto, to horse, to horse, for thou and I
Have thirty miles to ride yet ere dinnertime.

[*Exit Peto.*]

Jack, meet me tomorrow in the Temple Hall°
At two o'clock in the afternoon.
There shalt thou know thy charge, and there receive 160
Money and order for their furniture.°
The land is burning. Percy stands on high,
And either we or they must lower lie. [*Exit.*]

FALSTAFF:
Rare words! Brave° world! Hostess, my breakfast, come!
O, I could wish this tavern were my drum!° [*Exit.*] 165

---

142. **double labor:** i.e., the taking and the returning.   144–45. **with unwashed hands:** without wasting any time.   147. **charge of foot:** command of a company of infantry.   148. **one:** i.e., a companion in thievery. (Falstaff sees war as the opportunity for stealing and con-ning.)   150. **unprovided:** ill-equipped.   151. **they . . . virtuous:** i.e., the rebels, by providing the occasion of war, give dishonest men a chance to profiteer and hence offend only those who are honest.   158. **Temple Hall:** i.e., at the Inner Temple, one of the Inns of Court.   161. **fur-niture:** equipment, furnishing.   164. **Brave:** splendid.   165. **drum:** (Possibly Falstaff means that he wishes he could continue to enjoy this tavern instead of risking his life in battle. He may also be punning on *tavern/taborn*, i.e., *taborin*, a kind of drum.)

ACT IV, SCENE I°

[*Enter Hotspur, Worcester, and Douglas.*]

HOTSPUR:
　　Well said, my noble Scot. If speaking truth
　　In this fine age were not thought flattery,
　　Such attribution° should the Douglas have
　　As not a soldier of this season's stamp°
　　Should go so general current° through the world.　　　5
　　By God, I cannot flatter; I do defy°
　　The tongues of soothers!° But a braver° place
　　In my heart's love hath no man than yourself.
　　Nay, task me to my word;° approve me,° lord.
DOUGLAS:　　Thou art the king of honor.　　　10
　　No man so potent breathes upon the ground
　　But I will beard him.°

Enter one [a Messenger] with letters.

HOTSPUR:　　　　　　　　Do so, and 'tis well. —
　　What letters hast thou there? — I can but thank you.°
MESSENGER:
　　These letters come from your father.
HOTSPUR:
　　Letters from him? Why comes he not himself?　　　15
MESSENGER:
　　He cannot come, my lord. He is grievous sick.
HOTSPUR:
　　Zounds, how has he the leisure to be sick
　　In such a jostling° time? Who leads his power?
　　Under whose government° come they along?
MESSENGER:
　　His letters bears his mind, not I, my lord.　　[*Hotspur reads the letter.*]　　20
WORCESTER:
　　I prithee, tell me, doth he keep° his bed?

ACT IV, SCENE I. **Location:** The rebel camp near Shrewsbury.　**3. attribution:** praise, tribute.　**4. stamp:** coinage.　**5. go . . . current:** be so widely accepted and acclaimed. (Continues the metaphor of coinage.)　**6. defy:** proclaim against.　**7. soothers:** flatterers.　**braver:** better, dearer.　**9. task . . . word:** challenge me to make good my word.　**approve:** test.　**12. But . . . him:** but that I will defy him.　**13. I can . . . you:** (Said to Douglas.)　**18. jostling:** contending, clashing.　**19. government:** command.　**21. keep:** keep to.

MESSENGER:

He did, my lord, four days ere I set forth,
And at the time of my departure thence
He was much feared° by his physicians.

WORCESTER:

I would the state of time° had first been whole   25
Ere he by sickness had been visited.
His health was never better worth than now.

HOTSPUR:

Sick now? Droop now? This sickness doth infect
The very life-blood of our enterprise;
'Tis catching hither, even to our camp.   30
He writes me here that inward sickness —
And that his friends by deputation°
Could not so soon be drawn,° nor did he think it meet°
To lay so dangerous and dear a trust
On any soul removed but on his own.°   35
Yet doth he give us bold advertisement°
That with our small conjunction° we should on,°
To see how fortune is disposed to us;
For, as he writes, there is no quailing° now,
Because the King is certainly possessed°   40
Of all our purposes. What say you to it?

WORCESTER:

Your father's sickness is a maim° to us.

HOTSPUR:

A perilous gash, a very limb lopped off.
And yet, in faith, it is not! His present want°
Seems more° than we shall find it. Were it good   45
To set the exact wealth of all our states°
All at one cast?° To set so rich a main°
On the nice° hazard° of one doubtful hour?
It were not good, for therein should we read
The very bottom and the soul of hope,°   50

24. **feared**: feared for.   25. **time**: the times.   32. **by deputation**: through deputies.   33. **drawn**: assembled.   **meet**: appropriate.   35. **On . . . own**: on anyone other than himself.   36. **advertisement**: counsel, advice.   37. **conjunction**: joint force.   **on**: go on.   39. **quailing**: losing heart.   40. **possessed**: informed.   42. **maim**: injury.   44. **want**: absence.   45. **more**: more serious.   46. **To . . . states**: to stake the absolute total of our resources.   47. **cast**: throw of the dice.   **main**: stake in gambling; also, an army.   48. **nice**: precarious, delicate.   **hazard**: (1) game at dice (2) venture.   49–50. **should . . . hope**: we should discover the utmost foundation and basis of our hopes, the most we could rely on.

The very list,° the very utmost bound
Of all our fortunes.

DOUGLAS: Faith, and so we should;
Where now remains a sweet reversion,°
We may boldly spend upon the hope
Of what is to come in.
A comfort of retirement° lives in this.   55

HOTSPUR:
A rendezvous, a home to fly unto,
If that the devil and mischance look big°
Upon the maidenhead° of our affairs.

WORCESTER:
But yet I would your father had been here.   60
The quality and hair° of our attempt
Brooks° no division. It will be thought
By some that know not why he is away
That wisdom, loyalty,° and mere° dislike
Of our proceedings kept the Earl from hence.   65
And think how such an apprehension°
May turn the tide of fearful faction°
And breed a kind of question in our cause.
For well you know we of the offering side°
Must keep aloof from strict arbitrament,°   70
And stop all sight holes, every loop° from whence
The eye of reason may pry in upon us.
This absence of your father's draws° a curtain
That shows the ignorant a kind of fear
Before not dreamt of.

HOTSPUR: You strain too far.°   75
I rather of his absence make this use:
It lends a luster and more great opinion,°
A larger dare° to our great enterprise,
Than if the Earl were here; for men must think,
If we without his help can make a head°   80

---

51. **list:** limit. 53. **reversion:** (Literally, part of an estate yet to be inherited.) 56. **retirement:** something to fall back on. 58. **big:** threatening. 59. **maidenhead:** i.e., commencement. 61. **hair:** kind, nature. 62. **Brooks:** tolerates. 64. **loyalty:** i.e., to the crown. **mere:** absolute. 66. **apprehension:** (1) perception (2) apprehensiveness. 67. **fearful faction:** timid support. 69. **offering side:** side that attacks. 70. **strict arbitrament:** just inquiry or investigation. 71. **loop:** loophole. 73. **draws:** draws aside, opens. 75. **strain too far:** exaggerate. 77. **opinion:** renown. 78. **dare:** daring. 80. **make a head:** raise an armed force.

To push against a kingdom, with his help
We shall o'erturn it topsy-turvy down.
Yet° all goes well, yet all our joints° are whole.

DOUGLAS:
As heart can think. There is not such a word
Spoke of in Scotland as this term of fear.   85

Enter Sir Richard Vernon.

HOTSPUR:
My cousin Vernon, welcome, by my soul.

VERNON:
Pray God my news be worth a welcome, lord.
The Earl of Westmorland, seven thousand strong,
Is marching hitherwards; with him Prince John.

HOTSPUR:
No harm. What more?

VERNON: And further I have learned   90
The King himself in person is set forth,
Or hitherwards intended° speedily,
With strong and mighty preparation.

HOTSPUR:
He shall be welcome too. Where is his son,
The nimble-footed madcap Prince of Wales,   95
And his comrades, that doffed° the world aside
And bid it pass?

VERNON: All furnished,° all in arms;
All plumed like estridges,° that with the wind
Bated° like eagles having lately bathed,
Glittering in golden coats,° like images,°   100
As full of spirit as the month of May
And gorgeous as the sun at midsummer,
Wanton° as youthful goats, wild as young bulls.
I saw young Harry, with his beaver° on,
His cuisses° on his thighs, gallantly armed,   105
Rise from the ground like feathered Mercury,
And vaulted with such ease into his seat°

83. **Yet:** still. **joints:** limbs. 92. **intended:** on the verge of departure. 96. **doffed:** put aside with a gesture. 97. **furnished:** equipped. 98. **estridges:** ostriches. (Refers to ostrich plumes on crests.) 99. **Bated:** flapped their wings. (From falconry.) 100. **coats:** (1) coats of mail (2) heraldic coats of arms. **images:** gilded statues. 103. **Wanton:** sportive, frolicsome. 104. **beaver:** visor; hence, helmet. 105. **cuisses:** armor for the thighs. 107. **seat:** saddle.

As if an angel dropped down from the clouds
To turn and wind° a fiery Pegasus°
And witch° the world with noble horsemanship.   110

HOTSPUR:

No more, no more! Worse than the sun in March
This praise doth nourish agues.° Let them come.
They come like sacrifices° in their trim,°
And to the fire-eyed maid° of smoky war
All hot and bleeding will we offer them.   115
The mailèd° Mars shall on his altar sit
Up to the ears in blood. I am on fire
To hear this rich reprisal° is so nigh,
And yet not ours. Come, let me taste my horse,
Who is to bear me like a thunderbolt   120
Against the bosom of the Prince of Wales.
Harry to Harry shall, hot horse to horse,
Meet and ne'er part till one drop down a corse.
O, that Glendower were come!

VERNON: There is more news:
I learned in Worcester, as I rode along,   125
He cannot draw his power° this fourteen days.

DOUGLAS:

That's the worst tidings that I hear of yet.

WORCESTER:

Ay, by my faith, that bears a frosty sound.

HOTSPUR:

What may the King's whole battle° reach unto?

VERNON:

To thirty thousand.

HOTSPUR: Forty let it be!   130
My father and Glendower being both away,
The powers of us° may serve so great a day.
Come, let us take a muster speedily.
Doomsday is near; die all, die merrily.

---

109. **wind:** wheel about. **Pegasus:** winged horse of Greek mythology. 110. **witch:** bewitch. 111–112. **Worse . . . agues:** (The spring sun was believed to give impetus to chills and fevers, by drawing up vapors. Vernon's speech, says Hotspur, gives one the shudders.) 113. **sacrifices:** beasts for sacrifice. **trim:** fine apparel, trappings. 114. **maid:** i.e., Bellona, goddess of war. 116. **mailèd:** dressed in mail, armor. 118. **reprisal:** prize. 126. **draw his power:** muster his army. 129. **battle:** army. 132. **The . . . us:** our forces.

DOUGLAS:
> Talk not of dying. I am out of° fear 135
> Of death or death's hand for this one half year. *Exeunt.*

ACT IV, SCENE II°

Enter Falstaff, [and] Bardolph.

FALSTAFF: Bardolph, get thee before to Coventry; fill me a bottle of sack. Our soldiers shall march through; we'll to Sutton Coldfield° tonight.

BARDOLPH: Will you give me money, Captain?

FALSTAFF: Lay out, lay out.°

BARDOLPH: This bottle makes an angel.° 5

FALSTAFF: An if° it do, take it for thy labor; an if it make twenty, take them all; I'll answer° the coinage.° Bid my lieutenant Peto meet me at town's end.

BARDOLPH: I will, Captain. Farewell. *Exit.*

FALSTAFF: If I be not ashamed of my soldiers, I am a soused gurnet.° I have misused the King's press° damnably. I have got, in exchange of a 10 hundred and fifty soldiers, three hundred and odd pounds. I press me° none but good° householders, yeomen's° sons, inquire me out contracted° bachelors, such as had been asked twice on the banns° — such a commodity of warm° slaves as had as lief° hear the devil as a drum, such as fear the report of a caliver° worse than a struck° fowl or a hurt wild duck. 15 I pressed me none but such toasts-and-butter,° with hearts in their bellies no bigger than pins' heads, and they have bought out their services;° and now my whole charge° consists of ancients,° corporals, lieutenants, gentlemen of companies° — slaves as ragged as Lazarus in the painted cloth,° where the glutton's dogs licked his sores, and such as indeed were 20

---

135. **out of:** free from. **ACT IV, SCENE II. Location:** A public road near Coventry. 2. **Sutton Coldfield:** (in Warwickshire near Coventry.) 4. **Lay out:** i.e., pay for it yourself. 5. **makes an angel:** i.e., makes ten shillings I've spent for you. (But Falstaff answers as though *makes* means "produces," implying that Bardolph has profited from the transaction.) 6. **An if:** if. 7. **answer:** be responsible for. **the coinage:** i.e., the money produced. 9. **soused gurnet:** a kind of pickled fish. 10. **King's press:** royal warrant for the impressment of troops. 11. **press me:** draft, conscript. 12. **good:** i.e., wealthy. **yeomen's:** small freeholders'. **contracted:** engaged to be married. 13. **banns:** public announcements, declared on three Sundays in succession, of an intent to marry. 14. **warm:** i.e., loving their comfort. **lief:** willingly. 15. **caliver:** musket. **struck:** wounded. 16. **toasts-and-butter:** weaklings. 17. **bought . . . services:** i.e., paid, bribed, to be released from military duty. 18. **charge:** company, troop. **ancients:** ensigns, standard-bearers. (By appointing a disproportionate number of junior officers, Falstaff has made it possible to collect for himself their more substantial pay.) 19. **gentlemen of companies:** a kind of junior officer. 19–20. **painted cloth:** cheap hangings for a room. (For the story of Lazarus the beggar and Dives the rich man, see Luke 16:19–31.)

never soldiers, but discarded unjust° servingmen, younger sons to younger brothers,° revolted° tapsters, and hostlers trade-fallen,° the cankers° of a calm world and a long peace, ten times more dishonorable-ragged than an old feazed ancient.° And such have I, to fill up the rooms of them as have bought out their services, that you would think that I had a hundred and fifty tattered prodigals° lately come from swine keeping, from eating draff° and husks. A mad fellow met me on the way and told me I had unloaded all the gibbets° and pressed the dead bodies. No eye hath seen such scarecrows. I'll not march through Coventry with them, that's flat.° Nay, and the villains march wide betwixt the legs as if they had gyves° on, for indeed I had the most of them out of prison. There's not a shirt and a half in all my company, and the half shirt is two napkins tacked together and thrown over the shoulders like a herald's coat without sleeves; and the shirt, to say the truth, stolen from my host° at Saint Albans,° or the red-nose innkeeper of Daventry.° But that's all one;° they'll find linen enough on every hedge.°

Enter the Prince [and the] Lord of Westmorland.

PRINCE: How now, blown° Jack? How now, quilt?

FALSTAFF: What, Hal? How now, mad wag? What a devil dost thou in Warwickshire? My good lord of Westmorland, I cry you mercy.° I thought your honor had already been at Shrewsbury.

WESTMORLAND: Faith, Sir John, 'tis more than time that I were there, and you too; but my powers° are there already. The King, I can tell you, looks for us all. We must away° all night.

FALSTAFF: Tut, never fear° me. I am as vigilant as a cat to steal cream.

PRINCE: I think, to steal cream indeed, for thy theft hath already made thee butter.° But tell me, Jack, whose fellows are these that come after?

FALSTAFF: Mine, Hal, mine.

PRINCE: I did never see such pitiful rascals.

---

21. **unjust:** dishonest.   21–22. **younger ... brothers:** (i.e., with no possibility of inheritance).   22. **revolted:** runaway.   **trade-fallen:** whose business has fallen away.   23. **cankers:** cankerworms that destroy leaves and buds. (Used figuratively.)   24. **feazed ancient:** frayed flag.   26. **prodigals:** (See Luke 15:15–16.)   27. **draff:** hogwash.   28. **gibbets:** gallows.   30. **that's flat:** that's for sure.   31. **gyves:** fetters.   34. **my host:** the innkeeper.   34, 35. **Saint Albans, Daventry:** (Towns north and west of London, on the road to Coventry.)   35. **that's all one:** no matter.   36. **hedge:** (Where wet linen was spread out to dry.)   37. **blown:** swollen, inflated; also, short of wind.   39. **cry you mercy:** beg your pardon.   42. **powers:** soldiers.   43. **must away:** must march.   44. **fear:** worry about.   45–46. **thy ... butter:** i.e., all the cream (rich things) you have stolen has been churned into butterfat in your barrel-like belly.

FALSTAFF: Tut, tut, good enough to toss;° food for powder,° food for pow-
der. They'll fit a pit as well as better. Tush, man, mortal men, mortal men.　50
WESTMORLAND: Ay, but, Sir John, methinks they are exceeding poor and
bare,° too beggarly.
FALSTAFF: Faith, for° their poverty, I know not where they had that, and
for their bareness, I am sure they never learned that of me.
PRINCE: No, I'll be sworn, unless you call three fingers in the ribs° bare.　55
But, sirrah, make haste. Percy is already in the field.　　　　*Exit.*
FALSTAFF: What, is the King encamped?
WESTMORLAND: He is, Sir John. I fear we shall stay too long.　　*[Exit.]*
FALSTAFF: Well,
To the latter end of a fray and the beginning of a feast　　　　　60
Fits a dull fighter and a keen° guest.　　　　　　　　　　*Exit.*

Act IV, Scene III°

Enter Hotspur, Worcester, Douglas, [and] Vernon.

HOTSPUR:
We'll fight with him tonight.
WORCESTER:　　　　　　　　　It may not be.
DOUGLAS:
You give him then° advantage.
VERNON:　　　　　　　　　　Not a whit.
HOTSPUR:
Why say you so? Looks he not for supply?°
VERNON:
So do we.
HOTSPUR: His is certain; ours is doubtful.
WORCESTER:
Good cousin, be advised, stir not tonight.　　　　　　　　　5
VERNON:
Do not, my lord.
DOUGLAS:　　　　　　You do not counsel well.
You speak it out of fear and cold heart.

---

49. **toss:** toss on a pike. **food for powder:** cannon fodder.　**51–52. poor and bare:** inferior
and threadbare. (But Falstaff puns on the sense of "financially strapped and lean.")　**53. for:** as
for.　**55. three . . . ribs:** i.e., Falstaff's fat-covered ribs. (A *finger* was a measure of three-fourths
of an inch.)　**61. keen:** with keen appetite.　**ACT IV, SCENE III. Location:** The rebel camp
near Shrewsbury.　**2. then:** i.e., if you wait. (Addressed to Worcester, not Hotspur.)　**3. supply:** reinforcements.

VERNON:
Do me no slander, Douglas. By my life,
And I dare well maintain it with my life,
If well-respected° honor bid me on,   10
I hold as little counsel with weak fear
As you, my lord, or any Scot that this day lives.
Let it be seen tomorrow in the battle
Which of us fears.

DOUGLAS: Yea, or tonight.   15

VERNON: Content.

HOTSPUR: Tonight, say I.

VERNON:
Come, come, it may not be. I wonder much,
Being men of such great leading° as you are,
That you foresee not what impediments   20
Drag back our expedition.° Certain horse°
Of my cousin Vernon's are not yet come up.
Your uncle Worcester's horse came but today,
And now their pride and mettle° is asleep,
Their courage with hard labor tame and dull,   25
That not a horse is half the half of himself.

HOTSPUR:
So are the horses of the enemy
In general journey-bated° and brought low.
The better part of ours are full of rest.

WORCESTER:
The number of the King exceedeth our.   30
For God's sake, cousin, stay till all come in.

The trumpet sounds a parley.°

Enter Sir Walter Blunt.

BLUNT:
I come with gracious offers from the King,
If you vouchsafe me hearing and respect.°

HOTSPUR:
Welcome, Sir Walter Blunt; and would to God
You were of our determination!°   35

10. **well-respected:** well weighed or considered. 19. **leading:** leadership. 21. **expedition:** speedy progress. **horse:** cavalry (as also at line 23). 24. **pride and mettle:** spirit. 28. **journey-bated:** tired from the journey. s.d. *parley:* trumpet summons to a conference. 33. **respect:** attention. 35. **determination:** persuasion (in the fight).

Some of us love you well; and even those some°
Envy your great deservings and good name
Because you are not of our quality°
But stand against us like an enemy.

BLUNT:

And God defend° but still° I should stand so,   40
So long as out of limit° and true rule
You stand against anointed majesty.
But to my charge. The King hath sent to know
The nature of your griefs° and whereupon
You conjure from the breast of civil peace   45
Such bold hostility, teaching his duteous land
Audacious cruelty. If that° the King
Have any way your good deserts forgot,
Which he confesseth to be manifold,
He bids you name your griefs, and with all speed   50
You shall have your desires with interest
And pardon absolute for yourself and these
Herein misled by your suggestion.°

HOTSPUR:

The King is kind; and well we know the King
Knows at what time to promise, when to pay.   55
My father and my uncle and myself
Did give him that same royalty he wears,
And when he was not six-and-twenty strong,
Sick in the world's regard, wretched and low,
A poor unminded outlaw sneaking home,   60
My father gave him welcome to the shore;
And when he heard him swear and vow to God
He came but to be Duke of Lancaster,
To sue his livery° and beg his peace°
With tears of innocency and terms of zeal,   65
My father, in kind heart and pity moved,
Swore him assistance, and performed it too.
Now when the lords and barons of the realm

---

36. **even those some:** i.e., those same persons among us who love you. 38. **quality:** party. 40. **defend:** forbid. **still:** always. 41. **limit:** bounds of allegiance. 44. **griefs:** grievances. 47. **If that:** if. 53. **suggestion:** instigation. 64. **sue his livery:** sue as an heir come of age for the delivery of his lands. **beg his peace:** i.e., request to be reconciled to King Richard.

Perceived Northumberland did lean to him,
The more and less° came in with cap and knee,°   70
Met him in boroughs, cities, villages,
Attended° him on bridges, stood in lanes,°
Laid gifts before him, proffered him their oaths,
Gave him their heirs° as pages, followed him
Even at the heels in golden° multitudes.   75
He presently, as greatness knows itself,°
Steps me° a little higher than his vow°
Made to my father while his blood° was poor°
Upon the naked shore at Ravenspurgh,
And now, forsooth, takes on him to reform   80
Some certain edicts and some strait° decrees
That lie too heavy on the commonwealth,
Cries out upon abuses, seems to weep
Over his country's wrongs; and by this face,°
This seeming brow of justice, did he win   85
The hearts of all that he did angle for;
Proceeded further — cut me° off the heads
Of all the favorites that the absent King
In deputation left behind him here
When he was personal° in the Irish war.   90

BLUNT:
Tut, I came not to hear this.

HOTSPUR: Then to the point.
In short time after, he deposed the King,
Soon after that, deprived him of his life,
And in the neck of that° tasked° the whole state;
To make that worse, suffered his kinsman March —   95
Who is, if every owner were well placed,°
Indeed his king — to be engaged° in Wales,
There without ransom to lie forfeited;°

---

70. **more and less:** persons of all ranks.   **with . . . knee:** i.e., with cap in hand and with bended knee.   72. **Attended:** waited for.   **stood in lanes:** stood row-deep along the roads.   74. **Gave . . . heirs:** i.e., to serve him.   75. **golden:** (1) auspicious, celebrating (2) majestically attired.   76. **knows itself:** perceives its own strength.   77. **Steps me:** i.e., steps. (*Me* is used colloquially.)   **vow:** i.e., Henry's vow to seek no more than his inheritance.   78. **blood:** spirit, temper.   **poor:** i.e., unambitious.   81. **strait:** strict.   84. **face:** show, pretense.   87. **cut me:** i.e., cut.   90. **personal:** physically, in person.   94. **in . . . that:** next, immediately after.   **tasked:** laid taxes upon.   96. **if . . . placed:** if every claimant were given his proper place.   97. **engaged:** held as hostage.   98. **lie forfeited:** remain prisoner, unreclaimed.

Disgraced me° in my happy° victories,
Sought to entrap me by intelligence;°   100
Rated° mine uncle from the Council board;
In rage dismissed my father from the court;
Broke oath on oath, committed wrong on wrong,
And in conclusion drove us to seek out
This head of safety,° and withal° to pry   105
Into his title, the which we find
Too indirect for long continuance.

BLUNT:
Shall I return this answer to the King?

HOTSPUR:
Not so, Sir Walter. We'll withdraw awhile.
Go to the King; and let there be impawned°   110
Some surety for a safe return again,
And in the morning early shall mine uncle
Bring him our purposes.° And so farewell.

BLUNT:
I would you would accept of grace and love.

HOTSPUR:
And maybe so we shall.

BLUNT: Pray God you do.   [*Exeunt.*] 115

Act iv, Scene iv°

Enter [the] Archbishop of York, [and] Sir Michael.

ARCHBISHOP [*giving letters*]:
Hie, good Sir Michael, bear this sealèd brief°
With wingèd haste to the Lord Marshal,°
This to my cousin Scroop,° and all the rest
To whom° they are directed. If you knew
How much they do import, you would make haste.   5

---

99. **Disgraced me:** (by demanding the prisoners; see 1.3.23 ff.) **happy:** fortunate. 100. **intelligence:** secret information, i.e., from spies. 101. **Rated:** scolded. 105. **head of safety:** armed force for our protection. **withal:** also. 110. **impawned:** pledged. 113. **purposes:** proposals. **Act iv, Scene iv.** Location: York. The Archbishop's palace. 1. **brief:** letter, dispatch. 2. **Lord Marshal:** i.e., Thomas Mowbray, son of the Duke of Norfolk who is exiled in *Richard II*, and a longtime enemy of the new king. 3. **Scroop:** i.e., perhaps Sir Stephen Scroop of *Richard II*, 3.2.91–218, or Lord Scroop of Masham of *Henry V*, 2.2. 4. **To whom:** to those persons to whom.

SIR MICHAEL: My good lord, I guess their tenor.
ARCHBISHOP: Like enough you do.
   Tomorrow, good Sir Michael, is a day
   Wherein the fortune of ten thousand men
   Must bide the touch;° for sir, at Shrewsbury,   10
   As I am truly given to understand,
   The King with mighty and quick-raisèd power
   Meets with Lord Harry. And I fear, Sir Michael,
   What with the sickness of Northumberland,
   Whose power was in the first proportion,°   15
   And what with Owen Glendower's absence thence,
   Who with them was a rated sinew° too
   And comes not in, o'erruled by prophecies,
   I fear the power of Percy is too weak
   To wage an instant° trial with the King.   20
SIR MICHAEL:
   Why, my good lord, you need not fear;
   There is Douglas and Lord Mortimer.
ARCHBISHOP: No, Mortimer is not there.
SIR MICHAEL:
   But there is Mordake, Vernon, Lord Harry Percy,
   And there is my lord of Worcester, and a head°   25
   Of gallant warriors, noble gentlemen.
ARCHBISHOP:
   And so there is. But yet the King hath drawn
   The special head° of all the land together:
   The Prince of Wales, Lord John of Lancaster,
   The noble Westmorland, and warlike Blunt,   30
   And many more corrivals° and dear men
   Of estimation° and command in arms.
SIR MICHAEL:
   Doubt not, my lord, they shall be well opposed.
ARCHBISHOP:
   I hope no less, yet needful 'tis to fear;
   And, to prevent the worst, Sir Michael, speed.   35
   For if Lord Percy thrive not, ere the King
   Dismiss his power he° means to visit us,

---

10. **bide the touch:** be put to the test (like gold).   15. **in** . . . **proportion:** of the largest size.   17. **rated sinew:** main strength or support reckoned upon.   20. **instant:** immediate.   25. **head:** troop.   28. **special head:** notable leaders.   31. **corrivals:** partners in the enterprise.   32. **estimation:** reputation, importance.   37. **he:** i.e., the King.

For he hath heard of our confederacy,
And 'tis but wisdom to make strong against him.
Therefore make haste. I must go write again   40
To other friends; and so farewell, Sir Michael.

Exeunt [separately].

ACT V, SCENE I°

Enter the King, Prince of Wales, Lord John of Lancaster, Sir Walter Blunt, [and] Fal-staff.

KING:
How bloodily the sun begins to peer
Above yon bosky° hill! The day looks pale
At his distemperature.°
PRINCE: The southern wind
Doth play the trumpet° to his° purposes,
And by his hollow whistling in the leaves   5
Foretells a tempest and a blustering day.
KING:
Then with the losers let it sympathize,
For nothing can seem foul to those that win.

The trumpet sounds.

Enter Worcester [and Vernon].

How now, my lord of Worcester? 'Tis not well
That you and I should meet upon such terms   10
As now we meet. You have deceived our trust
And made us doff our easy° robes of peace
To crush our old limbs in ungentle steel.
This is not well, my lord, this is not well.
What say you to it? Will you again unknit   15
This churlish knot of all-abhorrèd war
And move in that obedient orb° again
Where you did give a fair and natural light,

ACT V, SCENE I. Location: The King's camp near Shrewsbury.   2. **bosky:** bushy.   3. **his dis-temperature:** i.e., the sun's unhealthy appearance.   4. **trumpet:** trumpeter.   **his:** its, the sun's.   12. **easy:** comfortable.   17. **orb:** orbit, sphere of action. (The King's subjects, like planets and stars in the Ptolemaic cosmos, were supposed to revolve around the kingly center, comparable to the earth, in fixed courses.)

And be no more an exhaled meteor,°
A prodigy of fear,° and a portent   20
Of broachèd° mischief to the unborn times?
WORCESTER: Hear me, my liege:
For mine own part, I could be well content
To entertain° the lag end of my life
With quiet hours, for I protest   25
I have not sought the day of this dislike.°
KING:
You have not sought it? How comes it, then?
FALSTAFF: Rebellion lay in his way, and he found it.
PRINCE: Peace, chewet,° peace!
WORCESTER:
It pleased Your Majesty to turn your looks   30
Of favor from myself and all our house;
And yet I must remember° you, my lord,
We were the first and dearest of your friends.
For you my staff of office did I break
In Richard's time, and posted° day and night   35
To meet you on the way, and kiss your hand,
When yet you were in place and in account
Nothing° so strong and fortunate as I.
It was myself, my brother, and his son
That brought° you home and boldly did outdare   40
The dangers of the time. You swore to us,
And you did swear that oath at Doncaster,
That you did nothing purpose 'gainst the state,
Nor claim no further than your new-fall'n° right,
The seat of Gaunt, dukedom of Lancaster.   45
To this we swore our aid. But in short space
It rained down fortune showering on your head,
And such a flood of greatness fell on you —
What with our help, what with the absent King,
What with the injuries° of a wanton° time,   50

---

19. **exhaled meteor:** (Meteors were believed to be vapors drawn up or *exhaled* by the sun and visible as streaks of light; they were regarded as ill omens.)   20. **prodigy of fear:** fearful omen.   21. **broachèd:** set flowing, already begun.   24. **entertain:** occupy.   26. **the . . . dislike:** this time of discord.   29. **chewet:** chough, jackdaw. (Here, a chatterer.)   32. **remember:** remind.   35. **posted:** rode swiftly.   38. **Nothing:** not at all.   40. **brought:** escorted.   44. **new-fall'n:** recently inherited (by the death of John of Gaunt).   50. **injuries:** abuses, evils.   **wanton:** lawless.

The seeming sufferances° that you had borne,
And the contrarious winds that held the King
So long in his unlucky Irish wars
That all in England did repute him dead —
And from this swarm of fair advantages   55
You took occasion° to be quickly wooed
To grip the general sway into your hand;
Forgot your oath to us at Doncaster;
And being fed by us, you used us so
As that ungentle gull, the cuckoo's bird,°   60
Useth the sparrow; did oppress our nest,
Grew by our feeding to so great a bulk
That even our love° durst not come near your sight
For fear of swallowing; but with nimble wing
We were enforced, for safety's sake, to fly   65
Out of your sight and raise this present head,°
Whereby we stand opposèd by such means°
As you yourself have forged against yourself
By unkind usage, dangerous countenance,°
And violation of all faith and troth   70
Sworn to us in your younger enterprise.

KING:

These things indeed you have articulate,°
Proclaimed at market crosses, read in churches,
To face° the garment of rebellion
With some fine color° that may please the eye   75
Of fickle changelings° and poor discontents,
Which gape and rub the elbow° at the news
Of hurly-burly innovation.°
And never yet did insurrection want°
Such water-colors° to impaint his° cause,   80
Nor moody° beggars, starving for a time
Of pell-mell havoc° and confusion.

---

51. **sufferances:** suffering, distress. 56. **occasion:** the opportunity. 60. **ungentle . . . bird:** rude nestling, the cuckoo's young offspring. (The cuckoo lays its eggs in other birds' nests.) 63. **our love:** we in our love. 66. **head:** armed force. 67. **opposèd . . . means:** goaded into opposition by such factors. 69. **dangerous countenance:** threatening behavior. 72. **articulate:** set forth, specified. 74. **face:** trim, adorn. 75. **color:** (1) hue (2) specious appearance. 76. **changelings:** turncoats. 77. **rub the elbow:** i.e., hug themselves with delight. 78. **innovation:** rebellion. 79. **want:** lack. 80. **water-colors:** i.e., thin excuses. (See *color,* line 75.) **his:** its. 81. **moody:** sullen, angry. 82. **havoc:** plundering.

PRINCE:
    In both your° armies there is many a soul
    Shall pay full dearly for this encounter,
    If once they join in trial. Tell your nephew   85
    The Prince of Wales doth join with all the world
    In praise of Henry Percy. By my hopes° —
    This present enterprise set off his head° —
    I do not think a braver gentleman,
    More active-valiant or more valiant-young,   90
    More daring or more bold, is now alive
    To grace this latter age with noble deeds.
    For my part, I may speak it to my shame,
    I have a truant been to chivalry;
    And so I hear he doth account me too.   95
    Yet this before my father's majesty:
    I am content that he shall take the odds
    Of his great name and estimation,°
    And will, to save the blood on either side,
    Try fortune with him in a single fight.   100
KING:
    And, Prince of Wales, so dare we venture° thee,
    Albeit° considerations infinite
    Do make against it. No, good Worcester, no.
    We love our people well; even those we love
    That are misled upon your cousin's° part;   105
    And, will they take the offer of our grace,°
    Both he and they and you, yea, every man
    Shall be my friend again, and I'll be his.
    So tell your cousin, and bring me word
    What he will do. But if he will not yield,   110
    Rebuke and dread correction wait on us,°
    And they shall do their office. So, begone.
    We will not now be troubled with reply.
    We offer fair; take it advisedly.

                Exeunt Worcester [and Vernon].

---

83. **both your:** i.e., your and our.   87. **hopes:** i.e., hopes of salvation.   88. **This . . . head:** i.e., if this present rebellion is taken from his account, not held against him.   98. **estimation:** reputation.   101. **venture:** hazard, risk.   102. **Albeit:** although it be that. (The subjunctive has the force of "were it not that.")   105. **cousin's:** i.e., nephew's.   106. **grace:** pardon. 111. **wait on us:** are in attendance upon us.

PRINCE:
It will not be accepted, on my life. 115
The Douglas and the Hotspur both together
Are confident against the world in arms.

KING:
Hence, therefore, every leader to his charge;
For on their answer will we set on them,
And God befriend us as our cause is just! 120

Exeunt. Manent° Prince, Falstaff.

FALSTAFF: Hal, if thou see me down in the battle and bestride° me, so;° 'tis a point of friendship.

PRINCE: Nothing but a colossus can do thee that friendship. Say thy prayers, and farewell.

FALSTAFF: I would 'twere bedtime, Hal, and all well. 125

PRINCE: Why, thou owest God a death.° *[Exit.]*

FALSTAFF: 'Tis not due yet; I would be loath to pay him before his day. What need I be so forward with him that calls not on me? Well, 'tis no matter; honor pricks° me on. Yea, but how if honor prick me off° when I come on? How then? Can honor set to° a leg? No. Or an arm? No. Or 130 take away the grief° of a wound? No. Honor hath no skill in surgery, then? No. What is honor? A word. What is in that word "honor"? What is that "honor"? Air. A trim reckoning! Who hath it? He that died o' Wednesday. Doth he feel it? No. Doth he hear it? No. 'Tis insensible, then? Yea, to the dead. But will it not live with the living? No. Why? De- 135 traction° will not suffer° it. Therefore I'll none of it. Honor is a mere scutcheon.° And so ends my catechism.°

Exit.

ACT V, SCENE II°

Enter Worcester [and] Sir Richard Vernon.

WORCESTER:
O, no, my nephew must not know, Sir Richard,
The liberal and kind offer of the King.

---

s.d. *Manent:* they remain onstage.   121. bestride: stand over in order to defend.   so: well and good.   126. thou . . . death: (Proverbial, with a pun on *debt.*)   129. pricks: spurs.   prick me off: mark me off (as one dead).   130. set to: rejoin or set.   131. grief: pain.   135–36. Detraction: slander.   136. suffer: allow.   137. scutcheon: heraldic emblem carried in funerals, displayed on coaches, etc.; it was the lowest form of symbol, having no pennon or other insignia.   catechism: the principles of faith given in the form of question and answer.   ACT V, SCENE II. Location: Near the rebel camp.

VERNON:
 'Twere best he did.

WORCESTER: Then are we all undone.
 It is not possible, it cannot be,
 The King should keep his word in loving us;   5
 He will suspect us still and find a time
 To punish this offense in° other faults.
 Suspicion all our lives shall be stuck full of eyes;°
 For treason is but trusted like the fox,
 Who, never so° tame, so cherished, and locked up,   10
 Will have a wild trick° of his ancestors.
 Look how we can, or sad° or merrily,
 Interpretation will misquote our looks,
 And we shall feed like oxen at a stall,
 The better cherished still the nearer death.   15
 My nephew's trespass may be well forgot;
 It hath the excuse of youth and heat of blood,
 And an adopted name of privilege° —
 A harebrained Hotspur, governed by a spleen.°
 All his offenses live upon my head   20
 And on his father's. We did train° him on,
 And, his corruption being ta'en from us,°
 We as the spring° of all shall pay for all.
 Therefore, good cousin, let not Harry know
 In any case the offer of the King.   25

 Enter Hotspur [and Douglas, with soldiers].

VERNON:
 Deliver° what you will; I'll say 'tis so.
 Here comes your cousin.

HOTSPUR: My uncle is returned.
 Deliver up° my lord of Westmorland.
 Uncle, what news?

WORCESTER:
 The King will bid you battle presently.   30

---

7. **in:** in punishing.   8. **stuck . . . eyes:** i.e., provided with many eyes, suspiciously inquisi-
tive.   10. **never so:** be he never so.   11. **trick:** trait.   12. **or sad:** either sad.   18. **an adopted
. . . privilege:** i.e., a nickname, "hotspur," to justify his rashness.   19. **spleen:** intemperate impulse.   21. **train:** incite, draw.   22. **his . . . us:** i.e., since his guilt originated in
us.   23. **spring:** source.   26. **Deliver:** report.   28. **Deliver up:** release (as hostage; see
4.3.110–111).

DOUGLAS:

Defy him by° the lord of Westmorland.

HOTSPUR:

Lord Douglas, go you and tell him so.

DOUGLAS:

Marry, and shall, and very willingly.   *Exit Douglas.*

WORCESTER:

There is no seeming mercy in the King.

HOTSPUR:

Did you beg any? God forbid!   35

WORCESTER:

I told him gently of our grievances,
Of his oath breaking, which he mended thus,
By now forswearing that he is forsworn.
He calls us rebels, traitors, and will scourge
With haughty arms this hateful name in us.   40

Enter Douglas.

DOUGLAS:

Arm, gentlemen, to arms! For I have thrown
A brave° defiance in King Henry's teeth,
And Westmorland, that was engaged,° did bear it;
Which cannot choose but bring him quickly on.

WORCESTER:

The Prince of Wales stepped forth before the King,   45
And, nephew, challenged you to single fight.

HOTSPUR:

O, would the quarrel lay upon our heads,
And that no man might draw short breath today
But I and Harry Monmouth!° Tell me, tell me,
How showed his tasking?° Seemed it in contempt?   50

VERNON:

No, by my soul. I never in my life
Did hear a challenge urged° more modestly,
Unless a brother should a brother dare
To gentle° exercise and proof of arms.°

---

31. **Defy him by:** send back your defiance with. 42. **brave:** proud. 43. **engaged:** held as hostage. 49. **Monmouth:** (A name for the Prince, taken from the Welsh town where he was born.) 50. **showed his tasking:** appeared his giving the challenge. 52. **urged:** put forward. 54. **gentle:** befitting noble birth. **proof of arms:** test of martial skill.

He gave you all the duties° of a man,   55
Trimmed up your praises° with a princely tongue,
Spoke your deservings like a chronicle,
Making you ever better than his praise
By still dispraising praise valued with you;°
And, which became him like a prince indeed,   60
He made a blushing cital° of himself,
And chid his truant youth with such a grace
As if he mastered there a double spirit
Of teaching and of learning instantly.°
There did he pause. But let me tell the world,   65
If he outlive the envy° of this day,
England did never owe° so sweet a hope,
So much misconstrued in his wantonness.°

HOTSPUR:
Cousin, I think thou art enamorèd
On his follies. Never did I hear   70
Of any prince so wild a liberty.°
But be he as he will, yet once ere night
I will embrace him with a soldier's arm,
That he shall shrink under my courtesy.°
Arm, arm with speed! And, fellows, soldiers, friends,   75
Better consider what you have to do
Than I, that have not well the gift of tongue,
Can lift your blood up with persuasion.

Enter a Messenger.

FIRST MESSENGER: My lord, here are letters for you.
HOTSPUR: I cannot read them now.   80
O gentlemen, the time of life is short!
To spend that shortness basely were too long
If° life did ride upon a dial's point,°
Still ending at the arrival of an hour.°
An if we live, we live to tread on kings;   85

---

55. **duties:** due merits.   56. **Trimmed . . . praises:** adorned his praise of you.   59. **still . . . you:** constantly disparaging praise itself compared with your true worth.   61. **cital:** account, citation.   64. **instantly:** simultaneously.   66. **envy:** hostility.   67. **owe:** own.   68. **wantonness:** playful sportiveness.   71. **liberty:** licentiousness.   74. **shrink under my courtesy:** (1) be daunted by my greater courtesy (2) fall back before my attack.   83. **If:** even if.   **dial's point:** hand of a watch.   84. **Still . . . hour:** ineluctably concluding within an hour's time.

If die, brave° death, when princes die with us!
Now, for° our consciences, the arms are fair.°
When the intent of bearing them is just.

Enter another [Messenger].

SECOND MESSENGER:
My lord, prepare. The king comes on apace.

HOTSPUR:
I thank him that he cuts me from my tale,   90
For I profess not talking. Only this —
Let each man do his best. And here draw I
A sword, whose temper I intend to stain
With the best blood that I can meet withal
In the adventure of this perilous day.   95
Now, *Esperance!°* Percy! And set on.
Sound all the lofty instruments of war,
And by that music let us all embrace;
For, heaven to earth,° some of us never shall
A second time do such a courtesy.   100

Here they embrace. The trumpets sound. [Exeunt.]

ACT V, SCENE III°

*The King enters with his power° [and passes over the stage]. Alarum° to the battle.
Then enter Douglas, and Sir Walter Blunt [dressed like King Henry].*

BLUNT:
What is thy name, that in the battle thus
Thou crossest me? What honor dost thou seek
Upon my head?

DOUGLAS: Know then my name is Douglas,
And I do haunt thee in the battle thus
Because some tell me that thou art a king.   5

BLUNT: They tell thee true.

DOUGLAS:
The lord of Stafford dear° today hath bought
Thy likeness,° for instead of thee, King Harry,

---

86. **brave:** glorious. 87. **for:** as for. **fair:** just. 96. *Esperance:* (The motto of the Percy family.) 99. **heaven to earth:** i.e., I'll wager heaven against earth. ACT V, SCENE III. Location: Shrewsbury field. The scene is virtually continuous. s.d. *power:* army. *Alarum:* trumpet signal to advance. 7. **dear:** dearly. 7–8. **bought Thy likeness:** paid for his resemblance to you.

This sword hath ended him. So shall it thee,
Unless thou yield thee as my prisoner.   10

BLUNT:
I was not born a yielder, thou proud Scot,
And thou shalt find a king that will revenge
Lord Stafford's death.   *They fight. Douglas kills Blunt.*

Then enter Hotspur.

HOTSPUR:
O Douglas, hadst thou fought at Holmedon thus,
I never had triumphed upon a Scot.   15

DOUGLAS:
All's done, all's won; here breathless° lies the King.

HOTSPUR: Where?

DOUGLAS: Here.

HOTSPUR:
This, Douglas? No. I know this face full well.
A gallant knight he was; his name was Blunt,
Semblably furnished° like the King himself.   20

DOUGLAS:
A fool go with thy soul,° whither it goes!
A borrowed title hast thou bought too dear.
Why didst thou tell me that thou wert a king?

HOTSPUR:
The King hath many marching in his coats.°   25

DOUGLAS:
Now, by my sword, I will kill all his coats!
I'll murder all his wardrobe, piece by piece,
Until I meet the King.

HOTSPUR: Up, and away!
Our soldiers stand full fairly for the day.°   [*Exeunt.*]

Alarum. Enter Falstaff, solus.

FALSTAFF: Though I could scape shot-free° at London, I fear the shot   30
here; here's no scoring° but upon the pate. Soft, who are you? Sir Walter

---

16. **breathless:** i.e., dead.   21. **Semblably furnished:** similarly accoutered.   22. **A . . . soul:** i.e.,
may the stigma of "fool" accompany your soul (for having dressed as a decoy of King
Henry).   25. **coats:** vests worn over armor embroidered with a coat of arms.   29. **stand . . . day:**
i.e., seem in an auspicious position, likely to win the victory.   30. **shot-free:** without paying the
tavern bill.   31. **scoring:** (1) cutting (2) marking up of charges, by notches on a stick or on the inn
door.

Blunt. There's honor for you. Here's no vanity!° I am as hot as molten lead, and as heavy too. God keep lead out of me! I need no more weight than mine own bowels. I have led my ragamuffins where they are peppered. There's not three of my hundred and fifty left alive, and they are 35 for the town's end,° to beg during life. But who comes here?

Enter the Prince.

PRINCE:
What, stands thou idle here? Lend me thy sword.
Many a nobleman lies stark and stiff
Under the hoofs of vaunting enemies,
Whose deaths are yet unrevenged. I prithee, 40
Lend me thy sword.

FALSTAFF: O Hal, I prithee, give me leave to breathe awhile. Turk Gregory° never did such deeds in arms as I have done this day. I have paid Percy, I have made him sure.°

PRINCE:
He is, indeed, and living to kill thee. 45
I prithee, lend me thy sword.

FALSTAFF: Nay, before God, Hal, if Percy be alive, thou gets not my sword; but take my pistol, if thou wilt.

PRINCE:
Give it me. What, is it in the case?

FALSTAFF: Ay, Hal, 'tis hot, 'tis hot.° There's that will sack a city. 50

The Prince draws it out and finds it to be a bottle of sack.

PRINCE:
What, is it a time to jest and dally now?

He throws the bottle at him. Exit.

FALSTAFF: Well, if Percy be alive, I'll pierce° him. If he do come in my way, so;° if he do not, if I come in his willingly, let him make a carbonado° of me. I like not such grinning honor as Sir Walter hath. Give me life, which I can save, so; if not, honor comes unlooked for, and there's an end.° [*Exit.*] 55

---

32. Here's no vanity: i.e. (ironically), if this doesn't show what I was saying about honor, then nothing does. **36. town's end:** i.e., city gate, frequented by beggars. **42–43. Turk Gregory:** (*Turk* is an abusive term signifying a tyrant, and *Gregory* refers probably to Pope Gregory XIII, who was assumed to have encouraged the Massacre of Saint Bartholomew [1572], in which many French Protestants were slain, and to have encouraged plots against Elizabeth.) **44. made him sure:** made sure of him. (But Prince Hal takes *sure* in a different sense, meaning "safe.") **50. hot:** (Falstaff implies he has been firing at the enemy.) **52. Percy . . . pierce:** (Elizabethan pronunciation rendered the pun more obvious than it is now.) **53. so:** well and good. **carbonado:** meat scored across for broiling. **55. there's an end:** (1) that concludes the subject of my catechism (see 5.1.128–137) (2) thus life ends.

ACT V, SCENE IV°

*Alarum. Excursions.° Enter the King, the Prince, Lord John of Lancaster, [and the]
Earl of Westmorland.*

KING: I prithee,
Harry, withdraw thyself; thou bleedest too much.
Lord John of Lancaster, go you with him.

LANCASTER:
Not I, my lord, unless I did bleed too.

PRINCE:
I beseech Your Majesty, make up,°   5
Lest your retirement° do amaze° your friends.

KING:
I will do so. My lord of Westmorland,
Lead him to his tent.

WESTMORLAND:
Come, my lord, I'll lead you to your tent.

PRINCE:
Lead me, my lord? I do not need your help.   10
And God forbid a shallow scratch should drive
The Prince of Wales from such a field as this,
Where stained nobility lies trodden on
And rebels' arms triumph in massacres!

LANCASTER:
We breathe° too long. Come, cousin Westmorland,   15
Our duty this way lies. For God's sake, come.
                    [Exeunt Prince John and Westmorland.]

PRINCE:
By God, thou hast deceived me, Lancaster!
I did not think thee lord of such a spirit.
Before, I loved thee as a brother, John,
But now I do respect thee as my soul.   20

KING:
I saw him hold Lord Percy at the point°
With lustier maintenance° than I did look for
Of such an ungrown warrior.

ACT V, SCENE IV. **Location:** Scene continues at Shrewsbury field. **s.d.** *Excursions:* sorties.
(The fallen body of Blunt may be removed at some point or may be onstage still at 5.4.76 when
Hal kills Hotspur.) **5. make up:** go forward. **6. retirement:** retreat. **amaze:** alarm.
15. breathe: rest, pause for breath (as also at line 47). **21. at the point:** at sword's
point. **22. lustier maintenance:** more vigorous bearing.

PRINCE:
O, this boy lends mettle to us all!   *Exit.*

[*Enter Douglas.*]

DOUGLAS:
Another king? They grow like Hydra's heads.°   25
I am the Douglas, fatal to all those
That wear those colors° on them. What art thou
That counterfeit'st the person of a king?

KING:
The King himself, who, Douglas, grieves at heart
So many of his shadows° thou hast met   30
And not the very King. I have two boys
Seek° Percy and thyself about the field;
But, seeing thou fall'st on me so luckily,
I will assay° thee; and defend thyself.

DOUGLAS:
I fear thou art another counterfeit;   35
And yet, in faith, thou bearest thee like a king.
But mine I am sure thou art, whoe'er thou be,
And thus I win thee.

              They fight; the King being in danger,
                         enter Prince of Wales.

PRINCE:
Hold up thy head, vile Scot, or thou art like°
Never to hold it up again! The spirits   40
Of Valiant Shirley, Stafford, Blunt, are in my arms.
It is the Prince of Wales that threatens thee,
Who never promiseth but he means to pay.°

              They fight. Douglas flieth.

Cheerly, my lord. How fares Your Grace?
Sir Nicholas Gawsey hath for succor sent,
And so hath Clifton. I'll to Clifton straight.   45

KING: Stay and breathe awhile.
Thou hast redeemed thy lost opinion,°
And showed thou mak'st some tender of° my life
In this fair rescue thou hast brought to me.   50

---

25. **Hydra's heads:** (The heads of the Lernaean Hydra grew again as fast as they were cut off.)   27. **colors:** i.e., the colors of the King's insignia.   30. **shadows:** having form without substance.   32. **Seek:** who seek.   34. **assay:** put to the test.   39. **like:** likely.   43. **pay:** (1) settle a debt (2) kill.   48. **opinion:** reputation.   49. **thou . . . of:** you have some care for.

PRINCE:
   O God, they did me too much injury
   That ever said I hearkened° for your death.
   If it were so, I might have let alone
   The insulting° hand of Douglas over you,
   Which would have been as speedy in your end   55
   As all the poisonous potions in the world,
   And saved the treacherous labor of your son.
KING:
   Make up° to Clifton; I'll to Sir Nicholas Gawsey.

                                          Exit King.

   Enter Hotspur.

HOTSPUR:
   If I mistake not, thou art Harry Monmouth.
PRINCE:
   Thou speak'st as if I would deny my name.   60
HOTSPUR:
   My name is Harry Percy.
PRINCE: Why then, I see
   A very valiant rebel of the name.
   I am the Prince of Wales; and think not, Percy,
   To share with me in glory any more.
   Two stars keep not their motion in one sphere,   65
   Nor can one England brook° a double reign
   Of Harry Percy and the Prince of Wales.
HOTSPUR:
   Nor shall it, Harry, for the hour is come
   To end the one of us; and would to God
   Thy name in arms were now as great as mine!   70
PRINCE:
   I'll make it greater ere I part from thee,
   And all the budding honors on thy crest
   I'll crop° to make a garland for my head.
HOTSPUR:
   I can no longer brook thy vanities.°   *They fight.*

   Enter Falstaff.

---

52. **hearkened:** listened (as for welcome news).   54. **insulting:** exulting.   58. **Make up:** advance.   66. **brook:** endure.   73. **crop:** pluck.   74. **vanities:** empty boasts.

FALSTAFF: Well said,° Hal! To it, Hal! Nay, you shall find no boy's play   75
here, I can tell you.

Enter Douglas. He fighteth with Falstaff, who falls down as if he were dead. [Exit
Douglas.] The Prince killeth° Percy.

HOTSPUR:
O Harry, thou hast robbed me of my youth!
I better brook the loss of brittle life
Than those proud titles thou hast won of me;
They wound my thoughts worse than thy sword my flesh.   80
But thoughts, the slaves of life, and life, time's fool,°
And time, that takes survey of all the world,
Must have a stop. O, I could prophesy,
But that the earthy and cold hand of death
Lies on my tongue. No, Percy, thou art dust,   85
And food for —   [*He dies.*]
PRINCE:
For worms, brave Percy. Fare thee well, great heart.
Ill-weaved ambition, how much art thou shrunk!
When that this body did contain a spirit,
A kingdom for it was too small a bound;   90
But now two paces of the vilest earth
Is room enough. This earth that bears thee dead
Bears not alive so stout° a gentleman.
If thou wert sensible of courtesy,°
I should not make so dear° a show of zeal;°   95
But let my favors° hide thy mangled face,
And, even in thy behalf, I'll thank myself
For doing these fair rites of tenderness.
                          [*He covers Hotspur's face with a scarf*
                                    or other favor.]
Adieu, and take thy praise with thee to heaven!
Thy ignominy sleep with thee in the grave,   100
But not remembered in thy epitaph!

                    He spieth Falstaff on the ground.

---

75. Well said: well done. **s.d.** *killeth:* mortally wounds. **81. thoughts . . . fool:** i.e., our men-
tal consciousness, which is dependent on physical existence, and our life itself, which is subject
to time. **93. stout:** valiant. **94. sensible of courtesy:** able to hear my praise. **95. dear:**
handsome, heartfelt. **zeal:** admiration. **96. favors:** plume, scarf, glove, or similar article.

What, old acquaintance, could not all this flesh
Keep in a little life? Poor Jack, farewell!
I could have better spared a better man.
O, I should have a heavy° miss of thee   105
If I were much in love with vanity.°
Death hath not struck so fat a deer today,
Though many dearer, in this bloody fray.
Emboweled° will I see thee by and by.
Till then in blood by noble Percy lie.   *Exit.*   110

Falstaff riseth up.

FALSTAFF: Emboweled? If thou embowel me today, I'll give you leave to
powder° me and eat me too tomorrow. 'Sblood, 'twas time to counterfeit,
or that hot termagant° Scot had paid° me, scot and lot° too. Counterfeit?
I lie, I am no counterfeit. To die is to be a counterfeit, for he is but the
counterfeit of a man who hath not the life of a man; but to counterfeit   115
dying, when a man thereby liveth, is to be no counterfeit but the true and
perfect image of life indeed. The better part° of valor is discretion, in the
which better part I have saved my life. Zounds, I am afraid of this gunpowder Percy, though he be dead. How if he should counterfeit too and
rise? By my faith, I am afraid he would prove the better counterfeit.   120
Therefore I'll make him sure; yea, and I'll swear I killed him. Why may
not he rise as well as I? Nothing confutes me but eyes,° and nobody sees
me. Therefore, sirrah [*stabbing him*], with a new wound in your thigh,
come you along with me.

He takes up Hotspur on his back.

Enter Prince [and] John of Lancaster.

PRINCE:
Come, brother John; full bravely hast thou fleshed°   125
Thy maiden sword.
LANCASTER: But soft, whom have we here?
Did you not tell me this fat man was dead?
PRINCE: I did; I saw him dead,
Breathless and bleeding on the ground. — Art thou alive?
Or is it fantasy that plays upon our eyesight?   130

---

105. **heavy:** (1) serious (2) corpulent.   106. **vanity:** frivolity.   109. **Emboweled:** disembow-
eled, i.e., for embalming and burial.   112. **powder:** salt.   113. **termagant:** violent and blustering, like the heathen god of the Saracens in medieval and Renaissance lore.   **paid:** i.e.,
killed.   **scot and lot:** i.e., in full. (Originally the phrase was the term for a parish
tax.)   117. **part:** constituent part, quality, role.   122. **Nothing . . . eyes:** i.e., nothing can contradict me but an eyewitness.   125. **fleshed:** initiated (in battle).

I prithee, speak. We will not trust our eyes
Without our ears. Thou art not what thou seem'st.

FALSTAFF: No, that's certain, I am not a double man;° but if I be not Jack
Falstaff, then am I a Jack.° There is Percy [*throwing the body down*]. If
your father will do me any honor, so; if not, let him kill the next Percy   135
himself. I look to be either earl or duke, I can assure you.

PRINCE:
Why, Percy I killed myself and saw thee dead.

FALSTAFF: Didst thou? Lord, Lord, how this world is given to lying! I
grant you I was down and out of breath, and so was he; but we rose both
at an instant° and fought a long hour by Shrewsbury clock. If I may be   140
believed, so; if not, let them that should reward valor bear the sin upon
their own heads. I'll take it upon my death° I gave him this wound in the
thigh. If the man were alive and would deny it, zounds, I would make
him eat a piece of my sword.

LANCASTER:
This is the strangest tale that ever I heard.   145

PRINCE:
This is the strangest fellow, brother John. —
Come, bring your luggage nobly on your back.
For my part, if a lie° may do thee grace,°
I'll gild it with the happiest° terms I have.

                                                    A retreat is sounded.

The trumpet sounds retreat; the day is our.   150
Come, brother, let us to the highest° of the field,
To see what friends are living, who are dead.

                              Exeunt [*Prince of Wales and Lancaster*].

FALSTAFF: I'll follow, as they say, for reward. He that rewards me, God reward him! If I do grow great, I'll grow less; for I'll purge,° and leave sack,
and live cleanly as a nobleman should do.   155

                                   Exit [*bearing off the body*].

ACT V, SCENE V°

The trumpets sound. Enter the King, Prince of Wales, Lord John of Lancaster, Earl of Westmorland, with Worcester and Vernon prisoners.

---

133. **double man:** (1) specter (2) two men.   134. **Jack:** knave.   140. **at an instant:** simultaneously.   142. **take . . . death:** i.e., swear with my eternal soul at risk.   148. **a lie:** i.e., this lie of
yours.   **grace:** credit.   149. **happiest:** most felicitous.   151. **highest:** highest vantage
point.   154. **purge:** (1) reduce in weight, using laxatives (2) repent.   **ACT V, SCENE V. Location:** The battlefield.

KING:

Thus ever did rebellion find rebuke.
Ill-spirited Worcester! Did not we send grace,
Pardon, and terms of love to all of you?
And wouldst thou turn our offers contrary?°
Misuse the tenor of thy kinsman's trust?°   5
Three knights upon our party slain today,
A noble earl, and many a creature else
Had been alive this hour,
If like a Christian thou hadst truly borne
Betwixt our armies true intelligence.°   10

WORCESTER:

What I have done my safety urged me to;
And I embrace this fortune patiently,
Since not to be avoided it falls on me.

KING:

Bear Worcester to the death and Vernon too.
Other offenders we will pause upon.   15

[*Exeunt Worcester and Vernon, guarded.*]

How goest the field?

PRINCE:

The noble Scot, Lord Douglas, when he saw
The fortune of the day quite turned from him,
The noble Percy slain, and all his men
Upon the foot of fear,° fled with the rest;   20
And falling from a hill, he was so bruised
That the pursuers took him. At my tent
The Douglas is; and I beseech Your Grace
I may dispose of him.

KING: With all my heart.

PRINCE:

Then, brother John of Lancaster,   25
To you this honorable bounty° shall belong.
Go to the Douglas, and deliver him
Up to his pleasure, ransomless and free.
His valors shown upon our crests° today

---

4. turn . . . contrary: reverse the intention of our offers. **5. Misuse . . . trust:** i.e., abuse Hotspur's confidence (by concealing the generosity of my offer, in your role as emissary). **10. intelligence:** information, report. **20. Upon . . . fear:** fleeing in panic. **26. bounty:** assignment, act of benevolence. **29. crests:** i.e., helmets.

Have taught us how to cherish such high deeds 30
Even in the bosom of our adversaries.

LANCASTER:
I thank Your Grace for this high courtesy,
Which I shall give away° immediately.

KING:
Then this remains, that we divide our power.
You, son John, and my cousin Westmorland 35
Towards York shall bend you° with your dearest° speed
To meet Northumberland and the prelate Scroop,
Who, as we hear, are busily in arms.
Myself and you, son Harry, will towards Wales,
To fight with Glendower and the Earl of March. 40
Rebellion in this land shall lose his° sway,
Meeting the check of such another day;
And since this business so fair° is done,
Let us not leave° till all our own be won.   *Exeunt.*

---

33. **give away:** pass along, confer on Douglas.   36. **bend you:** direct your course.   **dearest:** most urgent.   41. **his:** its.   43. **fair:** successfully.   44. **leave:** leave off.

TEXTUAL NOTES FOR
THE FIRST PART OF KING HENRY THE FOURTH

Copy text: the first complete Quarto of 1598 [Q1]; and, for 1.3.201 through 2.2.110, the fragment of an earlier Quarto [Q0]. The act and scene divisions, missing in Q0 and Q1, are based on F except that F provides no break at 5.3.
Act 1, Scene 1. 22. **levy:** leauy.   39. **Herdfordshire:** Herdforshire.   62. **a dear:** deere.   69. **blood, did:** bloud. Did.   70. **plains. Of:** plains, of.   76. **In faith, it is:** [assigned in Q1 to King].
Act 1, Scene 2. 19. **king:** a king.   27. **proof, now:** proofe. Now.   61. **similes:** smiles.   122. **thou:** the.   124. **Peto, Bardolph:** Haruey, Rossill.
Act 1, Scene 3. 194. **good night:** god-night.   201. s.p. **Hotspur:** [missing in Q0–Q4].   238. **whipped:** [Q1] whip [Q0].
Act 11, Scene 1. 27. s.p. **First Carrier:** Car.   38. s.d.: [at line 47 in Q0].   44. **Weald:** wild.
Act 11, Scene 11. s.d. *Poins, Peto: Poines, and Peto &c.*   11. **square:** squire.   16–17. **Bardolph:** Bardol [and thus, or "Bardoll," throughout the play].   27. **mine:** [Q1] my [Q1].   33. **Go hang:** [F] Hang [Q0].   41. s.p. and text BARDOLPH **What news:** [all assigned as continuation of Poins's speech in line 40].   42. s.p. **Gadshill:** Bar.   64. s.p. **First Traveler:** Trauel.   67. s.p. **Travelers:** Trauel.   71. s.p. **Travelers:** Tra.
Act 11, Scene 111. 1. s.p. **Hotspur:** [not in Q1].   2. **in:** in the.   38. **thee:** the.   59. **A roan:** Roane.
Act 11, Scene 1v. 26. **precedent:** present.   29. s.p. **Poins:** Prin.   140. s.p. **Prince:** Gad.   141. s.p. **Gadshill:** Ross. [also at lines 143 and 147].   185. **keech:** catch.   197. **eel-skin:** ellskin.   260. s.d.: [after line 321 in Q1].   272. **Owen:** O.   314. **tristful:** trustfull.   320. **yet:** so.   377. **lean:** lane.   421. **Good:** God [also at line 422].   428. s.d. *pockets: pocket.*   430. s.p. **Peto:** [not in Q1].   436. s.p. **Prince:** [not in Q1].

ACT III, SCENE I. 55. coz: coose [also at line 75]. 97. cantle: scantle. 126. meter: miter. 129. on: an. 259. hot Lord: Hot. Lord.
ACT III, SCENE II. 59. won: wan. 84. gorged: gordge. 96. then: than. 145. northern: Northren. 161. s.d.: [after line 162 in Q1].
ACT III, SCENE III. 26. that's: that. 43. tithe: tight. 94. no thing: nothing. 106. owed: ought. 136. guests: ghesse. 159. o'clock: of clocke.
ACT IV, SCENE I. 1. s.p. [and elsewhere] Hotspur: Per. 20. lord: mind. 55. is: tis. 96. doffed: daft. 105. cuisses: cushes. 108. dropped: drop. 116. altar: altars. 123. ne'er: neare. 126. cannot: can. 127. yet: it. 134. merrily: merely.
ACT IV, SCENE II. 2. Coldfield: cophill. 12. yeomen's: Yeomans. 24. feazed: fazd. 26. tattered: tottered. 61. s.d. Exit: Exeunt.
ACT IV, SCENE III. 23. horse: horses. 74. heirs ... followed: heires, as Pages followed. 84. country's: Countrey.
ACT IV, SCENE IV. 0. s.d. Michael: Mighell [and throughout]. 18. o'erruled: ouerrulde. 36. not, ere: not ere. 37. power he: power, he.
ACT V, SCENE I. s.d. Lancaster: Lancaster, Earle of Westmerland. 2. bosky: bulky. 3. southern: Southren. 88. off: of. 114. s.d. Exeunt: Exit. 135. will it: wil.
ACT V, SCENE II. 3. undone: vnder one. 8. Suspicion: Supposition. 12. merrily: merely. 25. s.d. Hotspur: Percy. 79. s.p. First Messenger: Mes. 89. s.p. Second Messenger: Mes. 94–95. withal / . . . day.: withall. / . . . day.
ACT V, SCENE III. 1. in the: in. 22. A: Ah. 34. ragamuffins: rag of Muffins.
ACT V, SCENE IV. 4. s.p. [and elsewhere] Lancaster: P. John. 68. Nor: Now. 76. s.d. who: he. 92. enough. This: inough, this. thee: the.
ACT V, SCENE V. 36. bend you: bend, you.

PART TWO

><

*Early Modern Documents
and Controversies*

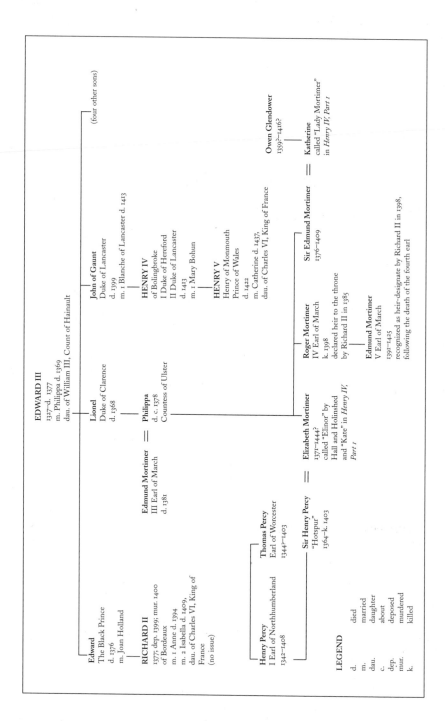

EDWARD III
1327–d. 1377
m. Philippa d. 1369
dau. of William III, Count of Hainault

Edward
The Black Prince
d. 1376
m. Joan Holland

RICHARD II
1377; dep. 1399; mur. 1400
of Bordeaux
m. 1 Anne d. 1394
m. 2 Isabella d. 1409,
dau. of Charles VI, King of France
(no issue)

Lionel
Duke of Clarence
d. 1368

Edmund Mortimer
III Earl of March
d. 1381

Philippa
d. c. 1378
Countess of Ulster

John of Gaunt
Duke of Lancaster
d. 1399
m. 1 Blanche of Lancaster d. 1413

HENRY IV
of Bolingbroke
I Duke of Hereford
II Duke of Lancaster
d. 1413
m. 1 Mary Bohun

HENRY V
Henry of Monmouth
Prince of Wales
d. 1422
m. Catherine d. 1437,
dau. of Charles VI, King of France

(four other sons)

Elizabeth Mortimer
1371–1444?
called "Elinor" by
Hall and Holinshed
and "Kate" in Henry IV,
Part 1

Roger Mortimer
IV Earl of March
k. 1398
declared heir to the throne
by Richard II in 1385

Edmund Mortimer
V Earl of March
1391–1425
recognized as heir-designate by Richard II in 1398,
following the death of the fourth earl

Sir Edmund Mortimer
1376–1409

Owen Glendower
1359?–1416?

Katherine
called "Lady Mortimer"
in Henry IV, Part 1

Henry Percy
I Earl of Northumberland
1342–1408

Thomas Percy
Earl of Worcester
1344?–k. 1403

Sir Henry Percy
"Hotspur"
1364?–k. 1403

LEGEND

d.   died
m.   married
dau.   daughter
c.   about
dep.   deposed
mur.   murdered
k.   killed

CHAPTER I

Historiography and the Uses of History

>‹

Sixteenth-century England witnessed a previously unknown interest in history as well as marked changes in historiography — that is, in ways of writing history, of conceptualizing its methodologies and protocols. The number of editions of historical works published in the period registers this interest: William Baldwin's *Mirror for Magistrates* saw seven editions between 1559 and 1587; Edward Hall's *Union*, popularly known as the *Chronicle*, had two editions in 1548 and another in 1550; John Stow's *Summary of English Chronicles* (1565) had ten editions by 1611; and Raphael Holinshed's compendious *Chronicles* (1577) was reissued in 1587, augmented and revised. Developments in the printing industry and the spread of literacy fueled this rapid expansion of available historical texts, and writers on education and conduct offered testimony to their importance. Sir Roger Ascham, Queen Elizabeth's tutor, wrote that history "could bring excellent learning and breed staid judgment in taking any like matter in hand" (129). The English humanist Sir Thomas Elyot put history at the center of his educational

◄ FIGURE 2 *This genealogical chart, in addition to showing the Mortimer claim to the throne and the relations of the Percies and Owen Glendower, through marriage, to that claim, cites the descendants of Edward III who figure by presence or parenthood in the play. It does not attempt to be a complete record of the families included.*

scheme: "Surely if a noble man do thus seriously and diligently read histories, I dare affirm there is no study or science for him of equal commodity and pleasure, having regard to every time and age" (1: 91).

But if there was general agreement about the salutary effects of *reading* history, precisely what it encompassed was problematic and fluid. Different writers used the term *history* in different contexts to mean different things. Usually, "history" involved a story of some sort: Elyot, for example, listed Holy Scripture, Homer's *Iliad* and *Odyssey,* and Aesop's fables in his catalogue of historical texts. Less commonly, history comprised an inventory of factual knowledge, such as Pliny's *Natural History,* one model for chorographies like William Harrison's *Description of England* (1587) and John Speed's *The Theatre of the Empire of Great Britain* (1611/12), which mapped histories of the land — its counties, cities, towns, villages, manors, and wards; its flora and fauna; and its people's habits. Furthermore, although the texts mentioned here are prose, a history could be a poem or, like Shakespeare's *Henry IV, Part 1,* a play.

The thinking of Renaissance humanists like Ascham and Elyot provided one impetus for the Elizabethans' interest in history; it also shaped a dominant strand of historical enquiry. Judged by present-day standards, these writers had less concern for "the past as it actually happened" than for discovering instructive analogues in the stories of great men that could offer examples, especially to contemporary princes and for contemporary situations, by which readers might learn virtuous behavior and right rule, judge their own actions, and avoid mistakes. For the sixteenth-century historian, *truth* meant moral, not factual veracity: the lesson drawn from an event had more importance than the event itself (Woolf 12). Not only could such lessons inspire men to emulate their predecessors and so achieve enduring fame, but the prospect of a lasting reputation might urge men to greatness and deter evil deeds, which the historian could also ensure would outlive the doer. Grounded in the assumption that "human nature" — as well as human experience — remains the same, the humanist model viewed individuals as capable of fashioning themselves to act in morally and socially productive ways that benefit themselves and the state.

Yet although the humanist conception of history and its uses gained widespread acceptance in the period, it competed with and was influenced by notions inherited from medieval chroniclers. Chief among these was the wheel of fortune, by means of which irrational occurrences could be rationalized as fate or chance. The wheel of fortune was ruled by the goddess Fortuna, whose feminine whims were thought to determine the outcome of battles and the rise and fall of men and nations. Fortuna's workings could be easily reconciled with those of her Christian counterpart, divine providence.

To subordinate fortune to God or providence was not, however, simply a matter of intellectual convenience but was necessary in the context of a Christian cosmology, which explained events by locating their first cause in divine purpose. Like Aristotle's view of nature, English historians' view of history was teleological: seeing events as directed toward an ultimate purpose, they wrote history accordingly, tracing outcomes back to their beginnings. Edward Hall, for instance, believed the union of the houses of Lancaster and York during the reign of Henry VII to be the climactic event toward which the civil conflicts of the fifteenth century that led to the Wars of the Roses had progressed. Men's fates were predetermined and worked to God's purpose, which was manifested in national history by the restoring of order to an England where the monarch was God's deputy. Yet another, more "modern" strand of thought, drawn primarily from Continental theorists such as Niccolò Machiavelli and Jean Bodin, offered a politically oriented rival to this tradition, one that did not focus on providentialist explanations but instead analyzed second causes, taking account of the effects of political situations and the impact of human will, agency, and capability. According to Machiavelli, Fortune could be mastered only by a strong man who knew not to rely on her.

To characterize history, however, as falling into a moral and a political school of thought or taking a progressive trajectory from one tradition to another would not only be highly schematic but would not make sense to late-sixteenth-century writers. Although the terms *moral* and *political* do serve to distinguish the attitudes writers took toward the past, both conceptions of history coexisted. Moreover, the writing of a single author sometimes endorsed radically different ideas of history and historiography. It is possible, for instance, to locate moments in Raphael Holinshed's *Chronicles* where a providential explanation of events occurs side by side with a more circumstantial one; and even in Hall's *Union,* the more providentially oriented of the two chronicle histories, providentialism competes with other explanations of the rebellion that marked the third and fourth years of what Hall terms Henry IV's "unquiet time" and that Shakespeare dramatizes in *Henry IV, Part 1.* Indeed, combining several strands of thought — history as a model for action and as God's will operating in human affairs — even extended beyond the boundaries of books to the sphere of public life, where, as in Sir Thomas Wyatt's confessional scaffold speech, made just before his execution for rebellion in 1554, a man might become his own historian:

> Lo, here see in me the same end which all other commonly had which have attempted like enterprise from the beginning. For peruse the Chronicles through, & you shall see that never rebellion attempted by subjects against

their Prince and country from the beginning did ever prosper or have better success, except the case of King Henry the Fourth, who, although he became a Prince, yet in his act was but a Rebel, for so I must call him. Usurpation [was] so sharply revenged afterward in his blood, as it well appeared, that the long delay of God's vengeance was supplied with more grievous plagues in the third and fourth generation. (qtd. in Campbell 218–19)

Wyatt's reference to Henry IV evokes a period that was of pressing interest to Elizabethans. For them, the previous century's Wars of the Roses, which had destroyed families, devastated the land, and disrupted ancient feudal allegiances and lineages, was *the* seminal event of their most recent past. Learning its lessons was especially important for an emergent nation-state that wished to preserve the peace and political stability of Elizabeth I's regime and to avoid the mistakes that had disrupted the security of the past. To this end, Tudor monarchs sponsored what might be called official histories, texts that constructed myths of ancestry and providential purpose that authenticated both the present ruler and his or her claim to the throne. These chronicle and verse accounts accomplished significant cultural work by restoring a sense of national unity and value that had been shaken by the persistent memory of the Wars of the Roses. The first of these histories, Polydore Vergil's 1534 account, was commissioned by Henry VII, who wished to trace his ancestry to King Arthur (though Henry did not survive to read it). Although Vergil's history attacked the historicity of Arthur, it clearly approved Henry IV's usurpation of Richard II's throne. In so favoring Lancastrian over Yorkist dynastic politics, Vergil's account calls attention to how historians of the Lancaster-York conflict, even as they celebrated the peace and prosperity of the Tudor dynasty and condemned civil dissension, kept the old quarrel alive by creating accounts which, in taking one side or the other, approached myth.

Edward Hall's *Union* (1548) is the most famous of these official histories. His title clearly signals the particular ideological investment of his project: *The Union of the Two Noble and Illustrious Families of Lancaster & York being long in continual dissension for the crown of this noble realm, with all the acts done in both the times of the Princes, both of the one lineage and of the other, beginning at the time of king Henry the fourth, the first author of this division, and so successively proceeding to the reign of the high and prudent prince, king Henry the eight, the undubitate flower and very heir of both the said lineages.* In taking union as his overarching theme, Hall brought an original emphasis to Vergil's account, from which he borrows heavily, often without specific acknowledgment. Although he wholeheartedly supports all favorable prophetic omens concerning Tudor rule (when providence appears, it consistently benefits Lancastrian kings), Hall does balance the claims of York and Lancaster against one another to produce a *dramatic*, though didactic, vision of fifteenth- and sixteenth-century history. Most significant, Hall's *Union* became crucial to the tradition of English historiography by following Vergil, for Vergil was the first of the humanist historians to set a pattern for the popular chronicles by writing history as a connected, unified narrative in which cause and effect were related, events interpreted, and their significance generalized to serve as useful lessons.

Of the texts reproduced in this volume, Hall's *Union* is the earliest; according to most scholars, it represents a *possible* source for Shakespeare's play. Raphael Holinshed incorporates parts of Hall's account into his massive *Chronicles of England* (1587), Shakespeare's central source; and Samuel Daniel's *The Civil Wars* (1595), from which Shakespeare borrows several crucial details, also relies on Hall. Differing in details and ideological assumptions, these selections represent history as a palimpsest — not just *one* history but several points of view on, or written over, the *same* history. Although these documents can be properly considered "histories," texts included elsewhere, such as the excerpts from William Harrison's *Description of England* (published as part of Holinshed's *First Volume of Chronicles*) and John Stow's *Survey of London* (1603) (see Chapter 3, "Cultural Territories"), John Speed's *History of Great Britain* (1611/12) (see Chapter 4, "The 'Education' of a Prince"), and John Foxe's *Acts and Monuments* (1563) (see Chapter 6, "The Oldcastle Controversy"), might also be read through the interpretive frameworks suggested here. In addition to the texts represented here, readers might explore William Baldwin's compilation, *The Mirror for Magistrates* (1559). Representing the clearest instance of Fortune's impact on humanist enquiry, *Mirror* offers ideological perspectives on Owen Glendower and the Earl of Northumberland widely different from those of Hall and Holinshed. Or, for an instance of how the events surrounding Henry IV's deposition of Richard II were appropriated to implicate, if not refigure, the troubled history of Robert Devereux, the Earl of Essex, and Queen Elizabeth, one might turn to John Hayward's *First Part of the Life and Reign of King Henry the IV* (1599).

→ EDWARD HALL

From The Union of the Two Noble and Illustrious Families of Lancaster and York   *1548*

→ RAPHAEL HOLINSHED

From The Chronicles of England, Scotland, and Ireland   *1587*

If Hall's *Union* can be seen as developing what present-day historians call a *grand récit*, or grand narrative, which favored the status quo, by the time Raphael Holinshed and his collaborators were compiling the *Chronicles*, they had little or no interest in legitimating the Tudor dynasty. To be sure, *Chronicles* does contain *grand récits*, but they are not presented, as in Hall's *Union, A Mirror for Magistrates*, or Samuel Daniel's *Civil Wars*, in a triumphal or tragic mode. Moreover, Holinshed's syndicate of writers were not servants of the Crown but middle-class citizens whose diversity of opinion appears reflected in the *Chronicles'* multivocal characteristics. Although Holinshed reproduces (often verbatim) earlier historians' work, he records to a greater degree than before what historians today call "history from below" — the doings of the artisanal and laboring classes — which, particularly with the inclusion of Harrison's *Description*, extend into anthropology. More than any historiographical writing produced in the period, the *Chronicles* was conceived as "documentary history," as part of a national archive, a project of civic consciousness. Indeed, the incoherence implied by the term "documentary history" can be thought of as giving the *Chronicles* positive, not negative, value (Patterson, *Reading* 7, 14). Holinshed's "Preface to the Reader" describes his purpose in conventionally didactic terms as "the encouragement of . . . worthy countrymen, by elders' advancements; and the daunting of the vicious, by sour penal examples, to which end (as I take it) chronicles and histories ought chiefly to be written"; but his method differs from Hall's didactic emphasis on dissension as the precursor to triumphant, celebratory union. In this regard, Holinshed can be seen not as Hall's successor but as offering a counterstatement to his vision of history.

For Holinshed and his collaborators, the diverse evidence discovered by historical enquiry "must not, at whatever cost to the historian, give way to principles of unity and order" (Patterson, *Reading* 15). The preface makes this clear:

Edward Hall, *The Union of the Two Noble and Illustrious Families of Lancaster and York . . .* [rev. ed. 1548], rpt. (London: J. Johnson, 1809) 27–32. Raphael Holinshed, *The Chronicles of England, Scotland, and Ireland Beginning at Duke William the Norman, Commonly Called the Conqueror; and Descending by Degrees of Years to All the Kings and Queens of England in Their Orderly Successions* [1587], rpt. (London: J. Johnson, 1808) 3: 17–26.

I have collected [the history] out of many and sundry authors, in whom what contrariety, negligence, and rashness sometime is found in their reports, I leave to the discretion of those that have perused their works. For my part, *I have in things doubtful rather chosen to show the diversity* of their writings than, by overruling them and using a peremptory censure, to frame them to agree to my liking, *leaving it nevertheless to each man's judgment to control them as he seeth cause.* (2: Preface to the Reader, emphases added)

What is perhaps most important here is Holinshed's insistence on a procedure whereby the reader becomes his (or her) own historian, what Annabel Patterson aptly calls "hands-off historiography" (*Reading* 14). In making such a statement, Holinshed bears witness to how extraordinarily complicated, even dangerous, life had become in post-Reformation England, where what at one moment was loyalty, obedience, and piety could at the next be redefined as treason or heresy. Certainly there was evidence that such redefinition applied to historians, for Queen Mary's 1555 proclamation enforcing the statute against heresy and "Prohibiting Seditious, Heretical Books" had listed "the book commonly called *Hall's Chronicles*" among them. Indeed, the general constraints on public expression in the period had particular relevance to Holinshed's own book: the 1587 edition was called in by the Privy Council and "castrated" (the language of the time) before being rereleased to booksellers. Although censorship certainly factored into the equation, the boundary between the state and individual self-determination, with its dependency on literacy, education, freedom of speech, and access to other media of persuasion (such as the historical drama), was increasingly difficult to police.

Reading Holinshed in conjunction with Hall, it is easy to discern how completely the former seems to have drawn on — or even plagiarized — the latter. But it is also instructive to note the (relative) care with which the *Chronicles* acknowledges its debt to "many and sundry authors." Parenthetical tags — "as some have said"; "saith Hall"; "as some write" — identify these borrowings and also serve to mark off previous writers' opinions, or politics, from Holinshed's. In addition, marginal notations name other authors (*Tho. Wals.*, for instance, is Thomas Walsingham) as well as offering interpretive commentary, as when Holinshed notes, alongside his account of the Percies' division of the realm, "A division of that which they had not" (p. 150). Also, noting precisely which materials Holinshed recycles and which he either omits or summarizes points to particular principles of selection. For instance, whereas Hall opens his account of the third year of Henry IV's reign with the prophetic appearance of Halley's comet (see Figure 5, p. 142) and moves directly to the beginnings of the Northern rebellion, Holinshed, after noting the "strange wonders" accompanying Glendower's birth, introduces accounts of Henry's Parliament and of various affairs touching relations between England and France.

Indeed, the *Chronicles* embeds histories of England's economic, governmental, religious, and legal institutions and of diplomatic affairs that extend beyond Hall's more parochial concerns (see, e.g., Patterson, *Reading* 99–127). Such detailed examination is also rewarding because it reveals two very different representations of the dangerous topic of rebellion, its causes and consequences. Unlike Holinshed, Hall avoids dealing with the vexed politics of Richard II's reign by beginning with that of Henry IV; throughout, his condemnatory tone enhances dissension and sharpens the "wrongs" of civil rebellion. Even though he may not fully endorse Henry IV's usurpation, he seems eager to censure the Northern rebels, an emphasis noticeable in his dismissive attitude toward Glendower's reliance on prophecy, which is somewhat ironic given Hall's own insistence, in line with his more overt providentialism, on reiterating prophecies of doom and the evils of civil discord and "intestine division." By contrast, whereas Holinshed sometimes retains Hall's emphasis on morality and political obedience and (especially in the second edition) includes editorial commentary, his account not only varies in tone but consistently registers a range of attitude and opinion.

For the battle of Shrewsbury, Hall's interest lies in outcomes and in judging the rebels. By contrast, Holinshed attempts to reconstruct the event by expanding existing sources into an analysis that alternates between Henry IV and the Percies, siding neither with one nor the other. In his account, Holinshed sometimes changes the narrative order of information gleaned from Hall; by putting particular details in a different context, such reordering opens up the possibility of alternative interpretations. One example is especially telling. Hall includes the full text of the articles sent by Northumberland and the Percies to Henry IV; these derive from Latin texts published in John Harding's *Chronicle* (1543) which Hall translated and imported into his account. Harding had been brought up from the age of twelve in Sir Henry Percy's household and, when twenty-five, "was with him armed" at Shrewsbury; in keeping with his Yorkist sympathies, he includes the documents "for truth, the cause why they rose against [Henry IV] may ever more be known" (Harding 351–53, addendum).

It is impossible to know whether these articles represent powerful eyewitness testimony or fit any protocol of verbatim reporting. Although Harding claims to have seen the articles at Warkworth Castle, his is clearly an opinionated history, and later (no less opinionated) historians have suspected their authenticity. Hall, however, lets them stand as evidence of the rebels' fractious and dissentious personalities and of Henry IV's falseness and perjury, notions that permit the chronicler to insulate his own opinions from any potentially dangerous currents in the political winds. Although Holinshed's *Chronicles* certainly records similar documents for other reigns, in this case the chronicler notes their "devising," offers a brief summary of their import, and ensures that readers know they were published abroad, making the Percies' rebellion an international matter. In this, as in the wide range of attitude and opinion that the *Chronicles* embraces, Holinshed's compilation moves in the direction of "modern" history.

EDWARD HALL

From *The Union of the Two Noble and Illustrious Families of Lancaster and York*

THE THIRD YEAR

In this year appeared a comet or blazing Star of a huge quantity by a long season which, as the Astronomers affirmed, signified great effusion of man's blood, which judgement was not frustrate, as you shall perceive. For Henry, Earl of Northumberland and Thomas, Earl of Worcester, his brother, and his son Lord Henry Percy called Hotspur, which were to King Henry in the beginning of his reign both fautors,[1] friends and aiders, perceiving now that he had pacified all domestical sedition and repressed his enemies, and reduced his realm to a convenient quietness, began somewhat to envy the glory of him, and grudged against his wealth and felicity. And specially grieved, because the King demanded of the Earl and his son such Scottish prisoners as they had taken at the conflicts fought at Holmedon and Nesbit, as you before have heard. For of all the captives which were there taken, there was delivered to the King's possession only Mordake, Earl of Fife, son to the Duke of Albany, Governor of Scotland, for the King them diverse and sundry times of the Earl and his son required. But the Percies, affirming them to be their own proper prisoners and their peculiar praies,[2] and to deliver them utterly denied, in so much that the King openly said that if they would not deliver them, he would take them without deliverance. Wherewith they, being sore discontent, by the counsel of Lord Thomas Percy, Earl of Worcester, whose study was ever to procure malice, and to set all things in broil and uncertainty, feigning a cause to prove and tempt the King, came to him to Windsor, requiring him by ransom or otherwise to cause to be delivered out of prison Edmund Mortimer, Earl of March, their cousin germain,[3] whom (as they reported) Owen Glendower kept in filthy prison shackled with irons, only for that cause that he took his part, and was to him faithful and true. The King began not a little to muse on this request, and not without a cause, for indeed it touched him as near as his shirt, as you well may perceive by the Genealogy rehearsed in the beginning of this story. For this Edmund was son to Earl Roger, which was son to Lady Philippa, daughter to Lionel, Duke of Clarence, the third son to King Edward the third, which Edmund, at King Richard's going into Ireland, was proclaimed heir apparent to the crown and realm, whose Aunt, called Elinor, this Lord

---

[1] **fautors:** partisans.   [2] **praies:** booty, spoils of war.   [3] **cousin germain:** close kin.

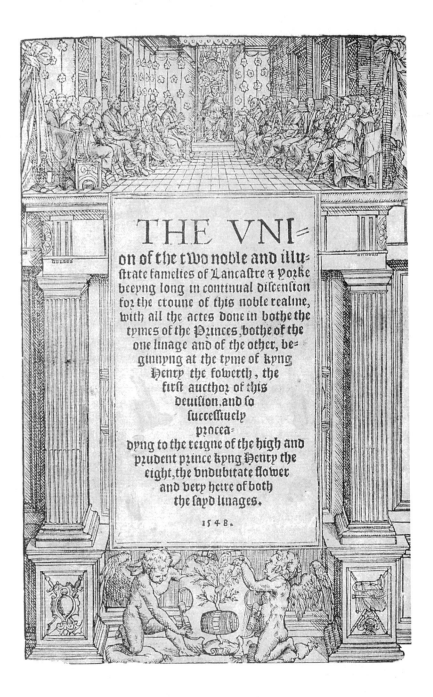

THE VNI=

on of the two noble and illu=
strate famelies of Lancastre ⁊ Yorke
beeyng long in continual discension
for the croune of this noble realme,
with all the actes done in bothe the
tymes of the Princes, bothe of the
one linage and of the other, be=
ginnyng at the tyme of kyng
Henry the fowerth, the
first aucthor of this
deuision, and so
successiuely
procea=
dyng to the reigne of the high and
prudent prince kyng Henry the
eight, the vndubitate flower
and very heire of both
the sayd linages.

1548.

Kyng Henry the fourthe.

Hat mischiefe hath insurged in real=
mes by intestine deuision, what depo=
pulacion hath ensued in countries by
ciuill discencion, what detestable mur=
der hath been committed in citees by se
perate faccions, and what calamitee
hath ensued in famous regios by do=
mestical discord & vnnaturall contro=
uersy: Rome hath felt, Italy can testi=
fie, Fraunce can bere witnes, Beame
can tell, Scotlande maie write, Den=
marke can shewe, and especially this
noble realme of Englande can appa=
rantly declare and make demonstracion. For who abhorreth not to ex=
presse the heynous factes comitted in Rome, by the ciuill war betwene
Julius Cesar and hardy Pompey by whose discorde the bright glory of
the triuphant Rome was eclipsed & shadowed: Who can reherce what
mischefes and what plages the pleasant countree of Italy hath tasted
and suffered by the sedicious faccions of the Guelphes and Gebely=
nes: Who can reporte the misery that daicly hath ensued in Fraunce,
by the discorde of the houses of Burgoyne and Orliens: Or in Scot=
land betwene the brother and brother, the vncle and the nephew: Who
can curiously endite the manifolde battailles that were fought in the
realme of Beame, betwene the catholikes and the pestiferus sectes of
the Adamites and others: What damage discencion hath dooen in
Germany and Denmarke, all christians at this daie can well declare.
And the Turke can bere good testimony, whiche by the discord of chri=
sten princes hath amplified greatly his seigniory and dominion. But
what miserie, what murder, and what execrable plagues this famous
region hath suffered by the deuision and discencion of the renoumed
houses of Lancastre and Yorke, my witte cannot comprehende nor my
toung declare nether yet my penne fully set furthe.

FOR what noble man liueth at this daie, or what gentleman of any
auncient stocke or progeny is clere, whose linage hath not ben infested
and plaged with this vnnaturall deuision. All the other discordes, sec=
tes and faccions almoste liuely florishe and continue at this presente
tyme, to the greate displesure and preiudice of all the christian publike
welth. But the olde deuided controuersie betwene the fornamed fami=
lies of Lancastre and Yorke, by the vnion of Matrimony celebrate and
consummate betwene the high and mighty Prince Kyng Henry the
seuenth and the lady Elizabeth his moste worthy Quene, the one bee=
yng indubitate heire of the hous of Lancastre, and the other of Yorke
was suspended and appalled in the person of their moste noble, puissat
and mighty heire kyng Henry the eight, and by hym clerely buried and

◄ FIGURE 3 (p. 130) *This title page from Edward Hall's* Union *(1548) shows the King seated on his throne, or state, flanked by courtiers. Their arrangement may intentionally illustrate Hall's theme, the union of two houses, but note that the two groups remain opposed, as in parliamentary debate. The columns supporting the picture are a common title-page device. The* putti *(angels) at the bottom surround a tree — possibly a rosebush — a genealogical device representing the joining of the two families.*

◄ FIGURE 4 (p. 131) *The first page of Hall's* Union *(1548) illustrates early modern spelling and typography. The device surrounding the initial letter is the royal seal, surrounded by the motto of the Order of the Garter, "Honi soit qui mal y pense" ("Shamed be he who thinks evil of it"). In the text, Hall sets England's "unnatural division" in relation to the history of other countries and points to its extinction in Henry VIII's time.*

Henry Percy had Married. And therefore the King little forced, although that that lineage were clearly subverted and utterly extinct.[4]

WHEN the King had long digested and studied on this matter, he made answer and said that the Earl of March was not taken prisoner neither for his cause nor in his service, but willingly suffered himself to be taken, because he would take no part against Owen Glendower and his [ac]complices, and therefore he would neither ransom nor relieve him, which fraud the King caused openly to be published and divulged, with which answer, if the parties were angry, doubt you not. But with the publishing of the cautell[5] that the Earl of March was willingly taken, they ten times more fumed and raged, in so much that Sir Henry Hotspur said openly: "Behold the heir of the realm is robbed of his right, and yet the robber, with his own, will not redeem him." So in this fury the Percies departed, nothing more minding than to depose King Henry from the high type of his regality, and to deliver and set in his throne their cousin, friend & confederate, Edmund, Earl of March, whom they not only delivered out of the captivity of Owen Glendower, but also entered into a league and amity with the said Owen against King Henry and all his friends and fautors, to the great displeasure and long unquieting of King Henry and his partakers. Here, I pass over to declare how a certain writer writeth that this Earl of March, the Lord Percy and Owen Glendower were unwisely made [to] believe by a Welsh Prophesier,

---

[4] **extinct:** Hall confuses two Mortimers: Sir Edmund Mortimer, son-in-law of Glendower, with his nephew, also named Edmund, the fifth Earl of March, proclaimed by Richard II as heir presumptive to the Crown in 1398. Shakespeare repeats Hall's error.   [5] **cautell:** trickery.

that King Henry was the Moldwarp,[6] cursed of God's own mouth, and that they three were the Dragon, the Lion and the Wolf, which should divide this realm between them, by the deviation and not divination of that mawmet[7] Merlin. I will not rehearse how they, by their deputies in the house of the Archdeacon of Bangor, seduced with that false feigned Prophesy, divided the realm amongst them, nor yet write how by a tripartite indenture sealed with their seals, all England from Severn and Trent South and Eastward, was assigned to the Earl of March: Nor how all Wales and the lands beyond Severn Westward, were appointed to Owen Glendower, and all the remnant from Trent Northward to the Lord Percy. But I will declare to you that which was not prophesied: that is, the confusion, destruction and perdition of these persons, not only giving credit to such a vain fable, but also setting it forward and hoping to attain to the effect of the same, which was especial of the Lord Percy and Owen Glendower. For the Earl of March was ever kept in the court under such a keeper that he could neither do or attempt any thing against the King without his knowledge, and died without issue, leaving his right title and interest to Anne, his sister and heir, married to Richard, Earl of Cambridge, father to the Duke of York, whose offspring, in continuance of time, obtained the game and got the garland. O, ye wavering Welshmen, call you these prophecies? Nay, call them unprofitable practices. Name you them divinations? Nay, name them diabolical devices. Say you they be prognostications? Nay, they be pestiferous publishings. For by declaring & credit giving to their subtle & obscure meanings, princes have been deceived, many a noble man hath suffered, and many an honest man hath been beguiled & destroyed.

KING Henry, knowing of this new confederacy, and nothing less minding then that that happened after, gathered a great army to go again into Wales, whereof the Earl of Northumberland and his son were advertised, by Lord Thomas, Earl of Worcester, and with all diligence raised all the power that they could make and sent to the Scots which before were taken prisoners at Holmedon for aid and men, promising the Earl Douglas the town of Berwick and a part of Northumberland, and to other Scottish lords great lordships and seigniories,[8] if they obtained the upper hand and superiority. The Scots, allured with desire of gain, and for no malice that they bare to King Henry, but somewhat desirous to be revenged of their old grieves,[9] came to the Earl with great company, and to make their cause seem good and just, they devised certain articles by the advice of Richard Scroop, Archbishop of York, brother to the Lord Scroop, whom King Henry caused to

---

[6] **Moldwarp:** mole; earth-thrower.   [7] **mawmet:** Mahomet; false god.   [8] **seigniories:** feudal domains.   [9] **grieves:** grievances.

be beheaded at Bristow, as you have heard before. Which articles they showed to diverse noblemen and prelates[10] of the realm, which, favoring and consenting to their purpose, not only promised them aid and succor by words, but by their writing and seals confirmed the same. Howbeit, whether it were for fear, either for that they would be lookers-on and no deed-doers, neither promise by word or by writing was performed. For all their confederates them abandoned, & at the day of the conflict left alone, the Earl of Stafford only except, which being of a haughty courage and high stomach, kept his promise & joined with the Percies, to his destruction.

THE Lord Percy, with the Earl Douglas and other earls of Scotland with a great army, departed out of the Northparties, leaving his father sick (which promised upon his amendment & recovery without delay to follow) and came to Stafford where his uncle the Earl of Worcester and he met, and there began to consult upon their great affairs and high attempted enterprise. There they exhorted their soldiers and companions to refuse no pain for the advancement of the commonwealth, nor to spare no travail for the liberty of their country: protesting openly that they made war only to restore the noble realm of England to his accustomed glory and freedom, which was governed by a tyrant and not by his lawful and right king. The captains swore and the soldiers promised to fight, yea & to die for the liberty of their country. When all things were prepared, they set forward toward Wales, looking every hour for new aid and succors, noising abroad that they came to aid the King against Owen Glendower. The King, hearing of the earls approaching, thought it policy to encounter with them before that the Welshmen should join with their army, and so include him on both parts, and therefore returned suddenly to the town of Shrewsbury. He was scantly entered into the town, but he was by his posts advertised that the earls, with banners displayed and battles ranged, were coming toward him, and were so hot and so courageous, that they with light horses began to skirmish with his host. The King, perceiving their doings, issued out and encamped himself without the East gate of the town. The earls nothing abashed, although their succors them deceived, embattled themselves not far from the King's army. And the same night they sent the articles whereof I spake before, by Thomas Caton and Thomas Salvain, esquires to King Henry, signed with their hands and sealed with their seals, which articles (because no Chronicler save one maketh mention what was the very cause and occasion of this great bloody battle, in the which on both parts were above forty thousand men assembled) I, word for word, according to my copy, do here rehearse.

WE Henry Percy, Earl of Northumberland, High Constable of England,

---

[10] **prelates:** ecclesiastical dignitaries of high rank; bishops, archbishops.

and Warden of the West Marches[11] of England toward Scotland, Henry Percy our eldest son, Warden of the East Marches of England toward Scotland, and Thomas Percy, Earl of Worcester, being proctors and protectors of the commonwealth, before our Lord Jesu Christ our supreme judge, do allege, say and intend to prove with our hands personally this instant day, against the Henry, Duke of Lancaster, thy [ac]complices and favorers, unjustly presuming and named King of England without title of right, but only of thy guile and by force of thy fautors: that when thou, after thine exile, didst enter England, thou madest an oath to us upon the holy Gospels, bodily touched and kissed by thee at Doncaster, that thou wouldest never claim the crown, kingdom or state royal but only thine own proper inheritance, and the inheritance of thy wife in England, and that Richard our sovereign lord the King and thine, should reign during the term of his life, governed by the good counsel of the lords spiritual and temporal. Thou hast imprisoned the same thy sovereign lord and our King within the Tower of London, until he had, for fear of death, resigned his kingdoms of England and France, and had renounced all his right in the foresaid kingdoms, and others his dominions and lands of beyond the sea. Under color of which resignation and renunciation, by the counsel of thy friends and [ac]complices, and by the open noising of the rascal people by thee and thy adherents assembled at Westminster, thou hast crowned thyself king of the realms aforesaid, and hast seized and entered into all the castles and lordships pertaining to the King's Crown, contrary to thine oath. Wherefore thou art forsworn and false.

ALSO we do allege, say and intend to prove, that where thou sworest upon the same Gospels in the same place and time to us, that thou wouldest not suffer any dismes[12] to be levied of the Clergy, nor fifteens[13] on the people, nor any other tallagies[14] and taxes to be levied in the realm of England to the behoffe[15] of the realm during thy life, but by the consideration of the three estates of the realm,[16] except for great need in causes of importance or for the resistance of our enemies, only and none otherwise. Thou, contrary to thine oath so made, hast done to be levied right many dismes and fifteens, and other impositions and tallagies, as well of the Clergy as of the commonality of the realm of England, & of the Merchants, for fear of thy majesty royal. Wherefore thou art perjured and false.

ALSO we do allege, say & intend to prove, that w[h]ere thou sworest to us upon the same Gospels in the foresaid place and time, that our sovereign

---

[11] **Marches:** borderlands between England and Wales. [12] **dismes:** tax of a tenth part of one's property; a tithe. [13] **fifteens:** tax of one-fifteenth of one's property. [14] **tallagies:** arbitrary taxes levied on feudal dependents by their superiors. [15] **behoffe:** on behalf of. [16] **three estates of the realm:** orders or classes of the body politic: nobles, clergy, and commons.

lord and thine, King Richard, should reign during the term of his life in his royal prerogative and dignity: thou hast caused the same our sovereign lord and thine, traitorously within the castle of Pomfret, without the consent or judgement of the lords of the realm, by the space of fifteen days and so many nights (which is horrible among Christian people to be heard) with hunger, thirst and cold to perish, to be murdered. Wherefore thou art perjured and false.

ALSO we do allege, say & intend to prove, that thou at that time when our sovereign lord and thine, King Richard, was so by that horrible murder dead, as above said, thou by extort power, didst usurp and take the kingdom of England, and the name and the honor of the kingdom of France, unjustly and wrongfully, contrary to thine oath, from Edmund Mortimer, Earl of March and of Ulster, then next and direct heir of England and of France, immediately by due course of inheritance after the decease of the foresaid Richard. Wherefore thou art perjured and false.

ALSO we do allege, say & intend to prove as aforesaid, that where thou madest an oath in the same place and time, to support and maintain the laws and good customs of the realm of England, and also afterward at the time of thy coronation thou madest an oath, the said laws and good customs to keep and conserve inviolate. Thou fraudulently and contrary to the law of England and thy fautors, have written almost through every shire in England to choose such knights for to hold a parliament as shall be for thy pleasure and purpose, so that in thy parliaments no justice should be ministered against thy mind in these our complaints now moved and showed by us, whereby at any time we might have any perfect redress, notwithstanding that we, according to our conscience (as we trust ruled by God), have often times thereof complained, as well can testify and bear witness the right reverend fathers in God, Thomas Arundell, Archbishop of Canterbury, and Richard Scroop, Archbishop of York. Wherefore now, by force and strength of hand before our Lord Jesu Christ, we must ask our remedy and help.

ALSO we do allege, say and intend to prove, that where Edmund Mortimer, Earl of March and Ulster, was taken prisoner by Owen Glendower in a pitched and foughten field, and cast into prison and laden with iron fetters, for thy matter and cause, whom falsely thou hast proclaimed willingly to yield himself prisoner to the said Owen Glendower, and neither wouldest deliver him thyself, nor yet suffer us his kinsmen to ransom and deliver him. Yet not withstanding, we have not only concluded and agreed with the same Owen for his ransom at our proper charges and expenses, but also for a peace between thee and the said Owen. Why hast thou then not only published and declared us as traitors, but also craftily and deceitfully imagined, purposed and conspired the utter destruction and confusion of our persons?

For the which cause we defy thee, thy fautors and [ac]complices as common traitors and destroyers of the realm, and the invaders, oppressors and confounders of the very true and right heirs to the Crown of England, which thing we intend with our hands to prove this day, almighty God helping us.

WHEN King Henry had overseen their articles and defiance, he answered the esquires that he was ready with dent[17] of sword and fierce battle to prove their quarrel false and feigned, and not with writing nor slanderous words, and so in his righteous cause and just quarrel he doubted not but God would both aid and assist him, against untrue persons and false forsworn traitors: with which answer the messengers departed. The next day in the morning early, which was the vigil of Mary Magdalene,[18] the King, perceiving that the battle was nearer than he either thought or looked for, lest that long tarrying might be a [di]minishing of his strength, set his battles in good order. Likewise did his enemies, which both in puissance[19] and courage were nothing to him inferior. Then suddenly the trumpets blew, and King's part cried "Saint George! Upon them!" The adversaries cried "Esperance Percie!" and so furiously the armies joined. The Scots, which had the forward on the lords' side, intending to be revenged of their old displeasures done to them by the English nation, set so fiercely on the King's forward, that they made them draw back, and had almost broken their array. The Welshmen also, which, since the King's departure out of Wales, had lurked and lain in woods, mountains and marshes, hearing of this battle toward, came to the aid of the earls, and refreshed the weary people with new succors. When a fearful messenger had declared to the King, that his people were beaten down on every side, it was no need to bid him stir, for suddenly he approached with his fresh battle, and comforted, heartened and encouraged his part so, that they took their hearts to them, and manly fought with their enemies. The Prince Henry that day helped much his father, for although he were sore wounded in the face with an arrow, yet he never ceased either to fight where the battle was most strongest, or to courage his men where their hearts w[ere] most daunted. This great battle continued three long hours with indifferent fortune on both parts. That at the last the King, crying "Saint George! Victory!" brake the array and entered into the battle of his enemies and fought fiercely, and adventured so far into the battle, that the Earl Douglas strake him down and slew Sir Walter Blunt, and three other appareled in the King's suit and clothing, saying, "I marvel to see so many kings so suddenly arise again." The King was raised and did that day many a noble feat of arms. For as the Scots write and Frenchmen affirm, although

---

[17] **dent:** dint; blow. [18] **vigil of Mary Magdalene:** the evening before the Feast Day, 22 July. [19] **puissance:** power.

that Englishmen keep silence, that he himself slew with his hands that day xxxvi. persons of his enemies, the other of his part,[20] encouraged by his doings, fought valiantly and slew the Lord Percy called Sir Henry Hotspur, the best captain on the part adverse. When his death was known, the Scots fled, the Welshmen ran, the traitors were overcome. Then neither woods letted,[21] nor hills stopped the fearful hearts of them that were vanquished to fly, and in that flight the Earl Douglas, which for hast[e], falling from the crag of a mountain, brake one of his genitals and was taken, and for his valiantness, of the King freely & frankly delivered. There was taken also Sir Thomas Percy, Earl of Worcester, & diverse other. On the King's part were slain Sir Walter Blunt and xvi.C.[22] other persons, but on the part of the rebels were slain the Earl of Stafford, the Lord Percy and above five thousand other, and as for the Scots, few or none escaped alive.

AFTER this glorious victory by the King obtained, he rendered to almighty God his humble and hearty thanks, and caused the Earl of Worcester, the morrow after Mary Magdalene, at Shrewsbury to be drawn, hanged and quartered, and his head to be sent to London, at which place many more captains were executed. After this great battle, he like a triumphant conqueror returned with great pomp to London, where he was by the senate and magistrates solemnly received, not a little rejoicing of his good fortune and fortunate victory. But before his departure from Shrewsbury, he, not forgetting his enterprise against Owen Glendower, sent into Wales with a great army Prince Henry, his eldest son, against the said Owen and his seditious fautors, which being dismayed and in manner desperate of all comfort by the reason of the King's late victory, fled in desert places and solitary caves, where he received a final reward, meet and prepared by God's providence for such a rebel and seditious seducer. For being destitute of all comfort, dreading to show his face to any creature, lacking meat to sustain nature, for pure hunger and lack of food miserably ended his wretched life. This end was provided for such as gave credence to false prophecies. This end had they that by diabolical divinations were promised great possessions and seigniories. This end happeneth to such as believing such fantastical follies, aspire and gape for honor and high promotions. When the Prince with little labor and less loss, had tamed & bridled the furious rage of the wild and savage Welshmen, and left governors to rule and govern the country, he returned to his father with great honor & no small praise. The Earl of Northumberland, hearing of the overthrow of his brother and son, came of his own free will to the King, excusing himself as one neither party [to]

---

[20] **other of his part:** others in Henry's army, not (as it has been interpreted) a reference to Prince Henry.   [21] **letted:** hindered.   [22] **xvi.C:** 1600.

nor knowing of their doing nor enterprise. The King neither accused him nor held him excused, but dissimulated the matter for ii. causes: one was he had Berwick in his possession, which the King rather desired to have by policy than by force; the other was that the Earl had his castles of Alnwick, Warkworth and other fortified with Scots, so that if the Earl were apprehended, all Northumberland were in jeopardy to become Scottish. For these causes the King gave him fair words & let him depart home, where he continued in peace a while, but after he rebelled, as you shall perceive by the sequel of this story.

RAPHAEL HOLINSHED

From *The Chronicles of England, Scotland, and Ireland*

In the king's absence, whilst he was forth of the realm in Scotland against his enemies, the Welshmen took occasion to rebel under the conduct of their captain Owen Glendower, doing what mischief they could devise, unto their English neighbors. This Owen Glendower was son to an esquire of Wales, named Griffith Vichan: he dwelled in the parish of Conway, within the county of Merioneth in North Wales, in a place called Glindour-wie, which is as much to say in English, as The valley by the side of the water of Dee, by occasion whereof he was surnamed Glindour Dew.

He was first set to study the laws of the realm, and became an utter barrister,[1] or an apprentice of the law (as they term him) and served King Richard at Flint Castle, when he was taken by Henry, Duke of Lancaster, though other have written that he served this King Henry the fourth, before he came to attain the crown, in room[2] of an esquire, and after, by reason of variance that rose betwixt him[3] and the Lord Reginald Grey of Ruthen, about the

[1400]

The Welshmen rebel by the setting on of Owen Glendower.

John Stow.

Owen Glendower what he was.

Tho. Wals.

---

[1] **utter barrister:** one called to the bar and having the privilege of practicing as advocate; utter barristers sat uttermost (outermost) on the forms called the bar, that is, in the most senior place next to the benchers. [2] **room:** position. [3] **him:** that is, Glendower.

lands which he claimed to be his by right of inheritance: when he saw that he might not prevail, finding no such favor in his suit as he looked for, he first made war against the said Lord Grey, wasting his lands and possessions with fire and sword, cruelly killing his servants and tenants. The King, advertised[4] of such rebellious exploits, enterprised by the said Owen, and his unruly [ac]complices, determined to chastise them, as disturbers of his peace, and so with an army entered into Wales; but the Welshmen with their captain withdrew into the mountains of Snowdon, so to escape the revenge, which the King meant towards them. The King therefore did much hurt in the countries with fire and sword, slaying diverse that with weapon in hand came forth to resist him, and so with a great booty of beasts and cattle he returned.

The occasion that moved him to rebel.

The king entreth into Wales, meaning to chastise the rebels.

[Holinshed reports the visit of the Emperor of Constantinople, who came seeking aid against the Turks; an act passed in Parliament against those holding opinions contrary to received doctrine of the Church of Rome. All refusing reform should be "delivered to the secular power, to be burnt to ashes": the first to be burned in Smithfield was William Hawtree or Sawtree, a priest. At this time, King Henry also sent commissioners to France to negotiate a league; Holinshed reports the return of Queen Isabel, Richard II's widow, to France.]

[1401]

About the same time, Owen Glendower and his Welshmen did much hurt to the King's subjects. One night as the King was going to bed, he was in danger to have been destroyed; for some naughty traitorous persons had conveyed into his bed a cerain iron made with smith's craft, like a caltrop,[5] with three long pricks, sharp and small, standing upright, it such sort, that when he had laid him down, & that the weight of his body should come upon the bed, he should have been thrust in with those pricks, and peradventure slain. But as God would, the King, not thinking of any such thing, chanced yet to feel and perceive the instrument before he laid him down, and so escaped the danger.

Anno Reg. 3.

Owen Glendower. The danger of the king to have been destroyed.

[4] **advertised:** informed, advised.   [5] **caltrop:** snare; trap.

Howbeit, he was not so soon delivered from fear; for he might well have his life in suspicion, & provide for the preservation of the same; since perils of death crept into his secret chamber, and lay lurking in the bed of down where his body was to be reposed and to take rest. Oh, what a suspected state therefore is that of a king holding his regiment with the hatred of his people, the heart grudgings of his courtiers, and the peremptory practices of both together? Could he confidently compose or settle himself to sleep for fear of strangling? Durst he boldly eat and drink without dread of poisoning? Might he adventure to show himself in great meetings or solemn assemblies without mistrust of mischief against his person intended? What pleasure or what felicity could he take in his princely pomp, which he knew by manifest and fearful experience, to be envied and maligned to the very death? The state of such a king is noted by the poet in Dionysius, as in a mirror, concerning whom it is said,

> *Districtus ensis cui super impia*
> *Cervice pendet, non Siculæ dapes*
> *Dulcem elaborabunt saporem,*
> *Non avium cytharæq. cantus.*[6]

Hor. lib, ca. 3.

Ode. 1

This year, the eight[h] day of April, deceased the Lord Thomas Beauchamp, Earl of Warwick. In the month of March appeared a blazing star, first between the east part of the firmament and the North, flashing forth fire and flames round about it, and lastly shooting forth fiery beams towards the north, foreshowing (as was thought) the great effusion of blood that followed, about the parts of Wales and Northumberland. For much about the same time, Owen Glendower (with his Welshmen) fought with the Lord Grey of Ruthen, coming forth to defend his possessions, which the same Owen wasted and destroyed: and as the fortune of that day's work fell out, the Lord Grey was taken prisoner, and many of his men were slain. This hap lifted the Welshmen into high pride, and increased marvelously their wicked and presumptuous attempts.

1402

The Earl of Warwick departeth this life.

A blazing star.

The Lord Grey of Ruthen taken in fight by Owen Glendower.

---

[6] **Districtus . . . cantus:** "To the man over whose impious neck the sword hangs, no Sicilian feasts will proffer a sweet savor nor songs of birds and of the cythera will bring repose."

FIGURE 5 *This drawing from* The Beauchamp Pageants *(c. 1485–90), a manuscript depicting the birth, life, and death of Richard Beauchamp, the Earl of Warwick (1389–1439), pictures Glendower's rising against the English and his defeat and capture of Lord Grey of Ruthen in 1402. The "blazing star" of which Holinshed speaks, identified later as Halley's Comet, appears at upper right. Glendower is at right center. The Earl of Warwick, in the left foreground, has his crest of the bear and ragged staff on his visored helmet.*

About Whitsuntide,[7] a conspiracy was devised by certain persons, that wished the King's death, maintaining and bruiting abroad, that King Richard was alive, and therefore exhorted men to stand with him, for shortly he would come to light, and reward such as took his part with just recompense. Herewith, there was a priest taken at Ware, or (as some books have) at Warwick, who had a calendar or roll, in which a great number of Names were written, more than were in any wise guilty of the fact, as afterwards appeared by the same priest's confession. For being examined, whether he knew such persons as he had so enrolled, & were there present before him, he said he never knew them at all; and being demanded wherefore he had then so recorded their names, he answered, because he thought they would gladly do what mischief they could against King Henry, upon any occasion offered in revenge of the injuries done to King Richard, by whom they had been advanced, and princely preferred. When therefore there appeared no more credit in the man, he was condemned, drawn, hanged, and quartered, and diverse that had been apprehended about that matter, were released, and set at liberty. Shortly after, the Prior of Laund (who for his evil government had been deprived of his state and dignity) was likewise executed, not for attempting any thing of himself, but only for that he confessed, that he knew evil counsel and concealed it. His name was Walter Baldocke, a canon sometime in Dunstable, and by King Richard promoted to the Priorship of Laund.

Also the same time, certain grey friars[8] were apprehended for treason which they had devised to bring to pass, and one of them, whose name was Richard Frisebie, being asked what he would do if King Richard had been alive, and present with them, answered stoutly, that he would fight against any man in his quarrel, even to death. Hereupon, he was condemned, drawn, and hanged in his friar's weed, to the great confusion of his brethren; but they made earnest instance to have his body taken down,

A bruit was spread abroad that King Richard was living.

A priest taken.

He is executed.

The prior of Laund apprehended.

Grey friars apprehended.

A grey friar hanged in his habit.

---

[7] **Whitsuntide:** the season of Whit Sunday, the seventh after Easter, commemorating the descent of the Holy Spirit to the Apostles at Pentecost. [8] **grey friars:** an order of Franciscan or Minor friars, founded by St. Francis of Assisi in 1210.

and buried with dirges and exequies,[9] and had their suit granted. Sir Roger of Claringdon, Knight, was also put to death about this conspiracy, with two of his servants, the one an esquire, the other a yeoman. He was base son (as was reported) unto Edward, eldest son to King Edward the third, surnamed the black prince. On Corpus Christi Day[10] at evensong time, the devil (as was thought) appeared in a town of Essex called Danbury, entering into the church in likeness of a grey friar, behaving himself very outrageously, playing his parts like a devil indeed, so that the parishioners were put in a marvellous great fright.

Sir Roger Claringdon.

The devil appeareth in likeness of a grey friar.

At the same instant, there chanced such a tempest of wind, thunder, and lightning, that the highest part of the roof of that church was blown down, and the chancel was all to shaken, rent, and torn in pieces. Within a small while after, eight of those grey friars that had practiced treason against the King were brought to open judgement, and convicted, were drawn and [be]headed at London; and two other suffered at Leicester, all which persons had published King Richard to be alive. Owen Glendower, according to his accustomed manner, robbing and spoiling within the English borders, caused all the forces of the shire of Hereford to assemble together against them, under the conduct of Edmund Mortimer, Earl of March. But coming to try the matter by battle, whether by treason or otherwise, so it fortuned, that the English power was discomfited, the Earl taken prisoner, and above a thousand of his people slain in the place. The shameful villainy used by the Welshwomen towards the dead carcasses, was such, as honest ears would be ashamed to hear, and continent tongues to speak thereof. The dead bodies might not be buried, without great sums of money given for liberty to convey them away.[11]

Eight friars executed.

The Earl of March taken prisoner in battle by Owen Glendower.

The King was not hasty to purchase the deliverance of the Earl March, because his title to the crown was well enough known, and therefore suffered him to remain in

The suspicion of K. Henry grounded upon a guilty conscience.

---

[9] **exequies:** funeral rites.   [10] **Corpus Christi Day:** the Feast of the Blessed Sacrament, or Body of Christ, observed on the Thursday after Trinity Sunday, the eighth after Easter.   [11] For a more detailed account, see the selection from the *Chronicles* on page 270.

miserable prison, wishing both the said Earl, and all other of his lineage out of this life, with God and his saints in heaven, so they had been out of the way, for then all had been well enough, as he thought. But to let these things pass, the King this year sent his eldest daughter Blanche, accompanied with the Earl of Somerset, the Bishop of Worcester, the Lord Clifford, and others, into Almanie, which brought her to Cologne, and there with great triumph she was married to William, Duke of Bavaria, son and heir to Lewis, the Emperor. About mid of August, the King, to chastise the presumptuous attempts of the Welshmen, went with a great power of men into Wales, to pursue the captain of the Welsh, rebel Owen Glendower, but in effect he lost his labor; for Owen conveyed himself out of the way, into his known lurking places, and (as was thought) through art magic, he caused such foul weather of winds, tempest, rain, snow, and hail to be raised, for the annoyance of the King's army, that the like had not been heard of; in such sort, that the King was constrained to return home, having caused his people yet to spoil and burn first a great part of the country. The same time, the Lord Edmund of Langley, Duke of York, departed this life, and was buried at Langley with his brethren. The Scots, under the leading of Patrick Hepborne, of the Hales the younger, entering into England, were overthrown at Nesbit, in the marches,[12] as in the Scottish chronicle ye may find more at large. This battle was fought the two and twentieth of June, in this year of our Lord 1402.

Archibald, Earl Douglas, sore displeased in his mind for this overthrow, procured a commission to invade England, and that to his cost, as ye may likewise read in the Scottish histories. For at a place called Holmedon, they were so fiercely assailed by the Englishmen, under the leading of the Lord Percy, surnamed Henry Hotspur, and George, Earl of March, that with violence of the English shot they were quite vanquished and put to flight, on the Rood Day[13] in harvest, with a great slaughter made by the Englishmen. We know that the Scottish writers note this

The King's daughter married into Germany.

Intemperate weather.

The decease of the Duke of York.

Scots overthrown.

Scots vanquished at Holmedon.

---

[12] **marches:** the borders between England and Wales.   [13] **Rood Day:** Holy Rood Day, the Exaltation of the Cross, 14 September.

battle to have chanced in the year 1403. But we, following Tho[mas] Walsingham in this place, and other English writers, for the accompt of times, have thought good to place it in this year 1402, as in the same writers we find it. There were slain of men of estimation, Sir John Swinton, Sir Adam Gordon, Sir John Leviston, Sir Alexander Ramsey of Dalhousie, and three and twenty knights, besides ten thousand of the commons: and of prisoners among other were these, Mordake, Earl of Fife, son to the Governor[14] Archibald, Earl Douglas, which in the fight lost one of his eyes, Thomas, Earl of Murray, Robert, Earl of Angus, and (as some writers have) the Earls of Atholl & Menteith,[15] with five hundred other of meaner degrees. After this, the Lord Percy, having bestowed the prisoners in sure keeping, entered Tividale, wasting and destroying the whole country, and then besieged the castle of Cocklawes, whereof was captain one Sir John Grenlow, who compounded with the Englishmen, that if the castle were not succoured within three months, then he would deliver it into their hands.

The number slain.

Prisoners taken.

The castle of Cocklawes besieged by the Lord Percy.

The first two months passed, and no likelihood of rescue appeared; but ere the third month was expired, the Englishmen being sent for to go with the King into Wales, raised their siege and departed, leaving the noblemen prisoners with the Earl of Northumberland, and with his son the Lord Percy, to keep them to the King's use. In this meanwhile, such as misliked with the doctrine and ceremonies then used in the church, ceased not to utter their consciences, though in secret, to those in whom they had affiance.[16] But as in the like cases it commonly happeneth, they were betrayed by some that were thought chiefly to favor their cause, as by Sir Lewis Clifford, Knight, who having leaned to the doctrine a long time, did now (as Thomas Walsingham writeth) disclose all that he knew unto the Archbishop of Canterbury, to show himself as it were to have erred rather of simpleness

The professors of Wycliffe's doctrine.

---

[14] Here, the lack of a comma led Shakespeare to identify Mordake as Douglas's son.   [15] **Menteith:** one of Mordake's titles; Shakespeare, however, assumes that Mordake is a separate person.   [16] **affiance:** confidence.

and ignorance, than of frowardness[17] or stubborn malice. The names of such as taught the articles and conclusions maintained by those which then they called Lollards or heretics, the said Sir Lewis Clifford gave in writing to the said Archbishop. Edmund Mortimer, Earl of March, prisoner with Owen Glendower, whether for irksomeness of cruel captivity, or fear of death, or for what other cause, it is uncertain, agreed to take part with Owen, against the King of England, and took to wife the daughter of the said Owen.

Sir Lewis Clifford betrayeth his fellows.

The Earl of March marrieth the daughter of Owen Glendower.

Strange wonders happened (as men reported) at the nativity of this man,[18] for the same night he was born, all his father's horses in the stable were found to stand in blood up to their bellies. The morrow after the Feast of Saint Michael,[19] a parliament began at Westminster, which continued the space of seven weeks, in the same was a tenth and a half granted by the clergy, and a fifteenth by the commonalty.[20] Moreover, the commons in this parliament besought the King to have the person of George, Earl of March, a Scottishman, recommended to his majesty, for that the same Earl showed himself faithful to the King & his realm.

Anno Reg. 4.
A parliament.

George Earl of March recommended to the King by parliament.

There was also a statute made, that the friars beggars should not receive any into their order, under the age of fourteen years. In this fourth year of King Henry's reign, ambassadors were sent over into Brittany, to bring from thence the Duchess of Brittany, the Lady Jane de Navarre, the widow of John de Montford, late Duke of Brittany, surnamed the conqueror, with whom by procurators the King had contracted matrimony. In the beginning of February, those that were sent returned with her in safety, but not without tasting the bitter storms of the wind and weather, that tossed them sore to and fro, before they could get to land. The King met her at Winchester, where, the seventh of February, the marriage was solemnized betwixt them.

1403

Ambassadors.

---

[17] **frowardness**: a disposition to go counter to what is demanded or seems reasonable. [18] **this man**: grammatically this seems to refer to Glendower, though Holinshed may be referring to the birth of Mortimer. [19] **Feast of Saint Michael**: 29 September. [20] **tenth ... fifteenth**: proportions of personal property granted as taxes to the King.

Whilest these things were those in doing in England, Waleran, Earl of Saint Paul, bearing still a deadly and malicious hatred toward King Henry, having assembled sixteen or seventeen hundred men of war, embarked them at Harfleur, and taking the sea, landed in the Isle of Wight, in the which he burned two villages, and four simple cottages, and for a triumph of so noble an act, made four knights.[21] But when he heard that the people of the Isle were assembled and approached to fight with him, he hasted to his ships and returned home: wherewith the noblemen of his company were displeased, considering his provision to be great and his gain small. In the same very season, John, Earl of Clermont, son to the Duke of Bourbon, won in Gascoigne out of the Englishmen's possession, the castles of Saint Peter, Saint Marie, and the New castle; and the Lord de la Bret won the castle of Carlassin, which was no small loss to the English nation.

> The Earl of Saint Paul in the Isle of Wight.

> The Earl of Clermont in Gascoigne.

Henry, Earl of Northumberland, with his brother Thomas, Earl of Worcester, and his son the Lord Henry Percy, surnamed Hotspur, which were to King Henry in the beginning of his reign, both faithful friends, and earnest aiders, began now to envy his wealth and felicity; and especially they were grieved, because the King demanded of the Earl and his son such Scottish prisoners as were taken at Holmedon and Nesbit. For of all the captives which were taken in the conflicts foughten in those two places, there was delivered to the King's possession only Mordake, Earl of Fife, the Duke of Albany's son, though the king did diverse and sundry times require deliverance of the residue, and that with great threatenings: wherewith the Percies being sore offended, for that they claimed them as their own proper prisoners, and their peculiar prize,[22] by the counsel of the Lord Thomas Percy, Earl of Worcester, whose study was ever (as some write) to procure malice, and set things in a broil, came to the King unto Windsor (upon a purpose to prove him) and there required of him, that either by ransom or otherwise, he would cause to be delivered out of prison Edmund

> The request of the Percies.

---

[21] **made . . . knights:** in creating knights, the Earl preempts the King's right.   [22] **prize:** spoils of war, booty.

Mortimer, Earl of March, their cousin germane,[23] whom (as they reported) Owen Glendower kept in filthy prison, shackled with irons, only for that he took his part, and was to him faithful and true.

The King began not a little to muse at this request, and not without cause: for indeed it touched him somewhat near, since this Edmund was son to Roger, Earl of March, son to the Lady Philippa, daughter of Lionel, Duke of Clarence, the third son of King Edward the third; which Edmund at King Richard's going into Ireland, was proclaimed heir apparent to the crown and realm, whose aunt called Elinor,[24] the Lord Henry Percy had married; and therefore King Henry could not well hear, that any man should be in earnest about the advancement of that lineage.[25] The King, when he had studied on the matter, made answer that the Earl of March was not taken prisoner for his cause, nor in his service, but willingly suffered himself to be taken, because he would not withstand the attempts of Owen Glendower and his [ac]complices, and therefore he would neither ransom him, nor relieve him.

The Percies with this answer and fraudulent excuse were not a little fumed, insomuch that Henry Hotspur said openly, "Behold, the heir of the realm is robbed of his right, and yet the robber with his own will not redeem him." So in this fury the Percies departed, minding nothing more than to depose King Henry from the high type of his royalty, and to place in his seat their cousin Edmund, Earl of March, whom they did not only deliver out of captivity, but also (to the high displeasure of King Henry) entered in league with the foresaid Owen Glendower. Herewith, they by their deputies in the house of the Archdeacon of Bangor, divided the realm amongst them, causing a tripartite indenture to be made and sealed with their seals, by the covenants whereof, all England

The saying of the L. Percy.

The conspiracies of the Percies with Owen Glendower. An indenture tripartite.

---

[23] **cousin germane:** close kinsman.   [24] **Elinor:** Actually, the sister of Sir Edmund Mortimer and of the fourth Earl of March was named Elizabeth. Shakespeare calls her Kate.   [25] **lineage:** Like Hall, Holinshed conflates Sir Edmund Mortimer, son-in-law of Glendower, with his nephew, also named Edmund, the fifth Earl of March, proclaimed by Richard II as heir presumptive to the Crown in 1398. Shakespeare repeats Holinshed's error.

from Severn and Trent, south and eastward, was assigned to the Earl of March; all Wales, & the lands beyond Severn westward, were appointed to Owen Glendower; and all the remnant from Trent northward, to the Lord Percy.

This was done (as some have said) through a foolish credit given to a vain prophecy, as though King Henry was the moldwarp,[26] cursed of God's own mouth, and they three were the dragon, the lion, and the wolf, which should divide this realm between them. Such is the deviation (saith Hall) and not divination of those blind and fantastical dreams of the Welsh prophesiers. King Henry, not knowing of this new confederacy, and nothing less minding than that which after happened, gathered a great army to go again into Wales, whereof the Earl of Northumberland and his son were advertised by the Earl of Worcester, and with all diligence raised all the power they could make, and sent to the Scots which before were taken prisoners at Holmedon, for aid of men, promising to the Earl of Douglas the town of Berwick, and a part of Northumberland, and to other Scottish lords great lordships and seigniories,[27] if they obtained the upper hand. The Scots, in hope of gain, and desirous to be revenged of their old griefs, came to the Earl with a great company well appointed.

The Percies, to make their part seem good, devised certain articles, by the advice of Richard Scroop, Archbishop of York, brother to the Lord Scroop, whom King Henry had caused to be beheaded at Bristol. These articles[28] being showed to diverse noblemen, and other states of the realm, moved them to favor their purpose, in so much that many of them did not only promise to the Percies aid and succour by words, but also by their writings and seals confirmed the same. Howbeit when the matter came to trial, the most part of the confederates abandoned them, and at the day of the conflict left them alone. Thus after that the conspirators had discovered themselves, the Lord Henry Percy, desirous to proceed in the

A division of that which they had not.

A vain prophecy.

The Percies raise their powers.

They crave aid of Scots.

The Archbishop of York of counsel with the Percies in conspiracy.

Thom. Wals.

---

[26] **moldwarp:** mole.   [27] **seigniories:** feudal dominions.   [28] **these articles:** for the text of the articles, see page 134.

enterprise, upon trust to be assisted by Owen Glendower, the Earl of March, & other, assembled an army of men of arms and archers forth of Cheshire and Wales. Incontinently,[29] his uncle, Thomas Percy, Earl of Worcester, that had the government of the Prince of Wales, who as then lay at London in secret manner, conveyed himself out of the Prince's house, and coming to Stafford (where he met his nephew) they increased their power by all ways and means they could devise. The Earl of Northumberland himself was not with them, but being sick, had promised upon his amendment to repair unto them (as some write) with all convenient speed.

The Earl of Worcester governor to the Prince slippeth from him. *Hall.*

These noblemen, to make their conspiracy seem excusable, besides the articles above mentioned, sent letters abroad, wherein was contained, that their gathering of an army tended to none other end, but only for the safeguard of their own persons, and to put some better government in the commonwealth. For whereas taxes and tallages[30] were daily levied, under pretense to be employed in defense of the realm, the same were vainly wasted, and unprofitably consumed: and where through the slanderous reports of their enemies, the King had taken a grievous displeasure with them, they durst not appear personally in the King's presence, until the prelates[31] and barons of the realm had obtained of the King license for them to come and purge themselves before him, by lawful trial of their peers, whose judgement (as they pretended) they would in no wise refuse. Many that saw and heard these letters, did commend their diligence, and highly praised their assured fidelity and trustiness towards the commonwealth.

The pretense of the Percies, as they published it abroad.

But the King, understanding their cloaked drift, devised (by what means he might) to quiet and appease the commons, and deface their contrived forgeries; and therefore he wrote an answer to their libels, that he marvelled much, since the Earl of Northumberland, and the Lord Henry Percy, his son, had received the most part of the

The King's answer to the Percies' libel.

---

[29] **incontinently:** immediately. [30] **tallages:** arbitrary taxes levied on feudal dependents by their superiors. [31] **prelates:** ecclesiastical dignitaries of high rank: bishops, archbishops.

sums of money granted to him by the clergy and commonalty, for defense of the marches, as he could evidently prove,
what should move them to complain and raise such manifest slanders. And whereas he understood, that the Earls of
Northumberland and Worcester, and the Lord Percy, had
by their letters signified to their friends abroad, that by reason of the slanderous reports of their enemies, they durst
not appear in his presence, without the mediation of the
prelates and nobles of the realm, so as they required
pledges, whereby they might safely come afore him, to declare and allege what they had to say in proof of their innocence, he protested by letters sent forth under his seal, that
they might safely come and go, without all danger, or any
manner of indamagement to be offered to their persons.

But this could not satisfy those men, but that resolved
to go forwards with their enterprise, they marched towards Shrewsbury, upon hope to be aided (as men
thought) by Owen Glendower, and his Welshmen, publishing abroad throughout the countries on each side, that
King Richard was alive, whom if they wished to see, they
willed them to repair in armor unto the castle of Chester,
where (without all doubt) he was at that present, and
ready to come forward. This tale being raised, though it
were most untrue, yet it bred variable motions in men's
minds, causing them to waver, so as they knew not to
which part they should stick; and verily, diverse were well
affected towards King Richard, specially such as had
tasted of his princely bountifulness, of which there was no
small number. And to speak a truth, no marvel it was, if
many envied the prosperous state of King Henry, since it
was evident enough to the world, that he had with wrong
usurped the crown, and not only violently deposed King
Richard, but also cruelly procured his death; for the
which undoubtedly, both he and his posterity tasted such
troubles, as put them still in danger of their states, till
their direct succeeding line was quite rooted out by the
contrary faction, as in Henry the sixt[h] and Edward the
fourth it may appear.

But now to return where we left. King Henry, advertised of the proceedings of the Percies, forthwith gathered
about him such power as he might make, and being

Poor K. Richard is still alive with them that wish K. Henry's over-throw.

earnestly called upon by the Scot, the Earl of March,[32] to make haste and give battle to his enemies, before their power by delaying of time should still too much increase, he passed forward with such speed, that he was in sight of his enemies, lying in camp near to Shrewsbury, before they were in doubt of [33] any such thing, for the Percies thought that he would have stayed at Burton-upon-Trent, till his council had come thither to him to give their advice what he were best to do. But herein the enemy was deceived of his expectation, since the King had great regard of expedition and making speed for the safety of his own person, whereunto the Earl of March incited him, considering that in delay is danger, & loss in lingering, as the poet in the like case saith:

The King's speedy diligence.

> *Tolle moras, nocuit semper differre paratis,*
> *Dum trepidant nullo firmatæ robore partes.*[34]

By reason of the King's sudden coming in this sort, they stayed from assaulting the town of Shrewsbury, which enterprise they were ready at that instant to have taken in hand, and forthwith the Lord Percy (as a captain of high courage) began to exhort the captains and soldiers to prepare themselves to battle, since the matter was grown to that point, that by no means it could be avoided, so that (said he) "This day shall either bring us all to advancement & honor, or else if it shall chance us to be overcome, shall deliver us from the King's spiteful malice and cruel disdain: for playing the men (as we ought to do), better it is to die in battle for the commonwealth's cause, than through cowardlike fear to prolong life, which after shall be taken from us, by sentence of the enemy."

The Percies troubled with the King's sudden coming.

The Lord Percy exhorteth his accomplices to stick to their tackle.

Hereupon, the whole army being in number about fourteen thousand chosen men, promised to stand with him so long as life lasted. There were with the Percies as chieftains of this army, the Earl of Douglas, a Scottish

The number of the Percies' army.

---

[32] **Scot . . . March:** that is, George Dunbar, Earl of March of Scotland, not to be confused with Edmund Mortimer, the Earl of March in England. [33] **were in doubt of:** anticipated, feared. [34] **Tolle . . . partes:** "While your foes are in confusion and before they have gathered strength, make haste; delay is always fatal to those who are prepared." Lucan *Pharsalia* 1:280–81.

man, the Baron of Kinderton, Sir Hugh Browne, and Sir
Richard Vernon, Knights, with diverse other stout and
right valiant captains. Now when the two armies were encamped, the one against the other, the Earl of Worcester
and the Lord Percy with their [ac]complices sent the articles (whereof I spake before) by Thomas Caton, and
Thomas Salvain, esquires to King Henry, under their
hands and seals, which articles in effect charged him with
manifest perjury, in that (contrary to his oath received
upon the evangelists at Doncaster, when he first entered
the realm after his exile) he had taken upon him the
crown and royal dignity, imprisoned King Richard,
caused him to resign his title, and finally to be murdered.
Diverse other matters they laid to his charge, as levying
of taxes and tallages, contrary to his promise, infringing
of laws & customs of the realm, and suffering the Earl of
March to remain in prison, without travailing[35] to have
him delivered. All which things they, as procurors & protectors of the commonwealth, took upon them to prove
against him, as they protested unto the whole world.

King Henry, after he had read their articles, with the
defiance which they annexed to the same, answered the
esquires, that he was ready with dint[36] of sword and fierce
battle to prove their quarrel false, and nothing else than a
forged matter, not doubting, but that God would aid and
assist him in his righteous cause, against the disloyal and
false forsworn traitors. The next day in the morning early,
being the even of Mary Magdalene,[37] they set their battles in order on both sides, and now whilst the warriors
looked when the token of battle should be given, the Abbot of Shrewsbury, and one of the clerks of the privy seal,
were sent from the King unto the Percies, to offer them
pardon, if they would come to any reasonable agreement.
By their persuasions, the Lord Henry Percy began to give
ear unto the King's offers, & so sent with them his uncle,
the Earl of Worcester, to declare unto the King the causes
of those troubles, and to require some effectual reformation in the same.

The Percies sent their articles to the King.

King Henry charged with perjuries.

Procurers & protectors of the commonwealth.

The King's answer to the messengers that brought the articles.

The King offereth to pardon his adversaries.

---

[35] **travailing:** laboring. [36] **dint:** blow. [37] **even ... Magdalene:** the eve
before the Feast Day of St. Mary Magdalene, 22 July.

It was reported for a truth, that now when the King had condescended unto all that was reasonable at his hands to be required, and seemed to humble himself more than was meet for his estate, the Earl of Worcester (upon his return to his nephew) made relation clean contrary to that the King had said, in such sort that he set his nephew's heart more in displeasure towards the King, than ever it was before, driving him by that means to fight whether he would or not. Then suddenly blew the trumpets, the King's crying "S[aint] George! Upon them!" The adversaries cried "Esperance! Percy!" and so the two armies furiously joined. The archers on both sides shot for the best game, laying on such load with arrows, that many died, and were driven down that never rose again.

The Earl of Worcester's double dealings in wrong reporting the King's words.

The Scots (as some write) which had the foreward[38] on the Percies' side, intending to be revenged of their old displeasures done to them by the English nation, set so fiercely on the King's foreward, led by the Earl of Stafford, that they made the same draw back, and had almost broken their adversaries' array. The Welshmen also, which before had lain lurking in the woods, mountains, and marshes, hearing of this battle toward, came to the aid of the Percies, and refreshed the wearied people with new succours. The King, perceiving that his men were thus put to distress, what with the violent impression of the Scots, and the tempestuous storms of arrows, that his adversaries discharged freely against him and his people, it was no need to will him to stir: for suddenly with his fresh battle, he approached and relieved his men; so that the battle began more fierce than before. Here the Lord Henry Percy, and the Earl Douglas, a right stout and hardy captain, not regarding the shot of the King's battle, nor the close order of the ranks, pressing forward together bent their whole forces towards the King's person, coming upon him with spears and swords so fiercely, that the Earl of March the Scot, perceiving their purpose, withdrew the King from that side of the field (as some write) for his great benefit and safeguard (as it appeared)

Hall.
The Scots.

The Welshmen come to aid the Percies.

The Earl of March.
Tho. Wals.

---

[38] **foreward:** vanguard.

for they gave such a violent onset upon them that stood about the King's standard, that slaying his standard-bearer, Sir Walter Blunt, and overthrowing the standard, they made slaughter of all those that stood about it, as the Earl of Stafford, that day made by the King Constable of the realm, and diverse other.

The Prince that day helped his father like a lusty young gentleman: for although he was hurt in the face with an arrow, so that diverse noblemen that were about him, would have conveyed him forth of the field, yet he would not suffer them so to do, lest his departure from amongst his men might happily have stricken some fear into their hearts: and so without regard of his hurt, he continued with his men; & never ceased, either to fight where the battle was most hot, or to encourage his men where it seemed most need. This battle lasted three long hours, with indifferent fortune on both parts, till at length, the King crying "Saint George! Victory!" brake the array of his enemies, and adventured so far, that (as some write) the Earl Douglas strake him down, & at that instant slew Sir Walter Blunt, and three other, appareled in the King's suit and clothing, saying: "I marvel to see so many kings thus suddenly arise one in the neck of another." The King indeed was raised, & did that day many a noble feat of arms, for as it is written, he slew that day with his own hands six and thirty persons of his enemies. The other on his part,[39] encouraged by his doings, fought valiantly, and slew the Lord Percy, called Sir Henry Hotspur. To conclude, the King's enemies were vanquished, and put to flight, in which flight, the Earl of Douglas, for haste, falling from the crag of an high mountain, brake one of his cullions,[40] and was taken, and for his valiantness, of the King frankly and freely delivered.

There was also taken the Earl of Worcester, the procuror and setter forth of all this mischief, Sir Richard Vernon, and the Baron of Kinderton, with diverse other. There were slain upon the King's part, beside the Earl of Stafford, to the number of ten knights, Sir Hugh Shirley,

Hall.
The valiance of the young Prince.

A sore battle & well maintained.

The valiant doings of the Earl Douglas.

The high manhood of the King.

The Lord Percy slain.

The Earl Douglas taken prisoner.

The Earl of Worcester taken.

Knights slain on the King's part.

---

[39] **other . . . part:** others in Henry's army, not (as it has been interpreted) a reference to Prince Henry.   [40] **cullions:** testicles.

Sir John Clifton, Sir John Cokayne, Sir Nicholas Gawsey, Sir Walter Blunt, Sir John Calverley, Sir John Massey of Podington, Sir Hugh Mortimer, and Sir Robert Gawsey, all the which received the same morning the order of knighthood: Sir Thomas Wensley was wounded to death, and so passed out of this life shortly after. There died in all upon the King's side sixteen hundred, and four thousand were grievously wounded. On the contrary side were slain, besides the Lord Percy, the most part of the knights and esquires of the county of Chester, to the number of two hundred, besides yeomen and footmen; in all there died of those that fought on the Percies' side, about five thousand. This battle was fought on Mary Magdalene even, being Saturday. Upon the Monday following, the Earl of Worcester, the Baron of Kinderton, and Sir Richard Vernon, Knights, were condemned and beheaded. The Earl's head was sent to London, there to be set on the bridge.

> The slaughter of Cheshire men at this battle.

> The Earl of Worcester and others beheaded.

→ **SAMUEL DANIEL**

From The First Four Books of the Civil Wars Between the Two Houses of Lancaster and York *1595*

Book III

Like many early modern writers, Samuel Daniel did not confine himself to one genre or form. He produced lyrics, narrative poetry, a sonnet sequence (*Delia* [1592]), verse epistles and treatises, tragedies, masques, pastorals, and a critical essay, *The Defence of Rhyme* (1607). Also like other writers, he wrote about the Lancaster-York conflict; but, unlike Hall's and Holinshed's histories, his is in verse. The first four books of *The Civil Wars* were published in 1595. A fifth book was added when it was republished in 1599, and a sixth, which brought the history up to Edward IV's coronation (1461), appeared in a heavily revised 1601 edition. Yet another edition appeared in 1609. Although his dedication to the 1601 edition indicates his plan to extend *The Civil Wars* "unto the glorious Union of Henry VII," Daniel never did so. When he did return to writing history, he wrote in prose (*The Collection of the History of England* [1612–18]).

Samuel Daniel, *The First Four Books of The Civil Wars Between the Two Houses of Lancaster and York* (London, 1595) Q7v–R4v.

The opening lines of the first book of *The Civil Wars* — "I sing the civil Wars, tumultuous Broils, / And bloody factions of a mighty Land" — evoke the conventions of epic, framing England's recent history in terms of classical models such as Virgil's *Aeneid* or Homer's *Iliad*. Borrowing or raiding conventions and exempla drawn from classical texts was, of course, a common practice in the period; among other things, it served to legitimate a writer's own authority. In *The Civil Wars*, Daniel's reliance on several other conventions aligns his text with Cicero's *De oratore*, which conceived history as a branch of oratory. In shaping what his 1609 dedication calls "that truth which is delivered in the Histories," Daniel himself takes on an "epic voice" that allows him to meditate on cause and effect, agent and act, motive and behavior; he also dramatizes the voices of Hotspur and Henry IV. Attributing the "poetical license of framing speeches to the persons of men according to their occasions" to ancient and modern authors, Daniel defends his strategy in familiar humanist terms. He has "drawn" his images "according to the portraiture of Nature," in which "Ambition, Faction, and Affections speak ever one Language, wear like colors (though in several fashions), feed, and are fed, with the same nutriments; and only vary but in time" (6–7). Such a practice blurs the boundaries between "history" and "poetry" — a term that, for writers of the period, encompassed what we today would call literature.

At least since Aristotle, history and poetry had been defined in opposition to each other, though many writers argued for traffic between them. In his famous *Defence of Poesy* (1583), Sir Philip Sidney, for instance, condemns the "historian in his bare *was*," claiming that "a feigned [invented] example hath as much force *to teach* as a true example" (20). He recalls how Herodotus, as well as later writers, "stole or usurped of poetry their passionate describing of passions, the many particularities of battles (which no man could affirm) . . . [and] long orations put in the mouths of great kings and captains (which it is certain they never pronounced)" (6). But Sidney, it must be remembered, was engaged in defending *poetry*, not history, and by the time Daniel was writing, the classical practice of composing speeches had already been discontinued by writers such as John Stow and Raphael Holinshed, whose historical projects were less invested in individuals than in examining a whole culture and its institutions. Viewed through this lens, Daniel seems to mount his own apology for relying on an outdated, perhaps inappropriate, practice. Indeed, elsewhere in the dedication, the apologetic note serves to justify his own "opinion" — a term commonly used to denote conflicting testimony that is neither debated nor resolved. Speaking of the dangers of violating "public Testimony" or introducing imaginative fictions, Daniel maintains that *"in these public actions, there are ever popular bruits and opinions, which run according to the time & the bias of men's affections. . . . It is the part of an Historian to recite them, not to rule them"* (6, emphasis added).

What is especially striking about *The Civil Wars* is Daniel's skill in reordering material drawn from Hall's *Union* to devise a dramatic account of Shrewsbury from various perspectives, including his own omniscient point of view, reflected in a series of curious oxymoronic phrases: "horrible good," "mischief necessary," "unjust-just scourge of our iniquity" (stanza 108). As though echoing

Sidney's condemnation of stage battles as "two armies . . . represented with four swords and bucklers," Ben Jonson complained that, for a history of civil war, Daniel's account was remarkably devoid of battles. Yet, like other historians of the period, Daniel was interested not in recording moment-by-moment military strategy but in celebrating valorous individuals' "great actions . . . openly presented on the Stage of the World." By stressing the Percies' kinship alliance, his epic evokes feudal aristocratic ideals that, in the last decade of Elizabeth's reign, were being reconfigured, giving way to the pressures of a rising middle class, a "new" monied aristocracy (see Chapter 5, "Honor and Arms").

Turning history toward heroic legend, Daniel's account is deeply nostalgic, especially in its focus on individual figures — Hotspur and Prince Henry, Henry IV, Douglas, the "Heroical Courageous" Sir Walter Blunt, the king's standard-bearer — and on the Hotspur-Prince Henry combat. In making the battle's outcome rest on an encounter between two *young* men, Daniel takes full advantage of poetic license, for at the time of the battle, the historical Hotspur was thirty-seven, two years older than Henry IV, and Prince Henry, recently named Lieutenant of Wales, was sixteen. Indeed, the figure of "Young *Henry*" arrives rather late in Daniel's "plot," which focuses primarily on Hotspur. And although Prince Henry arises as a "new-appearing glorious star / Wonder of Arms, the terror of the field" (stanza 110), he remains a cardboard cut-out — the lesser of two antagonists in King Henry's "losing victory" where "famous worth lies dead." Certainly, as he recounts Shrewsbury's aftermath, Daniel calls the King sharply to account and, in praising Hotspur's "great spirit," commends his honor and valor and laments that "this courage bold, / Had in some good cause been rightly shown" (stanza 114).

From *The First Four Books of The Civil Wars Between the Two Houses of Lancaster and York*

[Having seized the throne from Richard II, Henry IV faces political dissent and, in a series of challenges to his power, he fails to conquer either the Scots or the Welsh.]

86

And yet new *Hydras*[1] lo, new heads appear
T'afflict that peace reputed then so sure,
And gave him much to do, and much to fear,
And long and dangerous tumults did procure,

---

[1] *Hydras:* the Hydra was a mythical monster with many heads that grew again as soon as they were cut off.

And those even of his chiefest followers were
Of whom he might presume him most secure,
Who whether not so grac'd or so prefer'd
As they expected, these new factions stirr'd.

87

The *Percies* were the men, men of great might,
Strong in alliance, and in courage strong
That thus conspire, under pretense to right
The crooked courses they had suffered long:
Whether their conscience urg'd them or despight,[2]
Or that they saw the part they took[3] was wrong,
Or that ambition hereto did them call,
Or others envied grace, or rather all.

88

What cause soever were, strong was their plot,
Their parties great, means good, th'occasion fit:
Their practice close, their faith suspected not,
Their states far off and they of wary wit
Who with large promises draw in the Scot
To aid their cause, he likes, and yields to it,
Not for the love of them or for their good,
But glad hereby of means to shed our blood.

89

Then join they with the *Welsh*, who, fitly train'd
And all in arms under a mighty head
Great *Glendower*, who long warr'd, and much attain'd,
Sharp conflicts made, and many vanquished:
With whom was *Edmund Earl* of *March* retain'd
Being first his prisoner, now confedered,
A man the King much fear'd, and well he might
Lest he should look whether his Crown stood right.

---

[2] **despight:** contempt.   [3] **the part they took:** their role in supporting Bolingbroke against Richard II, the legitimate king.

90

For *Richard*, for the quiet of the state,
Before he took those *Irish* wars in hand
About succession doth deliberate,
And finding how the certain right did stand,
With full consent this man[4] did ordinate
The heir apparent in the Crown and land:
Then judge if this the King might nearly touch,
Although his might were small, his right being much.

91

With these the *Percies* them confederate
And as three heads they league in one intent,
And instituting a Triumvirate
Do part the land in triple government:
Dividing thus among themselves the state,
The *Percies* should rule all the *North* from *Trent*
And *Glendower Wales*, the *Earl* of *March* should be
Lord of the *South* from *Trent;* and thus they [a]gree.

92

Then those two helps which still such actors find —
Pretense of common good, the king's disgrace —
Doth fit their course, and draw the vulgar mind
To further them and aid them in this case:
The King they accus'd for cruel, and unkind
That did the state, and Crown, and all deface;
A perjured man that held all faith in scorn,
Whose trusted oaths had others made forsworn.

93

Besides the odious detestable act
Of that late murdered king they aggravate,

---

[4] **this man:** that is, Edmund, Earl of March. Like Hall and Holinshed (and Shakespeare), Daniel conflates the fifth Earl of March, claimant to the throne, with his uncle, Sir Edmund Mortimer, who was captured by Glendower and married his daughter.

Making it his[5] that so had will'd the fact
That he the doers did remunerate:
And then such taxes daily doth exact
That were against the orders of the state,
And with all these or worse they him assail'd
Who late of others with the like prevail'd.

94

Thus doth contentious proud mortality[6]
Afflict each other and itself torment:
And thus, O, thou mind-tort[u]ring misery
Restless Ambition, born in discontent,
Turn'st and retossest with iniquity
The unconstant courses frailty did invent:
And foul'st fair order and defil'st the earth
Fost[e]ring up War, father of blood and dearth.

95

Great seem'd the cause, and greatly to, did add
The people's love thereto, these crimes rehears'd,
That many gathered to the troops they had
And many more do flock from coasts dispers'd:[7]
But when the King had heard these news so bad,
Th'unlooked-for dangerous toil more nearly pers'd;[8]
For bent t[o]wards *Wales* t'appease those tumults there,
H[e] is forc'd [to] divert his course, and them forbear.

96

Not to give time unto th'increasing rage
And gathering fury, forth he hastes with speed,
Lest more delay or giving longer age
To th'evil grown, it might the cure exceed:[9]

---

[5] **his:** that is, Bolingbroke's.   [6] **mortality:** humankind.   [7] **from coasts dispers'd:** from far and near.   [8] **pers'd:** pierced.   [9] **Lest . . . exceed:** lest delays, permitting rebellion to heighten, might allow the disease to grow beyond any means to cure it.

All his best men at arms, and leaders sage
All he prepar'd he could, and all did need;
For to a mighty work thou goest, O King,
To such a field that power to power shall bring.

97

There shall young *Hotspur* with a fury led
Meet with thy forward[10] son as fierce as he:
There warlike *Worcester*, long experienced
In foreign arms, shall come t'encounter thee:
There *Douglas* to thy *Stafford* shall make head:
There *Vernon* for thy valiant *Blunt* shall be:
There shalt thou find a doubtful bloody day,
Though sickness keep *Northumberland* away.

98

Who yet reserv'd, though after quit[11] for this,
Another tempest on thy head to raise,
As if still-wrong revenging *Nemesis*
Did mean t'afflict all thy continual days:
And yet this field he happily[12] might miss
For thy great good, and therefore well he stays:
What might his force have done being join'd thereto
When that already gave so much to do?[13]

99

The swift approach and unexpected speed
The King had made upon this new-raised force
In th' unconfirmed troops much fear did breed,
Untimely hindring their intended course;
The joining with the *Welsh* they had decreed
Was hereby stopp'd, which made their part the worse,
Northumberland, with forces from the *North*
Expected to be there, was not set forth.

---

[10] **forward**: ardent, eager. [11] **after quit**: subsequently requited. [12] **happily**: perchance.
[13] **When ... do**: when the rebel forces, even without Northumberland, so troubled
Henry IV.

100

And yet undaunted *Hotspur* seeing the King
So near approach'd, leaving the work in hand,
With forward speed his forces marshaling,
Sets forth his farther coming to withstand:
And with a cheerful voice encouraging
By his great spirit his well-emboldened band,
Brings a strong host of firm-resolved might
And plac'd his troops before the King in sight.

101

"This day" (saith he), "O faithful valiant friends,
Whatever it doth give, shall glory give:
This day with honor frees our state, or ends
Our misery with fame, that still shall live.
And do but think how well this day he spends
That spends his blood his country to relieve:
Our holy cause, our freedom, and our right,
Sufficient are to move good minds to fight.

102

Besides th' assured hope of victory
That we may even promise on our side
Against this weak-constrained[14] company,
Whom force and fear, not will, and love, doth guide
Against a prince whose foul impiety
The heavens do hate, the earth cannot abide,
Our number being no less, our courage more,
What need we doubt if we but work therefore?"

103

This said, and thus resolv'd, even bent[15] to charge
Upon the King, who well their order view'd
And careful noted all the form at large

---

[14] **constrained:** forced to fight on Henry's side, not willingly. [15] **even bent:** ready.

Of their proceeding, and their multitude:
And deeming better if he could discharge
The day with safety, and some peace conclude,
Great proffers sends of pardon, and of grace
If they would yield, and quietness embrace.

104

But this refus'd, the King, with wrath incens'd,
Rage against fury doth with speed prepare:
And "O," saith he, "though I could have dispens'd
With this day's blood, which I have sought to spare
That greater glory might have recompens'd
The forward worth of these that so much dare,
That we might honor had by th'overthrown
That th'wounds we make, might not have been our own.

105

"Yet since that other men's iniquity
Calls on the sword of wrath against my will,
And that themselves exact this cruelty,
And I constrained am this blood to spill:
Then on, my masters, on courageously,
True-hearted subjects against traitors ill,
And spare not them who seek to spoil us all,
Whose foul confused end soon see you shall."

106

Straight moves with equal motion equal rage
The like incensed armies unto blood,
One to defend, another side to wage
Foul civil war. Both vows their quarrel good:
Ah, too much heat to blood doth now enrage
Both who the deed provokes and who withstood,
That valor here is vice, here manhood sin,
The forward'st hands doth, O, least honor win.[16]

---

[16] **That . . . win:** in civil war, valor and bravery prove dishonorable.

107

But now begin these fury-moving sounds
The notes of wrath that music brought from hell,
The rattling drums which trumpets' voice confounds,
The cries, th'encouragements, the shouting shrill;
That all about the beaten air rebounds,
Thundring confused, murmurs horrible,
To rob all sense except the sense to fight,
Well hands may work, the mind hath lost his sight.

108

O War! begot in pride and luxury,
The child of wrath and of dissension,
Horrible good; mischief necessary,
The foul reformer of confusion,
Unjust-just scourge of our iniquity,
Cruel recurer of corruption:
O, that these sin-sick states in need should stand
To be let blood with such a boisterous hand!

109

And O, how well thou hadst been spar'd this day
Had not wrong-counsel'd *Percy* been perverse,
Whose young undanger'd hand now rash makes way
Upon the sharpest fronts of the most fierce:
Where now an equal fury thrusts to stay
And rebeat-back that force and his disperse,
Then these assail, then those chase back again,
Till stayed with new-made hills of bodies slain.

110

There lo that new-appearing glorious star
Wonder of Arms, the terror of the field
Young *Henry,* laboring where the stoutest are
And even the stoutest forces back to yield,
There is that hand, boldened to blood and war,

That must the sword in woundrous[17] actions wield:
But better hadst thou learn'd with others' blood
A less expense to us, to thee more good.

III

Hadst thou not there lent present speedy aid
To thy endanger'd father nearly tired,
Whom fierce encountring *Douglas* overlaid,
That day had there his troublous life expired:
Heroical Courageous *Blunt* arrayed
In habit like as was the King attir'd
And deem'd for him, excus'd that fate with his,
For he had what his Lord did hardly miss.

112

For thought a king he would not now disgrace
The person then suppos'd, but princelike shows
Glorious effects of worth that fit his place,
And fighting dies, and dying overthrows:
Another of that forward name and race[18]
In that hot work his valiant life bestows,
Who bare the standard of the King that day,
Whose colors overthrown did much dismay.

113

And dear it cost, and O, much blood is shed
To purchase thee this losing victory
O travail'd[19] King: yet hast thou conquered
A doubtful day, a mighty enemy:
But O, what wounds, what famous worth lies dead!
That makes the winner look with sorrowing eye,
Magnanimous *Stafford* lost that much had wrought,
And valiant *Shorly*[20] who great glory got.

---

[17] **woundrous:** wondrous, with pun on wound. [18] **that . . . race:** another Blunt who also dies in battle. [19] **travail'd:** hard-pressed. [20] *Shorly:* Sir Hugh Shirley.

114

Such wrack of others' blood thou didst behold
O furious *Hotspur*, ere thou lost thine own!
Which now, once lost, that heat in thine wax'd cold,
And soon became thy Army overthrown;
And O, that this great spirit, this courage bold,
Had in some good cause been rightly shown!
So had not we thus violently then
Have term'd that rage, which valor should have been.

115

But now the King retires him to his peace,
A peace much like a feeble sickman's sleep,
(Wherein his waking pains do never cease
Though seeming rest his closed eyes doth keep)
For O, no peace could ever so release
His intricate turmoils, and sorrows deep,
But that his cares kept waking all his life
Continue on till death conclude the strife.

CHAPTER 2

Civic Order and Rebellion

><

From the outset, *Henry IV, Part 1* is concerned with threats to the stability of the kingdom. First and foremost is the opposition of the Northern lords — the Percies, the Earl of Northumberland and his son Hotspur, the Earl of Westmoreland, and Owen Glendower — to what they perceive as the king's treacherous double-dealing, especially his denial of what they consider to be their feudal rights, which the play configures in terms of familial as well as personal honor (see Chapter 5, "Honor and Arms"). That strand of the play's action culminates in Shrewsbury's battle, but it is juxtaposed with Hal's opposition to paternal authority, which occurs in London's tavern and theatrical culture, where a mock-Puritan Falstaff reigns as a Carnival Lord of Misrule. In both court and tavern, rebellious and riotous behavior threaten to turn the political and social order, in Hotspur's phrase, "topsy-turvy down." Throughout, the play raises or alludes to questions concerning the relations between kings and their subjects: the right use of power, the demands of loyalty and obedience, and the rights of subjects to rebel against, even to kill, a king. Although the play certainly works to put down rebellion and to affirm centralized monarchy, it also provides a range of opinion in questions of authority, obedience, and rebellion that reflect Tudor political and religious debates and controversies (see Bushnell, Strier, Pocock).

Basic to late medieval notions of political authority was the concept of natural law, which was thought to emanate from the reason or will of God and to exist independent of a ruler's individual will. The concept of natural law, however, is quite distinct from any notion of the divine right of kings (see Kantorowicz, Skinner). Grounded in the ordered creation of the universe and of society, natural law was unchangeable and eternally binding; from it all other law was derived. But existing side by side with this view was the idea, derived from Aristotelian rationalism, of a *natural* social and political order, one in which the part found its point and purpose in relation to the whole and where government originated in a pact between the ruler and the people for the common good. By the early sixteenth century, the concept of a monarch ruling as the vice-regent of God, independent of popular will or consent and unfettered by ecclesiastical checks on power, was growing in favor. Henry VIII's Reformation, for instance, had given divine sanction to princely authority. By midcentury, an absolutist view of civil authority that supported the construction of a state based on Christian virtues and values would prevail. Nonetheless, English monarchs found it convenient to use Parliament, which served as a constant reminder that the ruler was not the sole symbol of the commonwealth, to further their aims. After all, the ancestors of the contemporary Parliament — the barons who, in 1215, had forced King John to sign the Magna Carta — had asserted their authority over a king.

Criticism of and resistance to these absolutist tendencies appear throughout sixteenth-century writings on politics and statecraft. One strand of thought took form as a debate over naming: Was there a difference between a tyrant and a king? (See Bushnell 42–47.) Another, exemplified by the writing of Thomas Starkey, John Knox, George Buchanan, and John Ponet, questioned the basis for the controlling tendencies of monarchical power as well as specific abuses of power. In seeking means to advocate resistance to authoritarian government, some writers looked back to an essentially medieval concept, one based on the feudal contract in which the bargain between lord and tenant knights was extended to include the relations between prince and commonwealth. This kind of social structure was one in which the aristocracy, living in castles or great manor houses, gathered about them communities of dependent gentry and servants in feudal courts unified by their allegiance to a great family who dispensed the benefits of good lordship in return for fidelity and obedience. Although bonds of service were one means of ensuring absolute dependence and loyalty, ties of blood coupled to family name were equally, if not more, significant in cementing such feudal alliances, particularly in Northern society, where ties of kinship, blood, and lineage remained more tenacious and binding than loyalty to London's royal court (James 270–72). As late as the 1560s, the barony of Alnwick, one of several major Percy strongholds, held a Knights' Court; and the commonplace that the North "knew no king but a Percy" and that Percy tenants loved their earl "better than they do the Queen" was as evident during Elizabeth's reign as at the time of the 1403 rebellion that culminated at Shrewsbury (qtd. in James 292).

The feudal ties that gathered the Northumberlands together in 1403 can be understood in terms of similar conditions in 1569, when another Northern rising threatened the state. Briefly, the circumstances were these: in 1568, Mary, Queen of Scots, was dethroned by her subjects and fled to England, where she demanded her cousin Elizabeth's protection and help in recovering her crown. As Henry VII's great-granddaughter, Mary's claim to the English throne was arguably better than that of Elizabeth, and her presence in England stirred the Northern Catholic lords to support her cause under the pretense of defending Elizabeth's person and government from foreign invasion. Although mismanagement, divided aims, mutual jealousies, and failing nerve caused the rising to disintegrate, its roots, like those of the 1403 rebellion against Henry IV, lay in the tensions between competing loyalties: those demanded by the feudal ideas of the values of lineage and family bonds and wider notions of allegiance to a centralized nation-state or to a single monarch.

Although religious dissidence figured more prominently in the 1569 rebellion than in that represented in *Henry IV, Part 1*, a number of likenesses draw the two together, leading scholars to conjecture that the Elizabethan rebellion served as a pattern for Shakespeare's play. The 1569 rebellion, for instance, was instigated by descendants of the Northumberland Percies and the Earl of Westmoreland — Thomas Percy, Earl of Northumberland, Charles Neville, Earl of Westmoreland, and Christopher Neville, Westmoreland's uncle; moreover, the Catholic Bishop of Ross played a part more or less equivalent to that of the Archbishop of York in 1403. In Shakespeare's play, the Percies' resentment over Henry IV's refusal to ransom Mortimer, the pretender to the throne, and over his demand that they surrender Scots prisoners may well be patterned after the demands of the Northern lords in 1569 that Mary, the Scots pretender to the throne and Northumberland's prisoner, be left in the keeping of an Elizabethan Percy (Campbell 231–34).

Whether or not one finds such topical parallels compelling, the 1569 Northern rebellion certainly remained fresh in cultural memory. Except for the Earl of Essex's attempted honor revolt in 1601 (see James, Smith), it was the only instance of rebellion during Elizabeth's reign, and it proved threatening enough to prompt the Crown to issue a proclamation of treason against the Earls of Northumberland and Westmoreland and, in the rebellion's aftermath, an oath for those rebels seeking pardon that explicitly required them to "utterly renounce and forsake all foreign jurisdictions, powers, superiorities, and authorities [and] from henceforth bear faith and true allegiance to the Queen's majesty, her heirs and lawful successors" (12 Elizabeth 1, 18 February 1570, reprinted in Hughes and Larkin). As with Henry IV's judgment on the Percies' cause, "Thus ever did rebellion find rebuke" (5.5.1), so too with Elizabeth. And in 1571, the Crown issued *An Homily Against Disobedience and Willful Rebellion*, which was required to be read out in all churches.

One of the selections in this chapter, the *Homily*, marks the government's deeply anxious, even hysterical response to the 1569 Northern rebellion. The other, John Ponet's *Short Treatise of Politic Power* (1556), represents one strand of sixteenth-century political resistance. Here, Ponet questions the grounds for absolutist authority and proposes remedies designed to check its abuses. Together these texts offer a spectrum of positions on centralized state power and subjects' rights as well as on obedience and rebellion.

✦ *From* An Homily Against Disobedience and Willful Rebellion   *1571*

Third Part

The Anglican Church produced two official compilations of sermons. *Certain Sermons, or Homilies, Appointed by the King's Majesty, to Be Declared and Read, by All Parsons, Vicars, or Curates Every Sunday in Their Churches,* first published in 1547, was composed by Bishop Bonner, Archbishop Thomas Cranmer, and Nicholas Harpsfield and had gone through thirty-nine printings by 1640. *The Second Tome of Homilies, of Such Matters as Were Promised and Entitled in the Former Part of Homilies,* to which the *Homily Against Disobedience and Willful Rebellion* was later added, was first published in 1563. Printed twenty-two times by 1640, this volume was written by Archbishop Parker, Bishop Pilkington, Richard Taverner, and others, under the editorship of Bishop John Jewel.

These gatherings of sermons by influential clergy disseminated versions of orthodox Anglican positions to every church in the kingdom, making those views readily accessible. Literate churchgoers might consult the books, which were placed next to the Bible and *The Book of Common Prayer.* Those who could not read would, in all probability, hear many of these sermons read out over the course of a year; although some ministers wrote their own sermons, many used those already supplied in the two volumes of homilies. Moreover, regular church

---

An Homily Against Disobedience and Willful Rebellion, The Second Tome of Homilies, of Such Matters as Were Promised and Entitled in the Former Part of Homilies (London, 1623) 292–97.

attendance was obligatory, and those who refused to attend, such as Catholics or Protestant dissenters, could be fined or even imprisoned. In all likelihood, every English person was familiar with the *Homily Against Disobedience and Willful Rebellion*. This particular version replaces and considerably strengthens a 1547 text, "An Exhortation, concerning Good Order and Obedience to Rulers and Magistrates." It was included among the homilies in 1571, following the 1569 Northern Rebellion and the publication, in 1570, of a papal bull excommunicating Elizabeth and releasing her subjects from their oaths of allegiance and interdicting obedience to her laws (Camden, *Annales* 2: 245–48).

The *Homily* is in five parts, each followed by a prayer; it concludes with a "Thanksgiving for the suppression of the last rebellion." The first part explains the ordered creation of heaven and earth and the universal establishment of obedience: just as Lucifer, the first rebel, lost heaven, Adam lost Paradise. In order to reestablish obedience in the world, God ordained that the wife should be obedient to her husband, the child to the parent, the servant to the master, and that the people should obey governors and rulers who were God's deputies on earth. Biblical passages provide support, as in the first two verses of Romans 13: "Let every soul be subject unto the higher powers, for there is no power but of God, and the powers that be, are ordained of God. Whosoever therefore resisteth the power, resisteth the ordinance of God: and they that resist, shall receive to themselves damnation." The good ruler, says the *Homily*, is a blessing bestowed upon the people, the evil ruler a plague sent for their sins. The people may not choose to obey the good ruler and rebel against the evil, for what subject can judge his king? Even the tyrant, so the *Homily* argues, is better than the rebel. The second part of the *Homily* cites scriptural examples of obedience to civil authorities, the "good and gracious" as well as the "evil and unkind"; the third part depicts rebellion as the most dangerous violation of all God's commandments; the fourth focuses on the destruction of rebels, inviting worshippers to recall rebellions in England "yet fresh in memories" and to consider the great and noble families whose names appear in the chronicles and who "stood clean extinguished and gone" as a result of rebellion; and the fifth part links rebellion to the ambition of some and the ignorance of those easily led into evil.

The third part of the *Homily* represents rebellion as an all-encompassing, perilous fault, "the whole puddle and sink of all sins against GOD and man, against his Prince, his country, his countrymen, his parents, his children, his kinfolk, his friends, and against all men universally" (292). Repeatedly aligning God, prince, and country, it articulates an absolutist position based on the Ten Commandments that, in attempting to safeguard royal supremacy by the threat of divine retribution, suggests the perceived threats that rebellion posed to Elizabeth's own monarchy. While other homilies were repeatedly revised, and so demonstrate a somewhat fluid response to cultural change, the homily on disobedience and rebellion announces a static, authoritarian stance that is enhanced by its hellfire-and-brimstone rhetoric, which floods out to include the Catholic who rebels "for the maintenance of . . . Images and Idols" as well as the Protestant dissenter who (like Sir John Oldcastle) "assemble[s] and meet[s] armed in the field" rather than attending church (see Chapter 6, "The Oldcastle Controversy"). And by further defining rebels as those who, by "riotousness, gluttony, drunkenness, excess of apparel, and unthrifty games, have wasted their own goods unthriftily," the *Homily* even embraces the behaviors of subjects like Falstaff, Hal, and the denizens of Eastcheap's tavern community.

As it concludes, the *Homily* exploits the fear of plague that raged throughout the late sixteenth century, predicting disease and famine of epic proportions as one outcome of rebellion. Although elsewhere it invites listeners and readers to remember the dangers of foreign wars and the past century's civil war, the third part evokes rebellion's threats to social and familial structures, turning them upside down: "the brother to seek, and often to work the death of his brother, . . . the father to seek or procure the death of his sons . . . and by their faults to disinherit their innocent children." The fear that such conditions would recur, as well as the persistent memory of a horrible past, make this document an especially pertinent cultural context for all of Shakespeare's histories, which served as a theatrical means of reliving that past in contemporary memory.

From *An Homily Against Disobedience and Willful Rebellion*

As I have in the first part of this treatise showed unto you the doctrine of the holy Scriptures, as concerning the obedience of true subjects to their princes, even as well to such as be evil as unto the good, and in the second part of the same treaty confirmed the same doctrine by notable examples, likewise taken out of the holy Scriptures, so remaineth it now that I partly do declare unto you in this third part, what an abominable sin against GOD and man rebellion is, and how dreadfully the wrath of GOD is kindled and inflamed against all rebels, and what horrible plagues, punishments, and deaths, and finally eternal damnation, doth hang over their heads. As to us on the contrary part, good and obedient subjects are in GOD's favor, and be partakers of peace, quietness, and security, with other GOD's manifold blessings in this world, and by his mercies through our Savior Christ, of life everlasting, also in the world to come. How horrible a sin against GOD and man rebellion is, cannot possibly be expressed according unto the greatness thereof. For he that nameth rebellion, nameth not a singular or one only sin, as is theft, robbery, murder, and such like. But he nameth the whole puddle and sink of all sins against GOD and man, against his Prince, his country, his countrymen, his parents, his children, his kinfolk, his friends, and against all men universally, all sins I say against GOD and all men heaped together nameth he, that nameth rebellion. For concerning the offense of GOD's Majesty, who seeth not that rebellion riseth first by contempt of GOD and of his holy ordinances and laws, wherein he so straightly commandeth obedience, forbiddeth disobedience and rebellion: And besides the dishonor done by rebels unto GOD's holy Name, by their breaking of their oath made to their Prince, with the attestation of GOD's name, and calling of his Majesty to witness. Who heareth not the horrible oaths and blasphemies of GOD's holy name, that are used daily among rebels, that is either amongst them, or heareth the truth of their behavior: who knoweth not that rebels do not only themselves leave all works necessary to be done upon workdays, undone, whiles they accomplish their abominable work of rebellion, and to compel others that would gladly be well occupied, to do the same: but also how rebels do not only leave the Sabbath day of the Lord unsanctified, the Temple and Church of the Lord unresorted unto, but also do by their works of wickedness most horribly profane and pollute the Sabbath day, serving Satan, and by doing of his work, making it the devil's day, instead of the Lord's day? Besides that, they compel good men that would gladly serve the Lord assembling in his Temple and Church upon his day, as becometh the Lord's servants, to assemble and meet armed in the field, to resist the furies of such rebels. Yea, & many rebels, lest they should leave any part of GOD's commandments in the first table of his Law unbroken, or any sin against GOD undone, do make rebellion for the maintenance of their Images and Idols, and of their idolatry committed, or to be committed by them: and in despite of GOD, cut and tear in sunder his holy word, and tread it under their feet, as of late ye know was done.

As concerning the second table of GOD's law, and all sins that may be committed against man, who seeth not that they be contained in rebellion: For first the rebels do not only dishonor their Prince, the parent of their country, but also do dishonor and shame their natural parents, if they have any, do shame their kindred and friends, do disinherit & undo forever their children and heirs. Thefts, robberies, and murders, which of all sins are most loathed of most men, are in no men so much nor so perniciously and mischievously, as in rebels. For the most arrant thieves, cruellest murderers that ever were, so long as they refrain from rebellion, as they are not many in numbers, so spreadeth their wickedness and damnation unto a few, they spoil but a few, they shed the blood but of a few in comparison. But rebels are the cause of infinite robberies, and murders of great multitudes, and of those also whom they should defend from the spoil and violence of other: and as rebels are many in number, so doth their wickedness and damnation spread itself unto many. And if whoredom and adultery amongst such persons as are agreeable to such wickedness, are (as they indeed be most damnable), what are the forcible oppressions of matrons and men's wives, and the violating and deflowering of virgins and maids, which are most rife with rebels? How horrible and damnable, think you, are they? Now besides that: rebels by breach of their faith given, and the oath made to their Prince, be guilty of most damnable perjury: it is wondrous to see what false colors and feigned causes, by slanderous lies made upon their Prince, and the counselors, rebels will devise to cloak their rebellion withall, which is the worst and most damnable of all false witness-bearing that may be possible. For what should I speak of coveting or desiring of other men's wives, houses, lands, goods and servants in rebels, who by their wishes would leave unto no man anything of his own?

Thus you see that all good laws are by rebels violated and broken, and that all sins possible to be committed against GOD or man, be contained in rebellion: which sins if a man list to name by the accustomed names of the seven capital or deadly sins, as pride, envy, wrath, covetousness, sloth, gluttony, and lechery, he shall find them all in rebellion, and amongst rebels. For first, as ambition and desire to be aloft, which is the property of pride, stirreth up many men's minds to rebellion, so cometh it of a Luciferian pride and presumption, that a few rebellious subjects should set themselves up against the Majesty of their Prince, against the wisdom of the counselors, against the power and force of all Nobility, and the faithful subjects and people of the whole Realm. As for envy, wrath, murder, and desire of blood, and covetousness of other men's goods, lands, and livings, they are the inseparable accidents of all rebels, and peculiar properties that do usually stir up wicked men unto rebellion.

Now such as by riotousness, gluttony, drunkenness, excess of apparel, and unthrifty games, have wasted their own goods unthriftily, the same are most apt unto, and most desirous of rebellion, whereby they trust to come by other men's goods unlawfully and violently. And where other gluttons and drunkards take too much of such meats and drinks as are served to tables, rebels waste and consume in most space, all corn in barns, fields, or elsewhere, whole garners,[1] whole storehouses, whole cellars, devour whole flocks of sheep, whole droves of Oxen and Kine.[2] And as rebels that are married, leaving their own wives at home, do most ungraciously: so much more do unmarried men, worse than any stallions or horses (being now by rebellion set at liberty from correction of Laws which bridled them before) abuse by force other men's wives, and daughters, and ravish virgins and maidens, most shamefully, abominably, and damnably.

Thus all sins, by all names that sins may be nameth, and by all means that sins may be committed and wrought, do all wholly upon heaps follow rebellion, and are to be found altogether amongst rebels. Now whereas pesti-

---

[1] **garners:** granaries.   [2] **Kine:** cattle.

lence, famine, and war, are by the holy Scriptures declared to be the greatest worldly plagues and miseries that likely can be, it is evident, that all the miseries that all these plagues have in them, do wholly altogether follow rebellion, wherein, as all their miseries be, so is there much more mischief than in them all.

For it is known that in the resorting of great companies of men together, which in rebellion happeneth both upon the part of true subjects, and of the rebels, by their close lying together, and corruption of the air and place where they do lie, with ordure[3] and much filth, in the hot weather, and by unwholesome lodging, and lying often upon the ground, specially in cold and wet weather in winter, by their unwholesome diet, and feeding at all times, and often by famine and lack of meat and drink in due time, and again by taking too much at other times: It is well known, I say, that as well plagues and pestilences, as all other kinds of sicknesses and maladies by their means grow up and spring amongst men, whereby more men are consumed at the length, than are by dint of sword suddenly slain in the field. So that not only pestilences, but also all other sicknesses, diseases, and maladies, do follow rebellion, which are much more horrible than plagues, pestilences, and diseases sent directly from GOD, as hereafter shall appear more plainly.

And as for hunger and famine, they are the peculiar companions of rebellion: for while rebels do in short time spoil and consume all coin and necessary provisions, which men with their labors had gotten and appointed upon, for their finding[4] the whole year after, and also do let all other men, husbandmen and others, from their husbandry, and other necessary works, whereby provision should be made for times to come, who seeth not that extreme famine and hunger must needs shortly ensue and follow rebellion? Now whereas the wise King & godly Prophet David judged war to be worse than either famine or pestilence, for that these two are often suffered by GOD, for man's amendment, and be not sins of themselves: but wars have always the sins and mischiefs of men upon the one side or other joined with them, and therefore is war the greatest of these worldly mischiefs: but of all wars, civil war is the worst; and far more abominable yet is rebellion than any civil war, being unworthy the name of any war, so far it exceedeth all wars in all naughtiness, in all mischief, and in all abomination. And therefore our Savior Christ denounceth desolation and destruction to that Realm, that by sedition and rebellion is divided in itself.

Now as I have showed before, that pestilence and famine, so is it yet more evident that all the calamities, miseries, and mischiefs of war, be more griev-

---

[3] ordure: excrement.   [4] finding: support.

ous and do most follow rebellion, than any other war, as being far worse than all other wars. For not only those ordinary and usual mischiefs and miseries of other wars, do follow rebellion, as coin, and other things, necessary to man's use to be spoiled, Houses, Villages, Towns, Cities, to be taken, sacked, burned, and destroyed, not only many very wealthy men, but whole countries to be impoverished, and bitterly beggared, many thousands of men to be slain and murdered, women and maids to be violated and deflowered: which things when they are done by foreign enemies, we do much mourn, as we have great causes, yet are all these miseries without any wickedness wrought by any of our own countrymen. But when these mischiefs are wrought in rebellion by them that should be friends, by countrymen, by kinsmen, by those that should defend their country, and countrymen from such miseries, the misery is nothing so great, as is the mischief and wickedness when the Subjects unnaturally do rebel against their Prince, whose honor and life they should defend, though it were with the loss of their own lives: countrymen to disturb the public peace and quietness of their country, for defense of whose quietness they should spend their lives: the brother to seek, and often to work the death of his brother, the son of the father, the father to seek or procure the death of his sons, being at man's age, and by their faults to disinherit their innocent children and kinsmen their heirs forever, for whom they might purchase livings and lands, as natural parents do take care and pains, and to be at great costs and charges: and universally instead of all quietness, joy, and felicity, which do follow blessed peace & due obedience, to bring in all trouble, sorrow, disquietness of minds & bodies & all mischief & calamity, to turn all good order upside down, to bring all good laws in contempt, and to tread them under feet, to oppress all virtue and honesty, and all virtuous and honest persons, and to set all vice and wickedness, and all vicious and wicked men at liberty, to work their wicked wills, which were before bridled by wholesome Laws, to weaken, to overthrow, and to consume the strength of the Realm their natural Country, as well by the spending and wasting of money and treasure of the Prince and Realms, as by murdering the people of the same, their own countrymen, who should defend the honor of their Prince, and Liberty of their Country, against the invasion of foreign enemies: and so finally, to make their country thus by their mischief weakened, ready to be a prey and spoil to all outward enemies that will invade it, to the utter and perpetual captivity, slavery, and destruction of all their countrymen, their children, their friends, their kinsfolk left alive, whom by their wicked rebellion they procure to be delivered into the hands of the foreign enemies, as much as in them doth lie.

In foreign wars our countrymen in obtaining the victory win the praise of valiantness, yea and though they were overcome and slain, yet win they an honest commendation in this world, and die in a good conscience for serving GOD, their Prince, and their country, and be children of eternal salvation. But the rebellion how desperate and strong soever they be, yet win they shame here in fighting against GOD, their Prince and Country, and therefore justly do fall headlong into hell if they die, and live in shame and fearful conscience, though they escape.

But commonly they be rewarded with shameful deaths, their hands and carcasses set upon poles, and hanged in chains, eaten with kites[5] and crows, judged unworthy the honor of burial, and so their souls, if they repent not (as commonly they do not) the devil hurrieth them into hell, in the midst of their mischief. For which dreadful execution Saint Paul showeth the cause of obedience, not only for fear of death, but also in conscience to GOD-ward, for fear of eternal damnation in the world to come.

Wherefore good people, let us, as the children of obedience, fear the dreadful execution of GOD, and live in quiet obedience, to be the children of everlasting Salvation. For as heaven is the place of good obedient subjects, and hell the prison and dungeon of rebels against GOD and their Prince: so is that Realm happy where most obedience of subjects doth appear, being the very figure of heaven: and contrariwise where most rebellions and rebels be, there is the express similitude of hell, and the rebels themselves are the very figures of friends and devils, and their captain the ungracious pattern of Lucifer and Satan, the prince of darkness, of whose rebellion as they be followers, so shall they of high damnation in hell undoubtedly be partakers, and as undoubtedly children of peace the inheritors of heaven with GOD the father, GOD the Son, and GOD the holy Ghost: To whom be all honor and glory for ever and ever, Amen.

[5] **kites:** falcons, birds of prey.

→ JOHN PONET

From A Short Treatise of Politic Power 1556

Ponet was not named as the author of the *Treatise* until its republication in 1642. The title page of the 1556 edition prints only the initials D. I. P. B. R. W. ("Dr. John Ponet, Bishop of Rochester and Winchester"), which appear over an excerpt from Psalm 118: "It is better to trust in the Lords [*sic*] than to trust in

John Ponet, *A Short Treatise of Politic Power, and of the true Obedience which subjects owe to kings and other civil Governors, with an Exhortation to all true natural Englishmen* ([London], 1556) A2r–A5r, B5v–B7r, C6v–C8v, D3r, D7r, E3r–E3v, E7v, F1v–G3r, G4v–G6v, G9v–H1r, H3r–H7v.

Princes" — a fundamental principle of his theory. There was good reason for Ponet not to identify himself as the author of the *Treatise*, for his opposition to the Catholic Queen Mary's succession and her subsequent marriage with Philip of Spain had deprived him of his bishopric and sent him into exile in Strasbourg, where, with a community of other prelates, he helped to further the education of Protestant scholars. Unquestionably, the immediate aim of the *Treatise* was to justify the deposition of a Catholic prince, and his book may well have been included in Mary's 6 June 1558 proclamation banning "diverse books filled with heresy and treason" (Hudson 186). Unlike some of his contemporaries, however, Ponet does not oppose the Marian regime solely on matters of faith. Rather than speaking against the subversion of "true" — that is, Protestant — religion, he attacks the basic assumptions of absolutism itself and advocates basing resistance to authoritarian government upon *constitutional* principles.

In grounding his political philosophy on God's absolute sovereignty, Ponet shares the assumptions of the period that this law was manifestly known: it is "so plain, that none can gainsay it" (C2r). But within this divinely instituted framework, civil power is established for the welfare of the people, who have the determining voice as to the manner in which they are best served. Ultimately, sovereignty is mediated through the people — by whom Ponet means not simply the feudal aristocracy or lesser magistrates but the "poor people . . . of what state or degree in this world so ever they be" (A7v). Furthermore, Ponet argues for restraints on even the most arbitrary power: the first is God's divine law itself; the second, more subtle, maintains that no prince can do anything to hurt the people without their consent. Although the people may give the king authority to make positive laws — that is, those made and executed by men — the king cannot break or dispense with them, even by evoking tradition and precedent: "evil customs (be they never so old) are not to be suffered, but utterly to be abolished" (B5v). Ponet does not explicitly propose a concept of "natural rights" but writes instead of the duties of and limitations on a ruler. He nonetheless suggests that the people do have certain rights — to life, to a means of livelihood, to property, to equality before law, to freedom from invasions of personal liberty, and to resist and alter a government that infringes upon such rights.

Aristocracy and democracy, however, receive only brief mention. By implication, Ponet envisions only two possible forms of government: absolute monarchy and the mixed state or commonwealth — that is, a limited monarchy in which "the people" are theoretically present in a representative capacity, as in the English Parliament. Evoking the familiar Platonic analogy between the natural body and the body politic, he asserts that the ideal state cannot be attained until every member functions in complete harmony with the whole. Whereas a ruler's duty is to seek the best for his people, not for himself alone, the people owe duty to the country and to *the whole commonwealth* before any member of it — including the king. While he stresses the relation between order and obedience, Ponet breaks completely with the dominant view of absolute obedience proposed in the 1547 *Homily* (which preceded the even more stringent 1571 version) and grounds his doctrine of obedience — or, more appropriately, disobedience — on the right of individual judgment. If a civil authority demands obedience to God and to the wealth and benefit of the realm, all well and good, but if the ruler commands the individual to dishonor God, to commit idolatry, to kill an innocent, or to fight against his country, the individual should not obey such evil commandments.

Having established the possibility of disobedience, Ponet then counters the widely adopted providentialist view expressed four centuries earlier by John of Salisbury that "tyrants are the ministers of God . . . [and] by their means the wicked may be punished, and the good chastened" (quoted in Hudson 157). It is a superstitious blasphemy to say that God allowed tyranny as a punishment for sin, for this, Ponet claims, is to make God the author of evil. In describing the surveillance experienced by religious and political dissidents, from governmental seizure of possessions and arms to monitoring (and interpreting) speech as well as silence and to inflicting bodily punishment, Ponet alludes to his own history as well as that of other Marian exiles, such as Christopher Goodman. His emphasis on property rights and his identification of tyranny with theft clearly speaks to these contemporary conditions.

Although the *Treatise* is relatively free of metaphor, Ponet constructs the state as a "fair garden" spoiled by a domestic rogue animal (who just happens to be female). A bit later, this turns into a "state of nature" where the people become "game" and "prey" to an unscrupulous hunter; finally, the state is transformed into a site of popular public entertainment, where the people, muzzled and baited like bears, are at the mercy of bestial inquisitors (p. 190). A tyrannous ruler who visits such a "plague" upon his subjects, Ponet maintains, is not ordained by God; therefore, the people owe him no obedience. However, lacking an "express politic law" that supports either deposition or tyrannicide, he resorts to scriptural examples as well as to English history, where he justifies Edward II's brutal murder but cannily defers judgment on Richard II and Henry IV. Searching for a practical solution, he looks back to the ancient feudal office of High Constable (an office held, during Henry IV's reign, by the Earl of Northumberland), which carried with it the authority to summon the king before Parliament or other courts of judgment. Although he seems to dismiss the idea as soon as he brings it up, his move to convert feudal status into constitutional authority in order to check absolutist power anticipates the attempt at aristocratic reform of government that lay behind the Earl of Essex's 1601 rising against Queen Elizabeth and her ministers (see James).

Finally, Ponet's own remedy for expressing opposition to a regime rests on individual resistance. But since a doctrine of individual resistance advocating that a private man may kill a magistrate would support anarchy, he suggests a hierarchy of means for dealing with a prince who fails to recognize his responsibility to God and to his people. If such a tyrant refuses his duties, the people are to look to the nobility and Parliament for relief, and if this expedient fails, they should complain to some minister of God's word, who may excommunicate not only common people but kings and princes when they "spoil, rob, undo and kill their poor subjects without justice and good laws" (p. 193). If the minister shirks his duty, then, and only then, may the individual act. Lacking the courage to act, the individual's final resort lies in penance and prayer, for then God will intervene and revenge the cause of the oppressed.

The type of political thought Ponet expressed was almost completely submerged during Elizabeth's reign; after all, it would have been difficult to prove the "Protestant Princess" a godless tyrant. This is not to say, however, that the Queen's policies went unquestioned. Indeed, the major anti-absolutist voices came from those in Sir Philip Sidney's circle, among them the Scot, George Buchanan, and the notorious Earl of Essex, who based his opposition to centralized power on the kind of feudal principles Ponet advocated (see Chapter 5, "Honor and Arms"). Ponet's ideas also surface in Puritan thought, which advocated a limited monarchy embodying the representational principle. Certainly the religious goals of the Puritans were similar to those of the Marian exiles, but the means they advocated to achieve their aims took the form of public passive resistance and of attempting to achieve parliamentary sanction for their programs of reform rather than the radical expedients of rebellion and tyrannicide. Traces of Ponet's influence appear in Richard Hooker's *Laws of Ecclesiastical Polity* (1594–97), which adopts a sophisticated version of his political views but circumscribes them so as to render them nearly harmless to monarchy. But it was not until after the American Revolution, when a charge of rebellion made little difference, that Ponet would be recognized by another political theorist. Quoting from the 1556 edition of the *Treatise,* John Adams declared that it "contains all the essential principles of liberty which were afterwards dilated on by Sidney and Locke" (quoted in Hudson 216). For Adams, Ponet anticipated American democratic ideals.

From *A Short Treatise of Politic Power*

WHEREOF POLITIC POWER GROWETH, WHEREFORE IT WAS ORDAINED, AND THE RIGHT USE AND DUTY OF THE SAME: &C.

[Desiring to know a more perfect and reasonable governor than themselves, men turned to God.]

[God] hath taken upon him the order and government of man his chief creature, and prescribed him a rule, how he should behave himself, what he should do, and what he may not do.

This rule is the law of nature, first planted and graffed only in the mind of man, that after (for that his mind was through sin defiled, filled with darkness, and encumbered with many doubts) set forth in writing in the decalogue or ten commandments: and after reduced by Christ our savior to these two words: Thou shalt love thy lord God above all things, and thy neighbor as thy self. The latter part whereof he also thus expoundeth: what so ever ye will that men do unto you, do ye even so to them.

In this law is comprehended all justice, the perfect way to serve and glorify God, and the right mean to rule every man particularly, and all men generally: and the only stay to maintain every commonwealth. This is the touchstone to try every man's doings (be he king or beggar) whether they be good or evil. By this all men's laws be discerned, whether they be just or unjust, godly or wicked. [Ponet offers examples of just and unjust, ungodly laws, evoking the Ten Commandments and repeating the golden rule: whatsoever you would have men do unto you, do you unto them.]

Against the offenders of this law, there was no corporeal punishment ordained in this world, til after the destruction of the world with the great flood. For albeit Cain and Lamech had committed horrible murders, yet were they not corporally punished, but had a protection of God that none should lawfully hurt them. But after the flood, when God saw his gentleness and patience could not work his creatures to do their duties unforced [and sin prevailed], then was he constrained to change his lenity into severity, and to add corporeal pains to those that would not follow, but transgress his ordinances. And so he made this law, which he declared to Noah: He that Sheddeth the blood of man, his blood Shall be Shed by man. For man is made after the image of God.

By this ordinance and law he instituteth politic power and giveth authority to men to make more laws. [God would have men live quietly, yet giving man authority over goods and lands bred discord, so that He was not served and glorified.] This ordinance also teacheth makers of laws, how they should behave themselves in making laws: that is, to set apart all affections, and to observe an equality in pains, that they be not greater or less, than the fault deserveth, and that they punish not the innocent or small offender for malice, and let the mighty and great thief escape for affection. And out of this ordinance groweth and is grounded the authority for Magistrates to execute laws: for laws without execution, be no more profitable, than bells without clappers. But whether this authority to make laws, or the power to execute the same, shall be and remain in one person alone, or in many, it is not expressed, but left to the discretion of the people to make so many and so few, as they think necessary for the maintenance of the state. [Citing Moses, the Lacedemonians, Athens, and Rome, Ponet offers types of rule, either by one, by a chosen few, by the multitude, by "people of the lowest sort," and by "the king, nobility, and the people all together."]

And these diverse kinds of states or policies had their distinct names, as where one ruled, a Monarchy: where many of the best, Aristocracy: where the multitude, Democracy: and where all together, that is, a king, the nobility, and commons, a mixed state: which men by long continuance have judged to be the best sort of all. For where that mixed state was exercised, there did the commonwealth longest continue. But yet every kind of these states tended to one end, that is, to the maintenance of justice, to the wealth and benefit of the whole multitude, and not of the superior and governors alone. And when they saw, that the governors abused their authority, they altered the state.

[Ponet cites biblical and classical examples of changes in government and stresses the importance of politic power and authority, without which "mankind could not be preserved, nor the world continued." He offers additional examples of governmental forms — councils, diets, and parliaments — that safeguard the people's liberty against tyrants. Just as the man who does something for another while seeking his own profit should make recompense for any hurt, so too with rulers who deceive an entire realm, which is even worse. But politic power must be used properly: the ruler who oppresses the poor risks eternal damnation. Authorities must remember that they execute "not the judgment of man, but of God."]

WHETHER KINGS, PRINCES, AND OTHER GOVERNORS HAVE AN ABSOLUTE POWER AND AUTHORITY OVER THEIR SUBJECTS

[Since rulers would be taken for ministers of God, claiming absolute power and prerogative, it is necessary to examine whether they do so rightfully or wrongfully, for God will eventually "judge the world with equity, and revenge the cause of the oppressed." May kings and princes do things "contrary to the positive laws of their country"? Ponet here marks distinctions between tyrants who exercise power according to their own wills and the circumstances pertaining to the "mixed state," in which the people retain authority.]

True it is, that in matters indifferent, that is, that of themselves be neither good nor evil, hurtful, or profitable, but for a decent order, Kings and Princes (to whom the people have given their authority) may make such laws, and dispense with them. But in matters not indifferent, but godly and profitably ordained for the commonwealth, there can they not (for all their authority) break them or dispense with them. For Princes are ordained to do good, not to do evil; to take away evil, not to increase it; to give example of well doing, not to be procurers of evil; to procure the wealth and benefit of their subjects, and not to work their hurt or undoing. And in the empire where (by the civil laws) the emperors claim, that the people gave them their authority to make laws, albeit they have been willing, and often attempted to execute their authority, which some Pickthanks (to please them) say they have by the laws, yet have they been forced of themselves to leave off their enterprise. But such as be indifferent expounders of the laws, be of that mind that we before have declared: and therefore make this a general conclusion, and as it were a rule, that the emperor willing any thing to be done, there is no more to be done, than the laws permit to be done. For (say they) neither pope, Emperor, nor king may do any thing to the hurt of his people without their consent. King Antigonus' Chancellor, saying unto him, that all things were honest and lawful to kings: ye say true (quoth the king) but [only] to such kings as be beasts, barbarous and without humanity. But to true and good Princes, nothing is honest, but that is honest in deed, and nothing is just, but that is just in deed.

Antiochus the third king of Asia, considering that as he was above the people, so the laws were above him, wrote general letters to all the cities of his country, that if they should perceive that he, by any letters, should require anything contrary to the laws, they should think that such letters were obtained without his consent, and therefore they should not obey them.

Now if where the people have given their authority to their governor to make such laws, yet can he not break or dispense with the positive laws. How much less may such governors, kings, and princes to whom the people have not given their authority (but they with the people, and the people with them make the laws) break them or dispense with them? If this were tolerable, then were it in vain to make solemn assemblies of the whole state, long Parliaments &c? Yes (I beseech thee) what certainty should there be in anything, where all should depend on one's will and affection? But it will be said, that albeit kings and princes can not make laws, but with the consent of the people, yet may they dispense with any positive law, by reason that of long time they have used so to do, and prescribe so to do: for long custom maketh a law.

To this it may be answered, evil customs (be they never so old) are not to be suffered, but utterly to be abolished. And none may prescribe to do evil, be he king or subject, if the laws appoint thee the time of thirty or forty years to claim a sure and a perfect interest of that thou enjoyest, yet if thou know, that either thyself or those by whom thou claimest, came wrongfully by it, thou art not indeed a perfect owner of it, but art bounden to restore it. Although the laws of man do excuse and defend thee from outward trouble and punishment, yet can they not quiet the conscience, but what thy conscience remembreth, that thou enjoyest that is not thine, it will bite thee that thou hast done wrong: it will accuse thee before the judgment of God, and condemn thee. And if princes and governors would show themselves half so wise, as they would men should take them to be, and by the example of others learn what mischief might happen to themselves, they would not (if they might) claim, much less execute any such absolute authority. No, neither would their Counselors (if they loved them) maintain them in it: nor yet the subjects (if they did not consider their own safety and felicity in this life) would not, if they might suffer their Prince to do what him lusted. [The rulers of commonwealths neither have nor can claim absolute authority. Since the end of their authority is determined to maintain justice, to defend the innocent, and to punish evil, they should abstain from tyranny, do their duties, and glorify God.]

WHETHER KINGS, PRINCES, AND OTHER POLITIC GOVERNORS BE SUBJECT TO GOD'S LAWS, AND THE POSITIVE LAWS OF THEIR COUNTRIES

[Ponet reaffirms God's absolute sovereignty. Citing (among other scriptural examples) Saint Paul's admonition to rulers as subject to the principalities and powers, he argues that kings and princes, as executors of God's laws and men's just ordinances, are not exempt from them but "be bounden to be subject and obedient to them."]

For good and just laws of man be God's power and ordinances, and they are but ministers of the laws, and not the law's self. And if they were exempt from the laws, and so it were lawful for them to do what them lusteth, their authority being of God, it might be said, that God allowed their tyranny, robbery of their subjects, killing them without law, and so God [is] the author of evil: which were a great blasphemy. Justinian the emperor well considered, when he made this saying to be put into the body of the laws. It is a worthy saying (saieth he) for the Majesty of him that is in authority, to confess that the prince is subject to the laws, [for] the authority of the prince doth so much depend on the authority of the laws. And certainly it is more honor than the honor of the empire, to submit the principality unto the laws. For indeed laws be made, that the willful self-will of men should not rule, but that they should have a line to lead them, as they might not go out of the way of justice: and that (if any would say, they did them wrong) they might allege the law for their warrant and authority. It is also a principle of all laws grounded on the law of nature, that every man should use himself and be obedient to that law, that he will [have] others be bounden unto. For otherwise he taketh away that equality (for there is no difference between the head and foot, concerning the use and benefit of the laws) whereby commonwealths be maintained and kept up. What equality (I beseech you) should there be, where the subject should do to his ruler all the ruler would: and the ruler to the subject, that [which] the ruler lusted?

[Ponet cites Trajan, who was taken to be a god by the Roman Senate yet still remained subject to its laws, and Zaleuchus as examples of rulers who kept their own laws. Once again, he justifies his reasons for turning to Ethnike or pre-Christian rulers.]

Kings and princes ought, both by God's law, the law of nature, man's laws, and good reason, to be obedient and subject to the positive laws of their country, and may not break them. And that they be not exempt from them, nor may dispense with them, unless the makers of the laws give them express authority so to do.

Who shall be the kings' judges, hereafter thou shalt hear.

IN WHAT THINGS, AND HOW FAR SUBJECTS ARE BOUNDEN TO OBEY THEIR PRINCES AND GOVERNORS

[Ponet grounds his theory of obedience on the right of individual judgment.]

In man's commandments, men ought to consider the matter, and not the man. For all men what so ever ministery or vocation they exercise, are but men, and so may err. We see councils against councils, parliaments against parliaments, commandment against commandment; this day one thing, tomorrow another. It is not the man's warrant that can discharge thee, but it is the thing itself that must justify thee. It is the matter that will accuse thee, and defend thee, acquit thee, and condemn thee when thou shalt come before the throne of the highest and everlasting power, where no temporal power will appear for thee, to make answer or to defend thee: but thou thyself must answer for thyself, and for what so ever thou hast done. And therefore Christian men ought well to consider, and weigh men's commandments, before they be hasty to do them, to see if they be contrary or repugnant to God's commandments and justice: which if they be, they are cruel and evil, and ought not to be obeyed. We have this special commandment from God the highest power, often repeated by the holy ghost. Forbear to do evil, and do that is good.

[A ruler's duties exist within a cooperative, relational framework.]

And men ought to have more respect to their country, than to their prince: to the commonwealth, than to any one person. For the country and commonwealth is a degree above the king. Next unto God men ought to love their country, and the whole commonwealth before any member of it: as kings and princes (be they never so great) are but members; and commonwealths may stand well enough and flourish, albeit there be no kings, but contrariwise without a commonwealth there can be no king. Commonwealths and realms may live, when the head is cut off, and may put on a new head, that is, make them a new governor, when they see their old head seek too much his own will and not the wealth of the whole body, for the which he was only ordained.

[By the so-called justice and law lately executed in England, it appears that ministers of civil power do sometimes command that which subjects ought not to do. Among a series of examples drawn from English history, Ponet cites Lady Jane Gray's allowing herself to be called queen against her will and Archbishop Cranmer resisting Henry VIII's disinheritance of Mary and Elizabeth.]

For albeit the king or Queen of a realm have the Crown never justly, yet may they not dispose of the Crown or realm, as it pleaseth them. They have the Crown to minister justice, but the Realm being a body of free men and not of bondsmen, he nor she can not give or sell them as slaves and bondsmen. No, they can not give or sell away the holds and forts (at Calais and Berwick, or such like) without the consent of the Commons, for it was purchased with their blood and money.

[In an ideal state, Ponet argues, princes should be defenders of the people, and he cites numerous examples, biblical as well as contemporary, of persecution, oppression, and tyranny.]

And besides also they ought to consider, that princes be ordained for the wealth and benefit of the people, and not to their destruction: to maintain commonwealths and not to subvert them, which rather than any man should consent unto, he ought (being a faithful man to his country) to abide all losses, both of body and goods. For next after God, men be born to love, honor, and maintain their country.

WHETHER ALL THE SUBJECT'S GOODS BE THE KAISER'S AND KING'S OWN, AND THAT THEY MAY LAWFULLY TAKE THEM AS THEIR OWNER

[Ponet discusses several kinds of evil governors, including those that impose great taxes, saying, "All things be the kaiser's, all things be the king's, all things be the prince's."] Whereof cometh this common saying? It cannot come of nothing. But by that that is already said, ye see that every man may keep his own, and none may take it from him, so that it cannot be interpreted, that all things be the kaiser's or king's, as his own proper, or that they may take them from their subjects at their pleasure, but thus it is to be expounded, that they ought to defend, that every man hath, that he may quietly enjoy his own, and to see that they be not robbed or spoiled thereof. For as in a great man's house, all things be said to be the Steward's, because it is committed to his charge, to see that every man in the house behave himself honestly, and do his duty, to see that all things be well kept and preserved and may take nothing away from any man, nor misspend or waste, and of his doings he must render accompt to his lord for all: so in a Realm or other dominion, the realm and country are God's, he is the lord, the people are his servants, and the king or governor is but God's minister or Steward, ordained not to misuse the servants, that is, the people, neither to spoil them of that they have, but to see the people do their duty to their lord God, that the goods of this world be not abused but spent to God's glory, to the maintenance and defense of the commonwealth, and not to the destruction of it. The prince's watch ought to defend the poor man's house, his labor the subject's ease, his diligence the subject's pleasure, his trouble the subject's quietness. [A good prince does not seek his own profit but the wealth of those committed to his charge.]

WHETHER IT BE LAWFUL TO DEPOSE AN EVIL GOVERNOR, AND KILL A TYRANT

As there is no better nor happier commonwealth nor no greater blessing of God, than where one ruleth, if he be a good, just and godly man: so is there no worse nor none more miserable, nor greater plague of God than where one ruleth, that is evil, unjust and ungodly. [Like a physician, a shipmaster or a parent, a good governor neglects his own pleasure and profit and labors to see his office well discharged and to protect those under his care.] An evil person coming to the government of any state, either by usurpation, or by election or by succession, utterly neglecting the cause why kings, princes and other governors in commonwealths be made (that is, the wealth of the people) seeketh only or chiefly his own profit and pleasure. And as a sow coming into a fair garden, rooteth up all the fair and sweet flowers and wholesome simples [medicinal herbs], leaving nothing behind, but her own filthy dirt: so doth an evil governor subvert the laws and orders, or maketh them to be wrenched or racked to serve his affections, that they can no longer do their office. He spoileth the people of their goods, either by open violence, making his ministers to take it from them without payment therefore, or promising and never paying: or craftily under the name of loans, benevolences, contributions, and such like gay painted words, or for fear he getteth out of their possession that they have, and never restoreth it. [He spends these monies not for the commonwealth's benefit but on whores, dicing, banqueting, and unjust wars.] He spoileth and taketh away from them their armor and harness, that they shall not be able to use any force to defend their own right. And not contented to have brought them into such misery (to be sure of his state) seeketh and taketh all occasions to dispatch them of their lives. If a man keep his house, and meddle in nothing, then shall it be said, that he fretteth at the state. If he come abroad and speak to any other, forthwith it is taken for a just conspiracy. If he say nothing, and show a merry countenance, it is a token, that he despiseth the government. If he look sorrowfully, then he lamenteth the state of his country. How many so ever be for any cause, committed to prison, are not only asked, but be racked also to show whether he be privy of their doings. If he depart, because he would live quietly, then is he proclaimed an open enemy. To be short, there is no doing, no gesture, no behavior, no place can preserve or defend innocency against such a governor's cruelty. But as an hunter maketh wild beasts his prey, and useth toils, nets, snares, traps, dogs, ferrets, mining and digging the ground, guns, bows, spears, and all other instruments, engines, devises, subtleties, and means, whereby he may come by his prey: so doth a wicked governor make the people his game and prey, and useth all kinds of subtleties, deceits, crafts, policies, force, violence, cruelty and such like devilish ways, to spoil and destroy the people, that be committed to his charge. And when he is not able without most manifest cruelty to do by himself that he desireth, then feigneth he unjust causes to cast them into prison, where like as the bearwards muzzle the bears, and tie them to the stakes, whiles they be baited, and killed, of mastiffs and curs, so he keepeth them in chains, whilst the bishops and other his tormentors and heretical inquisitors do tear and devour them. Finally he saith and denieth, he promiseth and breaketh promise, he sweareth and forsweareth, and neither passeth on God nor the devil (as the common saying is) so he may bring to pass that he desireth. Such an evil governor properly men call a Tyrant.

Now for as much as there is no express positive law for punishment of a Tyrant among Christian men, the question is, whether it be lawful to kill such a monster and cruel beast covered with the shape of a man.

[Ponet offers Old Testament examples for the deposing of kings and killing of tyrants.]

And as Cardinal Pole truly citeth, England lacketh not the practice and experience of the same. For they deprived King Edward the second, because without law he killed his subjects, spoiled them of their goods, and wasted the treasure of the Realm. And upon what just cause Richard the second was thrust out, and Henry the fourth put in his place, I refer it to their own judgment.

[Ponet turns to Denmark, France, Hungary, and Portugal for other examples.]

If the fault be unsavory, it is good for no use, but to be cast out, and trodden under foot of all men. And again: If thy right eye be a let unto thee, pull it out, and cast it from thee. For it is better that one member perish, than that the whole body should be cast into hell. And again say the Canonists (the pope's lawyers) in rehearsing Christ's words: If our eye, foot, or hand offend us, let it be taken from the rest of the body: for it is better to lack members in this world, than that they should carry the rest of the body into hell. By [these] is understood the heads and rulers, and not the other members and subjects. And not only the heads and rulers in the church, but also in all policies and commonwealths.

[Ponet takes up the question of deposing and punishing a pope.]

But here ye see, the body of every state may (if it will) yea and ought to redress and correct the vices and heads of their governors. And forasmuch as ye have already seen whereof politic power and government groweth, and the end whereunto it was ordained. And seeing it is before manifestly and sufficiently proved, that kings and princes have not an absolute power over their subjects: that they are and ought to be subject to the law of God, and the wholesome positive laws of their country, and that they may not lawfully take or use their subjects' goods at their pleasure: the reasons, arguments and law that serve for the deposing and displacing of an evil governor, will do as much for the proof, that it is lawful to kill a tyrant, if they may be indifferently heard. As God hath ordained Magistrates to hear and determine private men's matters, and to punish their vices, so also will he, that the magistrates' doings be called to accompt and reckoning, and their vices corrected and punished by the body of the whole congregation or commonwealth.

As it is manifest by the memory of the ancient office of the High Constable of England, unto whose authority it pertained, not only to summon the king personally before the parliament or other courts of judgment (to answer and receive according to justice) but also upon just occasion to commit him unto ward.

Kings, Princes and governors have their authority of the people, as all laws, usages and policies do declare and testify.

For in some places and countries they have more and greater authority, in some places less. And in some the people have not given this authority to any other, but retain and exercise it themselves. And is any man so unreasonable to deny, that the whole may do as much as they have permitted one member to do? Or those that appointed an office upon trust, have not authority upon just occasion (as the abuse of it) to take away that they gave? All laws do agree, that men may revoke their proxies and letters of Attorney, when it pleaseth them: much more when they see their proctors and attorneys abuse it.

But now to pose the latter part of this question affirmatively, that it is lawful to kill a tyrant. [Although the Ethnikes had no right and perfect knowledge of God, they did know the law of nature.]

For it is no private law to a few or certain people, but common to all: not written in books, but graffed in the hearts of men; not made by man, but ordained of God, which we have not learned, received or read, but have taken, sucked and drawn it out of nature, whereunto we are not taught, but made, not instructed, but seasoned, and (as S[aint] Paul saith) man's conscience bearing witness of it.

This law testifieth to every man's conscience, that it is natural to cut away an incurable member, which (being suffered) would destroy the whole body.

Kings, Princes and other governors, albeit they are the heads of a politic body, yet they are not the whole body. And though they be the chief members, yet they are but members: neither are the people ordained for them, but they are ordained for the people.

[The Ethnikes encouraged men to kill tyrants and esteemed the deed of great reward, worth pardon and lasting fame. Ponet gives classical examples of those who delivered a country from tyranny and cites scriptural analogies on rooting out evil. The manner of punishing evildoers may not be similar among Christians and Ethnikes, yet the laws of many Christian regions permit private men to kill malefactors, even magistrates, for a number of offenses. Nevertheless, there is no allowance for private men to kill tyrannous and traitorous governors, unless by God's "special inward commandment," as given to Moses.]

But I beseech thee, what needeth to make one general law to punish by one name a great many offenses, when the law is already made for the punishment of every one of them particularly? If a prince rob and spoil his subjects, it is theft, and as a thief he ought to be punished. If he kill and murder them contrary or without the laws of his country, it is murder, and as a murderer he ought to be punished. If he commit adultery, he is an adulterer and ought to be punished with the same pains that others be. If he violently rav-

ish men's wives, daughters, or maidens, the laws that are made against rav-
ishers ought to be executed on him. If he go about to betray his country, and
to bring the people under a foreign power, he is a traitor, and as a traitor he
ought to suffer. And those that be judges in commonwealths ought (upon
complaint) to summon and cite them to answer to their crimes, and so to
proceed as they do with others. For the prophet speaking unto those that
have the rule in commonwealths, and that be judges and other ministers of
justice, saith: minister justice to the poor and orphan, pronounce the miserable and poor to be innocent, if he be innocent. Take the poor, and deliver
the needy out of the hands of the wicked. When ye sit to judge, ye shall not
have respect of persons, whether they be rich or poor, great or small. Fear no
man, for ye execute the judgement of God, saith the holy ghost by the
mouth of Moses. Judge not after the outward appearance of men, but judge
rightly, saith Christ.

[Ponet cites scriptural examples of evil governors and instances where such
justice did not prevail. Such states, he warns, will suffer the consequences, as
did Sodom and Gomorrah.]

And on the other side, where the nobility and people look diligently and
earnestly upon their authorities, and do see the same executed on their
heads and governors, making them to yield accompt of their doings, then
without fail will the princes and governors be as diligent to see the people
do their duty. And so shall the commonwealth be godly and prosper, and
God shall be glorified in all. But thou wilt say, what if the nobility, and those
that be called to common Counsels, and should be the defenders of the people, will not or dare not execute their authority? What is then to be done?
The people be not so destitute of remedy, but God hath provided another
mean, that is, to complain to some minister of the word of God, to whom
the keys be given to excommunicate not only the common people for all notorious and open evils but also kaisers, kings, princes, and all other governors, when they spoil, rob, undo and kill their poor subjects without justice
and good laws. [Ponet cites the example of Saint Ambrose, who excommu-
nicated the Emperor Theodosius and refused to absolve him until he had
passed a law requiring that the execution of revenge not be done in anger
but be delayed.]

But thou wilt say, what if the minister pass not on his duty, but be content to wink at all the vices of the governors, be they never so wicked, so he
may have a bishopric, a deanery, a prebend, or a good fat benefice, and live
unpunished in all abomination? Yea, and what if there be such special
grudges between the nobility and the commons that the one sort neither
trusteth nor loveth the other, so as the one dare not open the necessity and

mean of such correction and redress of the evil governor's vices, for fear lest, if the purpose come to light beforehand, the matter be dashed, and the motioner leap headless for his labor, as it is in these days often seen. What shift then?

[God many times delivered the Israelites from wicked tyrants, and when they forgot God's word, he punished them by replacing a good judge with an evil one. Ponet cites examples of individuals destined to save Israel by taking matters into their own hands, such as Jael and Mattathias.]

But if neither the whole state nor the minister of God's word will do their common duty, nor any other lawful shift before mentioned can be had, nor dare be attempted, yet are not the poor people destitute all together of remedy. But God hath left unto them two weapons, able to conquer and destroy the greatest Tyrant that ever was: that is, **Penance** and **Prayer**. Penance for their own sins, which provoke the anger and displeasure of God, and make him to suffer tyrants, wars, famine, pestilence and all plagues to reign among the people. And prayer, that He will withdraw His wrath and show his merciful countenance.

[By such means, God delivered the people of Israel from the Philistines. And when the apostles and people in the primitive church called on God for mercy, the angel of God struck Herod sitting in his throne. Emperor Julian, who persecuted the church, was also slain. And when Duke George of Saxony persecuted those who professed God's word and threatened to destroy the university at Wittenberg, Luther went into the pulpit and "exhorted every man to put on his armor: that is, Penance and prayer"; later, the whole country was converted to Christ's Gospel.]

These be the wonderful works of almighty God, whose power is as great and as ready at a pinch as ever it was, and his mercy as willing to be showed, if His poor afflicted people would do on their weapon: that is, be sorry for their sins, and desire Him to withdraw his scourges, and to hold His merciful hand over them.

CHAPTER 3

Cultural Territories

Right at the center of *Henry IV, Part 1* a sequence of two scenes (2.4, 3.1) juxtaposes two very different locales and embraces a range of class, gender, linguistic, and regional or national differences. Each scene records or alludes to features of a marginal culture far removed from Henry IV's court: that of London's underworld, located in the heart of the walled City, and that of Wales, in many respects a "foreign" or alien region or nation. Furthermore, just as Eastcheap's tavern is the site of a theatrical performance in which Hal and Falstaff rehearse various identities, so too with the Welsh outpost, where Glendower orchestrates both the rebels' plot and his daughter's musical performance. Nowhere else does the play so insistently represent an interplay between centers and margins and, especially at the level of language, stress distinctions between insiders and outsiders. In doing so, it (like other history plays) contributes to a wider discourse of national identity and also to a new self-consciousness concerning the diverse peoples and distinctive local cultures that constituted early modern England.

Mapping the Land and Its People

Cartography and chorography — the one devoted to mapping the land visually, the other descriptively — played a central role in sharpening perceptions of national identity and enhancing national pride. Whereas chronicle history told the story of England's kings, mapmakers and chorographers documented the story of the land. The printing circumstances of two such projects — William Harrison's *Description of England* (1587) and John Speed's *Theatre of the Empire of Great Britain* (1611/12) — join both histories. Neither project was exactly new — such social, topographical, and antiquarian descriptions have roots in classical writers such as Tacitus, and Harrison's and Speed's work parallels that of early modern Continental cosmographers such as Abraham Ortelius, a famous mapmaker. The tradition that shaped Harrison's *Description* in particular, and also led to its inclusion in the first volume of Holinshed's *Chronicles*, was a native one developed by English monastic chroniclers, especially Ranulf Higden, after whose popular fourteenth-century *Polychronicon* Harrison patterned his work (Edelen xv–xviii). Speed's *Theatre* owes a similar debt to Christopher Saxton's 1579 atlas of maps as well as to George Braun's and Frans Hogenberg's *Civitates Orbis Terrarum* (1572), which included bird's-eye views of eleven British cities. Speed, however, considered himself primarily as a historian: his maps, which turn the land into a stage for celebrating Britain's past and present, were designed to accompany his *History of Great Britain* (Nicholson 10–15). One implication of literally binding the history of the land together with that of its kings was that allegiance to one implied allegiance to the other. But by the early seventeenth century, royal history was increasingly marginalized. As the idea of the *country* — whether conceived as kingdom, nation, county, locality, or countryside — became more and more central, it gradually displaced the idea of loyalty to the king with that of loyalty to the land, not necessarily to the *whole* of England but rather to a particular division. Richard Helgerson writes that "maps let [sixteenth-century Englishmen] see in a way never before possible the country — both county and nation — to which they belonged and at the same time showed royal authority — or at least its insignia — to be a merely ornamental adjunct to that country." Furthermore, Helgerson argues, the cartographic representation of England had a particular ideological effect, for "in strengthening the sense of local and national identity at the expense of dynastic identity, it opened up a conceptual gap between land and ruler" (131–33, 114). *Henry IV, Part 1*'s Welsh scene, which brings a map onstage, offers an emblem of this pull between competing identities: just as the map marks disputes of individual ownership, it also defines that ownership as independent of, even challenging, the king's authority.

Speed's map, "The Kingdom of England," which shows the land's most prominent topographical features and also (in the original) marks shire boundaries in color, is probably more elaborate than that used by the Lord Chamberlain's Men, but it also calls attention to divisions within the country. Although the royal arms appear at the top of the map, the costumed figures framing the land, which mark social class distinctions and model the sumptuary laws governing apparel, are, if not more important than the land itself, an integral part of its image (see Figure 6). What Speed's maps represent visually, Harrison's *Description* portrays in language. In addition to chapters on topography, climate, and natural resources and an English "bestiary" of wild and domestic animals (including dogs), the *Description* records how England's people worked and traveled, ate and drank, clothed and sheltered themselves, and how they were educated, protected, organized, and governed. Moreover, in giving the locations of manors and monuments, the pedigrees and family histories of county gentry, and the names of properties, buildings, and institutions, chorographic catalogues not only insist on *ownership* but inscribe the land with the identities and accomplishments of individuals other than kings. As Helgerson argues, cartography and chorography helped in constructing England as a cultural entity. In this discourse, nationalism and individualism are deeply intertwined and interdependent: indeed, the emergence of the land parallels the emergence of the individual in the early modern period (120–22).

Certainly Harrison's account of the prejudices and passions of his generation writes his own identity onto the land. His observations clearly derive from his own experiences — as he puts it, from "conference with divers, either at the table or secretly alone" (vi). Writing with "an especial eye unto the truth of things," he records how the particularities of material culture map shifts in social mobility coincident with the massive redistribution of wealth characterizing the period (vii). "Of Degrees of People in the Commonwealth of England" (see p. 221), for instance, exhibits some anxiety about maintaining hierarchy and degree and holding fast to "ancient" forms in an age when new money could buy a patent of gentility from the heralds. Harrison's comments would include Shakespeare, an ambitious, upwardly mobile author whose purchase of a coat of arms for his father prompted Ben Jonson, in *Every Man Out of His Humour*, to parody his rival's motto, "Non Sans Droict," as "Not without Mustard," thus exposing the commoner's table condiment as the player's only right (Gurr, *Shakespearean Stage* 83). Moreover, those aristocrats who demean their status by becoming "graziers,

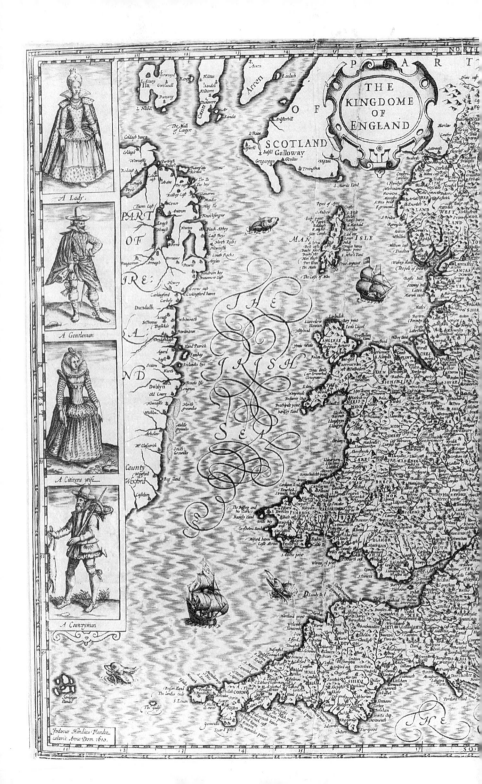

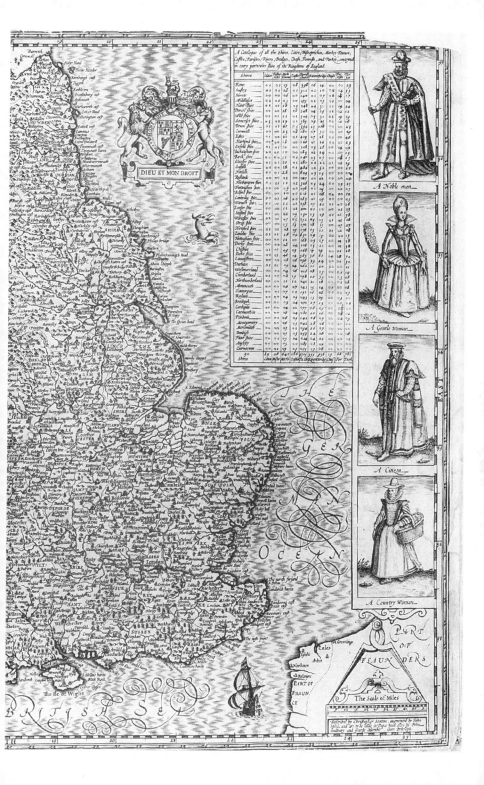

≺ FIGURE 6 (overleaf) *"The Kingdom of England" from John Speed,* The Theatre of the Empire of Great Britain *(1611/1612). The original is in color.*

butchers, tanners, sheepmasters, woodmen, . . . thereby to enrich themselves and bring all the wealth of the country into their own hands" are just as suspect. Troubled by evidence of a world turning upside down, Harrison writes that costly furnishings are to be found not just in noble houses but also in those of "inferior artificers and many farmers" who have "learned also to garnish their cupboards with plate, their joint beds with tapestry and silk hangings, and their tables with carpets and fine napery, whereby the wealth of our country . . . doth infinitely appear."

Just as possessions marked changing place and status, so did dress, which, by contributing to the power to constitute and imagine the person, served as another marker of emergent individualism. In "Of Their Apparell and Attire" (see p. 233), Harrison deplores the English penchant for "mutability" in fashions, calls attention to how women dressing as men blurs sex and gender lines, and upholds traditional alignments between social class and color in which scarlet and red crimson were ceremonial colors reserved for lords, russet for clergy, and blue for gentlemen. By pitting a growing desire for the strange, the fantastical, and the new against a conservative impulse to retain longstanding customs as markers of a "true" national identity, Harrison's moralizing registers the tensions and instabilities of a country emerging from the late Middle Ages into a nascent modernity. Like Harrison, present-day social historians differ on the extent of this instability. Some, like Steve Rappaport, view early modern England as a relatively stable society; others, such as Ian Archer, see a social fabric divided and shot through with the *pursuit* of stability. Significantly, however, both Rappaport and Archer stress that negotiation and adaptation to circumstances were crucial as the English began to reimagine their nation as a competitor on the European social stage.

London

Nowhere was evidence of such negotiation and adaptation more apparent than in London, the country's political and social capital and the seat of its rapidly expanding market economy. Serving as the hub of a transnational community of manufacturing and commercial exchange, London was not only the heart of the conspicuous consumption to which Harrison refers but also a mass market for human as well as financial capital. In the 1590s, London was on its way to becoming Europe's largest metropolitan city: by 1600, those living inside the city walls — an area barely exceeding one square mile — numbered approximately 100,000; counting the suburban sprawl beyond the city walls east of the Tower and west beyond the Inns of Court and the Strand, that number was probably closer to 200,000. All told, half of England's inhabitants lived in London, which also attracted European immigrants, or "alien vagrants," who tended to settle in the Liberties, areas outside the control of civic authorities and free of their regulation. The image of London in Speed's map of Middlesex provides little more than an overview: in the text that lies open just beneath the inset, he even apologizes for his inability to show all the grandeurs of this "most famous Citie LONDON" (see Figure 7). Notably, the absence of royal arms marks the city's independence of Crown control. The opposing arms of the City of Westminster and those of the City of London draw attention to two competing centers of authority, each shown with its major religious institution. A clearer sense of the City as a largely medieval fabric made up of densely jumbled buildings and houses, with a church every few hundred yards, appears in a map attributed to Ralph Agas (see Figure 8). Londoners were (and still are) identified by the area of the City in which they lived: each area constituted a community, or world, often organized around a particular trade. And it was not only geographically but structurally that early modern Londoners lived in a multitude of "worlds within worlds." The City itself was made up of precincts within wards and households within parishes, and individuals were also identified by membership in the livery companies (the major organizations of "handcraft men") or, like the denizens of Shakespeare's Eastcheap, with communities of "roisterers" (Rappaport 215; see "Of Lantern and Candlelight," p. 249).

John Stow's *Survey of London* (published in 1598 and amended in 1603), the first detailed, comprehensive history of the City, helps to flesh out the "Agas" map. Stow dedicated his book to London's Lord Mayor and its citizens, a patriotic tribute that has been repaid annually since 1828 at a communion service in the church of St. Andrew Undershaft. There, on the anniversary of his death, London's Lord Mayor places a new quill pen in the alabaster hand of Stow's burial monument, which shows him poised at a desk, writing his "discovery of London, my native soil and country" (Barker and Jackson 105). Anatomizing or analyzing the city, Stow's antiquarian

FIGURE 7 (overleaf) *Map of Middlesex from John Speed,* The Theatre of the Empire of Great Britain *(1611/1612). The original is in color. The back of each map contains topographical, administrative and historical comment and summarizes the main monuments of the county and its chief assets.*

LONDON

E-SEX
...ribed
...OST FAMOUS
...s of
...WESTMINSTER

LONDON

The large circuit w[i]... fmale circle; foe in this
multitude of ftreets be... rather conceit the mag-
fydes the beautifull &... nificens therof is wyde,
ftately buildings in this... then curioufely feeke
ayre, and moft famous... fatiffaction by the fight
Citie LONDON: can no... whofe pleafant fitua-
wife be demonftrated... tion, beautye, and rich
in foe little compafe,... bleffings both for foyll
as here I am inforced... and fea equals; yf not
to fhewe. But as Her-... exceeds any Citie un-
cules his bodye might... der Heaven. The
be meafured by his .t.... trew ploit whereof
foote, and the univer-... I purpofely referue to
fall Globe drawe in a... a further leafure & larger
Scale. And,

SAINT PAULS

**Described by Iohn Norden, Augmented by I. Speed
Sold in Popes head alley against the Exchange by
George Humble.**

Waltham Abbey
WalthamForest
EDMONTON HUDR
Enfield Chace
High Bernet
PART OF ESSEX
Woodford
Walthamſtow
Wanſted
Layton
FYNESBURY
WENLAXBARNE
AND
WESTMINSTER   LONDON   OSUSTON
LIBERTIES
Lambeth   Southwark   The Iſle of Dogges
HUNDRED
Greenwich
PART OF SUR... REY
PART OF KENT
Kingſton

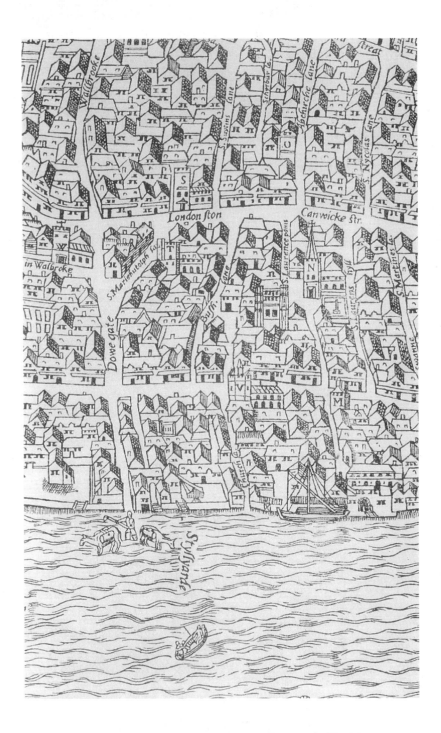

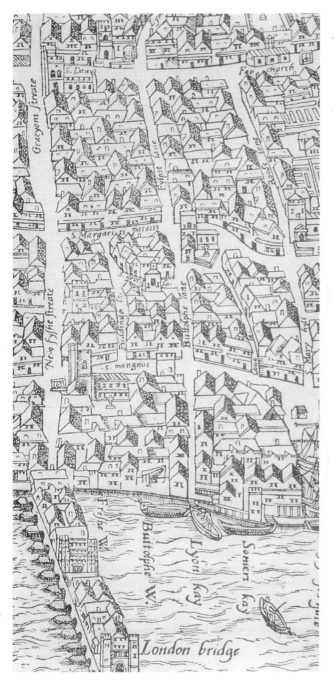

FIGURE 8 *Detail from the "Agas" map of London (drawn c. 1553–59, published c. 1604) shows the Eastcheap area just north of the Thames, described in further detail in John Stow's* Survey *(see p. 236). Although the map does not depict every dwelling, it provides a sense of Elizabethan London as a jumble of streets, alleys, and courtyards — a kind of rabbit warren.*

project offers a kind of early modern *Blue Guide* or travelers' handbook for a walking tour of London. But it is also a social and cultural history enlivened by the reminiscences of someone who had talked to old men who remembered Richard III (d. 1485), had lived through Elizabeth's entire reign, and would see James I come to the throne. Like Harrison, who worries over lost customs, Stow is concerned with preservation at a time when many buildings were being torn down and replaced, falling prey to the progressive ideologies of a turn-of-the-century market society. His is an elegaic archaeology, and his account of Candlewick Street Ward (see p. 236), *Henry IV, Part 1*'s Eastcheap locale, reveals his strategies for imprinting London's sites with social and cultural significance.

A drawing from Hugh Alley's *A Caveat for the City of London* (1598), which pictures thirteen of London's food markets, gives a close-up view of Eastcheap's cattle market (see Figure 9). An informer on malpractices for City authorities, Alley was a "projector" who hoped to establish himself as an enforcer of regulations that would protect consumers from wholesalers who played the market for easy profits (Archer, Barron, and Harding 15–27, 31–34). Although hardly photographically accurate, his drawing offers a lively view of closely packed houses with fretwork and finials and, on the ground floor, joints of meat set out for sale. The inscribed pillar names "engrossing" — the practice of buying goods with the intention of reselling — as the market's particular offense. As the site of profiteering associated with beef, Eastcheap is an especially appropriate place for Falstaff to reside, and its relation to Smithfield, where domestic animals were slaughtered and where heretics were burned, makes a resonant connection between the fat knight and the figure of the Protestant martyr, Sir John Oldcastle (see Chapter 6, "The Oldcastle Controversy"). And since hides and skins, the by-products of selling cattle and sheep for meat, were used by shoemakers, bookbinders, parchment makers, glovers, saddlers, cordwainers, purse-makers, girdlers and bottle-makers, Eastcheap and its environs were also central to London's commodity culture.

Henry IV, Part 1 makes pointed references to this world of getting and spending. In addition to specifically English commodities, such as gammons of bacon, races of ginger, bales of wool, and stockfish (a kind of dried cod), the play mentions Spanish leather, holland linen, and tapestry wall hangings (probably made from English wool but crafted on the Continent), and Falstaff drinks sack, a white wine imported from Spain, rather than English "small beer," or strong ale. Such traces of material culture reflect a changing economy, increasingly dependent on overseas trade, that brought wealth to a large "middling" class of merchants and retailers and contributed to the rise of professions, especially law and banking. Yet it would be a mis-

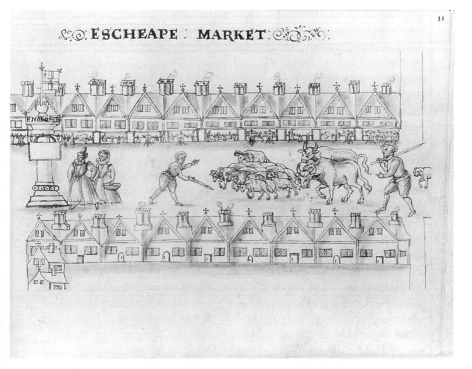

FIGURE 9 *This drawing of Eastcheap's Market is from Hugh Alley's* A Caveat for the City of London *(1598).*

take to assume that early modern Londoners experienced overwhelming economic prosperity, for the 1590s were the worst years of the century for its people. A deadly plague epidemic ravaged the city in 1593, bringing unemployment and homelessness to thousands, and 1594 saw the first of four successive harvest failures, causing severe inflation. From 1596 to 1598, the price of flour more than doubled, and overall food prices rose by 46 percent, a rate seventeen times faster than during the previous forty years. Furthermore, in the last fifteen years of Elizabeth's reign, armies were competing with the general population for consumables: enormous amounts went to provisioning troops and ships for campaigns on the Continent, on the Scots border, and in Ireland, where Tyrone's rebellion, which took nearly a decade to crush, cost two million pounds (Rappaport 13–14).

One response to these economic pressures was that foreigners, strangers, and vagrants became scapegoats for all the ills afflicting London: inflation, lack of food and housing, crippling unemployment, and escalating prices

(Archer, *Pursuit* 5). Both the Crown and the City imposed a number of restrictive vagrancy acts aimed not exclusively at the foreign population but also at "native vagrants" — those who had come to London from the provinces as well as "idlers" who earned their living by begging, thievery, cony-catching (gulling or cheating the unwary), prostitution — and playing. To many contemporaries, such "masterless men" threatened social norms. Not only did legislators ascribe a series of criminal abuses to vagrants, but writers of popular tracts as well as Puritan antitheatrical commentators promoted the image of a dangerous London counterculture. Although the most alarmist responses implied that inescapable moral and social evils lurked in every marketplace, street, and lane, most writers singled out brothels, theatres, and taverns or alehouses as the major locales of criminal activity. In crowding these venues into one space, *Henry IV, Part 1*'s tavern is ideally suited to embodying the subversive behaviors associated with all three.

Prostitution was one of the major types of organized crime in early modern London. One hundred brothels peppered the eastern and western wards of the City, extending across the river to Southwark's Liberties. Stow's description of the "Bear gardens and The Stew on the bank side" (p. 239) provides insight into the strict surveillance governing the trade, including the policing of women's bodies. Owners, for instance, were forbidden to "keep any woman that hath the perilous infirmities of burning" — that is, one with venereal diseases. Tellingly, Stow does not mention the great public amphitheatres — the Rose, the Swan, and, in 1599, the Globe — which also occupied prominent positions on Bankside near the bear baiting arena, nor does he mention the Theatre and the Curtain, both located north of the City in Moorfields, also one of the Liberties. Although his preference for celebrating traditional customs rather than contemporary cultural practices clearly reflects a nostalgic bent (see Manley, "Of Sites"; Archer, "Nostalgia"), his silence concerning the theatre seems curious, especially given the numerous voices raised against plays, players, and spectators as well as those who spoke in their defense.

Theatre in London: Sites and Controversies

Drama, of course, had flourished in the City, in innyards and private playhouses, for some decades. But the public playhouses, standing beyond London's municipal authority and arising at a time when traditional hierarchies were breaking down, were a new development. Whereas scholars have always focused on the physical characteristics of these buildings, the histories of the companies who played there, the makeup of their audiences, and the circumstances of sixteenth- and early-seventeenth-century performances (see McDonald), recent work has speculated on the theatre's ideological role in the culture and the function of plays as part of an entertainment industry. Although opinions vary, theatre historians and literary or cultural historians agree that the theatres were a site of cultural contradiction. Marginal in location, they were institutionally central to London's commercial milieu — in a position, as Jean Howard writes, "to embody and negotiate among a variety of competing ideological interests" (*Stage* 12). In terms of the history play, for instance, putting representations of monarchy on a public stage stripped away their sacred aura, making it possible to alter spectator-subjects' relations to royalty (see Howard, *Stage;* Montrose; Kastan, "Proud Majesty"). If the theatre's physical location outside regulatory jurisdiction enabled it to be singled out for attack, it was also the case that it came under surveillance precisely because it was central to the culture. Just as contradictorily, much of what we know about the theatre's cultural impact comes from those who rail against it. At the risk of drawing an ahistorical analogy between early modern popular theatre and today's mass culture entertainments, it is as though the only surviving records of film and television productions (besides the texts themselves) were those documenting their detrimental effects on the viewing public.

From the Lord Mayor's letter to John Whitgift, the Archbishop of Canterbury (p. 241), to the tracts of a Puritan activist, Stephen Gosson, this body of writing circulates common themes: the theatres promote disorder and corrupt youth; frequented by "the worst sorts of people," they exhibit "wanton and profane devices" and are antithetical to "sermons and other Christian exercises." Dedicated to the "Gentlewomen Citizens of London," Gosson's *School of Abuse* (1579) (p. 243) warns women that theatregoing marks them irrevocably. It is, he claims, an easy progress from theatre to tavern to brothel — and to being "noted" as a whore. In his later *Plays Confuted in Five Actions* (1582), Gosson calls theatres "snares unto fair women . . . full of secret adultery" and condemns both the playhouse practice of cross-dressing and the effeminizing effects of spectacle, which "soften[s] the hearts of men," teaching vice, not virtue. Rebutting the notion that plays stage the culture's worst abuses with a humanist argument, Thomas Heywood's *Apology for Actors* (1612) (p. 247) maintains that plays instruct and delight, are "an ornament to the City," and work to "refine the English tongue."

In this discourse of attack and defense, there seems to be little room for a middle ground between Heywood's image of theatre's ability to make "the ignorant more apprehensive" and the Puritan view of a "market of bawdry" that threatens a Christian commonwealth with the worst excesses of Rome and the devil. Significantly, in distancing himself from "licentious" players as well as "lascivious shows, scurrilous jests, or scandalous invectives," Heywood (himself a playwright) acknowledges some grounds for the antitheatrical position. Overall, however, the debate's polarized terms demonstrate that both playhouses and players occupied a distinctive position in cultural memory. Furthermore, both sides figure the theatre as a site for playing out a larger cultural debate between secular and religious authorities over the control of London's citizenry, a control especially directed at all who, in crossing social boundaries, refused to stay in their place.

In conflating theatre, brothel, and tavern or alehouse as haunts for an idle, itinerant population (one of the standard arguments used to justify civic action against all three (Archer, *Pursuit*, 206–07), the antitheatrical debate coincides with a popular rogue literature that warned Elizabethan readers of another notorious criminal pursuit, thievery. A 1567 act against pickpocketing speaks of "a certain Kind of evil-disposed Persons, commonly called Cutpurses or Pick-purses who do confeder together, making among themselves as it were a Brotherhood or Fraternity of an Art or Mystery, to live idly by the Secret Spoil of the good and true Subjects of the Realm" (8 Elizabeth I, rpt. in Hughes and Larkin). Smart's Quay, near Billingsgate market, was the home of a school for pickpockets (Weinstein 47), and Eastcheap's tavern inhabitants, although perhaps not quite so well organized, seem to have been part of just such a school or fraternity, which had its own articles, or code of honor (see Dekker, *O Per Se O;* Harman; see also the Segar selection from *Honor Military and Civil* on p. 336).

As though parodying Harrison's "Of Degrees of People in the Commonwealth," Thomas Dekker's *Lantern and Candlelight, or The Bellman's Second Night Walk* (1609) maps out an elaborate hierarchy within the vagrant population, listing the various malpractices through which its members gulled the public. His first chapter, "Of Canting" (p. 249), which lifts the vagabond idiom into linguistic history, provides a context for *Henry IV, Part 1*'s colloquialisms, its "strange tongues" and "gross terms." Describing the various types of vagabonds as though they were "tribes" from an exotic foreign land, Dekker appears to be imitating travel accounts of the period. Although other chapters focus on particular abuses, at times amounting to an instruction manual on how best to rob, cheat, and steal, neither Dekker's *Lantern* nor Robert Greene's *Second Part of Conny-Catching* (1597) is a serious documentation of London's organized crime. Rather, much like those about whom they wrote, they were taking advantage of a marketplace niche. Just as the cutpurse and the thief found a high concentration of available targets in London and its environs, the "rogue writers" were in the business of providing entertaining narratives that, like present-day tabloids, sensationalized both particular types of individual criminals and their accomplishments (Sharpe 114–16). For these writers as for the antitheatrical commentators, "caveat" (beware) was the watchword for those who, by entering London's underworld establishments, ran the risk of consorting with its transient communities of criminals and vagrants.

Alehouse and Tavern

If membership in a guild gave London tradesmen a sense of belonging as well as an identity (see Rappaport; Archer, *Pursuit*), there was another sense in which to be a Londoner in the 1590s was to be a vagrant, for many were detached from their homes, defined as a particular shire, county, town, or village. According to Patricia Fumerton, such a vagrant identity represented a position of experimentation, a way of configuring the individual outside of the fixed, secure boundaries of place. She argues that the alehouse was a response to vagrancy, a space of mobility and freedom where one could become part of a "family" without being tied down to the duties and disciplines of a domestic household. Moreover, home and alehouse were contradictory, opposed locales competing with each other across gendered lines. Whereas the household was a feminine stronghold, the alehouse, even when (as was often the case) run by a woman, was a predominantly male space (see Figures 10 and 11).

As the site of a new, more liberally permissive world of public drinking traversed by all classes (Clark 111–15), the alehouse represented a place where stomachs could be filled on the cheap and where one could feel "at home" but not be *at* home. Collapsing alehouse and tavern (a more upscale venue offering wine) under one roof, Shakespeare constructs just such a prodigal locale for both Falstaff and Hal: a "home-away-from-home" inhabited by members of London's criminal underworld where Falstaff can booze around the clock and where Hal, freed from the restraints of Westminster's domestic and political duties, can join a "family of vagrancy" encompassing a wide range of social backgrounds. Often identified (though never named) as the Boar's Head, Shakespeare's Eastcheap tavern may allude to a real Boar's Head (one of six London taverns by that name) that served as a theatre or "itinerant playhouse" long before the public amphitheatres gave companies of actors spaces of their own in which to play (Gurr, *Shakespearean Stage* 117; "Authority"). If so, *Henry IV, Part 1* traces a history of playing venues, spaces Shakespeare's company may at one time have considered a kind of home.

Just as Shakespeare's play evokes the all-male or homosocial economy shared by the early modern stage and the early modern alehouse, present-

'Tis Merrie vvhen Gossips meete.

NEWLY ENLARGED, With diuers merry Songes, sung by a Fidlers Boy.

Widdow *Wif* *Mayde*.

LONDON, Printed by *W.W.* Deane and are to b...

FIGURE 10 (left) *This drawing, "The Laws of Drinking" (1617), shows an upstairs room in which well-dressed gentlemen converse (apparently refreshing themselves at the "wells" of classical thought, as the banners surrounding them signify) and a lower chamber, with a rude table and benches, for the "ruder" classes. The classical "streams" are opposed to the sewers of Puddle Wharf, one of the major docks at the Thames. Note the alehouse sign, which resembles a Tudor rose.*

FIGURE 11 (above) *This frontispiece from Samuel Rowland's* 'Tis Merry When Gossips Meet *(1602), which shows a widow, a wife, and a maid meeting to converse in a tavern, suggests that even fashionable women patronized taverns. Here, they appear to sit in a private room.*

day stagings of *Henry IV, Part 1* represent the tavern milieu as a sort of idyllic male retreat (see Figures 12 and 13). Perhaps most richly and nostalgically detailed in Orson Welles's *Chimes at Midnight*, that image is appropriated by Kenneth Branagh's *Henry V* (1989), which uses flashbacks of *Henry IV*'s tavern scene to mark the distance between the "wild prince" and the "warrior king" in a film that rehabilitates the image of male heroism for a post-Vietnam, post-Falklands generation. When drawn forward into the present, as in Gus van Sant's *My Own Private Idaho* (1991) — in part an homage to Welles's film that raids many of its shot setups — van Sant's Boar's Head realizes, perhaps even more tellingly than Shakespeare's representation, the historical contours of its early modern contexts. Organized around a Falstaffian father figure named Bob, van Sant's film centers on the homoerotic attachments of a group of homeless, itinerant hustlers in the recognizably postmodern landscape of an urban drug culture (see Taubin).

Many critics have considered Falstaff as the "king" of Eastcheap's tavern community and as someone who is both father and mother. By occupying all of these positions, he to some extent displaces Mistress Quickly as the establishment's ruler and mutes the independent status of her historical counterparts. Although such businesses were usually family-run and were rarely a one-woman show, in a society with fairly limited economic opportunities for lower-class women, managing an alehouse or a tavern provided one of the few avenues for achieving social recognition or advancement. At the other end of the scale, prostitution was the other "mystery," or occupation, open to women. Alehouse keepers often rented chambers where the more mobile prostitutes operated, and Doll Tearsheet appears to be such a "customer." Although ballad literature circulates the image of the attractive alewife who plied customers not only with drink but, on occasion, with more intimate favors, stage Quicklys seem to be women "of a certain age," in direct contrast to younger and more inviting Dolls. A seventeenth-century drawing portrays the stereotype (see Figure 14), as does the ballad of the infamous Elinor Rumming (an alehouse keeper during Henry VIII's reign), which describes her as "all bowsy, comely crinkled, wondrously wrinkled" — much like Margaret Rutherford, Orson Welles's Quickly. Repeat-

◁ FIGURES 12 AND 13 *Two contrasting depictions of Eastcheap's tavern. Figure 12 (top), from the English Shakespeare Company's production* The Henrys, *shows Hal (Michael Pennington) and the others listening to John Woodvine's Falstaff (with wooden dagger) recount his exploits at Gadshill (2.4). Figure 13 (bottom), a production still from Orson Welles's 1965–66 film,* Chimes at Midnight, *features (from left) Welles as Falstaff, Margaret Rutherford as Mistress Quickly, and Jeanne Moreau as Doll Tearsheet.*

edly, popular literature emphasized the alewife's strong personality and depicted her as a larger-than-life figure, often a shrew who kept her husband under her thumb and who, like Quickly, was caught between the need to extend credit in bad times in order to attract business and the risk of being cheated by customers (Clark 111–15).

Women in *Henry IV, Part 1:*
Wives, Rebels, and Others

Although Quickly's knowledge of "harlotry players" aligns her with those historical women who attended the public playhouses while Doll resembles the prostitutes who visited the theatre to solicit customers, both are Shake-

FIGURE 14 *This drawing, attributed to David Loggan (c. 1650), shows "Mother Louse," an old-style alehouse keeper, probably from Oxfordshire. She holds two ale measures; her "arms" (shown at upper right) are three lice, topped by an ale measure.*

speare's inventions (see Howard, *Stage;* Gurr, *Playgoing;* Cook, *Players*). Unlike Lady Percy and Lady Mortimer, they stand outside of patriarchal chronicle history. Nonetheless, *Henry IV, Part I*'s women figures share representational characteristics that draw them together. Both the tavern's common women and the nobles' wives appear in locales — Eastcheap and Wales — associated with rebellion as well as with the illicit powers of female sexuality and theatrical performance (Rackin, "Foreign," 80–84; Highley; Wikander). In dramatizing a spectrum of positions, from the tavern's "loose" women (though Quickly maintains that she is "an honest man's wife") to the nobles' wives, the play points to a broad range of texts that attempted to prescribe and regulate the "place" of women in the culture (see Figure 15, p. 256). On the one hand, early modern conduct books on marriage map out the specific duties and behaviors of wives (as well as husbands); on the other, misogynist treatises portray women as dangerous gadabouts addicted to vanity, ultimate consumers whose wanton behavior spelled man's ruin. What both kinds of texts share is a tendency to construct "man" as a stable entity endowed with positive attributes and "woman" as his inconstant, negative opposite.

One of the most popular marriage manuals, John Dod and Robert Cleaver's *A Godly Form of Household Government* (1621) (p. 255), envisions a symmetrical interdependence between husband and wife based on love and, above all, mutual respect. To oversimplify somewhat, it also offers a strict division between public and private spheres of behavior in which the husband acts as hunter-gatherer, the wife as saver and keeper. Such a strict division of labor, however, may simply represent a desirable economic ideal, for even the most "well-governed" English wives were by no means totally enclosed within domestic space (see Powell 175). Furthermore, Dod and Cleaver's treatise aims less at being prescriptive than at describing the best model of bourgeois marriage as they knew it (Hutson 21–24; see also Belsey 159–60). Just as Lady Percy and Lady Mortimer function primarily to construct their husbands' attributes, so too with Dod and Cleaver's view of marriage, in which the woman's role supports concepts of masculinity central to the culture. Yet if such notions offer one context for the ideals of marriage lying behind its stage representation, it is also the case that both women risk being configured outside these ideals. When Kate Percy demands to know Hotspur's business and threatens to break his little finger (2.3), she behaves like the scold or shrew of misogynist literature. In the theatre, this scene is often played for its sexual innuendoes, much like the so-called wooing scene between Petruchio and another Kate in Shakespeare's *Taming of the Shrew* (2.1). And in Wales, Lady Mortimer becomes an eroticized figure similar to the "froward" creatures condemned by misogynist writers.

Whereas John Stow's recounting of rules governing brothels represents one pole of a discourse designed to police women's bodies and Stephen Gosson's antitheatrical polemic another, Joseph Swetnam's *Arraignment of Lewd, Idle, Froward, and Unconstant Women* (1615) (p. 264) offers further evidence of what became, in the latter decades of the sixteenth century and well into the seventeenth, a full-blown controversy about women (see Henderson and McManus). Like most misogynistic literature, Swetnam's pamphlet attempts to coerce men as well as women into exceptionally well-defined roles. The biblical notion of woman as helpmeet to man grounds Swetnam's treatise, automatically placing women in a subordinate position. But in figuring himself as idle and his book as a pastime, he betrays an obsession with pleasure that somewhat undermines his moral project. For him, not only do all women offer the same pleasure but they are figured as sexually open commodities that can be exchanged for money. Wanton, vain, and extravagant, women are portrayed as *naturally* incontinent; they represent a threat to a strictly masculine economy of pleasure that eventually emasculates (Purkiss 70–79). Just as a wife's expenditure of money means that she is neither virtuous nor properly "enclosed," her open mouth, with its nagging, scolding tongue, also identifies her sexual openness (see Boose). In figuring woman as a dangerous "other," Swetnam's treatise provides a context that embraces not only *Henry IV, Part 1*'s alehouse women, one of whom circulates her body all too freely while the other (Quickly) speaks indecorous malapropisms, but also its noble wives, one who sharply questions her husband's betrayal of marital duty, the other a seductress whose ravishing language highlights masculine sensuality and uxoriousness, traits condemned by early modern sexual mythology (Rackin, "Foreign Country" 172).

Wales

If Eastcheap's tavern is constructed as a "feminized" space devoted to fleshly pleasures, Wales is even more blatantly configured as a country of "the other" — of magic, prophecy, and witchcraft (usually, in the period, associated with women; see Dolan 171–236). The home of the rebels, Wales is also the seat of "true" legitimacy, in the person of Mortimer, and stands in direct contrast to the tavern, where Hal's legitimacy is called into question. Though Wales had been annexed to England by acts of Parliament in 1536 and 1543, at the time *Henry IV, Part 1* was written it was still conceived as a foreign land. Not only did the Welsh consider themselves the heirs and descendants of an ancient race who were Britain's rightful owners, but even after the failure of Glendower's rebellion, they cast their political ambitions within a secularized messianic tradition that expected the return of Arthur, its mythic hero, and refused to acknowledge England as their overlord (Williams 72–75, 130; see also Morgan, Rowse).

Since political as well as racial tensions characterized Welsh-English relations, and since sixteenth-century Welsh writers worked to capture power within English politics rather than insisting on their distinct national identity, one would not expect to find materials written in English that are favorable or sympathetic to the Welsh. Instead, early modern images of Wales come from those who had colonized it. Holinshed's representation of Glendower as someone who believed in prophecies reflects a stereotypical view of his desire to revive Welsh destiny, and Shakespeare's play, which debunks his preoccupations with magic and astrological signs, perhaps glances at a popular Catholicism considered suspicious by Protestant Englishmen. Wales was also associated, through similar struggles against English rule, with Ireland, whose rebel leader Tyrone much resembled Glendower (Canny 97–99, Highley 99). Moreover, Holinshed's account of the Welshwomen's violent assault on dead Englishmen's bodies (p. 270) resembles similar tales of atrocities attributed to Irishwomen (Palmer). Fusing images of disorderly women and Welsh rebels, and blaming "barbarous" Welshwomen in part for why the Welsh were so intractable, Holinshed's language fits into a pattern by which colonial powers and racial oppressors turn a particular group into "the other" and use resulting stereotypes to justify their behavior. When Holinshed first mentions the women mutilating the corpses, he passes over it, just as Westmoreland does in *Henry IV, Part 1* (1.1.43–46), but when it recurs after a later battle, the *Chronicles* includes a more precise description (attributed to Abraham Fleming) of what amounts to a ritual castration in which the woman "assume the kind of sexual dominance that the culture reserved for men while making it appear as if their male victims are sodomizing themselves" (Highley 102–3; see also Rackin, "Foreign Country" 82–86).

The barbarism Holinshed attributes to Welshwomen extended to the Welsh language. Addressing the "great Discord Variance Debate Division Murmur and Sedition" between England and Wales, Henry VIII outlawed the Welsh language in 1536, calling it "a Speech nothing like, nor consonant to the natural Mother Tongue within this Realm" (27 Henry 8 c. 26; repr. in Bowen 75). In spite of that prohibition, however, Welsh was spoken on the stage. Usually it was represented as "bad" or "deformed" English, an idiom of the conquerors' language that satirized Welsh speakers' sensitivity about their inability to pronounce consonants properly and their confusion of feminine and masculine pronouns. Parson Hugh and Doctor Caius in Shakespeare's *Merry Wives of Windsor* (1597) exemplify one comic stereotype of the stage Welshman. *Henry V*'s Fluellen embodies the passionate sense of honor and patriotism and the obsession with genealogy associated with the Welsh. Usually, too, stage Welsh speakers are male. An exception is the Welsh Gentlewoman who is also Sir Walter Whorehound's whore in Thomas Middleton's *A Chaste Maid in Cheapside* (1630). Her inability to understand a wooer who addresses her in Latin and assumes that she speaks Hebrew offers a more decidedly comic instance of the Mortimers' difficulties. Whereas the dialects spoken by *Henry V*'s Welsh, English, Irish, and Scots captains bolster class as well as national distinctions, in *Henry IV, Part 1*, language also functions as a primary marker of gender. Although the carefully dramatized language in which women speak often takes away or mutes the sounds of "real" women's voices (especially the scolding talk with which women accused one another in courts of law [Gowing, "Gender"]), *Henry IV, Part 1* does not conform to the usual practice of "deforming" Lady Mortimer's Welsh but instead insists on *hearing* the "pure" Welsh language.

That language is *textually* represented only in stage directions — "The Lady speaks in Welsh" or "Glendower speaks to her in Welsh, and she answers him in the same" — but the "forbidden" language does appear in present-day prompt books. In Royal Shakespeare Company practice, the Lady's speech, as well as her song, relies on a 1964 prompt book which has been copied right up to the 1990s (see p. 272). Even so, readers unfamiliar with Welsh as well as theatre audiences must, as Phyllis Rackin observes, rely on Glendower's translation ("Foreign Country" 86). By casting (but not *writing*) the Lady's lines in a foreign tongue, Shakespeare excludes her, like *Henry V*'s French Princess Katherine, from a linguistic community that includes all of the male characters in *Henry IV, Part 1* as well as those in *Henry V*, with the exception of Le Fer, the captured French soldier. However, while Princess Katherine learns the conqueror's English and so becomes crucial to constructing Henry V as a sovereign male subject, Mortimer — supposedly England's "true heir" — says that he will learn Welsh in order to understand his wife. As Rackin suggests, abandoning the King's English, "the language of patriarchal authority and of history," suspends him in a theatrical world, one represented by antitheatrical polemic as potentially emasculating ("Foreign Country" 85–86). As configured in *Henry IV, Part 1*, the matter of Wales draws together the dangers that female power and authority represented to late-sixteenth-century culture.

Although the regional, national, gender, and class divisions that trace through Shakespeare's play are not so irrevocably marked out in late-twentieth-century England, it is still the case that economic distinctions sharply divide city from country, north from south, and that old enmities between regions once considered "nations" prevail. For the most part, too, the linguistic distinctions that undoubtedly identified the players in Shakespeare's company, those "native vagrants" who came to London from various parts of the country, are wiped away on today's stages, where all but "low" comic figures speak in Received Standard Pronunciation, a "stage English" which suggests that something called a United Kingdom does indeed exist. Those early modern distinctions, however, are not entirely forgotten. In the English Shakespeare Company's *Henry IV, Part 1*, the actors speak in various idioms and accents, serving to remind theatre audiences that the territory or land called England is still made up of diverse and distinctive local cultures.

→ **WILLIAM HARRISON**

From The Description of England   *1587*
Of Degrees of People in the Commonwealth of England

CHAPTER V

We in England divide our people commonlie into foure sorts, as gentlemen, citizens or burgesses, yeomen, which are artificers, or laborers. Of gentlemen the first and chéefe (next the king) be the prince, dukes, marquesses, earls, viscounts, and barons: and these are called gentlemen of the greater sort, or (as our common usage of speech is) lords and noblemen: and next unto them be knights, esquiers, and last of all they that are simplie called gentlemen; so that in effect our gentlemen are divided into their conditions, wherof in this chapter I will make particular rehearsall.

The title of prince dooth peculiarlie belong with us to the kings eldest sonne, who is called prince of Wales, and is the heire apparent to the crown; as in France the kings eldest sonne hath the title of Dolphine, and is named peculiarlie Monsieur. So that the prince is so termed of the Latine word Princeps, sith he is (as I may call him) the cheefe or principall next the king. The kings yoonger sonnes be but gentlemen by birth (till they have received creation or donation from their father of higher estate, as to be either visconts, earles, or dukes) and called after their names, as lord Henrie, or lord Edward, with the addition of the word Grace, properlie assigned to the king

William Harrison, "Of Degrees of People in the Commonwealth of England" and "Of Their Apparell and Attire," from *The Description of England* in volume 1 of Raphael Holinshed, *The Chronicles of England, Scotland, and Ireland* (London, 1587; rpt. London: J. Johnson et al., 1808) 263–77; 289–90.

and prince, and now also by custome conveied to dukes, archbishops, and (as some saie) to marquesses and their wives.

The title of duke commeth also of the Latine word Dux, à ducendo,[1] bicause of his valor and power over the armie: in times past a name of office due to the emperour, consull, or chéefe governour of the whole armie in the Romane warres: but now a name of honor, although perished in England, whose ground will not long beare one duke at once; but if there were manie as in time past, or as there be now earles, I doo not thinke but that they would florish and prosper well inough.

In old time he onelie was called marquesse, Qui habuit terram limitaneam,[2] a marching[3] province upon the enimies countries, and thereby bound to kéepe and defend the frontiers. But that also is changed in common use, and reputed for a name of great honor next unto the duke, even over counties, and sometimes small cities, as the prince is pleased to bestow it.

The name of earle likewise was among the Romans a name of office, who had Comites sacri palatij, comites ærarij, comites stabuli, comites patrimonij, largitionum, scholarum, commerciorum, and such like.[4] [Harrison provides a further history of the title of earl and discusses the title of viscount.]

The baron, whose degrée answered to the dignitie of a senator in Rome, is such a frée lord as hath a lordship or baronie, whereof he beareth his name, & hath diverse knights or fréeholders holding of him, who with him did serve the king in his wars, and held théir tenures in Baronia, that is, for performance of such service. [A further history of the word *baron;* how the title may, like *lord,* be given to a person with his office.]

Unto this place I also referre our bishops, who are accounted honourable, called lords, and hold the same roome in the parlement house with the barons, albeit for honour sake the right hand of the prince is given unto them, and whose countenances in time past were much more glorious than at this present it is, bicause those lustie prelats sought after earthlie estimation and authoritie with farre more diligence than after the lost shéepe of Christ, of which they had small regard, as men being otherwise occupied and void of leisure to attend upon the same. Howbeit in these daies their estate remaineth no lesse reverend than before, and the more vertuous they are

---

[1] à ducendo: leading.   [2] **Qui habuit terram limitaneam:** who live at the borders of the lands — that is, in areas such as the marches, or border counties.   [3] **marching:** border.   [4] **Comites sacri palatij . . . and such like:** degrees of civil administrators: those who assisted the emperor in exercising his peculiar rights (*comites sacri palatij*), those who managed the treasury (*comites ærarij*), acted as masters of the horse (*comites stabuli,* whence "constable"), managed the emperor's private property (*comites patrimonij*) or his public revenues (*comites largitionum*), administered the imperial guard (*comites scholarum*) or trade (*comites commerciorum*).

that be of this calling, the better are they estéemed with high and low. They reteine also the ancient name (lord) still, although it be not a little impugned by such as love either to heare of change of all things, or can abide no superiours. For notwithstanding it be true, that in respect of function, the office of the eldership is equallie distributed betwéene the bishop and the minister,[5] yet for civill governements sake, the first have more authoritie given unto them by kings and princes, to the end that the rest maie thereby be with more ease reteined within a limited compasse of uniformitie, than otherwise they would be, if ech one were suffered to walke in his owne course. [Many wish to abolish the word *lord* as it refers to bishops, to remove bishops from civil authority, and to reform the church.] But whither am I digressed from my discourse of bishops, whose estates doo daily decaie, & suffer some diminution? Herein neverthelesse their case is growne to be much better than before, for whereas in times past the cleargie men were feared bicause of their authoritie and severe government under the prince, now are they beloved generallie for their painefull diligence dailie shewed in their functions and callings, except peradventure of some hungrie wombes, that covet to plucke & snatch at the loose ends of their best commodities; with whom it is (as the report goeth) a common guise, when a man is to be preferred to an ecclesiasticall living, what part thereof he will first forgo and part with to their use. Finallie, how it standeth with the rest of the clergie for their places of estate, I neither can tell nor greatlie care to know. [In former times, the clergy were set above earls and barons, but at the present time, their authority is limited. Harrison praises the learning of English clergymen.]

Dukes, marquesses, earles, visconts, and barons, either be created of the prince, or come to that honor by being the eldest sonnes or highest in succession to their parents. For the eldest sonne of a duke during his fathers life is an erle, the eldest sonne of an erle is a baron, or sometimes a viscont, according as the creation is. The creation I call the originall donation and condition of the honour given by the prince for good service doone by the first ancestor, with some advancement, which with the title of that honour is alwaies given to him and his heires males onelie. The rest of the sonnes of the nobilitie by the rigor of the law be but esquiers: yet in common spéech all dukes and marquesses sonnes, and earles eldest sonnes be called lords, the which name commonlie dooth agrée to none of lower degrée than barons, yet by law and use these be not esteemed barons.

The baronie or degrée of lords dooth answer to the degree of senators of Rome (as I said) and the title of nobilitie (as we use to call it in England) to

---

[5] **bishop . . . minister:** Harrison refers readers to 1 Samuel 15:30 and 1 Kings 8:13.

the Romane Patricij.[6] Also in England no man is commonlie created baron, except he maie dispend of yearelie revenues a thousand pounds, or so much as maie fullie mainteine & beare out his countenance and port. But visconts, erles, marquesses, and dukes excéed them according to the proportion of their degrée & honour. But though by chance he or his sonne have lesse, yet he kéepeth this degree: but if the decaie be excessive and not able to mainteine the honour, as Senatores Romani were amoti à senatu:[7] so sometimes they are not admitted to the upper house in the parlement although they keepe the name of lord still, which can not be taken from them upon anie such occasion. The most of these names have descended from the French invention, in whose histories we shall read of them eight hundred yeares passed.

[Following the French example, the Emperor Otto bestowed titles on those who had served in his wars. Harrison explains those titles, no longer used.]

Knights be not borne, neither is anie man a knight by succession, no not the king or prince: but they are made either before the battell, to incourage them the more to adventure & trie their manhood: or after the battell ended, as an advancement for their courage and prowesse alreadie shewed (& then are they called Milites;) or out of the warres for some great service doone, or for the singular vertues which doo appeare in them, and then are they named Equites aurati,[8] as common custome intendeth. They are made either by the king himselfe, or by his commission and roiall authoritie given for the same purpose: or by his lieutenant in the warres. . . . Sometime diverse ancient gentlemen, burgesses, and lawiers, are called unto knighthood by the prince, and neverthelesse refuse to take that state upon them, for which they are of custome punished by a fine, that redoundeth unto his cofers, and to saie truth, is oftentimes more profitable unto him than otherwise their service should be, if they did yeeld unto knighthood. And this also is a cause, wherefore there be manie in England able to dispend a knights living, which never come unto that countenance, and by their owne consents. [Harrison compares this practice to that of Rome and cites the manner of dubbing knights at present, following the French custom.]

At the coronation of a king or queene, there be other knights made with longer and more curious ceremonies, called knights of the bath. But how soever one be dubbed or made knight, his wife is by and by called madame or ladie, so well as the barons wife; he himselfe having added to his name in common appellation this syllable Sir, which is the title whereby we call our

---

[6] **Patricij:** patricians.   [7] **amoti à senatu:** banished from the Senate.   [8] **Equites aurati:** knights provided with gold, as in the gold spurs that marked their rank.

knights in England. His wife also of courtesie so long as she liveth is called my ladie, although she happen to marie with a gentleman or man of meane calling, albeit that by the cōmon law she hath no such prerogative. If hir first husband also be of better birth than hir second, though this later likewise be a knight, yet in that she pretendeth a privilege to loose no honor through courtesie yéelded to hir sex, she will be named after the most honorable or worshipfull of both, which is not séene elsewhere.

The other order of knighthood in England, and the most honorable is that of the garter, instituted by king Edward the third, who after he had gained manie notable victories, taken king Iohn of France, and king Iames of Scotland (and kept them both prisoners in the Tower of London at one time) expelled king Henrie of Castile the bastard out of his realme, and re-stored Don Petro unto it (by the helpe of the prince of Wales and duke of Aquitaine his eldest sonne called the Blacke prince) he then invented this societie of honour, and made a choise out of his owne realme and dominions, and throughout all christendome of the best, most excellent and renowmed persons in all vertues and honour, and adorned them with that title to be knights of his order, giving them a garter garnished with gold and pretious stones, to weare dailie on the left leg onlie: also a kirtle, gowne, cloke, chaperon,[9] collar, and other solemne and magnificent apparell, both of stuffe and fashion exquisite & heroicall to weare at high feasts, & as to so high and princelie an order apperteineth. [Harrison mentions the knights of the round table but dismisses King Arthur's legend as "invention"; instead, preferring "a true description of such ancient actions as were performed in deed," he recounts the origins of the Order of the Garter.]

The order of the garter therefore was devised in the time of king Edward the third, and (as some write) upon this occasion. The quéenes maiestie then living, being departed from his presence the next waie toward hir lodging, he following soone after happened to find hir garter, which slacked by chance and so fell from hir leg, unespied in the throng by such as attended upon hir. His groomes & gentlemen also passed by it, disdaining to stoope and take up such a triflé: but he knowing the owner, commanded one of them to staie and reach it up to him. Why and like your grace (saieth a gentleman) it is but some womans garter that hath fallen from hir as she followed the quéenes maiestie. What soever it be (quoth the king) take it up and give it me. So when he had received the garter, he said to such as stood about him: You my maisters doo make small account of this blue garter here (and therewith held it out) but if God lend me life for a few moneths, I will make the proudest of you all to reverence the like. And even upon this slen-

___

[9] **kirtle . . . chaperon:** kirtle, a tunic; chaperon, a hood.

der occasion he gave himselfe to the devising of this order. Certes I have not read of anie thing, that having had so simple a beginning hath growne in the end to so great honour and estimation. But to proceed. After he had studied awhile about the performance of his devise, and had set downe such orders as he himselfe invented concerning the same, he proclaimed a roiall feast to be holden at Windsore, whither all his nobilitie resorted with their ladies, where he published his institution, and foorthwith invested an appointed number into the afore said fellowship, whose names insue, himselfe being the sovereigne and principall of that companie. [A list of those knights assembled by Edward III at the institution of the Garter ceremonies. The order of election; preparations for installing a Garter Knight; the cloth given to and the apparel worn by various degrees of nobility. The four degrees of reproach which inhibit a person from entering into the order: heresy lawfully proved; high treason; flight from battle; "riot and prodigal excess of expenses." Rituals of offering, burial and degrading for Garter Knights. The motto, "Honi soit qui mal y pense" ("Shamed be he who thinks evil of it").]

There is yet an other order of knights in England called knights Bannerets, who are made in the field with the ceremonie of cutting awaie the point of his penant of armes, and making it as it were a banner, so that being before but a bacheler knight, he is now of an higher degree, and allowed to displaie his armes in a banner, as barrons doo. Howbeit these knights are never made but in the warres, the kings standard being unfolded.

Esquire (which we call commonlie squire) is a French word, and so much in Latine as Scutiger vel armiger, and such are all those which beare armes, or armoires, testimonies of their race from whence they be descended. They were at the first costerels or bearers of the armes of barons, or knights, & thereby being instructed in martiall knowledge, had that name for a dignitie given to distinguish them from common souldiers called Gregarij milites when they were together in the field.

Gentlemen be those whome their race and bloud, or at the least their vertues doo make noble and knowne. The Latines call them Nobiles & generosos, as the French do Nobles or Gentlehommes. [The etymology of the term *gentleman* traced to Rome.]

Moreover as the king dooth dubbe knights, and createth the barons and higher degrees, so gentlemen whose ancestors are not knowen to come in with William duke of Normandie (for of the Saxon races yet remaining we now make none accompt, much lesse of the British issue) doo take their beginning in England, after this manner in our times. Who soever studieth the lawes of the realme, who so abideth in the universitie giving his mind to his booke, or professeth physicke and the liberall sciences, or beside his service in the roome of a capteine in the warres, or good counsell given at home, whereby his common-wealth is benefited, can live without manuell labour, and thereto is able and will beare the port, charge, and countenance of a gentleman, he shall for monie have a cote and armes bestowed upon him by heralds (who in the charter of the same doo of custome pretend antiquitie and service, and manie gaie things) and thereunto being made so good cheape be called master, which is the title that men give to esquiers and gentlemen, and reputed for a gentleman ever after. Which is so much the lesse to be disalowed of, for that the prince dooth loose nothing by it, the gentleman being so much subiect to taxes and publike paiments as is the yeoman or husbandman, which he likewise dooth beare the gladlier for the saving of his reputation. Being called also to the warres (for with the government of the common-wealth he medleth litle) what soever it cost him, he will both arraie & arme himselfe accordinglie, and shew the more manly courage, and all the tokens of the person which he representeth. No man hath hurt by it but himselfe, who peradventure will go in wider buskens[10] than his legs will beare, or as our proverbe saith, now and then beare a bigger saile than his boat is able to susteine.

Certes the making of new gentlemen bred great strife sometimes amongst the Romans, I meane when those which were Novi homines,[11] were more allowed of for their vertues newlie séene and shewed, than the old smell of ancient race, latelie defaced by the cowardise & evill life of their nephues & defendants[12] could make the other to be. But as envie hath no affinitie with iustice and equitie, so it forceth not what language the malicious doo give out, against such as are exalted for their wisdomes. This neverthelesse is generallie to be reprehended in all estates of gentilitie, and which in short time will turne to the great ruine of our countrie, and that is the usuall sending of noblemens & meane gentlemens sonnes into Italie, from whence they bring home nothing but meere atheisme, infidelitie, vicious conversation, & ambitious and proud behaviour, wherby it commeth to passe that they returne far worsse men than they went out. A gentleman at this present is newlie come out of Italie, who went thither an earnest protestant, but comming home he could saie after this manner: Faith & truth is to be kept, where no losse or hinderance of a further purpose is susteined by holding of the same; and forgivenesse onelie to be shewed when full revenge is made. Another no lesse forward than he, at his returne from thence could ad thus much; He is a foole that maketh accompt of any

---

[10] **buskens:** foot and leg coverings reaching to the calf or knee; a half-boot.   [11] **Novi homines:** new men.   [12] **defendants:** in the margin, Harrison (questioning his sources) adds "dependants?"

religion, but more foole that will loose anie part of his wealth, or will come in trouble for constant leaning to anie: but if he yéeld to loose his life for his possession, he is stark mad, and worthie to be taken for most foole of all the rest. This gaie bootie gate[13] these gentlemen by going into Italie, and hereby a man may see what fruit is afterward to be looked for where such blossoms doo appéere. I care not (saith a third) what you talke to me of God, so as I may have the prince & the lawes of the realme on my side. Such men as this last, are easilie knowen; for they have learned in Italie, to go up and downe also in England, with pages at their héeles finelie apparelled, whose face and countenance shall be such as sheweth the master not to be blind in his choise. But least I should offend too much, I passe over to saie anie more of these Italionates and their demeanor, which alas is too open and manifest to the world, and yet not called into question.

Citizens and burgesses[14] have next place to gentlemen, who be those that are free within the cities, and are of some likelie substance to beare office in the same. But these citizens [or] burgesses [are] to serve the commonwealth in their cities and boroughs, or in corporat townes where they dwell. And in the common assemblie of the realme wherein our lawes are made, for in the counties they beare but little swaie (which assemblie is called the high court of parlement) the ancient cities appoint foure, and the boroughs two burgesses to have voices in it, and give their consent or dissent unto such things as passe or staie there in the name of the citie or borow, for which they are appointed.

In this place also are our merchants to be installed, as amongst the citizens (although they often change estate with gentlemen, as gentlemen doo with them, by a mutuall conversion of the one into the other) whose number is so increased in these our daies, that their onelie maintenance is the cause of the exceeding prices of forreine wares, which otherwise when everie nation was permitted to bring in hir owne commodities, were farre better cheape and more plentifullie to be had. Of the want of our commodities here at home, by their great transportation of them into other countries, I speak not, sith the matter will easilie bewraie it selfe. Certes among the Lacedemonians it was found out, that great numbers of merchants were nothing to the furtherance of the state of the commonwealth: wherefore it is to be wished that the huge heape of them were somewhat restreined, as also of our lawiers, so should the rest live more easilie upon their owne, and few honest chapmen[15] be brought to decaie, by breaking of the bankerupt. I doo not denie but that the navie of the land is in part mainteined by their

---

[13] **gate:** got. [14] **burgesses:** inhabitants of boroughs with full municipal rights; synonymous with citizens; also, a town magistrate. [15] **chapmen:** merchants.

traffike, and so are the high prices of wares kept up now they have gotten the onelie sale of things, upon pretense of better furtherance of the common-wealth into their owne hands: whereas in times past when the strange bot-toms were suffered to come in, we had sugar for foure pence the pound, that now at the writing of this treatise is well worth halfe a crowne, raisons or corints[16] for a penie that now are holden at six pence, and sometime at eight pence and ten pence the pound: nutmegs at two pence halfe penie the ounce: ginger at a penie an ounce, prunes at halfe penie farding:[17] great raisons[18] three pound for a penie, cinamon at foure pence the ounce, cloves at two pence, and pepper at twelve, and sixteene pence the pound. Whereby we may sée the sequele of things not alwaies but verie seldome to be such as is pretended in the beginning. The wares that they carrie out of the realme, are for the most part brode clothes[19] and carsies of all colours, likewise cot-tons, fréeses, rugs, tin, wooll, our best béere, baies, bustian, mockadoes tufted and plaine, rash,[20] lead, fells,[21] &c: which being shipped at sundrie ports of our coasts, are borne from thence into all quarters of the world, and there either exchanged for other wares or readie monie: to the great gaine and commoditie of our merchants. And whereas in times past their cheefe trade was into Spaine, Portingall, France, Flanders, Danske, Norwàie, Scot-land, and Iseland onelie: now in these daies, as men not contented with these iournies, they have sought out the east and west Indies, and made now and then suspicious voiages not onelie unto the Canaries, and new Spaine, but likewise into Cathaia, Moscovia, Tartaria,[22] and the regions thereabout, from whence (as they saie) they bring home great commodities. But alas I sée not by all their travell that the prices of things are anie whit abated. Certes this enormitie (for so I doo accompt of it) was sufficientlie provided for, An. 9 Edward 3. by a noble estatute made in that behalfe, but upon what occasion the generall execution thereof is staied or not called on, in good sooth I cannot tell.[23] This onelie I know, that everie function and severall vocation striveth with other, which of them should have all the water of commoditie run into hir owne cesterne.[24]

Yeomen are those, which by our law are called *Legales homines*, free men borne English, and may dispend[25] of their owne free land in yearelie rev-

---

[16] **raisons or corints:** currants.   [17] **farding:** farthing, the fourth part of a penny.   [18] **great raisons:** raisins as distinguished from currants.   [19] **brode clothes:** broadcloth; finely woven, plain black material used chiefly for men's clothing.   [20] **carsies . . . rash:** kerseys, friezes, baize, mockadoes, and rash are various woolen fabrics; bustian is a cotton fabric.   [21] **fells:** lead ore.   [22] **Cathaia, Moscovia, Tartaria:** Cathay (the name by which Northern China was known in medieval Europe), Muscovy or Russia, and Tartary (Tartar was the name applied to peoples and states of the thirteenth- and fourteenth-century Mongol Empire in Asia).   [23] **noble es-tatute . . . I cannot tell:** the statute of 1335 gave foreign merchants the right to trade freely in England.   [24] **cesterne:** cistern; sewer.   [25] **dispend:** expend.

enue, to the summe of fortie shillings sterling, or six pounds as monie goeth in our times. Some are of the opinion by Cap. 2. Rich. 2. an. 20. that they are the same which the French men call varlets,[26] but as that phrase is used in my time it is farre unlikelie to be so. The truth is that the word is derived from the Saxon terme Zeoman or Geoman, which signifieth (as I have read) a settled or staid man, such I meane as being maried and of some yeares, betaketh himselfe to staie in the place of his abode for the better maintenance of himselfe and his familie, whereof the single sort have no regard, but are likelie to be still fleeting now hither now thither, which argueth want of stabilitie in determination and resolution of iudgement, for the execution of things of anie importance. This sort of people have a certeine preheminence, and more estimation than labourers & the common sort of artificers, & these commonlie live wealthilie, kéepe good houses, and travell to get riches. They are also for the most part farmers to gentlemen (in old time called Pagani, & opponuntur militibus, and therfore Persius calleth himselfe Semipaganus)[27] or at the leastwise artificers, & with grasing,[28] frequenting of markets, and kéeping of servants (not idle servants as the gentlemen doo, but such as get both their owne and part of their masters living) do come to great welth, in somuch that manie of them are able and doo buie the lands of unthriftie gentlemen, and often setting their sonnes to the schooles, to the universities, and to the Ins of the court; or otherwise leaving them sufficient lands whereupon they may live without labour, doo make them by those meanes to become gentlemen: these were they that in times past made all France afraid. And albeit they be not called master as gentlemen are, or sir as to knights apperteineth, but onelie Iohn and Thomas, &c: yet have they beene found to have doone verie good service: and the kings of England in foughten battels, were woont to remaine among them (who were their footmen) as the French kings did amongst their horssemen: the prince thereby shewing where his chiefe strength did consist.

The fourth and last sort of people in England are daie labourers, poore husbandmen, and some retailers (which have no frée land) copie holders,[29] and all artificers, as tailers, shomakers, carpenters, brickmakers, masons, &c. As for slaves and bondmen we have none, naie such is the privilege of our countrie by the especiall grace of God, and bountie of our princes, that if anie come hither from other realms, so soone as they set foot on land they

---

[26] **varlets:** according to the statute, "no varlets, called yeomen, . . . shall use or bear livery, called livery of company, of any lord within the realm unless he be menial and familiar or continual officer of his said lord." [27] **Pagani . . . Semipaganus:** countrymen, as opposed to soldiers. Persius applies this epithet to himself in the prologue to his *Satires*, 1.6. [28] **grasing:** grazing; farmers who pasture cattle and sheep. [29] **copie holders:** freeholders, those with tenure of land.

become so frée of condition as their masters, whereby all note of servile bondage is utterlie remooved from them, wherein we resemble (not the Germans who had slaves also, though such as in respect of the slaves of other countries might well be reputed frée, but) the old Indians and the Taprobanes,[30] who supposed it a great iniurie to nature to make or suffer them to be bond, whome she in hir woonted course dooth product and bring foorth frée. This fourth and last sort of people therefore have neither voice nor authoritie in the common wealth, but are to be ruled, and not to rule other: yet they are not altogither neglected, for in cities and corporat townes, for default of yeomen they are faine to make up their inquests of such maner of people. And in villages they are commonlie made church-wardens, sidemen, aleconners, now and then constables, and manie times inioie the name of hedboroughes.[31] Unto this sort also may our great swarmes of idle serving men be referred, of whome there runneth a proverbe; Yoong serving men old beggers, bicause service is none heritage. These men are profitable to none, for if their condition be well perused, they are enimies to their masters, to their freends, and to themselves: for by them oftentimes their masters are incouraged unto unlawful exactions of their tenants, their fréends brought unto povertie by their rents inhanced, and they themselves brought to confusion by their owne prodigalitie and errors, as men that having not wherewith of their owne to mainteine their excesses, doo search in high waies, budgets, cofers, males,[32] and stables, which way to supplie their wants. How diverse of them also coveting to beare an high saile doo insinuate themselves with yoong gentlemen and noble men newlie come to their lands, the case is too much apparant, whereby the good na-tures of the parties are not onelie a little impaired, but also their livelihoods and revenues so wasted and consumed, that if at all yet not in manie yeares they shall be able to recover themselves. It were verie good therefore that the superfluous heapes of them were in part diminished. And sith necessitie in-forceth to have some, yet let wisdome moderate their numbers, so shall their masters be rid of unnecessarie charge, and the common wealth of manie théeves. No nation cherisheth such store of them as we doo here in Eng-land, in hope of which maintenance manie give themselves to idlenesse, that otherwise would be brought to labour, and live in order like subjects. Of their whoredomes I will not speake anie thing at all, more than of their swearing, yet is it found that some of them doo make the first a cheefe piller of their building, consuming not onelie the goods but also the health & wel-

---

[30] Taprobanes: Ceylonese. [31] sidemen, aleconners . . . hedboroughes: sidesmen, or church-wardens' assistants; inspectors of ale; petty constables. [32] budgets, cofers, males: pouches, cof-fers, and mail bags.

fare of manie honest gentlemen, citizens, wealthie yeomen, &c: by such un-
lawfull dealings. But how farre have I waded in this point, or how farre may
I saile in such a large sea? I will therefore now staie to speake anie more of
those kind of men. In returning therefore to my matter, this furthermore
among other things I have to saie of our husbandmen and artificers, that
they were never so excellent in their trades as at this present. But as the
workemanship of the later sort was never more fine and curious to the eie,
so was it never lesse strong and substantiall for continuance and benefit of
the buiers. Neither is there anie thing that hurteth the common sort of our
artificers more than hast, and a barbarous or slavish desire to turne the penie, and by ridding their worke to make spéedie utterance of their wares:
which inforceth them to bungle up and dispatch manie things they care not
how so they be out of their hands, whereby the buier is often sore defrauded,
and findeth to his cost, that hast maketh wast, according to the proverbe.

   Oh how manie trades and handicrafts are now in England, whereof the
common wealth hath no néed? How manie néedfull commodities have we
which are perfected with great cost, &c: and yet may with farre more ease
and lesse cost be provided from other countries if we could use the meanes.
I will not speake of iron, glasse, and such like, which spoile much wood, and
yet are brought from other countries better chéepe than we can make them
here at home, I could exemplifie also in manie other. But to leave these
things and procéed with our purpose, and herein (as occasion serveth) generallie by waie of conclusion to speake of the common-wealth of England, I
find that it is governed and mainteined by three sorts of persons.

   1   The prince, monarch, and head governour, which is called the king, or
(if the crowne fall to the woman) the quéene: in whose name and by whose
authoritie all things are administred.

   2   The gentlemen, which be divided into two sorts, as the baronie or estate of lords (which conteineth barons and all above that degree) and also
those that be no lords, as knights, esquiers, & simple gentlemen, as I have
noted alreadie. Out of these also are the great deputies and high presidents
chosen, of which one serveth in Ireland, as another did sometime in Calis,[33]
and the capteine now at Berwike; as one lord president dooth governe in
Wales, and the other the north parts of this Iland, which later with certeine
councellors and judges were erected by king Henrie the eight. But forsomuch as I have touched their conditions elsewhere, it shall be inough to
have remembred them at this time.

   3   The third and last sort is named the yeomanrie, of whom & their sequele, the labourers and artificers, I have said somewhat even now. Whereto

[33] **Calis:** Calais, a port in France.

I ad that they be not called masters and gentlemen, but goodmen, as goodman Smith, goodman Coot, goodman Cornell, goodman Mascall, goodman Cockswet, &c: & in matters of law these and the like are called thus,
Giles lewd yeoman, Edward Mountford yeoman, Iames Cocke yeoman,
Herrie Butcher yeoman, &c: by which addition they are exempt from the
vulgar and common sorts. Cato calleth them Aratores & optimos cives rei
publicæ,[34]) of whom also you may read more in the booke of common
wealth which sir Thomas Smith sometime penned of this land.

[34] **Aratores & optimos cives rei publicæ:** plowmen and best citizens of the state. For the
yeomen's names, Harrison includes the names of his parishioners.

→ WILLIAM HARRISON

From The Description of England   *1587*
Of Their Apparell and Attire

CHAPTER VII

An Englishman, indevoring sometime to write of our attire, made sundrie
platformes[1] for his purpose, supposing by some of them to find out one sted-
fast ground whereon to build the summe of his discourse. But in the end (like
an oratour long without exercise) when he saw what a difficult péece of
worke he had taken in hand, he gave over his travell,[2] and onelie drue the picture of a naked man, unto whom he gave a paire of sheares in the one hand,
and a peece of cloth in the other, to the end he should shape his apparell after such fashion as himselfe liked, sith he could find no kind of garment that
could please him anie while togither, and this he called an Englishman.
Certes this writer (otherwise being a lewd popish hypocrite and ungratious
priest)[3] shewed himselfe herein not to be altogether void of iudgement, sith
the phantasticall follie of our nation, even from the courtier to the carter is
such, that no forme of apparell liketh us longer than the first garment is in
the wearing, if it continue so long and be not laid aside, to receive some other
trinket newlie devised by the fickle headed tailors, who covet to have severall
trickes in cutting, thereby to draw fond customers to more expense of monie.
For my part I can tell better how to inveigh against this enormitie, than de-

[1] **platformes:** sketches.   [2] **travell:** travail.   [3] **ungratious priest:** Andrew Boorde, originally a
Carthusian monk, later a traveler and doctor, begins his *Introduction of Knowledge* with a chapter on the English.

scribe anie certeintie of our attire: sithence[4] such is our mutabilitie, that to daie there is none to the Spanish guise, to morrow the French toies are most fine and delectable, yer long no such apparell as that which is after the high Alman[5] fashion, by and by the Turkish maner is generallie best liked of, otherwise the Morisco[6] gowns, the Barbarian sléeves, the mandilion worne to Collie weston ward,[7] and the short French breches make such a comelie vesture, that except it were a dog in a doublet, you shall not sée anie so disguised, as are my countrie men of England. And as these fashions are diverse, so likewise it is a world to see the costlinesse and the curiositie: the excesse and the vanitie: the pompe and the braverie: the change and the varietie: and finallie the ficklenesse and the follie that is in all degrees: in somuch that nothing is more constant in England than inconstancie of attire. Oh how much cost is bestowed now adaies upon our bodies and how little upon our soules! how manie sutes of apparell hath the one and how little furniture hath the other? how long time is asked in decking up of the first, and how little space left wherein to féed the later? how curious, how nice also are a number of men and women, and how hardlie can the tailor please them in making it fit for their bodies? how manie times must it be sent backe againe to him that made it? what chafing, what fretting, what reprochfull language doth the poore workeman beare awaie? and manie times when he dooth nothing to it at all, yet when it is brought home againe it is verie fit and handsome; then must we put it on, then must the long seames of our hose be set by a plumbline, then we puffe, then we blow, and finallie sweat till we drop, that our clothes may stand well upon us. I will saie nothing of our heads, which sometimes are polled,[8] sometimes curled, or suffered to grow at length like womans lockes, manie times cut off above or under the eares round as by a wooden dish. Neither will I meddle with our varietie of beards, of which some are shaven from the chin like those of Turks, not a few cut short like to the beard of marques Otto,[9] some made round like a rubbing brush, other with a pique de vant[10] (O fine fashion!) or now and then suffered to grow long, the barbers being growen to be so cunning in this behalfe as the tailors. And therfore if a man have a leane and streight face, a marquesse Ottons cut will make it broad and large; if it be platter like, a long slender beard will make it séeme the narrower; if he be wesell becked,[11] then much heare left on

---

[4] **sithence:** since. [5] **Alman:** German. [6] **Morisco:** Moorish. [7] **mandilion worne to Collie weston ward:** A mandilion is a cape with sleeves; the style of wearing it sideways so that the sleeves hung in front and behind was known as Collyweston-ward. The term may be associated with Queen Elizabeth's manor of Collyweston in Northamptonshire. [8] **polled:** shorn; close-clipped. [9] **marques Otto:** Marquis Otto, from the French phrase *barbe faite à la marquisotte*, to shave all but the mustache. Harrison seems to refer to a close-cropped beard. [10] **pique de vant:** short Vandyke beard. [11] **wesell becked:** weasel-beaked.

the chéekes will make the owner looke big like a bowdled[12] hen, and so grim as a goose, if Cornelis of Chelmeresford[13] saie true: manie old men doo weare no beards at all. Some lustie courtiers also and gentlemen of courage, doo weare either rings of gold, stones, or pearle in their eares, whereby they imagine the workemanship of God not to be a little amended. But herein they rather disgrace than adorne their persons, as by their nicenesse in apparell, for which I saie most nations doo not uniustlie deride us, as also for that we doo séeme to imitate all nations round about us, wherein we be like to the Polypus[14] or Chameleon; and thereunto bestow most cost upon our arses, & much more than upon all the rest of our bodies, as women doo likewise upon their heads and shoulders. In women also it is most to be lamented, that they doo now farre excéed the lightnesse of our men (who neverthelesse are transformed from the cap even to the verie shoo) and such staring attire as in time past was supposed méet for none but light housewives onelie, is now become an habit for chast and sober matrones. What should I saie of their doublets with pendant codpéeses[15] on the brest full of iags[16] & cuts, and sléeves of sundrie colours? their galligascons[17] to beare out their bums & make their attire to sit plum round[18] (as they terme it) about them? their fardingals,[19] and diverslie coloured nether stocks[20] of silke, ierdseie,[21] and such like, whereby their bodies are rather deformed than commended? I have met with some of these trulles[22] in London so disguised, that it hath passed my skill to discerne whether they were men or women.

Thus it is now come to passe, that women are become men, and men transformed into monsters: and those good gifts which almightie God hath given unto us to reléeve our necessities withall (as a nation turning altogither the grace of God into wantonnesse, for

Luxuriant animi rebus plerunque secundis)[23]

not otherwise bestowed than in all excesse, as if we wist not otherwise how to consume and wast them. I praie God that in this behalf our sinne be not like unto that of Sodoma and Gomorha, whose errors were pride, excesse of diet, and abuse of Gods benefits aboundantlie bestowed upon them, beside want of charitie toward the poore, and certeine other points which the prophet shutteth up in silence. Certes the common-wealth cannot be said to florish where

---

[12] **bowdled:** ruffled. [13] **Cornelis of Chelmereseford:** An Essex barber? [14] **Polypus:** octopus. [15] **codpéeses:** bagged appendages, usually a part of male attire covering the genitals. [16] **iags:** slashes to show different-colored material beneath. [17] **galligascons:** galligaskins, or loose breeches. [18] **plum round:** plumb-round? [19] **fardingals:** farthingales, or hooped petticoats. [20] **nether stocks:** stockings. [21] **ierdseie:** jersey. [22] **trulles:** strumpets. [23] Luxuriant . . . se-cundis: "Desires usually run riot in prosperity" (Ovid, *Ars amatoria* 2: 437).

these abuses reigne, but is rather oppressed by unreasonable exactions made upon rich farmers, and of poore tenants, wherewith to mainteine the same. Neither was it ever merier with England, than when an Englishman was knowne abroad by his owne cloth, and contented himselfe at home with his fine carsie hosen,[24] and a meane slop:[25] his coat, gowne, and cloake of browne blue or puke,[26] with some pretie furniture of velvet or furre, and a doublet of sad tawnie,[27] or blacke velvet, or other comelie silke, without such cuts and gawrish[28] colours as are worne in these daies, and never brought in but by the consent of the French, who thinke themselves the gaiest men, when they have most diversities of iagges and change of colours about them. Certes of all estates our merchants doo least alter their attire, and therefore are most to be commended: for albeit that which they weare be verie fine and costlie, yet in forme and colour it representeth a great péece of the ancient gravitie apperteining to citizens and burgesses, albeit the yoonger sort of their wives both in attire and costlie housekeeping can not tell when and how to make an end, as being women in déed in whome all kind of curiositie is to be found and seene, and in farre greater measure than in women of higher calling. I might here name a sort of hewes devised for the nonce, wherewith to please phantasticall heads, as gooseturd gréene, pease porridge tawnie, popingaie blue, lustie gallant,[29] the divell in the head (I should saie the hedge)[30] and such like: but I passe them over thinking it sufficient to have said thus much of apparell generallie, when nothing can particularlie be spoken of anie constancie thereof.

[24] **carsie hosen:** kersey (woolen) hose.   [25] **meane slop:** wide breeches.   [26] **puke:** blue-black.
[27] **sad tawnie:** dark orange-brown.   [28] **gawrish:** garish.   [29] **lustie gallant:** light red.   [30] **hedge:** an off-shade of red.

→ JOHN STOW

From A Survey of London   *1603*

Candlewick Street Ward

Candlewick Street, or Candlewright street ward, beginneth at the East end of great Eastcheap; it passeth west through Eastcheap to Candlewright street, and through the same down to the north end of Suffolk lane, on the

---

John Stow, *A Survey of London. Containing the Original, Antiquity, Increase, Modern estate, and description of that City, written in the year 1598. by John Stow Citizen of London. Since by the same Author increased, with diverse rare notes of Antiquity, and published in the year 1603. Also an Apology (or defence) against the opinion of some men, concerning that City, the greatness thereof. With an appendix, containing in Latin* Libellum de situ & nobilitate Londini: *Written by William Fitzstephen, in the reign of Henry the second.* (London, 1603) 218–21, 407–409.

south side, and down that lane by the west end of Saint *Laurence* Church-yard, which is the farthest west part of that ward. The street of great Eastcheap is so called of the Market there kept, in the East part of the City, as West Cheap is a Market so called of being in the West.

This Eastcheap is now a flesh Market of Butchers, there dwelling on both sides of the street; it had sometime also Cooks mixed amongst the Butchers, and such other as sold victuals ready dressed of all sorts. For of old time when friends did meet, and were disposed to be merry, they went not to dine and sup in Taverns, but to the Cooks, where they called for meat what them liked, which they always found ready dressed at a reasonable rate, as I have before showed.

In the year 1410, the 11th of *Henry,* the fourth, upon the even of Saint *John Baptist,* the king's sons, *Thomas* and *John,* being in Eastcheap at supper (or rather at breakfast, for it was after the watch was broken up, betwixt two and three of the clock after midnight) a great debate happened between their men and other of the Court, which lasted one hour, till the Mayor and Sheriffs with other Citizens appeased the same. For the which afterwards the said Mayor, Aldermen and sheriffs were called to answer before the King, his sons, and diverse Lords, being highly moved against the City. At which time *William Gascoyne* chief Justice required the Mayor and Alder-men, for the Citizens, to put them in the king's grace. Whereunto they an-swered that they had not offended, but (according to the law) had done their best in stinting debate, and maintaining of the peace: upon which an-swer the king remitted all his ire and dismissed them.

And to prove this Eastcheap to be a place replenished with Cooks, it may appear by a song[1] called *London Lickpenny,* made by *Lidgate,* a Monk of Berry,[2] in the reign of *Henry* the fift, in the person of a Country man com-ing to London, and traveling through the same. In West Cheap (saith the song) he was called on to buy fine lawn, *Paris* thread, cotton Umble[3] and other linen clothes, and such like (he speaketh of no silks). In Cornhill to buy old apparel and household stuff, where he was forced to buy his own hood, which he had lost in Westminster hall.[4] In Candlewright street, Drapers proffered him cheap cloth; in East cheap the Cooks cried hot ribs of beef roasted, pies well baked, and other victuals. There was clattering of Pewter pots, harp, pipe, and sawtrie;[5] yea by cock, nay by cock,[6] for greater

---

[1] **song:** ballad.   [2] **Monk of Berry:** John Lydgate, of the Benedictine monastery of Bury St. Ed-munds; author of *The Falls of Princes* (1494), among many other works. Later scholars reject Lydgate's authorship.   [3] **lawn . . . Umble:** lawn and Paris thread are fine linen fabrics; cotton umble is fine cotton.   [4] **Westminster hall:** the old hall of Westminster Palace, where law courts were held.   [5] **sawtrie:** psaltery; a medieval stringed instrument similar to a dulcimer.   [6] **by cock:** a mild oath; perversion of "by God."

oaths were spared. Some sang of *Jenken*, and *Julian*,[7] &c., all which melody liked well the passenger, but he wanted money[8] to abide by it, and therefore gat him into Gravesend barge,[9] & home into Kent.

Candlewright (so called in old Records of the Guildhall,[10] of Saint Mary Overy,[11] and other) or Candlewick street took that name (as may be supposed) either of Chandlers, or makers of Candles, both of wax and tallow.[12] For Candlewright is a maker of Candles, or of Wick, which is the cotton or yarn thereof; or otherwise Wike, which is the place where they used to work them, as Scalding wike by the Stocks' Market was called of the Poulters scalding and dressing their poultry there. And in diverse Countries, Dairy houses, or Cottages, wherein they make butter and cheese, are usually called Wicks. There dwelled also of old time diverse Weavers of woolen clothes, brought in by *Edward* the third. For I read that in the 44th [year] of his reign the Weavers brought out of Flanders were appointed their meetings to be in the Churchyard of Saint *Laurence Poultney*, and the Weavers of Brabant[13] in the churchyard of Saint *Mary Somerset*. There were then in this city weavers of diverse sorts, to wit, of Drapery or Tapestry, and Napery.[14] These Weavers of Candlewright street being in short time worn out, their place is now possessed by rich Drapers, sellers of woolen cloth, &c. On the north side of this ward, at the west end of East cheap, have ye Saint *Clements* lane, a part whereof on both sides is of Candlewick street ward, to wit, somewhat North beyond the parish church of Saint *Clement* in Eastcheap. This is a small church, void of monuments,[15] other than of *Francis Barnam* Alderman, who deceased 1575, and of *Benedick Barnam* his son, alderman also, 1598. *William Chartney* and *William Overy* founded a Chantry[16] there. Next is Saint *Nicholas* lane for the most part on both sides of this ward, almost to Saint *Nicholas* church. Then is Abchurch lane, which is on both the sides, almost wholly of this ward, the parish Church there (called of Saint *Mary* Abchurch, Apechurch, or Upchurch, as I have read it) standeth somewhat near unto the south end thereof, on a rising ground. It is a fair Church: *Simon de Winchcomb* founded a Chantry there, [in] the 19th [year] of *Richard* the second. *John Littleton* founded another, and *Thomas Hondon* another, & [it] hath the monuments of *J[ohn] Long* Esquire of Bedfordshire, 1442; *William Wikenson* Alderman, 1519; *William*

---

[7] *Jenkin* and *Julian:* Jenken is a generic name for a commoner; Julian refers to Julius Caesar. The ballad tells of both commoners and nobility. [8] **wanted money:** lacked money to pay. [9] **Gravesend barge:** east of London, at the mouth of the Thames. [10] **Guildhall:** site of the City's offices, including those of the trade guilds. [11] **Saint Mary Overy:** parish church in Southwark; the records of that church. [12] **tallow:** animal fat. [13] **Brabant:** a city in Holland. [14] **Napery:** table linen. [15] **monuments:** graves with effigies. [16] **Chantry:** an endowment for priests to sing masses, usually for the soul of the founder; a chapel so endowed.

Jawdrell Tailor, 1440; Sir *James Hawes* Mayor, 1574; Sir *John Branch* Mayor, 1580; *John Miners, William Kettle,* &c.

On the south side of this ward, beginning again at the East, is Saint *Michaels* lane, which lane is almost wholly of this ward, on both sides down towards Thames street, to a Well or Pump there. On the East side of this lane is Crooked lane, aforesaid by Saint *Michaels* Church, towards new Fish street. One [of] the most ancient house[s] in this lane is called the leaden porch, and belonged sometime to Sir *John Merston* knight, [in] the first [year] of *Edward* the fourth. It is now called the swan in Crooked lane, possessed of[17] strangers, and selling of Rhenish wine. The parish church of this S[aint] *Michaels* was sometime but a small and homely thing, standing upon part of that ground, wherein now standeth the parsonage house: and the ground thereabout was a filthy plot, by reason of the Butchers in Eastcheap, who made the same their Laystall.[18] *William de Burgh* gave two messages[19] to that Church in Candlewick street [in] 1317. *John Loveken* stockfishmonger,[20] four times Mayor, built in the same ground this fair Church of Saint *Michael,* and was there buried in the Choir, under a fair tomb with the Images of him and his wife in Alabaster. The said Church hath been since increased with a new Choir and side chapels by Sir *William Walworth* Stockfishmonger, Mayor, sometime servant to the said *John Loveken.* Also, the tomb of *Loveken* was removed, and a flat stone of gray Marble garnished with plates of Copper laid on him, as it yet remaineth in the body of the Church. This *William Walworth* is reported to have slain *Jack Straw,*[21] but *Jack Straw* being afterward taken, was first adjudged by the said Mayor, and then executed by the loss of his head in Smithfield.

[17] **possessed of:** owned by.   [18] **Laystall:** place where refuse and dung are laid.   [19] **two messages:** sermons or proclamations.   [20] **stockfishmonger:** Stockfish is a kind of cod.   [21] **Jack Straw:** A leader in the various local rebellions over tenancy during Richard II's reign; in 1381, he set Highbury Manor on fire.

➔ JOHN STOW

From A Survey of London   *1603*

Borough of Southwark and Bridge Ward Without

Now to return to the West bank, there be two Bear gardens, the old and new places, wherein be kept Bears, Bulls and other beasts to be baited. As also Mastiffs in several kennels, nourished to bait them. These Bears and other Beasts are there baited in plots of ground, scaffolded about for the Beholders to stand safe.

Next on this bank was sometime the Bordello or stews, a place so called of certain stew houses privileged[1] there, for the repair of incontinent[2] men to the like women, of the which privilege I have read thus.

In a Parliament holden at Westminster the 8th [year] of *Henry* the second, it was ordained by the commons and confirmed by the king and Lords that diverse constitutions forever should be kept within that Lordship or franchise, according to the old customs that had been there used time out of mind. Amongst the which these following were some, *v[i]z.*

That no stewholder or his wife should let or stay any single Woman to go and come freely at all times when they listed.

No stewholder to keep any woman to board, but she to board abroad at her pleasure.

To take no more for the woman's chamber in the week than fourteen pence.

Not to keep open his doors upon the holy days.

Not to keep any single woman in his house on the holy days, but the Bailiff to see them voided out of the Lordship.

No single woman to be kept against her will that would leave her sin.

No stewholder to receive any Woman of religion, or any man's wife.

No single woman to take money to lie with any man, but she lie with him all night till the morrow.

No man to be drawn or enticed into any stewhouse.

The Constables, Bailiff, and others every week to search every stewhouse.

No stewholder to keep any woman that hath the perilous infirmity of burning, nor to sell bread, ale, flesh, fish, wood, coal, or any victuals, &c.

These and many more orders were to be observed upon great pain and punishment. I have also seen diverse Patents of confirmation, namely one dated 1345, the nineteenth [year] of *Edward* the third. Also I find that in the fourth [year] of *Richard* the second, these stew houses, belonging to *William Walworth* then Mayor of London, were farmed by Fraus of Flanders,[3] and spoiled by *Walter Tighler*,[4] and other rebels of Kent. Notwithstanding, I find that ordinances for the same place and houses were again confirmed in the

---

[1] **privileged:** given immunity from the law.   [2] **incontinent:** lacking sexual restraint.   [3] **Fraus of Flanders:** Dutchwomen.   [4] **Walter Tighler:** Stow refers to Wat Tyler, so named for his trade as a roofer. Tyler was a ringleader in the peasants' revolt against Richard II in 1381.

reign of *Henry* the sixth, to be continued as before. Also *Robert Fabian*[5] writeth that in the year 1506, the 21st of *Henry* the seventh, the said stew houses in Southwark were for a season inhibited, and the doors closed up, but it was not long, saith he, ere the houses there were set open again, so many as were permitted, for (as it was said) whereas before were eighteen houses, from thenceforth were appointed to be used but twelve only. These allowed stewhouses had signs on their fronts, towards the Thames, not hanged out, but painted on the walls, as a Boar's head, the Cross keys, the Gun, the Castle, the Crane, the Cardinal's Hat, the Bell, the Swan, &c. I have heard ancient men of good credit report that these single women were forbidden the rights of the Church, so long as they continued that sinful life, and were excluded from Christian burial, if they were not reconciled before their death. And therefore there was a plot of ground, called the single woman's churchyard, appointed for them, far from the parish church.

In the year of Christ, 1546, the 37th of *Henry* the eighth, this row of stews in Southwark was put down by the king's commandment, which was proclaimed by sound of Trumpet, no more to be privileged, and used as a common Brothel, but the inhabitants of the same to keep good and honest rule as in other places of this realm, &c.

[5] **Robert Fabian:** author of *New Chronicles of England and France* (1516).

➔ **LORD MAYOR OF LONDON**

Letter to John Whitgift, Archbishop of Canterbury
25 February 1591/1592

Our most humble duties to your Grace remembered. Whereas by the daily and disorderly exercise of a number of players & playing houses erected within this City, the youth thereof is greatly corrupted & their manners infected with many evil & ungodly qualities, by reason of the wanton & profane devices represented on the stages by the said players, the prentices & servants withdrawn from their works, & all sorts in general from the daily resort unto sermons & other Christian exercises, to the great hinderance of the trades & traders of this City & profanation of the good & godly religion established amongst us. To which places also do usually resort great num-

Lord Mayor of London, Letter to John Whitgift, Archbishop of Canterbury, 25 February 1592. Printed M. S. C. 1. 68, from *Remembrancia* 1: 635. Reprinted in E. K. Chambers, *The Elizabethan Stage* (Oxford: Clarendon Press, 1923) 4: 307–08.

bers of light & lewd disposed persons, as harlots, cutpurses, cozeners,[1] pilferers, & such like; & there, under the color of resort to those places to hear the plays, devise diverse evil & ungodly matches, confederacies, & conspiracies, which by means of the opportunity of the place cannot be prevented nor discovered, as otherwise they might be. In consideration whereof, we most humbly beseech your Grace for your godly care for the reforming of so great abuses tending to the offense of almighty god, the profanation & slander of his true religion, & the corrupting of our youth, which are the seed of the Church of god & the commonwealth among us, to vouchsafe us your good favor & help for the reforming & banishing of so great evil out of this City, which ourselves of long time though to small purpose have so earnestly desired and endeavored by all means that possibly we could. And because we understand that the Q[ueen's] Majesty is & must be served at certain times by this sort of people, for which purpose she hath granted her letters Patents to Mr. Tilney, Master of her Revels, by virtue whereof he, being authorized to reform, exercise, or suppress all manner of players, plays, & playing houses whatsoever, did first license the said playing houses within this City for her Majesty's said service, which before that time lay open to all the statutes for the punishing of these & such like disorders. We are most humbly & earnestly to beseech your Grace to call unto you the said Master of her Majesty's Revels, with whom also we have conferred of late to that purpose, and to treat with him if by any means it may be devised that her Majesty may be served with these recreations as hath been accustomed (which in our opinions may easily be done by the private exercise of her Majesty's own players in convenient place) & the City freed from these continual disorders, which thereby do grow & increase daily among us. Whereby your Grace shall not only benefit & bind unto you the politic state & government of this City, which by no one thing is so greatly annoyed & disquieted as by players & plays, & the disorders which follow thereupon, but also take away a great offense from the Church of god & hinderance to his gospel, to the great contentment of all good Christians, specially the preachers & ministers of the word of god about this City, who have long time & yet do make their earnest continual complaint unto us for the redress hereof. And thus recommending our most humble duties and service to your Grace, we commit the same to the grace of the Almighty. From London, the 25th of February, 1591.

Your Grace's most humble.

To the right reverend Father in God, my L[ord] the Archbishop of Canterbury his Grace.

---

[1] **cozeners:** tricksters.

→ STEPHEN GOSSON

From The School of Abuse   *1579*

[Gosson provides a history of abuses, citing classical examples and deploring the present condition of England compared to its "old discipline" — that is, before it was schooled with abuses.]

In our assemblies at plays in London, you shall see such heaving and shoving, such itching and shouldering, to sit by women; Such care for their garments, that they be not trod on; Such eyes to their laps, that no chips[1] light in them; Such pillows to their backs, that they take no hurt; Such masking[2] in their ears, I know not what; Such giving them Pippins[3] to pass the time; Such playing at foot Saunt without Cards;[4] Such tickling, such toying, such smiling, such winking, and such manning them home, when the sports are ended, that it is a right Comedy to mark their behavior, to watch their conceits,[5] as the Cat for the Mouse, and as good as a course[6] at the game itself, to bog[7] them a little, or follow aloof by the print of their feet, and so discover by [its] slot[8] where the Deer taketh soil.[9]

If this were as well noted, as ill seen, or as openly punished, as [it is] secretly practiced, I have no doubt but the cause would be feared to dry up the effect, and these pretty Rabbits[10] very cunningly ferreted from their burrows. For they that lack Customers all the week, either because their haunt is unknown, or the Constables and Officers of their Parish watch them so narrowly that they dare not queatch.[11] To Celebrate the Sabbath, [they] flock to Theaters, and there keep a general Market of Bawdry. Not that any filthiness in deed is committed within the compass of that ground, as was done in Rome, but that every wanton and his Paramour, every man and his Mistress, every John and his Joan, every knave and his quean,[12] are there first acquainted & cheapen the Merchandise in that place, which they pay for elsewhere as they can agree. These worms, when they dare not nestle in the Peascod[13] at home, find refuge

---

[1] **chips:** splinters from the sawdust on the floor.   [2] **masking:** whispering?   [3] **Pippins:** sweet apples.   [4] **playing . . . without Cards:** Saunt, or cent, was a counter in a two-handed card game resembling piquet; thus, playing "footsy."   [5] **conceits:** affectations.   [6] **course:** turn.   [7] **bog:** entangle.   [8] **slot:** tracks.   [9] **soil:** refuge.   [10] **Rabbits:** whores.   [11] **queatch:** stir, or move from one place to another; implying fear or submission.   [12] **quean:** whore.   [13] **worms . . . Peascod:** a peapod; Gosson hints at the spread of venereal diseases.

Stephen Gosson, *The School of Abuse, Containing a pleasant invective against Poets, Pipers, Players, Jesters, and such like Caterpillars of a Commonwealth; Setting up the Hag of Defiance to their mischievous exercise, & overthrowing their Bulwarks, by Prophane Writers, Natural reason, and common experience: A discourse as pleasant for Gentlemen that favor learning, as profitable for all that will follow virtue* (London, 1579) C1v–C3v, F1v–F4v.

abroad and are hid in the ears of other men's Corn. Every Tapster in one blind Tavern or other is Tenant at will, to which she tolleth resort, and plays the stale[14] to utter[15] their victuals and help them to empty their musty casks. There is she so entreated with words, and received with courtesy, that every back room in the house is at her commandment. Some that have neither land to maintain them nor good occupation to get their bread, desirous to strow[16] it with the best, yet disdaining to live by the sweat of their brows, have found out this cast of Ledgerdemain,[17] to play fast & loose among their neighbors. If any part of Music have suffered shipwreck, and arrived by fortune at their finger's ends,[18] with show of gentility they take by fair houses, receive lusty laughs at a price for boarders, and pipe[19] from morning to evening for wood and coal. By the brothers, cousins, uncles, great-grandsires, and such like acquaintance of their guests, they drink of the best, they sit rent free, they have their own Table spread to their hands, without wearing the strings of their purse,[20] or anything else, but household and honesty.

When resort so increaseth that they grow in suspicion, and the pots which are sent so often to the Tavern get such a knock before they come home that they return their Master a crack to his credit,[21] though he be called in question of his life, he hath shifts[22] enough to avoid the blank.[23] If their houses be searched, some instrument of Music is laid in sight to dazzle the eyes of every Officer, and all that are lodged in the house by night, or frequent it by day, come thither as pupils to be well schooled. Other there are which being so known that they are the byword of every man's mouth, and pointed at commonly as they pass the streets, either couch themselves in Alleys or blind Lanes, or take sanctuary in friaries, or live a mile from the City like Venus' Nuns[24] in a Cloister at Newington, Ratcliff, Islington, Hogsdon or some such place, where, like penitents, they deny the world and spend their days in double devotion.[25] And when they are weary of contemplation to comfort themselves, and renew their acquaintance, they visit Theaters, where they make full account of a play before they depart. Solon made no law for Parricides because he feared that he should rather put men in mind to commit such offenses than, by any strange punishment, give them a bit to keep them under.[26] And I intend not to show you all that I see, nor

---

[14] **stale:** prostitute used as a decoy.   [15] **utter:** hawk or sell.   [16] **strow:** flaunt.   [17] **Ledgerdemain:** trickery, sleight of hand.   [18] **arrived . . . ends:** that is, by picking pockets, stealing.   [19] **pipe:** call.   [20] **without . . . purse:** without paying for anything.   [21] **pots . . . credit:** implying that servants sent to taverns for ale or beer not only mishandle the pots but have themselves a drink on their master's tab.   [22] **shifts:** devices.   [23] **blank:** the white spot in the center of a target.   [24] **Venus' Nuns:** prostitutes; Venus is the goddess of sensual love.   [25] **double devotion:** sexual innuendo.   [26] **bit . . . under:** the mouthpiece of a horse's bridle; here, a restraint.

half that I hear of these abuses, lest you judge me more willful to teach them than willing to forbid them.

[Plays and players only seem to please, but they cannot be trusted. Although Queen Elizabeth made laws regarding apparel and degree and has restrained the theatres, still we attend. Plays that show virtuous lessons are tolerable, but players must be called to account for "the abuses that grow at their assemblies." Gosson rails against vanity and condemns dancers, tumblers, dicers, card-players, bowlers, fencers, and unruly soldiers.]

To the Gentlewomen Citizens of London, Flourishing Days with Regard of Credit[27]

The reverence that I owe you Gentlewomen, because you are Citizens, & the pity wherewith I tend your case, because you are weak, hath thrust out my hand, at the breaking up of my School, to write a few lines to your sweet selves. Not that I think you to be rebuked as idle housewives, but commended and encouraged as virtuous Dames. The freest horse, at the whisk of a wand, girds forward; The swiftest Hound, when he is halloed, strips forth; The kindest Master, when he is clapped on the back, fighteth best; The stoutest Soldier, when the Trumpet sounds, strikes fiercest; The gallantest Runner, when the people shout, getteth ground, and the perfectest livers, when they are praised, win greatest credit.

I have seen many of you which were wont to sport yourselves at Theatres, when you perceived the abuse of those places, school yourselves, & of your own accord abhor Plays. And sith you have begun to withdraw your steps, continue so still, if you be chary of your good name. For this is general, that they which show themselves openly, desire to be seen. It is not a soft shoe that healeth the Gout, nor a golden Ring that driveth away the Cramp, nor a crown of Pearl that cureth the Megrims,[28] nor your sober countenance that defendeth your credit, nor your friends which accompany your person that excuse your folly, nor your modesty at home that covereth your lightness, if you present yourselves in open Theatres. Thought is free: you can forbid no man that vieweth you to note you, and that noteth you, to judge you, for entering to places of suspicion. Wild Colts, when they see their kind, begin to bray; & lusty bloods, at the show of fair women, give a wanton sigh or a wicked wish. Blazing marks are most shot at; glistering faces chiefly marked; and what followeth? Looking eyes have liking hearts; liking hearts may burn in lust. We walk in the Sun many times for pleasure, but our faces

---

[27] This "open letter" to the Gentlewomen of London concludes Gosson's tract.   [28] **Megrims:** sick headaches.

are tanned before we return: though you go to theatres to see sport, Cupid may catch you ere you depart. The little God hovereth about you & fanneth you with his wings to kindle fire: when you are set as fixed whites,[29] Desire draweth his arrow to the head & flicketh it up to the feathers, and Fancy bestirreth him to shed his poison through every vein. If you do but listen to the voice of the Fowler, or join looks with an amorous Gazer, you have already made yourselves assaultable, & yielded your Cities to be sacked. A wanton eye is the dart of **Cephalus:**[30] where it leveleth, there it lighteth; & where it hits, it woundeth deep. If you give but a glance to your beholders, you have vailed the bonnet[31] in token of obedience: for the bolt[32] is fallen ere the Air clap; the Bullet past, ere the Piece crack; the cold taken, ere the body shiver; and the match made, ere you strike hands.

[All sorts of people come to plays; to avoid being beguiled, stay at home and, rather than going to the theatre, remember God, who "will succor you still in time of need."]

Be ever busied in godly meditations: seek not to pass over the gulf with a tottering plank that will deceive you. When we cast off our best clothes, we put on rags, when our good desires are once laid aside, wanton will begins to prick. Being pensive at home, if you go to Theatres to drive away fancies, it is as good Physic as, for the ache of your head, to knock out your brains; or when you are stung with a Wasp, to rub the sore with a Nettle. When you are grieved, pass the time with your neighbors in sober conference; or, if you can read, let Books be your comfort. Do not imitate those foolish Patients which, having sought all means of recovery & are never the nearer, run unto witchcraft. If your grief be such that you may not disclose it, & your sorrow so great that you loath to utter it, look for no salve at Plays or Theaters, lest that laboring to shun **Scylla,** you light on **Charybdis;**[33] to forsake the deep, you perish in sands, to ward [off] a light stripe,[34] you take a death's wound; and to leave Physic, you flee to enchanting. You need not go abroad to be tempted: you shall be enticed at your own windows. The best counsel that I can give you is to keep home & shun all occasion of ill speech. The virgins of **Vesta**[35] were shut up fast in stone walls to the same end. You must keep your sweet faces from scorching in the Sun, chapping in the wind, and warping with the weather, which is best performed by staying within. And

---

[29] set . . . whites: that is, at the center of the target.   [30] **Cephalus:** Cephalus remained so faithful to his wife Procris that Aurora, who held him captive, had to relinquish him.   [31] **vailed . . . bonnet:** took off one's hat as a sign of respect or submission.   [32] **bolt:** thunderbolt.   [33] **Scylla . . . Charybdis:** a rock and a whirlpool on the Sicilian coast; by avoiding one peril, one runs into its opposite.   [34] **stripe:** blow with a staff or sword.   [35] **Vesta:** the Roman goddess of households; the Vestal Virgins of Rome had charge of the sacred fire in Vesta's temple.

if you perceive yourselves in any danger at your own doors, either allured by courtesy in the day, or assaulted with Music in the night, close up your eyes, stop your ears, tie up your tongues. When they speak, answer not; when they halloo,[36] stoop not; when they sigh, laugh at them; when they sue, scorn them. Shun their company: never be seen where they resort; so shall you neither set them props when they seek to climb, nor hold them the stirrup when they proffer to mount.

These are hard lessons which I teach you. Nevertheless, drink up the potion, though it like not your taste, and you shall be eased; resist not the Surgeon, though he strike in his knife, and you shall be cured. The Fig tree is sour, but it yieldeth sweet fruit: **Thyme** is bitter, but it giveth Honey; my School is tart, but my counsel is pleasant, if you embrace it. Shortly I hope to send out the discourses of my **Phialo,**[37] by whom (if I see you accept this) I will give you one dish for your own tooth. Farewell.

Yours to serve at Virtue's call,
Stephen Gosson.

[36] **halloo:** call out.   [37] **Phialo:** *Ephemerides of Phialo* (1579), Gosson's further defense of his attack on plays and playing.

→   THOMAS HEYWOOD

From An Apology for Actors   *c. 1608*

Of Actors, and the True Use of Their Quality

[The quality of stage plays is not to be condemned because of the theatre's abuses.]

First, playing is an ornament to the City, which strangers of all Nations, repairing hither, report of in their Countries, beholding them here with some admiration: for what variety of entertainment can there be in any City of Christendom more than in *London?* But some will say, this dish might be very well spared out of the banquet. To him I answer, *Diogenes*, that used to feed on roots, cannot relish a Marchpane.[1] Secondly, our *English* tongue, which hath been the most harsh, uneven, and broken language of the world, part *Dutch*, part *Irish, Saxon, Scotch, Welsh*, and indeed a gallimaufry of many,

[1] **Marchpane:** marzipan, a paste of ground almonds.

Thomas Heywood, *An Apology for Actors. Containing three brief Treatises. 1. Their Antiquity. 2. Their ancient Dignity. 3. The true use of their quality.* (London, 1612) F3r–F4r.

but perfect in none, is now by this secondary means of playing, continually refined, every writer striving in himself to add a new flourish unto it; so that in process, from the most rude and unpolish'd tongue, it is grown to a most perfect and composed language, and many excellent works and elaborate Poems writ in the same, that many Nations grow enamored of our tongue (before despised). Neither Sapphic, Ionic, Iambic, Phalaecean, Adonic, Glyconic, Hexameter, Tetrameter, Pentameter, Asclepiadean, Choriambic, nor any other measured verse used amongst the *Greeks, Latins, Italians, French, Dutch,* or *Spanish* writers, but may be express'd in English, be it in blank verse, or meter, in Distichon, or Hexastichon, or in what form or feet, or what number you can desire.[2] Thus you see to what excellency our refined *English* is brought, that in these days we are ashamed of that *Euphony* & eloquence which, within these 60 years, the best tongues in the land were proud to pronounce. Thirdly, plays have made the ignorant more apprehensive, taught the unlearned the knowledge of many famous histories, instructed such as cannot read in the discovery of all our *English* Chronicles. And what man have you now, of that weak capacity, that cannot discourse of any notable thing recorded even from *William* the *Conqueror,* nay from the landing of *Brut*[3] until this day, being possess'd of their true use. For, or because, Plays are writ with this aim and carried with this method: to teach the subjects obedience to their King, to show the people the untimely ends of such as have moved tumults, commotions, and insurrections, to present them with the flourishing estate of such as live in obedience, exhorting them to allegiance, dehorting them from all traitorous and felonious strategems.

If we present a Tragedy, we include the fatal and abortive ends of such as commit notorious murders, which is aggravated and acted with all the Art that may be, to terrify men from the like abhorred practices. If we present a foreign History, the subject is so intended, that in the lives of *Romans, Grecians,* or others, either the virtues of our Countrymen are extolled, or their vices reproved. [A list of classical tragedies and their teaching.] If a moral, it is to persuade men to humanity and good life, to instruct them in civility and good manners, showing them the fruits of honesty, and the end of villainy.

> *Versibus exponi Tragicis res Comica non vult.*
> Again, *Horace, Arte Poëtica.*
> *Et nostri proavi Plautinos & numeros et*
> *Laudavere sales —* [4]

---

[2] **Sapphic . . . can desire:** Heywood names various classical verse forms.   [3] *Brut:* Brutus; a mythical founder of Britain.   [4] Horace, *De Arte Poetica,* 2:89, 270–71. "Comic matter refuses to be expressed in tragic metres. But, you may say, our ancestor praised the metrics and wit of Plautus — "

If a Comedy, it is pleasantly contrived with merry accidents, and inter-mixt with apt and witty jests, to present before the Prince at certain times of solemnity, or else merrily fitted to the stage. And what is then the subject of this harmless mirth? Either, in the shape of a Clown, to show others their slovenly and unhandsome behavior, that they may reform that simplicity in themselves which others make their sport, lest they happen to become the like subject of general scorn to an auditory; else it entreats of love, deriding foolish inamorates[5] who spend their ages, their spirits, nay themselves, in the servile and ridiculous employments of their Mistresses. And these are mingled with sportful accidents, to recreate such as of themselves are wholly devoted to Melancholy, which corrupts the blood; or to refresh such weary spirits as are tired with labor, or study, to moderate the cares and heavyness of the mind, that they may return to their trades and faculties with more zeal and earnestness, after some small soft and pleasant retirement. Some-times they discourse of Pantaloons,[6] Usurers that have unthrifty sons, which both the fathers and sons may behold to their instructions; sometimes of Courtesans, to divulge their subtleties and snares, in which young men may be entangled, showing them the means to avoid them. If we present a Pas-toral, we show the harmless love of Shepherds diversely moralized, distin-guishing betwixt the craft of the City and the innocency of the sheep-cote. Briefly, there is neither Tragedy, History, Comedy, Moral or Pastoral from which an infinite use cannot be gathered. I speak not in the defense of any lascivious shows, scurrilous jests, or scandalous invectives. If there be any such, I banish them quite from my patronage.

---

[5] **inamorates:** lovers.   [6] **Pantaloons:** a stock character from the Italian commedia dell'arte; a lean, foolish old man.

→ THOMAS DEKKER

From Of Lantern and Candlelight   1609

Of Canting, How Long It Hath Been a Language: How It Comes to Be a Language; How It Is Derived, and by Whom It Is Spoken

When all the *World* was but *one Kingdom,* all the *People* in that Kingdom spake but one language. A man could travel in those days neither by Sea nor land but he met his Countrymen & none others.

Two could not then stand gabbling with strange tongues and conspire together (to his own face) how to cut a third man's throat, but he might understand them. There was no *Spaniard* (in that Age) to Brave his enemy in the Rich and Lofty *Castilian;* no *Roman* Orator to plead in the *Rhetorical* and *Fluent Latin;* no *Italian* to court his Mistress in the sweet and Amorous *Tuscan;* no *Frenchman* to parley in the full and stately phrase of *Orleans;* no *German* to thunder out the high and rattling *Dutch.* The unfruitful crabbed *Irish* and the Voluble significant *Welsh* were not then so much as spoken of; the quick *Scottish* Dialect (sister to the *English*) had not then a tongue. Neither were the strings of the *English* speech (in those times) untied. When she first learn'd to speak, it was but a broken language: the singlest and the simplest *Words* flowed from her utterance, for she dealt in nothing but in *Monosyllables* (as if to have spoken words of greater length would have crack'd her Voice); by which means her *Eloquence* was poorest, yet hardest to learn, and so (but for necessity) not regarded amongst *Strangers.* Yet afterwards those Noblest Languages lent her *Words* and phrases, and turning those *Borrowings* into *Good husbandry,* she is now as rich in *Elocution* and as abundant as her proudest & *Best-stored* Neighbors.

Whilst thus (as I said before) there was but one *Alphabet of Letters,* for all the world to *Read* by, the people that then lived might have wrought upon one piece of work in countries far distant asunder without mistaking one another, and not needing an *interpreter* to run between them. Which thing *Nimrod* (the first Idolater) perceiving, and not knowing better how to employ so many thousand Millions of *Subjects* as bowed before him, a fire of *Ambition* burned within him, to climb up so high that he might see what was done in heaven. And for that purpose, workmen were summoned from all the corners of the *Earth,* who presently were set to *Build the Tower of Ba-*

Thomas Dekker, *Of Lantern and Candlelight, or The Bellman's Second Night's Walk* (London, 1609).

bel. But the *Master workman* of this *Great Universe* (to check the *Insolence* of such a *Saucy builder*) that durst raise up *Pinnacles* equal to His own (above) commanded the self-same *Spirit* that was both bred in the *Chaos* and had maintained it in disorder to be both *Surveyor* of those works and *Comptroller* of the *Laborers*. This *Messenger* was called *Confusion*. It was a *Spirit* swift of flight, & faithful of service. Her looks wild, terrible and inconstant. Her attire carelessly loose, and of a thousand several colors. In one hand she gripped a heap of storms with which (at her pleasure) she could trouble the waters. In the other she held a whip, to make three *Spirits* that drew her to gallop faster before her. The *Spirits'* names were *Treason, Sedition, & War,* who at every time when they went abroad were ready to set *Kingdoms* in an uproar. She rode upon a Chariot of Clouds, which was always furnished with *Thunder, Lightning, Winds, Rain, Hailstones, Snow,* & all the other Artillery belonging to the service of *Divine Vengeance,* & when she spake, her *Voice* sounded like the roaring of many *Torrents,* boisterously struggling together, for between her Jaws did she carry 1,000,000 *Tongues*.

This strange *Linguist,* stepping to every Artificer that was there at work, whispered in his ear, whose looks were thereupon (presently) filled with a strange distraction: and on a sudden, whilst every man was speaking to his fellow, his language altered, and no man could understand what his fellow spake. They all stared one upon another, yet none of them all could tell wherefore so they stared. Their *Tongues* went, and their hands gave action to their *Tongues*: yet neither words nor action were understood. It was a Noise of a thousand sounds, and yet the sound of the noise was nothing. He that spake knew he spake well: and he that heard was mad that the other could speak no better. In the end they grew angry one with another, as thinking they had mocked one another of purpose. So that the *Mason* was ready to strike the *Bricklayer,* the *Bricklayer* to beat out the brains of his *Laborer,* the *Carpenter* took up his Axe to throw at the *Carver,* whilst the *Carver* was stabbing at the *Smith* because he brought him a *Hammer* when he should have made him a *Chisel*. He that called for *Timber* had *Stones* laid before him, & when one was sent for *Nails,* he fetched a *Tray of Mortar*.

Thus *Babel* should have been raised, and by this means *Babel fell*. The Frame could not go forward, the stuff was thrown by, the workmen made holiday. Everyone packed up his tools to be gone, yet not to go the same way that he came. But glad was he that could meet another whose speech he understood: for to what place soever he went, others (that ran madding up and down), hearing a man speak like themselves, followed only him, so that they who when the work began were all countrymen, before a quarter of it was finished fled from one another as from enemies & strangers. And in this manner did Men at the first make up nations. Thus were words coined into *Languages,* and out of those *Languages* have others been molded since, only by the mixture of nations after kingdoms have been subdued.

But I am now to speak of a *People* & a *Language,* of both which (many thousands of years since that *Wonder* wrought at *Babel*) the world till now never made mention. Yet confusion never dwelt more amongst any *Creatures.* The *Bellman* (in his first *Voyage* which he made for *Discoveries*) found them to be *savages,* yet living in an Island very temperate, fruitful, full of a Noble Nation, and rarely governed. The Laws, Manners and habits of these *Wild-men* are plainly set down, as it were in a former painted *Table.* Yet lest haply a *stranger* may look upon this second *Picture* of them who never beheld *The first,* it shall not be amiss (in this place) to repeat over again the *Names* of all the *Tribes* into which they *Divide* themselves, both when they *Serve* abroad in the open fields and when they lie in garrison within *Towns* & walled *Cities.*

And these are their Ranks as they stand in order, *viz.*

Rufflers.	Prigs.
Upright-men.	Swadders.
Hookers, *alias* Anglers.	Curtalls.
Rogues.	Irish Toyles.
Wild Rogues.	Swigmen.
Priggers of Prancers.	Jarkmen.
Paillards.	Patricoes.
Fraters.	Kinchin-Coes.
Abraham-men.	Glymmerers.
Mad Tom *alias of* Bedlam.	Bawdy-Baskets.
Whip-Jacks.	Autem-Morts.
Counterfeit Cranks.	Doxies.
Dommerats.	Dells.
	Kinchin-Morts.

Into thus many *Regiments* are they now divided. But in former times (above four hundred years now past) they did consist of five Squadrons only, *viz.*

1. Cursitors, alias Vagabonds.

2. Faytors.

3. Robert's men.

4. Draw-latches.

5. Sturdy Beggars.

And as these people are strange both in names and in their conditions, so do they speak a Language (proper only to themselves) called *canting*, which is more strange. By none but the soldiers of *These tattered bands* is it familiarly or usually spoken, yet within less than fourscore years (now past) not a word of this Language was known. The first Inventor of it was hanged, yet left he apt scholars behind him who have reduced that into *Method* which he on his death-bed (which was a pair of gallows) could not so absolutely perfect as he desired.

It was necessary that a people (so fast increasing & so daily practicing new & strange *Villainies*) should borrow to themselves a speech which (so near as they could) none but themselves should understand: & for that cause was this Language (which some call *Peddler's French*) Invented, to th' intent that (albeit any Spies should secretly steal into their companies to discover them) they might freely utter their minds one to another, yet avoid the danger. The Language therefore of *canting* they study even from their Infancy, that is to say, from the very first hour that they take upon them the names of *Kinchin Coes*, till they are grown *Rufflers* or *Upright men*, which are the highest in degree amongst them.

This word *canting* seems to be derived from the Latin *verb* (*canto*) which signifies in English, to sing, or to make a sound with words, that's to say, to speak. And very aptly may *canting* take his derivation *a cantando*, from singing, because amongst these beggarly consorts that can play upon no better instruments, the language of *canting* is a kind of music, and he that in such assemblies can *cant* best is counted the best Musician.

Now as touching the Dialect or phrase itself, I see not that it is grounded upon any certain rules. And no marvel if it have none, for since both the *Father* of this new kind of Learning, and the *children* that study to speak it after him, have been from the beginning and still are the *Breeders* and *Nourishers* of a base disorder in their living and in their *Manners*, how is it possible they should observe any *Method* in their speech, and especially in such a Language as serves but only to utter discourses of villainies?

And yet (even out of all that *Irregularity*, unhandsomeness, & Fountain of *Barbarism*) do they draw a kind of form: and in some words (as well simple as compounds) retain a certain salt, tasting of some wit and some Learning. As for example, they call a cloak (in the *canting* tongue) a *Togeman*, and in Latin, *Toga* signifies a gown, or an upper garment. *Pannam* is bread; & *Panis* in Latin is likewise bread; *cassan* is cheese, and is a word barbarously coined out of the substantive *caseus*, which also signifies a cheese. And so of others.

Then by joining of two simples do they make almost all their compounds. As for example, *Nab* (in the *canting* tongue) is a head, & *Nab-cheat* is a hat or cap. Which word *cheat*, being coupled to other words, stands in very good stead and does excellent service: for a *Smelling cheat* signifies a Nose, a *Prattling cheat* is a tongue. *Crashing cheats* are teeth, *Hearing cheats* are Ears, *Fambles* are Hands, and thereupon a ring is called a *Fambling cheat*. A *Muffling cheat* signifies a Napkin. A *Belly cheat* an Apron, A *Grunting cheat* a Pig, A *Cackling Cheat* a Cock or a Capon, A *Quacking cheat* a duck, A *Lowing cheat* a Cow, A *Bleating cheat* a Calf or a Sheep: and so may that word be married to many others besides.

The word *Cove*, or *Cofe*, or *Cuffin* signifies a Man, a Fellow, &c. But differs something in his property according as it meets with other words. For a Gentleman is called a *Gentry Cove* or *Cofe*, A good fellow is a *Bene Cofe*, a Churl is called a *Queer Cuffin* — *Queer* signifies naught, and *Cuffin* (as I said before) a man. And in *Canting* they term a Justice of peace (because he punisheth them belike) by no other name than by *Queer cuffin*, that is to say a Churl, or a naughty man. And so, *Ken* signifying a house, they call a prison a *Queer ken*, that's to say, an ill house.

Many pieces of this strange coin could I show you, but by these small stamps you may judge of the greater.

[Dekker includes another example of canting rhythms before translating the following instance of "broken French."]

Two *Canters*, having wrangled a while about some idle quarrel, at length growing friends, thus one of them speaks to the other, *viz.*

A Canter in prose

Stow you, bene cofe, and cut benar whids and bing we to Romeville to nip a bung: so shall we have lower for the bowzing ken, and when we bing back to the Deuce-a-ville we will filch some Duds off the Ruffmans or mill the Ken for a lag of Duds.

Thus in English

Stow you, bene cofe:	hold your peace, good fellow.
And cut benar whids:	and speak better words.

And bing we to Romeville:	and go we to London.
To nip a bung:	to cut a purse.
So shall we have lower:	so shall we have money.
For the bowzing ken:	for the Alehouse.
And when we bing back:	and when we come back.
To the Deuce-a-ville:	to the Country.
We will filch some Duds:	we will filch some clothes.
Off the Ruffmans:	from the hedges.
Or mill the Ken:	or rob the house.
For a lag of Duds:	for a buck of clothes.

[Dekker provides a "Canter's Dictionary" of eighty-eight terms.]

To give [this commodity] a little more weight, you shall have a *Canting song*, wherein you may learn how *This cursed Generation* pray, or (to speak truth) curse such Officers as punish them.

A Canting Song

The Ruffian cly the nab of the Harmanbeck,
If we maund pannam, lap or Ruff-peck,
Or poplars of yarum: he cuts, bing to the Ruffmans,
Or else he swears by the lightmans,
To put our stamps in the Harmans.
The ruffian cly the ghost of the Harmanbeck;
If we heave a booth, we cly the Jerk.

If we niggle, or mill a bowzing Ken,
Or nip a bung that has but a win,
Or dup the gigger of a Gentry cofe's ken,
To the queer cuffing we bing,
And then to the queer Ken to scour the Cramp-ring,
And then to be Trined on the chates, in the lightmans:
The Bube & Ruffian cly the Harmanbeck & harmans.

Thus Englished

The Devil take the Constable's head,
If we beg Bacon, Buttermilk or bread,
Or Pottage: to the hedge he bids us hie,
Or swears (by this light) i' th' stocks we shall lie.
The Devil haunt the Constable's ghost;
If we rob but a Booth, we are whipped at a post.

If an alehouse we rob, or be ta'en with a whore,
Or cut a purse that has just a penny and no more,

Or come but stealing in at a Gentleman's door,
To the Justice straight we go,
And then to the Jail to be shackled, And so
To be hang'd on the gallows i' th' day-time:
The pox and the Devil take the Constable and his stocks.

We have *Canted* (I fear) too much.

→ JOHN DOD AND ROBERT CLEAVER

From A Godly Form of Household Government *1621*

WHAT THE DUTY OF A WIFE IS TOWARDS HER HUSBAND

This duty is comprehended in these three points. First, that she reverence her husband. Secondly, that she submit herself, and be obedient unto him. And lastly, that she do not wear gorgeous apparel, beyond her degree and place, but that her attire be comely and sober, according to her calling. The first point is proved by the Apostles *Peter* and *Paul,* who set forth the wives' duties to their husbands, commanding them to be obedient unto them, although they be profane and irreligious; yea, that they ought to do it so much the more, that by their honest life and conversation, they might win them to the obedience of the Lord.[1]

Now for so much as the Apostle would have Christian wives, that are matched with ungodly husbands, and such as are not yet good Christians to reverence and obey them: much more they should show themselves thankful to God, and willingly and dutifully perform this obedience and subjec-

◄ FIGURE 15 *This frontispiece from Richard Brathwaite's* The English Gentlewoman *(London, 1631), a conduct book detailing appropriate public and private behaviors for women, pictures (from upper right, clockwise) scenes exemplifying the ideals of honor, gentility, fancy, estimation, decency, complement, behavior, and apparel, each accompanied with a bannered phrase of advice. These scenes surround a central figure and another banner — "Grace my guide, glory my goal" — which summarizes the book's overall moral argument.*

[1] **Marginal note:** 1 Peter 3:1; Ephesians 5:22; Colossians 3:18; 1 Corinthians 7:3.

John Dod and Robert Cleaver, *A Godly Form of Household Government: For the Ordering of Private Families According to the Direction of God's Word* (London, 1621) O4v–Q3r.

tion, when they are coupled in marriage with godly, wise, discreet, learned, gentle, loving, quiet, patient, honest, and thrifty husbands. And therefore they ought evermore to reverence them, and to endeavor with true obedience and love to serve them; to be loath in any wise to offend them, yea, rather to be careful and diligent to please them, that their soul may bless them.[2] And if at any time it shall happen that the wife shall anger or displease her husband, by doing or speaking anything that shall grieve him, she ought never to rest until she hath pacified him, and gotten his favor again. And if he shall chance to blame her without a cause, & for that which she could not help or remedy (which thing sometimes happeneth even of the best men), yet she must bear it patiently and give him no uncomely or unkind words for it: but evermore look upon him with a loving and cheerful countenance, and so rather let her take the fault upon her, than seem to be displeased. Let her be always merry and cheerful in his company, but yet not with too much lightness. She must beware in any wise of swelling, pouting, lowering, or frowning: for that is a token of a cruel and unloving heart, except it be in respect of sin, or in time of sickness. She may not be sorrowful for any adversity that God sendeth: but must always be careful that nothing be spilt, or go to waste, through her negligence. In any wise she must be quick and cleanly about her husband's meat and drink, preparing him the same according to his diet in due season.[3] Let her show herself in word and deed wise, humble, courteous, gentle, and loving towards her husband, and also towards such as he doth love; and then shall she lead a blessed life. Let her show herself not only to love no man so well as her husband; but also to love none other at all, but him, unless it be for her husband's sake. Wherefore let the wife remember that (as the Scripture reporteth[4]) she is one body with her husband; so that she ought to love him none otherwise than herself. For this is the greatest virtue of a married woman; this is the thing that wedlock signifieth and commandeth, that the wife should reckon to have her husband for both father, mother, brother, and sister, like as *Adam* was unto *Eve*. And as the most noble and chaste woman *Andromache* said her husband *Hector* was unto her:

> *Thou art unto me both father and mother,*
> *Mine own dear husband, and well-beloved brother.*[5]

---

[2] **Marginal note:** "Wives must be serviceable and obedient unto their husbands, & stand in a reverend awe of them. Ephesians 5:33." [3] **Marginal note:** Genesis 27:9. [4] **Marginal note:** Genesis 2:23, 24; Matthew 19:5; 1 Corinthians 6:16; Ephesians 5:31. [5] Homer, *Iliad*, bk.6, 429–432. Dod and Cleaver's point is that the husband should be all to his wife; Andromache, after recounting the deaths of her father, her mother, and her seven brothers, urges Hector to remain in Troy rather than going into battle.

And if it be true that men do say, that friendship maketh one heart of two: much more truly and effectually ought wedlock to do the same, which far passeth all manner both friendship and kindred. Therefore it is not said, that marriage doth make one man, or one mind, or one body of two, but clearly one person. Wherefore matrimony requireth a greater duty of the husband towards his wife, and the wife towards her husband, than otherwise they are bound to show to their parents. [Dod and Cleaver develop these ideas, citing biblical texts to support their argument for a well-ordered household in which "communication and consent of counsel and will" characterize marital relations. Even when a wife is more wise and discreet than her husband, she must acknowledge her husband as her head.]

So that this modesty and government ought to be in a wife: namely, that she should not speak but to her husband, or by her husband. And as the voice of him that soundeth a trumpet is not followed, as the sound that it yieldeth: so is the wisdom and word of a woman of greater virtue and efficacy, when all that she knoweth, and can do, is, as if it were said and done by her husband. The obedience that the wife oweth to her husband dependeth upon this subjection of her will and wisdom unto him. As 1 Peter 3:6; Ephesians 5:33; Esther 1:1, 2 &c. 12. So that women may not provoke their husbands by disobedience, in matters that may be performed without offence to GOD: neither presume over them either in kindred or wealth, or obstinately to refuse in a matter that may trouble household peace and quiet. For disobedience begetteth contempt of the husband, and contempt, wrath, and is many times the cause of troubles between the man and the wife. If the obedience importeth any difficulty, she may for her excuse gently propound the same: yet upon condition to obey (in case the husband should persist in his intent) so long as the discommodity importeth no wickedness. For it is better to continue peace by obedience, than to break it by resistance. And indeed it is natural in the members to obey the conduct and government of the head. Yet must not this obedience so far extend, as that the husband should command any thing contrary to her honor, credit, and salvation, but as it is comely in the Lord: Colossians 3:18; Ephesians 5:22. Therefore, as it were a monstrous matter, and the means to overthrow the person, that the body should, in refusing all subjection and obedience to the head, take upon it to guide itself and to command the head: so were it for the wife to rebel against the husband. Let her then beware of disordering and perverting the course which God in His wisdom hath established: and withal let her understand that, going about it, she riseth not so much against her husband, as against GOD, and that it is her good and honor to obey God in her subjection and obedience to her husband. If in the practice of this duty, she find any difficulty or trouble through the inconsiderate course of her husband, or otherwise, let her remember, that the same proceedeth not of the order established by the Lord, but through some sin afterward crept in, which hath mixed gall among the honey of the subjection and obedience, that the woman should have enjoyed in that estate, wherein, together with *Adam,* she was created after the image of God. And so let her humble herself in the sight of God, and be well assured that her subjection and obedience is acceptable unto him: and that the more that the image of God is restored in her, and her husband, through the regeneration of the holy Ghost, the less difficulty she shall find in that subjection and obedience; as many in their marriage have indeed tried, to their great contentment and consolation.

[Women are directed to please the "nature, inclinations, and manners of their husbands, so long as the same import no wickedness."]

Moreover, a modest and chaste woman that loveth her husband must also love her house, as remembering that the husband that loveth his wife cannot so well like of the sight of any tapestry as to see his wife in his house. For the woman that gaddeth from house to house to prate, confoundeth herself, her husband, and family: Titus 2:5. But there are four reasons why the woman is to go abroad. First, to come to holy meetings, according to the duty of godliness. The second, to visit such as stand in need, as the duty of love and charity require. The third, for employment and provision in household affairs committed to her charge. And lastly, with her husband, when he shall require her: Genesis 20:1 &c. The evil and unquiet life that some women have, and pass with their husbands, is not so much for that, they commit with, and in their persons, as it is for that they speak with their tongues. If the wife would keep silence when her husband beginneth to chide, he should not have so unquiet dinners, neither she the worse supper. Which surely is not so: for at the same time that the husband beginneth to utter his grief, the wife beginneth to scold and chafe; whereof doth follow, that now and then, most unnaturally they come to handy gripes, more beastlike than Christianlike, which their so doing is both a great shame, and a foul discredit to them both. The best means therefore that a wife can use to obtain, and maintain the love and good liking of her husband is to be silent, obedient, peaceable, patient, studious to appease his choler if he be angry, painful and diligent in looking to her business, to be solitary and honest. The chief and special cause why most women do fail in not performing this duty to their husbands, is, because they be ignorant of the word of God, which teacheth the same and all other duties: and therefore their souls and consciences not being brought into subjection to God and his word, they can never until then, yield and perform true subjection and obedience to their husbands, and behave themselves so every way, as Christian wives are in duty bound to do. But if wives be not so dutiful, serviceable, and subject to their husbands, as in conscience they ought, the only cause thereof, for the most part, is through the want and neglect of the wise, discreet, and good government that should be in the husbands: besides the want of good example that they should give unto their wives both in word and deed. For as the common saying is: Such a husband, such a wife; a good Jack maketh a good Jill. For so much as marriage maketh of two persons one, therefore the love of the husband and wife may the better be kept and increased, and so continued, if they remember the duties last spoken of, as also not forget these three points following.

1. They must be of one heart, will, and mind, and neither to upbraid, or cast the other in the teeth with their wants and imperfections any ways, or to pride themselves in their gifts: but rather the one to endeavor to supply the other's wants, that so they, both helping and doing their best together, may be one perfect body.

2. It doth greatly increase love, when the one faithfully serveth the other: when in things concerning marriage the one hideth no secrets nor privities from the other, and the one doth not utter or publish the frailties or infirmities of the other; and when of all that ever they obtain or get, they have but one common purse together, the one locking up nothing from the other; and also when the one is faithful to the other's business in all their [. . .]⁶ and affairs. Likewise, when the one harkneth to the other, and when the one thinketh not scorn of the other, and when in matters concerning the government of the house, the one will be counseled and advised by the other: the one of them being always loving, kind, courteous, plain, and gentle unto the other in words, manners and deeds.

3. Let the one learn ever to be obsequious, diligent, and serviceable to the other in all honest things. And this will the sooner come to pass, if the one observe and mark what thing the other can away withal, or cannot away withal,⁷ and what pleaseth or displeaseth them: and so from thenceforth to do the one, and to leave the other undone. And if one of them be angry and offended with the other, then let the party grieved open and make known to the other their grief in due time, and with discretion. For the longer a dis-

---

⁶ A word is missing in the text. ⁷ **can . . . withal:** what behavior one can or cannot tolerate.

pleasure, or evil will rageth in secret, the worse will be the discord. And this must be observed, that it be done in a fit and convenient time: because there is some season, in the which if griefs were showed, it should make greater debate. As if the wife should go about to tell or admonish her husband when he is out of patience, or moved with anger, it should then be no fit time to talk with him. Therefore *Abigail* perceiving *Nabal* her husband to be drunk, would not speak to him until the morning.[8] Both the husband and wife must remember, that the one be not so offended and displeased with the manners of the other, that they should thereupon forsake the company one of the other: for that were like to one that, being stung with the Bees, would therefore forsake the honey.[9] And therefore no man may put away his wife for any cause, except for whoredom,[10] which must be duly proved before a lawful judge. But all godly and faithful married folks are to commend their state and marriage to God by humble and fervent prayer, that He for His beloved son's sake would so bless them and their marriage, that they may so Christianly and dutifully agree between themselves, that they may have no cause of any separation or divorcement. For like as all manner of medicines (and specially they that go nighest death, as to cut off whole members, &c.) are very loathsome and terrible: even so is divorcement indeed a medicine, but a perilous and terrible medicine. Therefore every good Christian husband and wife ought with all care and heedfulness so to live in marriage that they have no need of such a medicine.

[Examples from Scripture of wicked and ungodly women as well as those who were devout, religious, and virtuous. God's word, write Dod and Cleaver, praises more good women than men. After reiterating that wives should submit themselves to their husbands as to the Lord, Dod and Cleaver turn to more particular duties: the "special duty" of a mother to nurse her own children and the duties of stepfathers and stepmothers.]

The third and last point that appertaineth to the duty of wives, is, that they do not wear gorgeous and sumptuous apparel, or braided hair trimmed with gold: but that, after the example of holy women which trusted in God, they be sober in outward apparel, and garnished and decked inwardly with virtues of their minds: as with gentleness, meekness, quietness, and chastity, which indeed are most precious things in the sight of God. This point is plainly spoken of by the Apostle to *Tim-*

---

[8] **Marginal note:** 1 Samuel 25:36, 37.　[9] **Marginal note:** 1 Corinthians 7:10–16; Matthew 19:6; Matthew 19:9 & 5:33.　[10] **Marginal note:** Luke 16:18.

othy, chap. 2, vers[es] 9–10, in which place he so flatly condemneth both the excess and pride of apparel, as also the pomp, curiosity and wantonness which women use in trimming their heads by plaiting, crisping, braiding, curling, & curiously laying out, that no man can say more against it, in so few words, than he hath spoken to the utter dislike thereof. For if a man should occupy himself, & give liberty to his pen to write of the horrible abuse and excessive pride, that many women commit in this behalf, he should rather want time to write than matter to speak. Therefore such women as will not reform themselves herein, we leave them to the Lord, who (no doubt) will in his appointed time, not only severely punish them, but also their husbands, for suffering this great wickedness and dissoluteness in their wives, as he did the Jews for the same sin, as plainly may be seen in Isaiah 3:16 &c. For so it falleth out, according to the common proverb, That pride goeth before, & shame and destruction cometh after. And on the contrary part, we hope that such women as be true professors of Christ and his religion, will both attire and dress their heads so decently, and also content themselves with such comely apparel, as best beseemeth their calling and degree: so as by their good example, they may draw on other women to reform themselves in this behalf, and so rather to come short of that, which their ability and place would serve to maintain, than any ways to exceed therein, to the slander of their profession. And let them not so much regard what thing they would fain have, but rather what they cannot well be without: so that whatsoever they have need of, is too dear of a farthing.[11]

---

[11] **whatsoever . . . farthing:** so that what they have need of is too costly at the price of a farthing, the fourth part of a penny.

→ JOSEPH SWETNAM

From The Arraignment of Lewd, Idle, Froward, and Unconstant Women

1615

Chapter II

The Second Chapter showeth the manner of such Women as live upon evil report: It also showeth that the beauty of Women hath been the bane of many a man, for it hath overcome valiant and strong men, eloquent and subtle men. And, in a word, it hath overcome all men, as by examples following shall here appear.

First that of *Solomon,* unto whom God gave singular wit & wisdom, yet he loved so many women that he quite forgot his God, which always did guide his steps, so long as he lived godly and ruled Justly. But after he had glutted himself with women, then he could say, Vanity of vanity, all is but vanity. He also, in many places of his book of Proverbs, Exclaims most bitterly against lewd women, calling them all that naught is, and also displayeth their properties. And yet I cannot let men go blameless although women go shameless; but I will touch them both, for if there were not receivers, then there would not be so many stealers; if there were not some knaves, there would not be so many whores, for they both hold together to bolster each other's villany, for always birds of a feather will flock together, hand in hand, to bolster each other's villainy.

Men, I say, may live without women, but women cannot live without men: For Venus, whose beauty was excellent fair, yet when she needed man's help, she took *Vulcan,* a clubfooted Smith. And therefore if a woman's face glister, and her Gesture pierce the marble wall; or if her tongue be so smooth as oil or so soft as silk, and her words so sweet as honey; or if she were a very Ape for wit or a bag of gold for wealth; or if her personage have stolen away all that nature can afford; and if she be decked up in gorgeous apparel, then a thousand to one but she will love to walk where she may get acquaintance. And acquaintance bringeth familiarity, and familiarity setteth all follies abroach; and twenty to one that if a woman love gadding but that she will pawn her honor to please her fantasy.

Man must be at all the cost and yet live by the loss; a man must take all

Joseph Swetnam, *The Arraignment of Lewd, idle, froward, and unconstant women: Or the vanity of them, choose you whether. With a Commendation of wise, virtuous and honest Women. Pleasant for married Men, profitable for young Men, and hurtful to none* (London, 1615) C3v–F1r.

the pains, and women will spend all the gains. A man must watch and ward, fight and defend, till the ground, labor in the vineyard, and look what he getteth in seven years: a woman will spread it abroad with a fork[1] in one year, and yet little enough to serve her turn, but a great deal too little, to get her good will. Nay, if thou give her never so much and yet if thy personage please not her humor, then will I not give a halfpenny for her honesty at the year's end.

For then her breast will be the harborer of an envious heart, & her heart the storehouse of poisonous hatred; her head will devise villainy, and her hands are ready to practice that which their heart desireth. Then who can but say that women sprung from the Devil, whose heads, hands & hearts, minds & souls are evil, for women are called the hook of all evil, because men are taken by them as fish is taken with the hook.

For women have a thousand ways to entice thee, and ten thousand ways to deceive thee, and all such fools as are suitors unto them: some they keep in hand with promises, and some they feed with flattery, and some they delay with dalliances, and some they please with kisses. They lay out the folds of their hair to entangle men into their love; betwixt their breasts is the vale of destruction; & in their beds there is hell, sorrow, & repentance. Eagles eat not men till they are dead, but women devour them alive, for a woman will pick thy pocket & empty thy purse, laugh in thy face and cut thy throat. They are ungrateful, perjured, full of fraud, flouting and deceit, unconstant, waspish, toyish, light, sullen, proud, discourteous, and cruel. And yet they were by God created, and by nature formed, and therefore by policy and wisdom to be avoided. For good things abused are to be refused, or else for a month's pleasure she may hap to make thee go stark naked. She will give thee roast meat, but she will beat thee with the spit. If thou hast crowns in thy purse, she will be thy heart's gold until she leave thee not a whit of white money.[2] They are like summer birds, for they will abide no storm, but flock about thee in the pride of thy glory, and fly from thee in the storms of affliction, for they aim more at thy wealth than at thy person, and esteem more thy money than any man's virtuous qualities, for they esteem of a man without money as a horse doth of a fair stable without meat. They are like Eagles which will always fly where the carrion is.

They will play the horse-leech to suck away thy wealth, but in the winter of thy misery she will fly away from thee, Not unlike the Swallow, which in

---

[1] **fork:** a farm implement; *fork* was a term for a spendthrift.   [2] **white money:** silver coins.

the summer harboreth herself under the eaves of an house and against winter flieth away, leaving nothing but dirt behind her.

[Citing Old and New Testament sources condemning whores and lewd women, Swetnam claims that harlots use up men's strength, destroy the body's beauty, and shorten life. Women bring both pleasure and displeasure to men, yet still men desire them, to their ruin. Swetnam recounts stories of biblical and classical courtesans and the men they have ensnared: David, Solomon, Samson, Holofernes, Herod, Hercules, Socrates, Plato, Hannibal, and Julius Caesar.]

But yet happily some may say unto me: if thou shouldst refuse the company or the courtesy of a woman, then she would account thee a soft-spirited fool, a milksop, & a meacock.[3] But alas, fond fool, wilt thou more regard their babble than thine own bliss, or esteem more their frumps than thine own welfare? Dost thou not know that women always strive against wisdom, although many times it be to their utter overthrow? Like the Bee which is often hurt with her own honey, even so women are often plagued with their own conceit, weighing down love with discourtesy, giving him a weed, which presents them with flowers, as their catching in jest, and their keeping in earnest. And yet she thinks that she keeps herself blameless, and in all ill vices she would go nameless. But if she carry it never so clean, yet in the end she will be accounted but for a cony-catching quean,[4] and yet she will swear that she will thrive, as long as she can find one man alive, for she thinks to do all her knavery invisible. She will have a fig leaf to cover her shame, but when the fig leaf is dry and withered, it doth show their nakedness to the world. For take away their painted clothes, and then they look like ragged walls; take away their ruffs, and they look ruggedly; their coifs and stomachers,[5] and they are simple[6] to behold; their hair untrussed, and they look wildly. And yet there are many which lay their nets to catch a pretty woman, but he which getteth such a prize gains nothing by his adventure, but shame to the body and danger to the soul, for the heat of the young blood of these wantons leads many unto destruction for this world's pleasure. It chants[7] your minds, and enfeebleth your bodies with diseases; it also scandaleth your good names, but most of all it endangereth your souls. How can it otherwise choose, when lust and unclean-

---

[3] **meacock:** weakling. [4] **cony-catching quean:** a swindling prostitute. [5] **coifs and stomachers:** close-fitting caps and embroidered, jeweled bodices covering the chest and stomach. [6] **simple:** plain. [7] **chants:** enchants.

ness continually keeps them company, gluttony and sloth serveth them at the table, pride and vainglory appareleth them? But these servants will wax weary of their service, and in the end they shall have no other servants to attend them, but only shame, grief, and repentance. But then, oh then (you will say) when it is too late, Oh, would to God that we had been more careful of true glorious modesty, and less cunning to keep wantons company. Oh, therefore remember and think beforehand, that every sweet hath his sour. Then buy not with a drop of honey a gallon of gall; do not think that this world's pleasure will pass away with a trifle and that no sooner done but presently forgotten. No, no, answer yourselves that the punishment remaineth eternally, and therefore better it were to be an addle[8] egg than an evil bird. For we are not born for ourselves to live in pleasure, but to take pains and to labor for the good of our Country. Yet so delightful is our present sweetness, that we never remember the following sour, for youth are too too easy won and overcome with the world's vanities. Oh, too soon (I say) is youth in the blossoms devoured with the caterpillars of foul lust and lascivious desires. The black Fiend of Hell by his enticing sweet sin of lust draws many young wits to confusion, for in time it draws the heart blood of your good names, & that, being once lost, is never gotten again.

Again, Lust causeth you to do such foul deeds, which makes your foreheads forever afterwards seem spotted with black shame and everlasting infamy, by which means your graves after death are closed up with time's scandal. And yet women are easily wooed and soon won, got with an apple and lost with the paring. Young wits are soon corrupted; women's bright beauty breeds curious thoughts; and golden gifts easily overcome wantons' desires, with changing modesty into pastimes of vanity, and being once delighted therein, continues in the same without repentance. You are only the people's wonder, and misfortune's bandying ball tossed up and down the world with woe upon woe. Yea, ten thousand woes will be galloping hard at your heels and pursue you whersoever you go, for those of ill report cannot stay long in one place, but roam and wander about the world, and yet ever unfortunate, prospering in nothing, forsaken and cast out from all civil companies, still in fear lest authority with the sword of Justice bar them of liberty. Lo, thus your lives are despised, walking like night Owls in misery, and no comfort shall be your friend, but only repentance coming too late and overdear

---

[8] **addle:** rotten.

bought: A penance and punishment due to all such hated creatures as these are.

Therefore believe, all you unmarried wantons, and in believing, grieve that you have thus unluckily made yourselves neither maidens, widows, nor wives, but more vile than filthy channel dirt fit to be swept out of the heart and suburbs of your Country. Oh, then suffer not this world's pleasure to take from you the good thoughts of an honest life: But down, down upon your knees, you earthly Serpents, and wash away your black sin with the crystal tears of true sorrow and repentance, so that when you wander from this enticing world, you may be washed and cleansed from this foul leprosy of nature.

Lo, thus in remorse of mind my tongue hath uttered to the wantons of the world the abundance of my heart's grief, which I have perceived by the unseemly behavior of unconstant both men and women. Yet men for the most part are touched but with one fault, which is drinking too much, but it is said of women that they have two faults: that is, they can neither say well nor yet do well.

For commonly women are the most part of the forenoon painting themselves, and frizzling their hairs, and prying in their glass, like Apes to prank up themselves in their gaudies; like Puppets, or like the Spider which weaves a fine web to hang the fly. Amongst women, she is accounted a slut which goeth not in her silks. Therefore if thou wilt please thy Lady, thou must like and love, sue and serve, and in spending thou must lay on load, for they must have maintenance howsoever they get it, by hook or by crook, out of *Judas'* bag or the Devil's budget, thou must spare neither lands nor living, money nor gold.

[Women not only criticize men but steal from them: although men raise animals and farm for gainful purpose, they can gain nothing from women. Some women are not even faithful; as soon as they have depleted a man's wealth, they will leave him. Swetnam draws the picture of a courtesan: "a fair young man blind, and in his arms a beautiful woman with one hand in his pocket, showing her theft, and a knife in the other hand to cut his throat."]

Now peradventure thou maist say unto that thou dost not know one woman from another without some trial, because all women are in shape alike, for the sour crab is like the sweet pippin: true it is, so the Raven is a bird, and the Swan is but a bird. Even so, many women are in shape Angels, but in qualities Devils, painted coffins with rotten bones; the Ostrich carrieth fair feathers but rank flesh; the herb *Molia* carrieth a flower as white as snow, but a root as black as ink.

Although women are beautiful, showing pity, yet their hearts are black, swelling with mischief, not much unlike unto old trees, whose outward leaves are fair and green and yet the body rotten. If thou haunt their houses thou wilt be enamoured, and if thou do but hearken to these *Sirens,* thou wilt be enchanted, for they will allure thee with amorous glances of lust, and yet kill thee with bitter looks of hate: they have dimples in their cheeks to deceive thee, & wrinkles in their brows to betray thee; they have eyes to entice, smiles to flatter, embracements to provoke, becks to recall, lips to enchant, kisses to enflame, and tears to excuse themselves.

If God had not made them only to be a plague to men, he would never have called them necessary evils, and what are they better? For what do they either get or gain, save or keep? Nay, they do rather spend and consume all that which man painfully getteth: a man must be at all the cost and yet live by the loss.

It is very easy for him which never experienced himself in that vain pleasure, or repenting pleasure, choose you whether. I mean the accompanying of lewd women, but such as are exercised and experimented in that kind of drudgery. They, I say, have a continual desire, and temptation is ready at hand. Therefore take heed at the first, suffer not thyself to be led away into lustful folly, for it is more easy for a young man or maid to forbear carnal acts than it is for a widow, and yet more easy for a widow than for her that is married and hath her husband wanting. Then take heed at the first, for there is nothing gotten by women but repentance.

For women are like the bay tree which is ever green but without fruit, or like the unprofitable thorn which beareth as trim a blossom as the apple. This is nothing but to tell thee that thou must not judge of gold by the color, nor of women's qualities by their faces, nor by their speeches, for they have delicate tongues which will ravish and tickle the itching ears of giddy-headed young men, so foolish, that they think themselves happy if they can but kiss the daisy whereon their love doth tread; who if she frown, then he descends presently into hell, but if she smile, then is he carried with wings up into heaven. There is an old saying that when a dog wags his tail he loves his master.

Some think that if a woman smile on them, she is presently over head and ears in love. One must wear her glove, another her garter, another her colors of delight, and another shall spend and live upon the spoil which she getteth from all the rest. Then if thou wilt give thy body to the Surgeon and thy soul to the Devil, such women are fit for thy diet. Many creatures of every kind resemble women in conditions, for some horse an unskillful rider can hardly disorder, and some again, in despite of the best rider that is, will have a jadish trick: some Hawk, although he be ill served, yet will sit quiet, and some, if never so well served, yet will continually fly at check; again, some hounds by no means will forsake their undertaken game, and some again, in despite of the huntsman, will continually run at random; and some men will steal if their hands were bound behind them, and some again will rather starve than steal. Even so, some women will not be won with seven years loving, and some again will offend with an hour's liberty.

Therefore if thou study a thousand years, thou shalt find a woman nothing else but a contrary unto man; nay, if thou continue with her a hundred years, yet thou shalt find in her new fancies and contrary sorts of behavior. Therefore if all the world were paper, and all the sea ink, and all the trees and plants were pens, and every man in the world were a writer, yet were they not able with all their labor and cunning to set down all the crafty deceits of women.

Now methinks I hear some of you say that young wits are soon corrupted, and that women's bright beauty breedeth curious thoughts in men; also, golden gifts easily overcometh wanton women's desires, and thereby makes them become Venus' darlings, quite changing customs of modesty into passions of vanity, wherein once delighted they continue in the same without repentance or sorrow. But out alas, you lascivious Dames: these lewd conditions of yours will speedily bring all your joys to sorrow.

→ RAPHAEL HOLINSHED

From The Chronicles of England, Scotland, and Ireland 1587

On Welsh Women

This was a shrewd discomfiture to the Welsh by the English, on whome sinister lot lowred, at such time as more than a thousand of them were slaine in a hot skirmish; and such shamefull villanie executed upon the carcasses of the dead men by the Welshwomen; as the like (I doo belieue) hath never or sildome beene practised. For though it was a cruell déed of Tomyris quéene of the Massagets in Scythia, against whome when Cyrus the great king of Persia came, and had slaine hir sonne, she by hir policie

Abr. Fl. out of *Thom. Wals. Hypod.* pag. 159.

Iust. lib 1 *Herod. lib.* 1 *Val. Mar. lib.* 8. *sep. 7.*

trained him into such streicts,[1] that she slue him and all
his host; and causing a great vessel to be filled with the
bloud of Cyrus and other Persians, did cast his head there-
into, saieng; Bloud thou hast thirsted and now drinke
thereof thy fill: againe, though it was a cruell déed of Fulvia the wife of Marcus Antonius (at whose commande-
ment Popilius cut off the head and hands of that golden
mouthed orator Tullie, which afterwards were nailed up
over the place of common plées at Rome) to hold in her
hands the toong of that father of eloquence cut out of his
head after the same was parted from his shoulders, and to
pricke it all over with pins and néedels: yet neither the crueltie of Tomyris nor yet of Fulvia is comparable to this of
the Welshwomen; which is worthie to be recorded to the
shame of a sex pretending the title of weake vessels, and
yet raging with such force of fiercenesse and barbarisme.
For the dead bodies of the Englishmen, being above a
thousand lieng upon the ground imbrued in their owne
bloud, was a sight (a man would thinke) greevous to looke
upon, and so farre from exciting and stirring up affections
of crueltie; that it should rather have mooved the beholders to commiseration and mercie: yet did the women of
Wales cut off their privities, and put one part thereof into
the mouthes of everie dead man, in such sort that the cullions hoong downe to their chins; and not so contented,
they did cut off their noses and thrust them into their
tailes as they laie on the ground mangled and defaced.
This was a verie ignominious déed, and a woorsse not
committed among the barbarous: which though it make
the reader to read it, and the hearer to heare it, ashamed:
yet bicause it was a thing doone in open sight, and left tes-
tified in historie; I see little reason whie it should not be
imparted in our mother toong to the knowledge of our
owne countrimen, as well as unto strangers in a language
unknowne. And thus much by waie of notifieng the inhu-
manitie and detestable demeanour of those Welshwomen,
after the conflict betwéene the English and the Welsh,
whereof desultorie mention is made before pag. 520,[2] where
Edmund Mortimer earle of March was taken prisoner.

[1] **streicts:** straits. [2] see page 144.

❖ *From* Act III, Scene I of *Henry IV, Part 1*: Prompt Copy Excerpts of Welsh Passages   *1964*

GLENDOWER:
My daughter weeps. She'll not part with you;
She'll be a soldier too, she'll to the wars.

MORTIMER:
Good father, tell her that she and my aunt Percy
Shall follow in your conduct speedily.

GLENDOWER:
Bydd ddewr, fy merch.
Rhaid i filwr ateb si alwad.
Cei ddilyn yn fy ngofal i gyda dy fodryb
Persi, ac fe weli dy Fortimer[1] annwyl yn fuan eto.
[Be brave, my girl, a soldier must answer the call.
We leave you in the care of Percy's aunt.
You will follow and not be parted for long.][2]

LADY MORTIMER:
Ond pwy a wyr na welaf mohono byth.
O, fy nhad, gadewch i mi fynd gydag ef.
Nid oes arnag ofn yn wir.
[I may never see him again.
Oh, my father, let me go with him!
I fear not the wars.]

GLENDOWER:
Na, nid lle i wragedd yw rhyfeloedd, fy ngeneth i.
Rhaid i ti aros a chanlyn gyde mi.
[No, the battlefield is no place for my daughter.
You must stay awhile, be guided by me.]

---

[1] **Fortimer:** In Welsh *Mortimer* becomes *Fortimer.* The letter *m* mutates to *f* in certain grammatical positions; *f* here is pronounced as *v.*   [2] Although the Welsh is translated here, these passages would have been as incomprehensible to early modern auditors as they are, in all probability, to most readers (for Americans, perhaps the best analogue would be a Native American language). The eruption of Welsh onto the stage in this play signals a serious concern: as the sign of a foreign force that resists incorporation, it represents an obstacle to the cultural and ideological project of constructing a unified entity called "England" or "Great Britain" (Terence Hawkes, private communication).

Prompt Copy for the Royal Shakespeare Company's 1964 production of *Henry IV, Part One.* Song by the Reverend Fred Lewis. Translation by Barbara Fitton. The Shakespeare Centre Library, Stratford-upon-Avon.

LADY MORTIMER:

Nis gallaf aros hebddo.

Mae'n rhaid i mi gael mynd, a chaiff neb fy ngwahardd chwaith.

[I can't be parted from him.

I must go, no one shall prevent me.]

GLENDOWER:

She is desperate here; a peevish self-will'd harlotry,

One that no persuasion can do good upon.

LADY MORTIMER:

[*to Mortimer*]: Syll f'annwylyd, i ddwfn fy llygaid,

A gwel ynddynt iaith fy nghalon.

Iaith cariad yw, cariad sy'n llosgi'm bron.

Mor felys dy wefusau!

Fel mel a gesglir rhwng petalau'r haf.

[Look, dearest, deeply into my eyes

And see in them the language of my heart,

The language of lovers it is.

Love that burns in my heart sweeter than honey

That comes from the summer petals.]

MORTIMER:

I understand thy looks . . .

. . . to her lute.

GLENDOWER:

Nay, if you melt, then will she run mad.

LADY MORTIMER:

Gorffwys f'annwylyd yma ar y brwyn,

A, dod dy ben yn esmwyth yn fy ngôl.

Fe, ganaf i ti'r gân a geraist gynt

Sy'n hudo cwsg a hiraeth yn eu hôl.

[Rest, dear one, on the rushes;

Put your head in my lap.

I will sing to you the song of love

That brings sweet sleep and fills

The longing of my heart.]

MORTIMER:

Oh, I am ignorance itself in this!

GLENDOWER:

She bids you on the wanton rushes lay you down . . .

LADY PERCY:

Go, ye giddy goose.

GLENDOWER:
    Tarwch dant ar y Delyn.
        [Play on the harp.]

[The prompt copy proceeds as in the text of the play. At line 241, "Peace, she sings," the song begins.]

THE SONG

Gwyry dir oeddwn
Yn nolydd Fenws, clyd,
Cyn cwympo had serch
I'm swyno a' i hud.
Beraidd wyth! Creu toreth lle bunewyn.

Gordd Blodau, ffynaf
Mewn hinsawdd gwynfa las
Ond anial fy myd
Pe cefnau fy ngwas,
Gwae'r dynged! Fai'r haul yn marw yntan.

[A virgin I was,
Sheltered in a cozy home,
Before falling in love.

I was bewitched and happy
From an abundance of love.
Wild flowers flourished
In my green paradise.

But I'll desert my world
If my husband does not return.
Down, dangers! Fair sun shine on him
Lest he die.]

CHAPTER 4

The "Education" of a Prince

><

According to critical tradition, *Henry IV, Part 1* represents Hal's "education" for kingship. That education, however, has little or nothing to do with schoolrooms or "book learning"; instead, it is conceived in terms of experience, and it takes place in a tavern community of drunkards, thieves, and whores. Descending "from prince to prentice," Hal learns the manners and morals of those Falstaff calls "the tattered prodigals of the land" — an acquaintance that enables Hal to become a "complete man," one who knows himself and his future subjects. In this account, the play, together with *Henry IV, Part 2,* details Hal's "reformation" from an early modern juvenile delinquent to the model monarch chroniclers called "the mirror of all Christian kings." Two key moments in *Henry IV, Part 1* frame the initial stages of that interpretive narrative: the soliloquy in which Hal announces that his "loose behavior" is a calculated action (1.2.161) and his promise to his father that he will "hereafter . . . Be more myself" (3.2.92–93). Most of the time Hal is a prince in disguise who appears to enjoy his fellow revelers. It is only at the end of the play that he puts on a Shrewsbury "self" that bests his chivalric rival Hotspur, restores his reputation in his father's eyes, and feeds his future legend as Agincourt's hero.

Like the chronicle accounts that look back to the past from the achievements of an Elizabethan moment, the *Henry* plays seem to tell a history that anticipates Hal's accession as Henry V. Several kinds of texts are important

275

to understanding Shakespeare's representation of Hal's coming of age, his political and psychological development. Some, like the legendary stories of his early manhood, bear directly on the play and are incorporated in it. Others, which explore the ideas about education in post-Reformation England put forward in conduct books, manuals of statecraft, and the literature of fathers' advice to sons, point to cultural contexts that intersect with the play.

Accounts of Prince Henry's "wild youth" appear in all of the chronicles. John Stow, William Camden, John Speed, and Raphael Holinshed each record one or more incidents of Hal's notorious past: beating the king's watch, robbing passengers, brawling in Eastcheap, boxing the ears of the Lord Chief Justice. Although reported as fact, these mythologized tales are also cultural constructions that mask a real history of political antagonism between Henry IV and his heir. Turning briefly to that history will help to explain this transformation.

Following the Percies' Northern rebellion and a breakdown in Henry IV's health, Prince Henry's attention turned from military to domestic affairs. According to Parliamentary Rolls, he put royal finances in order and restored diplomatic relations with foreign powers. Impatient with his father's weakness and with his attempts to short-circuit the Privy Council's influence and so take single-handed control of government, the Prince found ready allies among the nobility. When the Council was reconstituted in 1410, it was composed entirely of his supporters and clearly enjoyed the confidence of the Commons. Until November 1411, the Prince's Council and the Commons controlled the government, and the November Parliament brought forward a proposal that Henry abdicate in favor of his twenty-four-year-old son. Fearing that the Prince was contemplating armed rebellion, Henry IV removed him and his friends from the Council and from all offices of state and, announcing that he intended "to stand as free in his prerogative as any of his predecessors," resumed his personal rule (McFarlane, *Lancastrian Kings* 92–93, 121–23). Dismissed from the court and from political responsibility, the Prince was open to attacks that soon materialized into the wild prince legends; although he appealed to the King to punish his slanderers, father and son were only partially reconciled.

The equivalent of early modern gossip, these legends have a counterpart in present-day popular curiosity about the lives of the royal family and in the tabloid newspapers that have exposed those lives — especially that of the current Prince of Wales and Princess Diana — to public view. For Elizabethans, the stories of Hal's youth ranked with the biblical parable of the prodigal son (Luke 15:11–32) as the most familiar versions of adolescent rebellion, and they were put to use, by chroniclers and dramatists alike, to support Henry V's Tudor reputation. The anonymous, episodically organized *Famous Victories of*

Henry V (c. 1583–88), Shakespeare's major dramatic source for all three *Henry* plays, capitalized extensively on these stories' popularity. *Famous Victories* belongs to a genre of comic historical drama that incorporates materials drawn from a still largely oral popular culture. In such plays, ballads, romances, songs, folktales, myths, and fairy stories jostle beside details from written history. Many contain a king who, posing as a common man, crosses barriers of class and hierarchy to mingle with a variety of folk heroes and London citizens in mutual harmony. By imagining a true equality between kings and subjects, such plays affirm monarchy. But their comic-romantic mode could also make sharp distinctions between the ideal commonwealth represented in the play and the real social conditions that fantasy denied.

In both *Famous Victories* and *Henry IV, Part 1* Hal is a full participant in a joyful lowlife community of masterless men, thieves, and apprentices; both, too, locate this community in London and its environs (see Chapter 3, "Cultural Territories"). But there are important differences between the two. The earlier play, in which Hal clearly appears as his father's antagonist, seems to acknowledge that his escapades are a cover for political ambition. He cannot wait for the "old King" to die, and both he and his companions imagine a utopian, anarchic state just over the horizon, one where hanging and whipping will be abolished, prisons will become fencing schools, and thieves will receive annual pensions. Were the King dead, claims Hal, "we would all be Kings" — a statement that not only alludes to a conception of rule resembling a constitutional monarchy but also seems to predict the moment some sixty years later when, with the execution of King Charles I, the "common weal" would indeed, for a time, rule. By contrast, *Henry IV, Part 1* displaces the father-son antagonism in several ways. It is Hal's "vile participation," not his rebellious desire for the throne, that vexes his father; moreover, the play further complicates the issue by giving Henry IV a rival father, Falstaff-Oldcastle, and Hal a rival son, Hotspur. And by stressing Hal's reformation from tavern roustabout to chivalric hero, the rivalry between sons becomes the dramatically significant encounter that brings about the apparent reconciliation between Henry IV and his heir.

At first glance, Hal's tavern education can appear to be simply an element of local color that incorporates familiar stories in order to ensure the play's box-office success. But if one way in which those stories functioned was to substitute one history for another, they also allude to cultural practices and debates pertinent to Shakespeare's own historical moment. When Henry IV refers to Hal as an "unthrifty son," a "young wanton and effeminate boy" who supports a desperate and dissolute crew of companions (*Richard II*, 5.3.1–20), he describes an adolescence of riot and license that was as familiar in the sixteenth century as it is today. In many respects, Hal behaves like those gentlemen's sons at university who, according to William Harrison's *Description of England* (1587), "ruffle and roist it out, . . . haunting riotous company (which draweth them from their books unto another trade)" (252). It was a commonplace that learning was not highly valued or greatly sought after. Allegedly, Tudor nobility preferred to give their sons a traditional chivalric upbringing, which involved training for military life and was carried out under a master of henchmen who taught young men to ride, joust, and wear armor and instructed them in the formalities of courtly tenure and household service, with particular attention to their table manners. By the early sixteenth century, however, social critics were calling attention to the lacks in such training. Describing the nobility as "customably brought up in hunting & hawking, dicing & carding, eating & drinking & in conclusion in all vain pleasure, pastime & vanity," Thomas Starkey advocated education as the means to achieving a "very true commonwealth," an ideal state (*Dialogue* 84r, 121v). Just as Henry IV considers Hal's behavior a political problem, one that damages his own reputation as well as the future of the realm, Tudor moral and social reformers expressed the hope that schooling could be used to promote godliness and loyalty, combat such vices as idleness and unruliness, and advance the economy.

Two especially influential treatises circulated these ideas. Sir Thomas Elyot's *Book Named the Governor* (1531), which went through five editions before 1558, advanced the belief in court circles that a humanist education for the aristocracy would benefit members of that class individually while leading to the improvement of society as a whole. His program for the nurture and training of young aristocrats sets out a course of study grounded in classical examples and defines the virtues and qualities necessary for governors, among which are benevolence, liberality, justice, faith, fortitude, magnanimity, and continence. Roger Ascham's *The Schoolmaster* (1570) represents a more workaday model that ranges from idealistic precepts to more practical concerns. Both writers argue that experience must be augmented by wisdom and virtue and that it is a primary task of rulers and counselors to know themselves as well as their subjects. Elyot, for example, maintains that governors should "repair in the diverse parts of their jurisdiction or province" in order to ascertain "what is commonly or privately spoken concerning the estate of the country or persons." The ruler will then be able to identify those best disposed toward "the public weal" as well as those whose "boldness to transgress [or] to condemn the laws" deserves "right grievous punishment" (408–16).

If Shakespeare's Hal seems to be unusually adept at upholding idleness for a while and at studying popular life and base companions, his education differs markedly from that of the historical Prince Henry — one of six children, four sons and two daughters. The Prince's education anticipated that advocated a century or more later by the humanists. He was learning Latin at eight, and a list of books he owned suggests that he kept a well-stored and much-read library, which included the church fathers; chronicles of the Crusades; works on law, ancient history, and hunting; and copies of Seneca's letters, Cicero's *Rhetoric*, and Chaucer's *Troilus and Crysede*, all bearing marginal notations in Latin, French, and English. When he became king, the language of his state papers, written in his own hand, was English. He was the first English monarch to conduct business in the vernacular tongue and to encourage its use by others; indeed, the phrase "the King's English" dates from his reign (McFarlane, *Lancastrian Kings* 116–19). At least in this respect, Shakespeare's Hal, who boasts that he "can drink with any tinker in his own language" (2.4.15), touches base with his historical counterpart and also intersects with a sixteenth-century moment when learned culture itself was in the midst of an extraordinary linguistic shift from Latin to the competing tongue called "the vernacular." In the taverns of Eastcheap, Hal studies "his companions / Like a strange tongue" — English in all its various idioms, dialects, and grammars (*Henry IV, Part 2*, 4.4.69–70). Stephen Mullaney argues that such learning, which takes Hal through a series of marginal or alien worlds, represents the activity of a culture in the process of extending its boundaries and reformulating itself (76–82).

For the Elizabethans, acknowledging and incorporating all that was strange took place as part of a larger reformation of manners, one that would eventually produce what Mullaney calls "a fundamental reconfiguration of the subject, in both political and psychoanalytical terms" (131). At the same time that humanists like Elyot, Ascham, and Erasmus (*The Education of a Christian Prince*, 1516) saw it as a primary task to guide the kings and counselors who now wielded growing power in emergent European states, those same humanist ideas were breaking through the walls of feudal privilege to construct a new nobility based on learning. Learning, it was thought, could in itself confer nobility — a nobility of mind that ranked higher than any nobility of blood and that was demonstrated by service to the public good. In his *Little Book of Good Manners for Children* (translated in 1532), the Dutch humanist Erasmus wrote: "Let others paint on their escutcheons lions, eagles, bulls, leopards. Those are the possessors of true nobility who can use on their coats of arms ideas which they have thoroughly learned from the liberal arts" (quoted in Simon 69). The Reformation had revived an old popular query — "When Adam delved and Eve span, who was then the gentleman?" — and advice books, conduct manuals, and sermons all urged the individual to view himself or herself in a new light. With notions of inherited nobility set aside, one might fashion one's own identity, learn the attributes of a courtier or a statesman.

When the Catholic humanist Juan Luis Vives defined the desirable arts as those necessary "for the aims of either this or the eternal life," he was speaking primarily of grooming those who were to become lawyers, clergymen, statesmen, and soldiers, professions to which women (except in rare cases) did not have access (*On Education*, quoted in Simon 118). Learning in the liberal arts was not, however, entirely limited to boys and men. The goal of promoting Christian virtues could justify the liberal education of women, whose assigned roles in life were confined to domestic skills and management and to private pleasures such as music; it could also, however, serve to limit their studies to only those subjects that specifically contributed to piety and Christian virtues, primary among which were chastity and obedience. Vives's influential *Instruction of a Christian Woman* (1523), for example, prescribes a course of study that includes the Bible, Greek and Roman moral philosophers — Plato, Cicero, Seneca, Plutarch, and Aristotle — and certain rhetoricians, such as Quintilian. But, since women are not destined, as men are, to govern or teach, Vives states that they have no need of history, grammar, and logic. Nor should they read romances, filled with foolish lies and encouraging illicit love; similarly, they should not read classical love poetry, particularly Ovid's *Remedia Amores*, which Vives would also keep from men, for it encourages lust (56–63). Although this curriculum applied more to aristocratic women than to those lower on the social scale, even women from the lower gentry could read and write Latin as well as Greek and had some knowledge of classical authors and culture. Queen Elizabeth, of course, was able to integrate a liberal education with her public and private life: ignoring Vives's advice that women need not study history or politics, she read Xenophon as well as Machiavelli's *The Prince* (1513) and was able to converse with European diplomats in Latin, French, and Italian. If she was an exception who countered the notion that the full range of humanist learning was meant only for men, few were in a position to imitate her (see Henderson and McManus 81–93; Kelly, *Women*).

Although Baldessare Castiglione's *Book of the Courtier* (1528, translated into English by Sir Thomas Hoby in 1561) pointedly includes women in its conversations on courtiership, it devotes most attention to advancing the model of a "complete" or all-around man, one whose behavior could be learned and *imitated*. Setting forth the characteristics of the ideal courtier — his training in sports and the military arts, his ethical and intellectual qualities, his apparel and his conversation — *The Courtier* became a second Bible for many in Elizabeth's court: allegedly, Sir Philip Sidney never went out without a copy in his pocket (Simon 369). Hoby's translation made a particular point of arguing that in order to attain the degree of civilization Castiglione imagined, English gentlemen must first cultivate their own language so that "we alone of the world may not be still counted barbarous in our tongue, as in time out of mind we have been in our manners. And so shall we perchance in time become as famous in England, as the learned men of other nations have been and presently are" (quoted in Simon 340). While Castiglione's idealized guide to courtly politics, relationships, and learning developed one idea of the protean self, Niccolò Machiavelli's *The Prince* considered the humanist advice books unrealistic and dangerously idealized. Emphasizing statecraft and diplomacy as theatre, dissimulation, and feigning, he claims that although it is good to possess all of the qualities of an admirable ruler, it is essential that one should *appear* to do so, for a populace can be best controlled through strategies of political manipulation and through constructing an artificial identity in the service of power (Greenblatt, *Renaissance Self-Fashioning* 162–63).

Although critics differ over how these ideas have left their mark on the early modern drama, and on Shakespeare's history plays in particular, Machiavelli's pragmatic philosophy, based entirely on the actions of men, offers a conception of history as social process which is attuned to issues of theatrical representation. Like the ideal prince who uses his virtue not to combat Fortune but to adapt himself to political exigencies, Hal manages to relate his ways of acting to the character — and characters — of the times. Playing the prodigal, he takes on a role that conceals his princely self; appraising "the lives of other[s]," he turns "past evils to advantages" (*Henry IV, Part 2*, 4.4.77–78).

→ ROGER ASCHAM

From The Schoolmaster   *1570*

In the best humanist tradition, Roger Ascham combined scholarship with state service and had considerable influence in the court. As one of Queen Elizabeth's tutors, he maintained a close relationship with her throughout his life. Published the same year that Ascham died, *The Schoolmaster* was dedicated to Sir William Cecil, Elizabeth's chief minister. Margaret Ascham, who wrote that dedication, offers the book as a testimony to "such good as my husband was able to do and leave to the commonweal." Divided into two parts — a first book "teaching the bringing up of youth" and a second "teaching the ready way to the Latin tongue" — Ascham's treatise represents a manual of private advice for young aristocrats that is far more accessible than Sir Thomas Elyot's weighty "book of virtues" for future governors. First and foremost, Ascham sees himself as a teacher. But, unlike the impressive figure shown in the frontispiece to *A Catechism* (see Figure 16), his teaching was not confined to the schoolroom. De-

FIGURE 16 *Title page from* A Catechism, *a Latin primer (1571). The drawing shows one student reciting while others sit in ranks before their schoolmaster, whose commanding position reproduces the hierarchical relation of king and court (see Figure 3). Note the bundle of switches beside his "throne."*

scribing himself as someone who has stepped out of his school and moved "from teaching a young scholar to admonish[ing] great and noble men," he views his book as a service to future aristocrats, as advice "written not for great men, but for great men's children." By so limiting its audience, Ascham also implies that education pertains only to aristocrats: although he never explicitly says so, he seems to share the fears expressed by Elyot and others that extending education to all might upset the social hierarchy by schooling people above their station.

The section reproduced here gives Ascham's views on the relation between experience and learning. Like other educational writers of the period, he mourns the lack of discipline that he sees as characteristic of the times. "Disobedience," he writes, "doth overflow the banks of good order, almost in every place, almost in every degree of man," and ill company not only corrupts "good wits" but produces a "graceless Grace" that demeans religious duty and threatens orderly life. Ascham measures England's contemporary conditions against those of Athens, which he depicts as an ideal commonwealth of "worthy wits," famous for nobility in war, "excellent and matchless masters of all manner of learning."

The attempt to construct, or reconstruct, the present in terms of a classical Golden Age appears in many early modern texts: indeed, such nostalgia for the past seems to be a particular hallmark of cultures undergoing rapid and widespread social, economic, and political change. In the conduct and advice books of the period as well as in texts by educational reformers, evoking that classical past supports the writers' insistence that learning Latin and Greek provides a discipline that grounds the entire educational enterprise. Yet if young scholars learned their rhetoric and history in Latin, they learned their alphabet, as well as their duties toward God, in English texts "set forth by public authority": the *ABC*, the *Catechism*, the *Psalter* and *Book of Common Prayer*, the New Testament, and the *Queen's Grammar*.

However central to the humanist curriculum, immersion in classical languages represents only one strand of Ascham's advice to young aristocrats. His interest, like Castiglione's, lies in shaping a whole man or "perfect courtier," one who is not only learned but who can converse easily, play an instrument, dance, ride, and write — and who does all these things *con sprezzatura*, that is, with no show of effort. Whereas some writers dismiss traditional chivalric training or deemphasize military arts, Ascham not only retains it but recommends turning to Castiglione's *Courtier* for instruction on combining learning with "comely exercises." Although he laments the excesses of Italian fashions and scorns the practice of sending young men to Italy, it is clearly important to *read* Castiglione — in English translation.

For Ascham as for William Harrison (see "Of Degrees of People in the Commonwealth of England," p. 221), order and hierarchy are organic principles by which men live. The two, he argues, are interdependent, so that when men are "called forth to the execution of great affairs, in service of their prince and country," they may be able to *order* their experiences according to wisdom, learning, and virtue. As this particular section closes, he evokes the example of Queen Elizabeth, the prince he has served most closely, as the figure "young Gentlemen of England" should emulate, calling them to account "that one maid should go beyond you all, in excellency of learning, and knowledge of diverse tongues."

From *The Schoolmaster*

[The youth of England are brought up with too much liberty. Ascham compares the Persians and also cites the example of Samson's obedience to his parents concerning marriage.]

Roger Ascham, *The Schoolmaster, or plain and perfect way of teaching children the Latin tongue. The first book teaching the bringing up of youth* (London, 1570).

Our time is so far from that old discipline and obedience, as now, not only young gentlemen but even very girls dare without all fear, though not without open shame, where they list, and how they list, marry themselves in spite of father, mother, God, good order, and all. The cause of this evil is, that youth is least looked unto, when they stand [in] most need of good keep and regard. It availeth not to see them well taught in young years, and after, when they come to lust and youthful days, to give them license to live as they lust themselves. For if ye suffer the eye of a young Gentleman once to be entangled with vain sights, and the ear to be corrupted with fond or filthy talk, the mind shall quickly fall sick, and soon vomit and cast up all the wholesome doctrine that he received in childhood, though he were never so well brought up before. And being once glutted with vanity, he will straightway loathe all learning, and all good counsel to the same. And the parents, for all their great cost and charge, reap only, in the end, the fruit of grief and care.

This evil is not common to poor men, as God will have it, but proper to rich and great men's children, as they deserve it. Indeed, from seven to seventeen, young gentlemen commonly be carefully enough brought up. But from seventeen to seven and twenty (the most dangerous time of all a man's life, and most slippery to stay well in), they have commonly the reign of all license in their own hand, and specially such as do live in the Court. And that which is most to be marveled at commonly, [is that] the wisest and also best men be found the fondest[1] fathers in this behalf. And if some good father would seek some remedy herein, yet the mother (if the house hold of our Lady) had rather, yea, & will, too, have her son cunning & bold, in making him to live trimly when he is young, [and] then by learning and travel, to be able to serve his Prince and his country, both wisely in peace and stoutly in war, when he is old.

The fault is in yourselves, ye noble men's sons, and therefore ye deserve the greater blame, that commonly the meaner men's children come to be the wisest counselors and greatest doers in the weighty affairs of this Realm. And why? for God will have it so, of his providence: because he will have it no otherwise, by your negligence.

[Nobility without virtue and wisdom is too weak to bear the burden of weighty affairs. Ascham evokes the metaphor of a well-run ship to stress the need for governing with wisdom.]

But Nobility, governed by learning and wisdom, is indeed most like a fair ship, having tide and wind at will, under the rule of a skillful master. When

---

[1] **fondest:** most permissive.

contrarywise, a ship, carried, yea with the highest tide & greatest wind, lacking a skillful master, most commonly doth either sink itself upon sands, or break itself upon rocks. And even so, how many have been either drowned in vain pleasure or overwhelmed by stout willfulness, the histories of England be able to afford over many examples unto us. Therefore, ye great and noble men's children, if ye will have rightfully that praise, and enjoy surely that place which your fathers have, and elders had, and left unto you, ye must keep it, as they got it, and that is, by the only way of virtue, wisdom, and worthiness.

For wisdom, and virtue, there be many fair examples in this Court, for young Gentlemen to follow. But they be, like fair marks in the field, out of a man's reach, too far off, to shoot at well. The best and worthiest men, indeed, be sometimes seen but seldom talked withal: a young Gentleman may sometime kneel to their person, [but] smally[2] use their company, for their better instruction.

But young Gentlemen are feign commonly to do in the Court as young Archers do in the field: that is, take such marks as be nigh them, although they be never so foul to shoot at. I mean, they be driven to keep company with the worst: and what force ill company hath to corrupt good wits, the wisest men know best.

And not ill company only, but the ill opinion also of the most part, doth much harm, and namely of those which should be wise in the true deciphering of the good disposition of nature, of comeliness in Courtly manners, and all right doings of men.

But error and fantasy do commonly occupy the place of truth and judgment. For if a young gentleman be demure and still of nature, they say he is simple and lacketh wit. If he be bashful, and will soon blush, they call him a babyish and ill-brought-up thing [as Xenophon notes in *Cyrus*]. If he be innocent and ignorant of ill, they say he is rude and hath no grace, so ungraciously do some graceless men misuse the fair and godly word GRACE.

But if ye would know what grace they mean, go, and look, and learn among them, and ye shall see that it is: First, to blush at nothing. And blushing in youth, sayeth *Aristotle*, is nothing else but fear to do ill, which fear being once lustily frayed away[3] from youth, then followeth: to dare do any mischief, to condemn stoutly any goodness, to be busy in every matter, to be skillful in everything, to acknowledge no ignorance at all. To do thus in Court, is counted of some the chief and greatest grace of all, and termed by the name of a virtue called Courage & boldness [as Cicero notes].

Moreover, where the swing goeth, there to follow, fawn, flatter, laugh and

---

[2] **smally:** rarely.   [3] **frayed away:** rubbed out.

lie lustily at other men's liking. To face, stand foremost, shove back, and to the meaner man, or unknown in the Court, to seem somewhat solemn, coy, big, and dangerous of look, talk, and answer. To think well of himself, to be lusty in condemning of others, to have some trim grace in a privy mock. And in greater presence, to bear a brave look: to be warlike, though he never looked enemy in the face in war, yet some warlike sign must be used, either a slovenly busking,[4] or an overstaring frounced[5] head, as though out of every hair's top should suddenly start out a good big oath, when need requireth. Yet praised be God, England hath at this time many worthy Captains and good soldiers, which be in deed so honest of behavior, so comely of conditions, so mild of manners, as they may be examples of good order, to a good sort of others which never came in war. But to return, where I left. In place also, to be able to raise talk, and make discourse of every risk, to have a very good will, to hear himself speak, to be seen in Palmistry,[6] whereby to convey to chaste ears some fond or filthy talk.

And if some Smithfield Ruffian[7] take up some strange going,[8] some new mowing with the mouth,[9] some wrenching with the shoulder, some brave proverb, some fresh new oath that is not stale but will run round in the mouth, some new disguised garment, or desperate hat, fond in fashion or garish in color, whatsoever it cost, how small soever his living be, by what shift soever it be gotten, gotten must it be, and used with the first,[10] or else the grace of it is stale and gone. [Ascham cites a "rude verse" on courtly excesses.]

Would to God this talk were not true, and that some men's doings were not thus. I write not to hurt any but to profit some; to accuse none but to admonish such who, allured by ill counsel, and following ill example, contrary to their good bringing up, and against their own good nature, yield overmuch to these follies and faults. I know many serving men of good order, and well staid; and again, I hear say there be some serving men do but ill service to their young masters. [For the enticements of lewd servants, read the comedies of Terence and Plautus. Even the best-brought-up wits are corrupted by mischievous servants.]

But I marvel the less, that these misorders be amongst some in the Court, for commonly in the country also everywhere, innocence is gone; Bashfulness is banished; much presumption in youth; small authority in age. Reverence is neglected; duties be confounded; and to be short, disobedience

---

[4] **busking**: dress. [5] **frounced**: curled. [6] **Palmistry**: chiromancy; divination by means of reading palms. Here, apparently, lewd gestures. [7] **Smithfield Ruffian**: sharp bargainer. [8] **strange going**: odd gait. [9] **mowing with the mouth**: exaggerated expression. [10] **the first**: those who introduce new fashions.

doth overflow the banks of good order, almost in every place, almost in every degree of man.

[These misorders are God's just plagues for condemning God's word, as in biblical times. We must fear God and learn true doctrine, which will preserve us.]

The remedy of this doth not stand only in making good common laws for the whole Realm, but also (and perchance chiefly) in observing private discipline, every man carefully in his own house. And namely, if special regard be had to youth, and that not so much in teaching them what is good as in keeping them from that that is ill.

Therefore, if wise fathers be not as well ware in weeding from their Children ill things and ill company, as they were before, in grafting in them learning, and providing for them good schoolmasters, what fruit they shall reap of all their cost & care, common experience doth tell.

[Ascham develops this argument further, citing classical examples. Some ignorance, he maintains, is as good as knowledge; and innocence in youth should be cultivated. Following an anecdote of a child of "ill parents" who could not say grace but could swear "many ugly oaths," he repeats his warnings about the "company of Ruffians" and then evokes the example of Athens, where youths were strictly disciplined and tutored in proper manners. He praises Athenian learning, citing authors of philosophy, eloquence and civil law, history, and poetry, and attributing all good learning and virtue to "those worthy wits of Athens." Since learning is "chiefly contained in the Greek and in no other tongue," English gentlemen should be condemned for adopting the French custom of "count[ing] it their shame to be counted learned."]

Some other, having better nature but less wit (for ill [persons] commonly have overmuch wit) do not utterly dispraise learning, but they say that without learning, common experience, knowledge of all fashions, and haunting all companies shall work in youth both wisdom and ability to execute any weighty affair. Surely long experience doth profit much, but most, and almost only to him (if we mean honest affairs) that is diligently before instructed with precepts of well doing. For good precepts of learning be the eyes of the mind, to look wisely before a man, which way to go right, and which not.

Learning teacheth more in one year than experience in twenty. And learning teacheth safely, when experience maketh more miserable than wise. He hazardeth sore that waxeth wise by experience. An unhappy Master he is that is made cunning by many shipwrecks, a miserable merchant that is neither rich or wise, but after some bankrupts. It is costly wisdom that is bought by experience. We know by experience itself that it is a marvelous pain to find out but a short way by long wandering. And surely he that would prove wise by experience, he may be witty in deed, but even like a swift runner that runneth fast out of his way, and upon the night, he knoweth not whither. And verily they be fewest of number that be happy or wise by unlearned experience. And look well upon the former life of those few, whether your example be old or young, who without learning have gathered, by long experience, a little wisdom and some happiness. And when you do consider what mischief they have committed, what dangers they have escaped (and yet twenty for one, do perish in the adventure), then think well with yourself whether ye would that your own son should come to wisdom and happiness by the way of such experience or no.

It is a notable tale that old Sir Roger Chamloe, sometime chief Justice, would tell of himself. When he was Ancient[11] in Inn of Court, Certain young Gentlemen were brought before him to be corrected for certain misorders. And one of the lustiest said, "Sir, we be young gentlemen, and wise men before us have proved all fashions and yet those have done full well." This they said, because it was well known that Sir Roger had been a good fellow in his youth. But he answered them very wisely. "Indeed," saith he, "in youth I was as you are now, and I had twelve fellows like unto myself, but not one of them came to a good end. And therefore follow not my example in youth but follow my counsel in age, if ever ye think to come to this place, or to these years, that I am come unto, lest ye meet either with poverty or Tyburn[12] in the way."

Thus experience of all fashions in youth being, in proof, always dangerous, in issue, seldom lucky, is a way, indeed, to overmuch knowledge, yet used commonly of such men which be either carried by some curious affection of mind or driven by some hard necessity of life to hazard the trial of over many perilous adventures.

Erasmus, the honor of learning of all our time, said wisely that experience is the common schoolhouse of fools, and ill men. Men of wit and honesty be otherwise instructed. For there be [those] that keep them out of fire, and yet was never burned; that beware of water, and yet was never nigh drowning; that hate harlots, and was never at the stews;[13] that abhor falsehood, and never brake promise themselves.

But will ye see a fit Similitude of this adventured experience. A Father

---

[11] **Ancient:** a senior member of the Inns of Court, the seat of London's legal profession.
[12] **Tyburn:** the place of public execution for Middlesex County, outside London's walls.
[13] **stews:** brothels.

that doth let loose his son to all experiences is most like a fond Hunter that letteth slip a whelp to the whole herd. Twenty to one, he shall fall upon a rascal,[14] and let go the fair game. Men that hunt so be either ignorant persons, privy stealers, or night walkers.[15]

Learning, therefore, ye wise fathers, and good bringing up, and not blind & dangerous experience, is the next and readiest way that must lead your Children, first, to wisdom, and then to worthiness, if ever ye purpose they shall come there.

And to say all in short, though I lack Authority to give counsel, yet I lack not good will to wish that the youth in England, especially Gentlemen, and namely nobility, should be by good bringing up, so grounded in judgment of learning, so founded in love of honesty, as, when they should be called forth to the execution of great affairs, in service of their Prince and country, they might be able to use and to order all experiences, were they good, were they bad; and that, according to the square, rule, and line of wisdom, learning, and virtue.

And I do not mean by all this my talk that young Gentlemen should always be poring on a book, and by using good studies should lease[16] honest pleasure, and haunt no good pastime. I mean nothing less. For it is well known that I both like and love, and have always and do yet still use, all exercises and pastimes that be fit for my nature and ability. And beside natural disposition, in judgment also, I was never either Stoic in doctrine or Anabaptist in Religion[17] to mislike a merry, pleasant, and playful nature, if no outrage be committed against law, measure, and good order.

[Ascham advocates joining knowledge of languages and learning with "courtly exercises and gentlemanlike pastimes," as in Athens.]

Therefore, to ride comely, to run fair at the tilt or ring, to play at all weapons, to shoot fair in bow, or surely in gun, to vault lustily, to run, to leap, to wrestle, to swim, to dance comely, to sing, and play of instruments cunningly, to Hawk, to hunt, to play at tennis, & all pastimes generally, which be joined with labor, used in open place, and [in] the daylight, containing either some fit exercise for war, or some pleasant pastime for peace, be not only comely and decent, but also very necessary, for a Courtly Gentleman to use.

[Ascham, a notorious gambler, refers readers to his comments on cockfighting for more on appropriate pastimes. Anticipating criticism for writing about such trifles rather than matters of religion or civil discipline, he justi-

---

[14] **rascal:** an inferior example of the herd.   [15] **night walkers:** thieves.   [16] **lease:** leave.   [17] **Stoic . . . in Religion:** The Stoics espoused indifference to pleasure or pain. The Anabaptists, a strict Protestant sect, disavowed all fleshly pleasures.

fies his practice by noting that Homer's *Iliad* and *Odyssey* contain much learning in a "small Argument, of one harlot, and of one good wife."]

To join learning with comely exercises, *Count Baldessar Castiglione* in his book, *The Courtier*, doth trimly teach. Which book, advisedly read and diligently followed but one year at home in England, would do a young gentleman more good, I think, than three years travel abroad spent in *Italy*. And I marvel this book is no more read in the Court than it is, seeing it is so well translated into English by a worthy Gentleman Sir Thomas Hoby, who was many ways well furnished with learning, and very expert in knowledge of diverse tongues.

And besides good precepts in books in all kinds of tongues, this Court also never lacked many fair examples for young gentlemen to follow. And surely one example is more valuable, both to good and ill, than twenty precepts written in books, and so *Plato*, not in one or two but diverse places, doth plainly teach.

[Ascham mentions, among others, King Edward VI and Sir John Cheke of St. John's College, Cambridge.]

Present examples of this present time I list not to touch. Yet there is one example for all the Gentlemen of this Court to follow, that may well satisfy them, or nothing will serve them, nor no example move them to goodness and learning.

It is your shame (I speak to you all, you young Gentlemen of England) that one maid should go beyond you all, in excellency of learning, and knowledge of diverse tongues. Point forth six of the best given Gentlemen of this Court, and all they together show not so much good will, spend not so much time, bestow not so many hours, daily, orderly, & constantly, for the increasing of learning & knowledge, as doth the Queen's Majesty herself. Yea, I believe that besides her perfect readiness in *Latin, Italian, French, & Spanish*, she readeth here now at Windsor more Greek every day than some Prebendary[18] of this Church doth read *Latin* in a whole week. And that which is most praiseworthy of all, within the walls of her privy chamber, she hath obtained that excellency of learning to understand, speak, & write both wittily with head, and fair with hand, as scarce one or two rare wits in both the Universities have in many years reached unto. Amongst all the benefits that God hath blessed me withal, next the knowledge of Christ's true Religion, I count this the greatest, that it pleased God to call me to be one poor minister in setting forward these excellent gifts of learning in this most excellent Prince. Whose only example,

---

[18] **Prebendary**: canon.

if the rest of our nobility would follow, then might England be, for learning and wisdom in nobility, a spectacle to all the world beside. But see the mishap of men: the best examples have never such force to move to any goodness, as the bad, vain, light and fond, have to all illness.

→ ANONYMOUS

From The Famous Victories of Henry the Fifth   *1598*

This Queen's Men's play, which perpetuates the "wild prince" legends of Hal's (supposedly) misspent youth, continues beyond the scenes reproduced here to dramatize Henry V's conquest of France. Scholars believe the published text is corrupt and probably much cut, which has led to speculation about whether an imagined original was one play or two and whether that play (or plays) contained more political scenes. To some extent, such notions seem driven by a wish to impose Shakespearean form on the earlier play and so explain the relations between *Henry IV, Parts 1 and 2* and *Henry V,* as well as to speculate on Shakespeare's composing process (see Hawkins, Melchiori). Whatever the case, the play was probably performed before 1588, when the great comedian Richard Tarleton died, for an anecdote in *Tarleton's Jests* (1638) describes Hal's insult to the Lord Chief Justice (scene 4), with Tarleton apparently playing several "clown" parts. Yet *Famous Victories* does not appear on the Stationers' Register until 1594 and was not published until 1598, suggesting that it may have been brought into print in order to capitalize on the decade-long popularity of English history plays.

In a cryptic aside, Karl Marx suggested that the major events of history occur twice: once as tragedy and again as farce. If the political antagonism between Henry IV and his son can be considered a tragic action, then this drama, which turns political rebellion to comic carnivalesque and, with Hal's reformation and his French victories, to romance, represents its farcical counterpart. Throughout, the character named Henry 5 demonstrates a scapegrace energy that carries forward into the second half, where it wins him Agincourt and a Princess Bride. The play's "mingling of kings and clowns," a feature of the drama that Sir Philip Sidney labeled a violation of decorum, places *Famous Victories* securely within a comic-popular tradition, and in dramatizing events that occur in the City of London and its environs, it demonstrates a concern with specific locales similar to that in John Stow's *Survey of London* (see Chapter 3, "Cultural Territories").

Given the objections from the Cobham family that required Shakespeare to change the name of the character once identified as Sir John Oldcastle to Fal-

Anonymous, *The Famous Victories of Henry the Fifth: Containing the Honorable Battle of Agincourt:* As it was played by the Queen's Majesty's Players (London, 1598 [written and performed c. 1583–88]), A2r–C3r.

staff, it may seem curious that the Office of the Revels permitted *Famous Victories*, which names Oldcastle as one of Hal's roistering companions, to be licensed without any change (see Chapter 6, "The Oldcastle Controversy"). One explanation might be that a Cobham was not in a political position to urge the change; another might involve the distinction between printing an old anonymous play and printing one by Shakespeare. Perhaps more important, however, is that Oldcastle's role in *Famous Victories* is neither as potentially subversive nor as central as it is in *Henry IV, Part 1*. Most of the time he is referred to as "Jockey"; no hint of the historical Oldcastle's reputation appears in the play, where much of the fun, as well as the disaffection with authority, depends on Derick and Ned — the "base, common, and popular" clown figures. It is they, not Oldcastle, who "take the stage."

Dramatic texts such as *Famous Victories* are often read primarily for what they can reveal about Shakespeare's own texts; rarely, if ever, are they performed. In 1982, however, Trevor Nunn's staging of both parts of *Henry IV* for the Royal Shakespeare Company included the scenes leading up to and away from Hal's insult to the Lord Chief Justice as a lively intermission entertainment. Performed as street theatre and in knockabout, slapstick style by members of the company who took minor roles in the productions, it gave particular point to the moment in *Henry IV, Part 2* when, after his father's death, Henry V reminds the Lord Chief Justice that he had "roughly sen[t] to prison / Th' immediate heir of England" and then reaffirms his office, naming him "a father to my youth" (5.2.70–71, 112–18). By choosing to pay homage to Shakespeare's dramatic source as well as to a *popular* acting tradition, Nunn's production re-staged the theatrical history of a play long associated with the Royal Shakespeare Company's own history, and particularly with the opening of a new theatre. In this case, the occasion marked the opening of the RSC's new Barbican Theatre, the first time since the sixteenth century that "Shakespeare" had found a home within the City of London's ancient walls.

From *The Famous Victories of Henry the Fifth*

[SCENE 1]

Enter the young Prince, Ned, and Tom.

HENRY 5:° Come away, *Ned* and *Tom.*
BOTH: Here, my Lord.
HENRY 5:   Come away, my Lads:
   Tell me, sirs, how much gold have you got?
NED: Faith, my Lord, I have got five hundred pound.   5
HENRY 5:   But tell me, *Tom,* how much hast thou got?

---

1. **Henry 5:** the Prince is called Henry 5 throughout.

TOM: Faith, my Lord, some four hundred pounds.

HENRY 5: Four hundred pounds! Bravely spoken, Lads.
But tell me, sirs, think you not that it was a villainous part of me to rob
my father's Receivers? 10

NED: Why no, my Lord, it was but a trick of youth.

HENRY 5: Faith, *Ned*, thou sayest true.
But tell me, sirs, whereabouts are we?

TOM: My Lord, we are now about a mile off *London*.

HENRY 5: But sirs, I marvel that Sir *John Oldcastle* 15
Comes not away. S'ounds,° see where he comes.

Enters Jockey.°

How now *Jockey*, what news with thee?

JOCKEY: Faith, my Lord, such news as passeth,
For the Town of Detfort° is risen,
With hue and cry after your man, 20
Which parted from us the last night,
And has set upon, and hath robb'd a poor Carrier.

HENRY 5: S'ounds, the villain that was wont to spy
Out our booties.

JOCKEY: Aye my Lord, even the very same. 25

HENRY 5: Now, base-minded rascal to rob a poor carrier,
Well, it skills not,° I'll save the base villain's life:
Aye, I may. But tell me, *Jockey*, whereabout be the Receivers?°

JOCKEY: Faith, my Lord, they are hard by,
But the best is, we are a horseback and they be a foot,
So we may escape them. 30

HENRY 5: Well, I[f] the villains come, let me alone with them.
But tell me, *Jockey*, how much got thou from the knaves?
For I am sure I got something, for one of the villains
So belam'd me about the shoulders, 35
As I shall feel it this month.

JOCKEY: Faith, my Lord, I have got a hundred pound.

HENRY 5: A hundred pound! Now, bravely spoken, *Jockey*:
But come, sirs, lay all your money before me.
Now, by heaven, here is a brave show: 40
But as I am true Gentleman, I will have the half

---

16. **S'ounds:** by his (Christ's) wounds; an oath. Printed as "sounds," "sownes," "sowns," and
"sownds"; regularized throughout to "S'ounds." **s.d.** *Jockey:* Oldcastle. 19. **Detfort:** Dept-
ford, south of the Thames, near Greenwich. 27. **skills not:** matters not. 28. **Receivers:**
treasury officials.

Of this spent tonight. But sirs, take up your bags,
Here comes the Receivers. Let me alone.

Enters two Receivers.

ONE: Alas, good fellow, what shall we do?
    I dare never go home to the Court, for I shall be hanged.   45
    But look, here is the young Prince. What shall we do?
HENRY 5:   How now, you villains, what are you?
ONE RECEIVER: Speak you to him.
OTHER: No, I pray, speak you to him.
HENRY 5:   Why, how now, you rascals, why speak you not?   50
ONE: Forsooth, we be — Pray speak you to him.
HENRY 5:   S'ounds, villains, speak, or I'll cut off your heads!
OTHER: Forsooth, he can tell the tale better than I.
ONE: Forsooth, we be your father's Receivers.
HENRY 5:   Are you my father's Receivers?   55
    Then I hope ye have brought me some money.
ONE: Money! Alas, sir, we be robb'd.
HENRY 5:   Robb'd? How many were there of them?
ONE: Marry, sir, there were four of them,
    And one of them had Sir *John Oldcastle's* bay Hobby,   60
    And your black Nag.
HENRY 5:   Gog's wounds,° how like you this, *Jockey?*
    Blood,° you villains! My father robb'd of his money abroad,
    And we robb'd in our stables!
    But tell me, how many were of them?   65
ONE RECEIVER: If it please you, there were four of them,
    And there was one about the bigness of you.
    But I am sure I so belam'd him about the shoulders,
    That he will feel it this month.
HENRY 5:   Gog's wounds, you lam'd them fairly,   70
    So that they have carried away your money.
    But come, sirs, what shall we do with the villains?
BOTH RECEIVERS: I beseech your grace, be good to us.
NED: I pray you, my Lord, forgive them this once.
[HENRY 5:]   Well, stand up and get you gone,   75
    And look that you speak not a word of it,
    For if there be, s'ounds, I'll hang you and all your kin.

                                         [Exeunt Receivers]

---

62. **Gog's wounds:** God's wounds.   63. **Blood:** by (Christ's) blood: an oath.

HENRY 5:   Now sirs, how like you this?
Was this not bravely done?
For now the villains dare not speak a word of it,   80
I have so feared them with words.
Now, whither shall we go?
ALL: Why, my Lord, you know our old hostess
At *Feversham.°*
HENRY 5:   Our hostess at *Feversham!* Blood, what shall we do there?   85
We have a thousand pound about us,
And we shall go to a petty Alehouse?
No, no: you know the old Tavern in Eastcheap,
There is good wine: besides, there is a pretty wench
That can talk well, for I delight as much in their tongues,   90
As any part about them.
ALL: We are ready to wait upon your grace.
HENRY 5:   Gog's wounds, wait: we will go altogether,
We are all fellows, I tell you, sir, and [if] the King
My father were dead, we would be all Kings;   95
Therefore, come, away.
NED: Gog's wounds, bravely spoken, *Harry.*

[Scene ii]

Enter John Cobler, Robin Pewterer, Lawrence Costermonger.°

JOHN COBLER: All is well here, all is well, masters.
[LAWRENCE]:   How say you, neighbor *John Cobler?*
I think it best that my neighbor
Robin Pewterer went to Pudding Lane end,
And we will watch here at Billingsgate ward,°   5
How say you, neighbor *Robin,* how like you this?
ROBIN: Marry, well, neighbors:
I care not much if I go to Pudding Lane's end.
But neighbors, and you hear any ado about me,
Make haste: and if I hear any ado about you,   10
I will come to you.
                                                          Exit Robin.

---

84. **Feversham:** Faversham, not far from Canterbury, near the main London road.   s.d. *Costermonger:* apple-seller.   4–5. **Pudding Lane . . . Billingsgate ward:** Pudding Lane and Billingsgate Ward are between Eastcheap and the river. Billingsgate was the principal London dock.

LAWRENCE: Neighbor, what news hear you of the young Prince?

JOHN: Marry, neighbor, I hear say he is a toward young Prince,
    For if he meet any by the highway,
    He will not let° to talk with him.   15
    I dare not call him thief, but sure he is one of these taking fellows.

LAWRENCE: Indeed, neighbor, I hear say he is as lively
    A young Prince as ever was.

JOHN: Aye, and I hear say, if he use it long,
    His father will cut him off from the Crown: 20
    But neighbor, say nothing of that.

LAWRENCE: No, no, neighbor, I warrant you.

JOHN: Neighbor, methinks you begin to sleep.
    If you will, we will sit down,
    For I think it is about midnight.   25

LAWRENCE: Marry, content, neighbor, let us sleep.

Enter Derick roving.

DERICK: Who, who there, who there?

                                                      Exit Derick.

Enter Robin.

ROBIN: O neighbors, what mean you to sleep,
    And such ado in the streets?

[BOTH]:   How now, neighbor, what's the matter?   30

Enter Derick again.

DERICK: Who there, who there, who there?

COBLER: Why, what ailst thou? here is no horses.

DERICK: O alas, man, I am robb'd! who there? who there?

ROBIN: Hold him, neighbor *Cobler.*

ROBIN: Why, I see thou art a plain Clown.   35

DERICK: Am I a Clown? S'ounds, masters,
    Do Clowns go in silk apparel?
    I am sure all we gentlemen Clowns in *Kent*° scant go so
    Well. S'ounds, you know clowns very well!
    Hear you, are you master Constable? And you be, speak,   40
    For I will not take it at his hands.

JOHN: Faith, I am not master Constable,
    But I am one of his bad° officers, for he is not here.

---

15. **let:** hesitate.   38. *Kent:* county south of London.   43. **bad:** sworn.

DERICK: Is not master Constable here?
   Well, it is no matter, I'll have the law at his hands.   45
JOHN: Nay, I pray you, do not take the law of us.
DERICK: Well, you are one of his beastly officers.
JOHN: I am one of his bad officers.
DERICK: Why, then, I charge thee look to him.
COBLER: Nay, but hear ye, sir, you seem to be an honest   50
   Fellow, and we are poor men, and now 'tis night,
   And we would be loath to have anything ado,
   Therefore I pray thee put it up.
DERICK: First, thou saiest true, I am an honest fellow,
   And a proper handsome fellow, too,   55
   And you seem to be poor men, therefore I care not greatly.
   Nay, I am quickly pacified:
   But and you chance to spy the thief,
   I pray you lay hold on him.
ROBIN: Yes, that we will, I warrant you.   60
DERICK: 'Tis a wonderful thing to see how glad the knave
   Is, now I have forgiven him.
JOHN: Neighbors, do ye look about you.
   How now, who's there?

Enter the Thief.

THIEF: Here is a good fellow. I pray you, which is the   65
   Way to the old Tavern in Eastcheap?
DERICK: Whoop, halloo! Now, Gadshill, knowest thou me?
THIEF: I know thee for an Ass.
DERICK: And I know thee for a taking fellow,
   Upon Gad's Hill° in *Kent:*   70
   A bots° light upon ye.
THIEF: The whoreson villain would be knock'd.
DERICK: Masters, [a] villain! And ye be men, stand to him,
   And take his weapon from him, let him not pass you.
JOHN: My friend, what make you abroad now?   75
   It is too late to walk now.
THIEF: It is not too late for true men to walk.
LAWRENCE: We know thee not to be a true man.
THIEF: Why, what do you mean to do with me?
   S'ounds, I am one of the King's liege people.°   80

70. **Gad's Hill:** several miles from Rochester on the London-Dover road.   71. **bots:** disease
of horses.   80. **liege people:** faithful subjects.

DERICK: Hear you, sir, are you one of the King's liege people?

THIEF: Aye, marry am I, sir, what say you to it?

DERICK: Marry, sir, I say you are one of the King's filching people.

COBLER: Come, come, let's have him away.

THIEF: Why, what have I done?   85

ROBIN: Thou hast robb'd a poor fellow,
And taken away his goods from him.

THIEF: I never saw him before.

DERICK: Masters, who comes here?

Enter the Vintner's boy.

BOY: How now, good man Cobler?   90

COBLER: How now, *Robin,* what makes thou abroad
At this time of night?

BOY: Marry, I have been at the Counter,°
I can tell such news as never you have heard the like.

COBLER: What is that, *Robin,* what is the matter?   95

BOY: Why, this night about two hours ago, there came the young Prince,
and three or four more of his companions, and called for wine good store,
and then they sent for a noise of Musicians, and were very merry for the
space of an hour, then whether their Music liked them not, or whether
they had drunk too much Wine or not, I cannot tell, but our pots flew   100
against the walls, and then they drew their swords, and went into the
street and fought, and some took one part, & some took another, but for
the space of half an hour, there was such a bloody fray as passeth, and
none could part them until such time as the Mayor and Sheriff were sent
for, and then at the last with much ado, they took them, and so the young 105
Prince was carried to the Counter, and then about one hour after, there
came a Messenger from the Court in all haste from the King, for my
Lord Mayor and the Sheriff, but for what cause I know not.

COBLER: Here is news indeed, *Robert.*

LAWRENCE: Marry, neighbor, this news is strange indeed. I think it best, 110
neighbor, to rid our hands of this fellow first.

THIEF: What mean you to do with me?

COBLER: We mean to carry you to the prison, and there to remain 'til the
Sessions day.

THIEF: Then I pray you let me go to the prison where my master is.   115

COBLER: Nay, thou must go to the country prison, to Newgate,
Therefore, come away.

---

93. **Counter:** a London prison, mainly for debtors.

THIEF: I prithee, be good to me, honest fellow.

DERICK: Aye, marry, will I, I'll be very charitable to thee,
For I will never leave thee, 'til I see thee on the Gallows.   120

[SCENE III]

Enter Henry the fourth, with the Earl of Exeter, and the Lord of Oxford.

OXFORD: And please your Majesty, here is my Lord Mayor and the Sheriff of London to speak with your Majesty.

KING HENRY 4: Admit them to our presence.

Enter the Mayor and the Sheriff.

Now, my good Lord Mayor of London,
The cause of my sending for you at this time is to tell you of a matter   5
which I have learned of my Council. Herein, I understand that you have
committed my son to prison without our leave and license. What, although he be a rude youth, and likely to give occasion, yet you might
have considered that he is a Prince, and my son, and not to be hauled to
prison by every subject.   10

MAYOR: May it please your Majesty to give us leave to tell our tale?

KING HENRY 4: Or else God forbid, otherwise you might think me an unequal Judge, having more affection to my son, than to any rightful judgment.

MAYOR: Then I do not doubt but we shall rather deserve commendations   15
at your Majesty's hands than any anger.

KING HENRY 4: Go to, say on.

MAYOR: Then if it please your Majesty, this night betwixt two and three of
the clock in the morning, my Lord the young Prince, with a very disordered company, came to the old Tavern in Eastcheap, and whether it was   20
that their Music liked them not, or whether they were overcome with
wine, I know not, but they drew their swords, and into the street they
went, and some took my Lord the young Prince's part, and some took the
other, but betwixt them there was such a bloody fray for the space of half
an hour, that neither watchmen nor any other could stay them, til my   25
brother the Sheriff of London & I were sent for, and at the last with
much ado we stayed them, but it was long first, which was a great disquieting to all your loving subjects thereabouts. And then, my good
Lord, we knew not whether your grace had sent them to try us, whether
we would do justice, or whether it were of their own voluntary will or   30
not, we cannot tell. And therefore in such a case we knew not what to do,
but for our own safeguard we sent him to ward, where he wanteth noth-

ing that is fit for his grace, and your Majesty's son. And thus most
humbly beseeching your Majesty to think of our answer.

KING HENRY 4: Stand aside until we have further deliberated on your an- 35
swer.

Exit Mayor.

KING HENRY 4: Ah, *Harry, Harry,* now thrice accursed *Harry,*
That hath gotten a son, which with grief
Will end his father's days.
Oh, my son, a Prince thou art, aye, a Prince indeed, 40
And to deserve imprisonment.
And well have they done, and like faithful subjects:
Discharge them and let them go.

EXETER: I beseech your Grace, be good to my Lord the young Prince.

KING HENRY 4: Nay, nay, 'tis no matter; let him alone. 45

OXFORD: Perchance the Mayor and the Sheriff have been too precise in
this matter.

KING HENRY 4: No: they have done like faithful subjects.
I will go myself to discharge them, and let them go.

Exeunt omnes.

[SCENE IV]

Enter Lord Chief Justice, Clerk of the Office, Jailer, John Cobler, Derick, and the Thief.

JUDGE: Jailer, bring the prisoner to the bar.

DERICK: Hear you, my Lord, I pray you bring the bar to the prisoner.

JUDGE: Hold thy hand up at the bar.

THIEF: Here it is, my Lord.

JUDGE: Clerk of the Office, read his indictment. 5

CLERK: What is thy name?

THIEF: My name was known before I came here,
And shall be when I am gone, I warrant you.

JUDGE: Aye, I think so, but we will know it better before thou go.

DERICK: S'ounds, and you do but send to the next Jail, 10
We are sure to know his name,
For this is not the first prison he hath been in, I'll warrant you.

CLERK: What is thy name?

THIEF: What need you to ask, and have it in writing.

CLERK: Is not thy name *Cutbert Cutter?* 15

THIEF: What the Devil need you ask, and know it so well.

CLERK: Why then, *Cutbert Cutter,* I indict thee by the name of *Cutbert
Cutter,* for robbing a poor carrier the 20th day of May last past, in the

fourteenth year of the reign of our sovereign Lord King *Henry* the
fourth, for setting upon a poor Carrier upon Gads Hill in *Kent,* and hav- 20
ing beaten and wounded the said Carrier, and taken his goods from him.

DERICK: Oh masters, stay there. Nay, let's never belie the man, for he hath
not [only] beaten and wounded me also, but he hath beaten and
wounded my pack, and hath taken the great rase° of Ginger, that bounc-
ing Bess with the jolly buttocks should have had; that grieves me most. 25

JUDGE: Well, what sayest thou? art thou guilty, or not guilty?

THIEF: Not guilty, my Lord.

JUDGE: By whom wilt thou be tried?

THIEF: By my Lord the young Prince, or by myself, whether you will.

Enter the young Prince, with Ned and Tom.

HENRY 5:   Come away, my lads. Gog's wounds, ye villain, what make you here? 30
I must go about my business myself, and you must stand loitering here.

THIEF: Why, my Lord, they have bound me, and will not let me go.

HENRY 5:   Have they bound thee, villain? why, how now, my Lord?

JUDGE: I am glad to see your grace in good health.

HENRY 5:   Why, my Lord, this is my man, 35
'Tis marvel you knew him not long before this,
I tell you he is a man of his hands.

THIEF: Aye, Gog's wounds, that I am, try me who dare.

JUDGE: Your Grace shall find small credit by acknowledging him to be
your man. 40

HENRY 5:   Why, my Lord, what hath he done?

JUDGE: And it please your Majesty, he hath robbed a poor Carrier.

DERICK: Hear you, sir, marry, it was one *Derick,*
Goodman *Hobling's* man of *Kent.*

HENRY 5:   What, was't you, button-breech? 45
Of my word, my Lord, he did it but in jest.

DERICK: Hear you, sir, is it your man's quality to rob folks in jest? In faith,
he shall be hanged in earnest.

HENRY 5:   Well, my Lord, what do you mean to do with my man?

JUDGE: And [it] please your grace, the law must pass on him, 50
According to justice. Then he must be executed.

DERICK°:   Hear you, sir, I pray you, is it your man's quality to rob folks in
jest? In faith, he shall be hanged in jest.

---

24. rase: root.   **52.** The next five lines repeat what has just been said; this time, however, Derick undoes his joke. Although the repeat may be a printing error, it is just as likely that the text
reflects playhouse practice, where exchanges that drew applause were repeated and/or impro-
vised upon.

HENRY 5:   Well, my Lord, what mean you to do with my man?

JUDGE: And please your grace, the law must pass on him,   55
   According to justice. Then he must be executed.

HENRY 5:   Why then, belike you mean to hang my man?

JUDGE: I am sorry that it falls out so.

HENRY 5:   Why, my Lord, I pray ye, who am I?

JUDGE: And [it] please your Grace, you are my Lord the young Prince, our   60
   King that shall be after the decease of our sovereign Lord, King *Henry*
   the fourth, whom God grant long to reign.

HENRY 5:   You say true, my Lord:
   And you will hang my man?

JUDGE: And [it] like your grace, I must needs do justice.   65

HENRY 5:   Tell me, my Lord, shall I have my man?

JUDGE: I cannot, my Lord.

HENRY 5:   But will you not let him go?

JUDGE: I am sorry that his case is so ill.

HENRY 5:   Tush, case me no casings, shall I have my man?   70

JUDGE: I cannot, nor I may not, my Lord.

HENRY 5:   Nay, and I shall not say, & then I am answered?

JUDGE: No.

HENRY 5:   No: then I will have him.

He giveth him a box on the ear.

NED: Gog's wounds, my Lord, shall I cut off his head?   75

HENRY 5:   No, I charge you draw not your swords,
   But get you hence, provide a noise of Musicians,
   Away, be gone.

                                        [*Exit Ned and Tom.*]

JUDGE: Well, my Lord, I am content to take it at your hands.

HENRY 5:   Nay, and you be not, you shall have more.   80

JUDGE: Why, I pray you, my Lord, who am I?

HENRY 5:   You? Who knows not you?
   Why, man, you are Lord Chief Justice of England.

JUDGE: Your Grace hath said truth, therefore in striking me in this place,
   you greatly abuse me, and not me only but also your father, whose lively   85
   person here in this place I do represent. And therefore to teach you what
   prerogatives mean, I commit you to the Fleet, until we have spoken with
   your father.

HENRY 5:   Why, then, belike you mean to send me to the Fleet?

JUDGE: Aye, indeed, and therefore carry him away.   90

                                        Exeunt Hen[ry] 5 with the Officers.

JUDGE: Jailer, carry the prisoner to Newgate again, until the next Sises.°
JAILER: At your commandment, my Lord, it shall be done.

[Exit Jailer and Thief; exit Judge.]

[SCENE V]

Enter Derick and John Cobler.

DERICK: S'ounds, masters, here's ado,
    When Princes must go to prison:
    Why *John*, didst ever see the like?
JOHN: O *Derick*, trust me: I never saw the like.
DERICK: Why *John*, thou maist see what princes be in choler.   5
    A Judge a box on the ear! I'll tell thee *John*, O *John*,
    I would not have done it for twenty shillings.
JOHN: No nor I. There had been no way but one with us,
    We should have been hang'd.
DERICK: Faith, *John*, I'll tell thee what: thou shalt be my   10
    Lord Chief Justice, and thou shalt sit in the chair,
    And I'll be the young prince, and hit thee a box on the ear,
    And then thou shalt say, "To teach you what prerogatives
    Mean, I commit you to the Fleet."
JOHN: Come on, I'll be your Judge,   15
    But thou shalt not hit me hard.
DERICK: No, no.
JOHN: What hath he done?
DERICK: Marry, he hath robb'd, *Derick*.
JOHN: Why then, I cannot let him go.   20
DERICK: I must needs have my man.
JOHN: You shall not have him.
DERICK: Shall I not have my man? Say no and you dare:
    How say you, shall I not have my man?
JOHN: No, marry, shall you not.   25
DERICK: Shall I not, *John?*
JOHN: No, *Derick*.
DERICK: Why then, take you that till more come!
    S'ounds, shall I not have him?
JOHN: Well, I am content to take this at your hand.   30
    But I pray you, who am I?

91. **Sises:** assizes; court sessions for administering civil and criminal justice.

DERICK: Who art thou? S'ounds, dost not know thy self?
JOHN: No.
DERICK: Now away, simple fellow,
    Why man, thou art *John* the Cobler.   35
JOHN: No, I am my Lord Chief Justice of England.
DERICK: Oh, *John,* Mass,° thou saiest true, thou art indeed.
JOHN: Why then, to teach you what prerogatives mean,
    I commit you to the Fleet.
DERICK: Well, I will go, but i'faith, you graybeard knave, I'll course you. 40

Exit. And straight enters again.

Oh *John,* Come, come out of thy chair! Why, what a clown wert thou, to
let me hit thee a box on the ear! and now thou seest they will not take me
to the Fleet. I think that thou art one of these Worenday° Clowns.
JOHN: But I marvel what will become of thee.
DERICK: Faith, I'll be no more a Carrier.   45
JOHN: What wilt thou do then?
DERICK: I'll dwell with thee and be a Cobler.
JOHN: With me? Alas, I am not able to keep thee,
    Why, thou wilt eat me out of doors.
DERICK: Oh *John,* no *John,* I am none of these great slouching fellows, that 50
    devour these great pieces of beef and brews.° Alas, a trifle serves me: a
    Woodcock, a Chicken, or a Capon's leg, or any such little thing serves me.
JOHN: A Capon! Why man, I cannot get a Capon once a year, except it be
    at Christmas, at some other man's house, for we Coblers be glad of a dish
    of roots.   55
DERICK: Roots! Why, are you so good at rooting?
    Nay, Cobler, we'll have you ring'd.°
JOHN: But *Derick,* though we be so poor,
    Yet will we have in store a crab° in the fire,
    With nut-brown Ale, that is full stale,°   60
    Which will a man quail, and lay in the mire.
DERICK: A bots° on you, and be — ; but for your Ale,
    I'll dwell with you. Come, let's away as fast as we can.   *Exeunt.*

---

37. **Mass:** by the mass; an oath.   43. **Worenday:** workaday?   51. **brews:** browls; meat broth.
57. **ring'd:** ringed through the nose like a pig, to keep him from rooting.   59. **crab:** crabap-
ple.   60. **stale:** old and strong.   62. **bots:** literally, a worm or maggot; Derick hopes that
Cobler will get a disease.

[SCENE VI]

Enter the young Prince, with Ned and Tom.

HENRY 5:   Come away, sirs! Gog's wounds, *Ned,*
Didst thou not see what a box on the ear
I took my Lord Chief Justice?
TOM: By gog's blood, it did me good to see it,
It made his teeth jar in his head.   5

Enter Sir John Oldcastle.

HENRY 5:   How now, Sir *John Oldcastle,*
What news with you?
JOHN OLDCASTLE: I am glad to see your grace at liberty,
I was come, I, to visit you in prison.
HENRY 5:   To visit me? Didst thou not know that I am a Prince's son? Why,   10
'tis enough for me to look into a prison, though I come not in myself. But
here's much ado nowadays: here's prisoning, here's hanging, whipping,
and the devil and all. But I tell you, sirs, when I am King, we will have no
such things. But my lads, if the old King my father were dead, we would
be all kings.   15
JOHN OLDCASTLE: He is a good old man, God take him to his mercy the
sooner.
HENRY 5:   But *Ned,* so soon as I am King, the first thing
I will do shall be to put my Lord Chief Justice out of office,
And thou shalt be my Lord Chief Justice of England.   20
NED: Shall I be Lord Chief Justice?
By gog's wounds, I'll be the bravest Lord Chief Justice
That ever was in England.
HENRY 5:   Then *Ned,* I'll turn all these prisons into fence Schools, and I
will endow thee with them, with lands to maintain them withal: then   25
I will have a bout with my Lord Chief Justice. Thou shalt hang
none but pickpurses and horse-stealers, and such base-minded villains, but that fellow that will stand by the highway side courageously
with his sword and buckler and take a purse, that fellow give him commendations; besides that, send him to me, and I will give him an an-   30
nual pension out of my Exchequer, to maintain him all the days of his
life.
JOHN OLDCASTLE: Nobly spoken, *Harry.* We shall never have a merry
world til the old King be dead.
NED: But whither are ye going now?   35

HENRY 5:   To the Court, for I hear say, my father lies very sick.°

TOM: But I doubt he will not die.

HENRY 5:   Yet will I go thither, for the breath shall be no sooner out of his mouth, but I will clap the Crown on my head.

JOCKEY: Will you go to the Court with that cloak so full of needles?   40

HENRY 5:   Cloak, eyelet-holes, needles, and all was of mine own devising, and therefore I will wear it.

TOM: I pray you, my Lord, what may be the meaning thereof?

HENRY 5:   Why man, 'tis a sign that I stand upon thorns, til the Crown be on my head.   45

JOCKEY: Or that every needle might be a prick to their hearts that repine at your doings.

HENRY 5:   Thou saiest true, *Jockey,* but there's some will say, the young Prince will be a well-toward young man and all this gear,° that I had as leave they would break my head with a pot, as to say any such thing. But   50 we stand prating here too long. I must needs speak with my father. Therefore, come away.

PORTER: What a rapping keep you at the King's Court gate?

HENRY 5:   Here's one that must speak with the King.

PORTER: The King is very sick, and none must speak with him.   55

HENRY 5:   No? you rascal, do you not know me?

PORTER: You are my Lord the young Prince.

HENRY 5:   Then go and tell my father, that I must and will speak with him.

NED: Shall I cut off his head?

HENRY 5:   No, no, though I would help you in other places, yet I have noth-   60 ing to do here, what° you are in my father's Court.

NED: I will write him in my Tables, for so soon as I am made Lord Chief Justice, I will put him out of his Office.

The Trumpet sounds.

HENRY 5:   Gog's wounds, sirs, the King comes.
Let's all stand aside.   65

Enter the King, with the Lord of Exeter.

KING HENRY 4:   And is it true, my Lord, that my son is already sent to the Fleet? Now truly that man is more fitter to rule the Realm than I, for by

---

36. father . . . sick: from this point forward, the scene concerns events dramatized in *Henry IV, Part 2,* especially 4.3.   **49. well-toward . . . gear:** a promising young man and such nonsense.   **61. what:** since.

no means could I rule my son, and he by one word hath caused him to be ruled. Oh my son, my son, no sooner out of one prison, but into another. I had thought once, whiles I had lived to have seen this noble Realm of 70 England flourish by thee, my son, but now I see it goes to ruin and decay.

He weepeth.

Enters Lord of Oxford.

OXFORD: And please your grace, here is my Lord your son,
That cometh to speak with you.
He saith, he must and will speak with you.
KING HENRY 4:   Who? my son *Harry?*   75
OXFORD: Aye, and please your Majesty.
KING HENRY 4:   I know wherefore he cometh,
But look that none come with him.
OXFORD: A very disordered company, and such as make
Very ill rule in your Majesty's house.   80
KING HENRY 4:   Well, let him come,
But look that none come with him.   *He goeth.*
OXFORD: And please your grace,
My Lord the King sends for you.
HENRY 5:   Come away, sirs, let's go all together.   85
OXFORD: And please your grace, none must go with you.
HENRY 5:   Why, I must needs have them with me,
Otherwise I can do my father no countenance,°
Therefore, come away.
OXFORD: The King your father commands   90
There should none come.
HENRY 5:   Well sirs, then be gone,
And provide me three Noise of Musicians.   *Exeunt knights.*

Enters the Prince with a dagger in his hand.

KING HENRY 4:   Come, my son, come on, a God's name,
I know wherefore thy coming is.   95
Oh my son, my son, what cause hath ever been,
That thou shouldst forsake me, and follow this vile and
Reprobate company, which abuseth youth so manifestly?
Oh my son, thou knowest that these thy doings
Will end thy father's days.   *He weeps.* 100

___

88. **no countenance:** show him no proper respect.

Aye so, so, my son, thou fearest not to approach the presence of thy sick father, in that disguised sort. I tell thee, my son, that there is never a needle in thy cloak, but is a prick to my heart, & never an eyelet-hole, but it is a hole to my soul. And wherefore thou bringest that dagger in thy hand I know not, but by conjecture. *He weeps.* 105

HENRY 5: My conscience accuseth me, most sovereign Lord, and well-beloved father, to answer first to the last point — that is, whereas you conjecture that this hand and this dagger shall be arm'd against your life — no. Know, my beloved father, far be the thoughts of your son — son, said I, an unworthy son for so good a father — but far be the 110 thoughts of any such pretended mischief. And I most humbly render it to your Majesty's hand, and live, my Lord and sovereign forever: and with your dagger arm show like vengeance upon the body of that your son — I was about [to] say and dare not, ah, woe is me, therefore — that your wild° slave. 'Tis not the Crown that I come for, sweet father, because 115 I am unworthy, and those vile & reprobate company I abandon, & utterly abolish their company forever. Pardon, sweet father, pardon: the least thing and most desir'd. And this ruffianly cloak, I here tear from my back, and sacrifice it to the devil, which is master of all mischief. Pardon me, sweet father, pardon me — Good my Lord of *Exeter,* speak for 120 me — pardon me, pardon, good father. Not a word. Ah, he will not speak one word! A[h] *Harry,* now thrice unhappy *Harry!* But what shall I do? I will go take me into some solitary place, and there lament my sinful life, and when I have done, I will lay me down and die. *Exit.*

KING HENRY 4: Call him again, call my son again. 125

[*The Prince returns.*]

HENRY 5: And doth my father call me again? Now *Harry,*
Happy be the time that thy father calleth thee again.

KING HENRY 4: Stand up, my son. And do not think thy father,
But at the request of thee, my son, will pardon thee,
And God bless thee, and make thee his servant. 130

HENRY 5: Thanks, good my Lord, & no doubt but this day,
Even this day, I am born new again.

KING HENRY 4: Come, my son and Lords, take me by the hands.

Exeunt omnes.

---

115. **wild:** possibly vile, as in underling; but "wild slave" seems just as appropriate in describing Hal's shame.

→ NICCOLÒ MACHIAVELLI

From The Prince   *1513*

First dedicated to Giuliano de' Medici and, later, to his nephew Lorenzo, Machiavelli's "little book" represents the response of a longtime government servant to problems in late-fifteenth- and early-sixteenth-century Florentine politics, especially the conduct of a prince newly come to power. Like the English humanist writers on education who aimed at curing the social ills of the body politic, Machiavelli addressed specific historical conditions. Although he hoped that his book would bring him favorable attention from the Medicean government, that was not the case, for he was never entrusted with public office after its publication. However, *The Prince* had and continues to exert a profound influence on subsequent political thought.

The ideas Machiavelli expresses concerning statecraft and the uses of history are less a literary or historical source for Shakespeare than a cultural locus for ideas of statecraft that trace through his plays. *The Prince* resembles a political manager's or corporate executive's handbook, a practicum of advice on successful rule that explores the workings and limits of power. Rather than basing his thinking on the idealized entities imagined by humanist theorists, Machiavelli's ideas come from observing the behavior of rulers and their subjects. "How men live," he writes, "is so different from how they should live that a ruler who . . . persists in doing what ought to be done, will undermine his power rather than maintain it." It is necessary, Machiavelli claims, for princes to cultivate two natures: a good one to be followed when possible and a bad one that they must be prepared to follow as necessity dictates.

Largely because they represented an incisive critique of humanism, these ideas, shockingly radical at the time they were written, have spawned somewhat reductive interpretations of Machiavelli's thought. Perhaps the most widely circulated of these is the assumption that politics is a deceitful practice in which "anything goes": the end justifies the means. Such a reading assumes that human nature — which, in Machiavelli's view, always remains the same — is *essentially* evil and works to validate malice as a dominant human characteristic. Several Elizabethan appropriations of Machiavelli reflected variations of these notions. It was assumed, for instance, that the Machiavellian state was one in which religious principles are subordinated to civil policy. On this basis, it was possible to criticize the "new men" who were coming to power during Elizabeth's reign as political opportunists who had overthrown all the providentialist assumptions of the past. Another applied to the drama, specifically in the term *Machiavel,* which came to describe the kind of character (for example, Shakespeare's Richard III or Iago) who relishes his own villainy and gloats over his success in lengthy soliloquies.

Nicholas Machiavel's Prince, translated out of Italian into English; by E[dward] D[acres], With some Animadversions noting and taxing his errors (London, 1640), 117–20, 135–41.

That character type, however, has a theatrical and cultural history that stretches back to the old Vice of the morality plays and to Senecan traditions; the association with Machiavelli — at least as his thought was understood to imply malicious, all-knowing opportunism — was written on top of an existing theatrical tradition. But what that association makes possible is a reconceptualization of *theatrical* power, and it is in this way that Machiavelli's thought most directly touches the early modern drama. In advising princes to construct an artificial identity in the service of power, Machiavelli opens up ways of thinking about how characters — and actors who play such fictionalized selves — can manipulate both an onstage and an offstage audience. Seen through the lens of the popular theatre, the ideas expressed in these chapters from *The Prince* suggest that power lies in self-concealment — in knowing how to put on a necessary, at times unreadable, guise and, above all, in knowing how to read others.

From *The Prince*

CHAPTER XV. OF THOSE THINGS, IN RESPECT WHEREOF, MEN, AND ESPECIALLY PRINCES, ARE PRAISED, OR DISPRAISED

It now remains that we consider what the conditions of a Prince ought to be, and his terms of government over his subjects and towards his friends. And because I know that many have written hereupon, I doubt, lest I, venturing also to treat thereof, may be branded with presumption, especially seeing I am like enough to deliver an opinion different from others. But my intent being to write for the advantage of him that understands me, I thought it fitter to follow the effectual truth of the matter, than the imagination thereof. And many Principalities and Republics have been in imagination which neither have been seen nor known to be indeed. For there is such a distance between how men do live, and how men ought to live, that he who leaves that which is done, for that which ought to be done, learns sooner his ruin than his preservation. For that man who will profess honesty in all his actions must needs go to ruin, among so many that are dishonest. Whereupon it is necessary for a Prince, desiring to preserve himself, to be able to make use of that honesty, and to lay it aside again, as need shall require.

Passing by, then, things that are only in imagination belonging to a Prince, to discourse upon those that are really true, I say that all men, whensoever mention is made of them, and especially Princes, because they are plac'd aloft in the view of all, are taken notice of for some of these qualities, which procure them either commendations or blame. And this is, that some one is held liberal, some miserable (miserable, I say, not covetous, for the covetous desire to have, though it were by rapine, but a miserable man is he, that too much forbears to make use of his own); some free givers, others extortioners; some cruel, others piteous; the one a League breaker, another faithful; the one effeminate and of small courage, the other fierce and courageous; the one courteous, the other proud; the one lascivious, the other chaste; the one of fair dealing, the other wily and crafty; the one hard, the other easy; the one grave, the other light; the one religious, the other incredulous, and such like.

I know that every one will confess it were exceedingly praiseworthy for a Prince to be adorned with all these above nam'd qualities that are good. But because this is not possible, nor do human conditions admit such perfection in virtues, it is necessary for him to be so discreet, that he know how to avoid the infamy of those vices which would thrust him out of his State. And if it be possible, beware of those also which are not able to remove him thence, but where it cannot be, let them pass with less regard. And yet, let him not stand much upon it, though he incur the infamy of those vices without which he can very hardly save his State. For if all be thoroughly considered, some things we shall find which will have the color and very face of Virtue, and following them, they will lead thee to thy destruction. Whereas some others, that shall as much seem vice, if we take the course they lead us, shall discover unto us the way to our safety and well-being.

[Chapter XVI treats of liberality and miserableness, Chapter XVII of clemency and cruelty. Here, Machiavelli claims that it is more politically sound to rule by fear than by love.]

CHAPTER XVIII. IN WHAT MANNER PRINCES OUGHT TO KEEP THEIR WORDS

How commendable in a Prince it is to keep his word, and live with integrity, not making use of cunning and subtlety, everyone knows well. Yet we see by experience in these our days, that those Princes have effected great matters who have made small reckoning of keeping their words, and have known by their craft to turn and wind men about, and in the end have overcome those who have grounded [their statecraft] upon the truth.

You must then know, there are two kinds of combating or fighting: the one by right of the laws, the other merely by force. That first way is proper to men; the other is also common to beasts. But because the first many times suffices not, there is a necessity to make recourse to the second, wherefore it behooves a Prince to know how to make good use of that part which belongs to a beast, as well as that which is proper to a man. This part hath been covertly show'd to Princes by ancient writers, who say that *Achilles* and many others of those ancient Princes were instructed to *Chiron* the Centaur, to be brought up under his discipline. The moral of this, having for their teacher one that was half a beast and half a man, was nothing else but that it was needful for a Prince to understand how to make his advantage of the one and the other nature, because neither could subsist without the other. A Prince, then, being necessitated to know how to make use of that part belonging to a beast, ought to serve himself of the conditions of the Fox and the Lion, for the Lion cannot keep himself from snares, nor the Fox defend himself against the Wolves. He had need then be a Fox, that he may beware of the snares, and a Lion, that he may scare the Wolves. Those that stand wholly upon the Lion understand not well themselves.

And therefore a wise Prince cannot, nor ought not keep his faith given, when the observance thereof turns to disadvantage, and the occasions that made him promise are past. For if men were all good, this rule would not be allowable. But being they are full of mischief, and would not make it good to thee, neither art thou tied to keep [faith] with them; nor shall a Prince ever want lawful occasions to give color to this breach. Very many modern examples hereof might be alleg'd, wherein might be showed how many peaces concluded, and how many promises made, have been violated and broken by the infidelity of Princes; and ordinarily things have best succeeded with him that hath been nearest the Fox in condition. But it is necessary to understand how to set a good color upon this disposition, and to be able to feign and dissemble thoroughly. And men are so simple and yield so much to the present necessities, that he who hath a mind to deceive shall always find another that will be deceived. I will not conceal any one of the examples that have been of late. *Alexander* the sixth never did anything else than deceive men, and never meant otherwise, and always found whom to work upon. Yet never was there man would protest more effectually, nor aver anything with more solemn oaths, and observe them less than he. Nevertheless, his cosenages[1] all thriv'd well with him, for he knew how to play this part cunningly.

Therefore is there no necessity for a Prince to be endowed with all these above written qualities, but it behooves well that he seem to be so. Or rather I will boldly say this: that having these qualities, and always regulating himself by them, they are hurtful. But seeming to have them, they are advantageous, as to seem pitiful, faithful, mild, religious, and of integrity, and indeed to be so, provided withal thou beest of such a composition, that if need require thee to use the contrary, thou canst, and know'st how to apply thyself thereto. And it suffices to conceive this, that a Prince, and especially

---

[1] **cosenages:** deceits; trickery.

a new Prince, cannot observe all those things for which men are held good, he often being forc'd, for the maintenance of his State, to do contrary to his faith, charity, humanity, and religion. And therefore it behooves him to have a mind so dispos'd as to turn and take the advantage of all winds and fortunes, and, as formerly I said, not forsake the good, while he can, but to know how to make use of the evil upon necessity.

A Prince then ought to have a special care that he never let fall any words but what are all season'd with the five above-written qualities, and let him seem to him that sees and hears him, all pity, all faith, all integrity, all humanity, all religion. Nor is there anything more necessary for him to seem to have than this last quality, for all men in general judge thereof, rather by the sight than by the touch. For [although] every man may come to the sight of him, few come to the touch and feeling of him. Every man may come to see what thou seemest; few come to perceive and understand what thou art; and those few dare not oppose the opinion of many, who have the majesty of State to protect them. And in all men's actions, especially those of Princes, wherein there is no judgment to appeal unto, men forbear to give their censures til the events, and ends of things. Let a Prince therefore take the surest courses he can to maintain his life and State. The means shall always be thought honorable, and commended by everyone, for the vulgar is overtaken with the appearance and event of a thing. And for the most part of people, they are but the vulgar; the others that are but few, take place where the vulgar have no subsistence. A Prince there is in these days, whom I shall not do well to name, that preaches nothing else but peace and faith; but had he kept the one and the other, several times had they taken from him his State and reputation.

✛ *From* The Brut, or The Chronicles of England *Fifteenth century*

✛ JOHN SPEED

From The History of Great Britain *1611/12*

Although these selections bear only tangentially on Hal's education, both concern the relations between Henry IV and his son. The first, taken from an early chronicle, reveals a glimpse of Prince Henry's history that historians such as Hall and Holinshed do not record. When Richard II exiled Bolingbroke in

---

The Brut, or The Chronicles of England, ed. Friedrich W. D. Brie (c. 1450? London, 1908). John Speed, *The History of Great Britain* (London, 1611/1612), 762–63.

1398, he took Prince Henry into his household as surety for his father's good behavior; Henry went with him to Ireland in 1399 and was knighted at the age of twelve. The encounter recorded in *The Brut* occurred at Chester, where Bolingbroke found his son when he came to speak with Richard. Written by a partisan of Richard II, this account may exaggerate the affection between Prince Henry and Richard II, but it is possible to speculate that the prince's loyalty to the king whom his father had deposed and murdered lay behind the estrangement between Henry IV and his son. The moment described here also offers a further explanation for one of Henry V's actions once he was crowned, which was to have Richard's body brought from the Black Friars church at Langley in Hertfordshire for reburial in Westminster Abbey (McFarlane, *Lancastrian Kings* 121–22; see also *Henry V* 4.1.95).

The second selection represents one account of the deathbed reconciliation between Henry IV and Hal, a part of the "wild prince" legend that Shakespeare's *Henry IV, Part 2* dramatizes (4.5). Although not in the form of a letter, it resembles letters of advice from fathers to their sons, many of which drew from the influential conduct books and manuals of the period. Perhaps the most notorious of these was Lord Burghley's "Certain Precepts for the Well Ordering of a Man's Life" (c. 1584), a list of ten secular commandments thought by some to be a source for Polonius's parting advice to Laertes (*Hamlet* 1.3.59–81).

From *The Brut, or The Chronicles of England*

[When Richard II hears that Henry Bolingbroke, Duke of Hereford, has returned to England, the King leaves Ireland for Flint Castle in Wales.]

And then was there sent unto the Castle of Flint, Master Thomas Arundel, Archbishop of Canterbury, and Sir Henry Percy, Earl of Northumberland, and other lords, both spiritual and temporal; and there was much thing spoken of between the King and them, by great oaths and sureties made, that he should come unto Chester safely, and speak with the Duke, and be delivered safely again to the said castle: which oaths and sureties were not all performed. And so came the King riding unto Chester and young Henry with him, that was the eldest son of the said Duke of Hereford and was lodged in the outerward of the Castle of Chester. Then King Richard understood and knew well that it was not well on their side. And the same night, after that King Richard was gone to Chester, Sir Thomas Percy, Earl of Worcester and steward of the King's household, came into the hall among the people, and there he broke the rod of his office, and bade every man do his best. And so went each man his way.

Then the King and the Duke met and spoke together in the hall of the said Castle, that was in the outerward, a long while, and after departed. And in the departing, Henry, the son and heir of the said Duke, come to his father, and knelt down before him, and welcomed him, as he ought to do. And there forthwith his father him charged the next day to come from the King, and wait upon him. Then this young knight Henry brought the King to his chamber with a sorrowful heart, because he should depart from his godfather and his Sovereign Lord, for he loved him entirely. And when he came unto the King's chamber, he told the King how he must, the next day after, wait upon his father, by straight and hard commandment. And then the King said to him these words: "Good son Henry, I give thee good leave to do thy father's commandment; but I know well there is one Henry shall do me much harm; and I suppose it is not thou. Wherefore I pray thee be my friend, for I wot not how it will go." And so on the next day after, Henry took his leave of the King his godfather with a heavy heart, and went to his father, Duke of Hereford. And after that, was the King arrested in the same Castle by the said Duke, and all his men that were about him put away; and such men were put about him as the Duke would. Then from thence he was brought to London, and, by assent of all the lords, put in the Tower.

JOHN SPEED

From *The History of Great Britain*

The vulgar Chronicles tell us a strange Story, the truth whereof must rest upon the reporters. The King, say they, lying dangerously sick, called his Crown to be set on a Pillow at his bed's head, when suddenly the pangs of his *Apoplexy* seizing on him so vehemently that all supposed him dead, the Prince coming in, took away the Crown; which, his Father reviving, soon missed; and calling for his son, demanded, what he meant, to bereave him of that, whereto he had yet no right? The Prince boldly replied: "Long may you live, Sovereign Father, to wear it yourself; but all men deeming you were departed to inherit another Crown, this being my right, I took as mine own; but now do acknowledge for none of mine"; and thereupon he set the Crown again where he found it. "Oh son," (quoth he) "with what right I got it, God only knoweth, who forgive me the sin." "Howsoever it was got," said the Prince, "I mean to keep and defend it, (when it shall be mine) with my Sword, as you by Sword have obtained it." Which the King hearing, he entered discourse of advice, showing him that he feared some discord would arise betwixt him and his brother *Thomas* Duke of *Clarence*, who with better respect had borne forth his youth than Prince *Henry* had done, and whose distemper was like to breed great troubles, if it were not in time

FIGURE 17 *This frame still from Orson Welles's* Chimes at Midnight *(1965–66), showing Henry IV (John Gielgud) and Hal (Keith Baxter) in "private conference," emphasizes the distance between father and son as well as the hierarchical relationship between the two. The high, bare walls, together with the strong side lighting, perfectly convey the King's icy majesty.*

stayed. "If my Brethren" (quoth *Henry*) "will be true subjects, I will honor them as my Brethren, but if otherwise, I shall as soon execute justice upon them, as on the meanest of birth in my Kingdom." The King rejoicing at this unexpected answer both prudently and Christianly charged him before God, to minister the law indifferently, to ease the oppressed, to beware of flatterers, not to desert justice, nor yet to be sparing of mercy. "Punish" (quoth he) "the oppressors of thy people, so shall thou obtain favor of God, and love and fear of thy Subjects, who whiles they have wealth, so long shalt thou have their obedience, but made poor, by oppressions, will be ready to make insurrections. Rejoice not so much in the glory of thy Crown, as meditate on the burthenous care which accompanieth it; mingle love with fear, so thou, as the heart, shalt be defended in the midst of the body: but know, that, neither the heart without the members, nor a King without his Subjects' help, is of any force. Lastly, my son, love and fear God, ascribe all thy victories, strength, friends, obedience, riches, honor, and all, unto him, and with the *Psalmist* say with all thanks, *Not unto us Lord, not unto us, but to thy holy Name be given the Laud and praise.*"

CHAPTER 5

Honor and Arms:
Elizabethan Neochivalric Culture
and the Military Trades

><

*H*enry IV, Part 1 dramatizes a spectrum of perspectives on honor and arms, the intertwined legacy of medieval chivalry, and on the military profession and the conduct of warfare. Henry IV desires to go on a crusade, the formal epitome of chivalric activity for a fifteenth-century king or noble; he also desires a son like Hotspur, "the theme of honor's tongue," and is contemptuous of a Hal whose brow is "stain[ed]" with "riot and dishonor" (1.1.80, 84). Yet if Hotspur's courage and insistence on fellowship align him with archaic chivalric ideals, his martial image as "the king of honor" is also undercut by his near-comic enthusiasm for war, which Hal even burlesques (2.4.85–90). In his guise as tavern layabout, Hal seems at first to be Hotspur's polar opposite, but in the last stages of the action he turns into Hotspur's worthy challenger in honor and arms. Vowing to his father that he will "redeem [his honor] on Percy's head," he employs terms — "engross up," "strict account," "reckoning," "smallest parcel" — that turn his honorable oath into "a marketplace transaction" (3.2.129–59; Cohen 80). As Phyllis Rackin points out, Hal does not come by his honor through blood or lineage, but, like the newly made gentry in Elizabeth's England who (as did Shakespeare) bought their coats of arms, he must *earn* his legitimacy (*Stages* 77–78). For Falstaff, however, honor is an empty word: "a mere scutcheon" (5.1.136–37), like the painted pageant shields carried by knights in the ceremonial competitions of Elizabeth's court. Like Hotspur, he knows that honor is gained by martial deeds; like Hal, he uses Shrewsbury to gain the King's favor as well as a title to garnish his knighthood. And at the bottom of this hierarchy stand Falstaff's foot soldiers — some hauled out of prison and forced to serve, others totally unfit for combat — men with no voice whose dramatic function is to represent their captain's corrupt military practices.

Such conflicting attitudes and postures mirror contradictions apparent in the last decades of Elizabeth's reign, and the play repeatedly measures the distance between the ideals its characters profess or attempt to enact and real historical conditions or cultural practices. Mapping these distinctions is yet another instance of how *Henry IV, Part 1* records a double history. Although the events it dramatizes are based on fifteenth-century history, their representation remains firmly rooted in the sociopolitical forms and conditions of late-sixteenth-century culture. Three related contextual strands are of particular importance in understanding the concepts of honor and arms in the period: the idea and ideals of chivalry that shaped the lineage culture of England's Northern counties, the ancestral home of the Percies; the extravagantly symbolic *political* chivalry of Elizabeth's court; and the persistent focus, in the last two decades of the century, on war and warfare as a *profession*.

The Chivalric Heritage

Medieval chivalry fused military, noble, and religious beliefs into an ethos based on internal virtues and ideals of personal conduct that embraced a ritualistically ordered way of life. Rooted in the warrior culture of the early Middle Ages as well as in Christianity, its cult of martial virtues drew strength from the disordered sociopolitical conditions of medieval Europe; its individualistic bent, from fragile governmental controls that threw the nobility back upon their own resources. The rise of feudal courts (like those portrayed in Thomas Malory's *Morte Darthur* [1469–70]) as aristocratic fellowships dedicated to a communal quest and united in faithful obedience to a lord provided the context for chivalry to become remodeled from a warrior's code into a sophisticated secular ethic with its own mythology and its own body of heraldic knowledge and ritual (James 270–72; Keen 253).

Although the concept of honor is chivalry's most important legacy to the sixteenth century, that heritage also led to contradictions between feudal notions about the values of lineage, nobility, and the importance of family alliances and wider notions of fealty to a centralized nation-state. Inherited through blood lines, honor was coupled to family name. "Better to die in honor than live in shame" — with a blot on one's arms — was a key concept; and, since the shedding of blood had specific chivalric value, honor not only sanctioned a politics of violence but also supported noble rebellion (James 276, 309–11, 342–43). In 1403, the Northern nobles rebelled because honor was at stake: once the Percies had sent Henry IV a challenge, offering to prove it "with our own hand," they had abandoned any show of respect for the Crown's central authority (see Chapter 2, "Civic Order and Rebellion").

The ideology of honor upheld by the Northern lineage culture differed considerably from that of London's court, which attempted to synthesize honor with humanistic learning and Protestant religion. Although reconciling a code that glorified self-esteem and individual will with Protestant Christianity posed difficulties, Sir Thomas Elyot's *Book of the Governor* (1531), directed to a noble audience, attempted to incorporate honor values into a universalized moral and religious system — precisely what the church had once attempted to do for chivalry in adapting it to serve the purposes of the Crusades. Elyot's honor ideology, which joined the virtues of the humanist scholar with those of the medieval knight, appears in texts such as Sir Philip Sidney's *The Countess of Pembroke's Arcadia* (1590); Ophelia's list of the attributes of the "noble mind" — the "courtier's, soldier's, scholar's eye, tongue, sword" (*Hamlet* 3.1.151) — aptly condenses the balance of martial discipline, humanist learning, and civic virtue codified in courtesy manuals such as Baldessare Castiglione's *Book of the Courtier* (1528) and perceived as central to fashioning the ideal late Tudor aristocrat.

More significantly, by imagining that members of an honor fellowship could become transformed into a literate magistracy, Elyot accommodates the feudal meanings of obedience to the demands of the state (I: 24–25). But set against this idea, the dissident position of honor, with its emphasis on warrior values, political autonomy, and individual will, persisted, not only in the North and the West but also at the court itself, where it became the code of political activists such as Robert Devereux, the Earl of Essex, and the members of his circle (James 338–39). Essex was perhaps the most famous, or notorious, "Hotspur" among Elizabeth's courtiers and the only one to which a Shakespearean play (*Henry V*, 5. Cho. 25–35) explicitly refers. Like Essex, Hotspur is active in the two spheres of conduct recognized in the period: the court and the wars. First seen in Henry IV's palace, he is required to justify his actions — a situation in which Essex, the military commander of expeditions to Cadiz and the Netherlands, repeatedly found himself. Not only did Essex frequently disobey the Queen's orders, but he also established feudal bonds of loyalty that encroached on the allegiance due to the Crown (McCoy; Smith). Like Essex, Hotspur embraces ideas of bravery and military prowess deriving from the lineage cult of honor. It is precisely these traits that envelop both in a somewhat archaic ideology that mystifies their figures, setting them apart from ordinary mortals. It also makes them potentially dangerous, for both espouse individual honor at the expense of national well-being.

Elizabethan Rites and Chivalric Rights

If the martial, individualistic values of lineage honor culture conflicted with the total Christianization of the codes of war, they were also at odds in the elaborate pageantry that surrounded the Queen, especially in the Accession Day Tilts, held yearly on 17 November, the day on which Elizabeth assumed the throne in 1558 (see Figure 18). Though feudalism as a working social or military structure was extinct, its forms and conventions were appropriated, in such pageants, to support Elizabeth's sovereign image. A substitution for or displacement of the "Pope's holidays," the Tilts combined patriotic devotion to a popular monarch with Protestant zeal in a chivalric ritual of worship centered on the Queen as the virgin of reformed religion (see Strong; Yates 88–111). Evoking an imagined, highly romanticized past in which "courtiers became medieval knights and their queen became a lady of medieval romance," these extravagant, ostentatious spectacles had a potent influence on the Elizabethan socio-cultural imaginary (Helgerson 50).

In the fourteenth and fifteenth centuries, there had been a close connection between warfare and such tournaments, where prowess with sword and lance represented training for actual military combat (see Figure 19). But in the late sixteenth century, the tournament became ceremonial, highly ritualized, focused almost exclusively on appearances and on the desire to be "well seen in arms." Embodying conflict as well as compliment, competition as well as stately ceremony, such mock combats allowed for "a socially sanctioned and carefully regulated release of aggressive energies" (McCoy 23–24). In a period that saw the knight's military status declining in the face of the domestic need to fashion competent bureaucrats, lawyers, and merchants, the tournaments allowed a kind of compromise between the conflicting interests of Elizabeth and her courtiers as well as between personal and political factions among the courtly ranks (McCoy 20–26). On the one hand, the tilts served as means for the Queen to tame a fractious nobility to her own will (Yates 110). On the other, those who performed in them hoped to reclaim some of the power and glory of the chivalric warrior: Robert Dudley, the Earl of Leicester, Sir Philip Sidney, and Essex used these rites to assert their own rights and ambitions (McCoy 26). A miniature of Essex,

the Queen's glove tied to his arm and his elaborately plumed helmet close by, portrays him as the Queen's Knight against a background depicting a medieval battlefield, where a squire holds his armored horse (Figure 20). His engraved, pearl-encrusted armor (which never saw a battlefield) is only one index of the conspicuous consumption on show in the tilts: the cost of a suit of ceremonial armor alone was roughly equivalent to that of today's executive jet and accorded its wearer a similar degree of status.

Henry IV, Part 1's representation of martial combat resembles these courtly rites more than it does the actual conditions of fifteenth- or sixteenth-century warfare. As in the tournaments, paired participants enter and engage in individual battle (see Peele, Nichols); the play even calls attention to the heraldic devices of coat-armor (see Figure 21): "the king has many marching in his coats," a practice common in the period that deflects attention from the royal commander. But the play's most important debt to Elizabethan neochivalric tournaments is the ritualized combat between Harry Percy and Harry of Lancaster, which occurs within the pointed context of a clash between the values of Northern lineage culture and the centralized power of the state.

On the stage, that encounter can show both combatants "playing by the rules" set down in treatises like Sir William Segar's *Honor Military and Civil* (1602) or George Silver's *Paradoxes of Defense* (1599) or, as in one recent production, pit a chivalric Hotspur against a Hal who abuses the laws of arms. In Michael Bogdanov's 1987–89 English Shakespeare Company staging, Hal and Hotspur, both wearing heraldic tabards and chain mail, slash at each other with heavy broadswords. Losing his (according to Segar, the most dishonorable martial act), Hal curls into a fetal position as though overcome by fear. With a grin, Hotspur returns the sword, and Hal charges at him, sweeps the weapon across his gut, and plunges the sword down from Hotspur's shoulder straight to his heart; not satisfied, he stabs him once more, this time from the rear (Hodgdon, *End* 165). By contrast, Adrian Noble's

◄ FIGURE 18 (top) *This pen and ink drawing of a tilt with lances, from a manuscript in the College of Arms (MS M6, c. 1565–75), shows the judges seated in a pavilion keeping score of the lances each combatant shatters (a broken lance appears in the foreground). Surrounding the tilt yard, or lists, with its central rail barrier, are scaffolds and stands where spectators could gain admittance for twelve pence.*

◄ FIGURE 19 (bottom) *This pen and ink drawing of a combat with swords (College of Arms MS M6, c. 1565–75) shows two combatants, with others waiting, and the judges' pavilion. The watching crowd consists of elegantly dressed courtiers, prosperous citizens, children and animals. Scholars estimate that the crowds for such combats could number in the thousands.*

FIGURE 20 *Robert Devereux, the Earl of Essex, in ceremonial tilt armor (c. 1593–95). This miniature by Nicholas Hilliard shows Essex in fancy dress as the Queen's Knight. Her favor, a glove, is tied to his arm, and the bases over his armor are embroidered with a formalized pattern of eglantine roses, one of the Queen's symbolic flowers. According to Roy Strong, this portrait may celebrate the spectacular Philautia tilt of 1595 (65).*

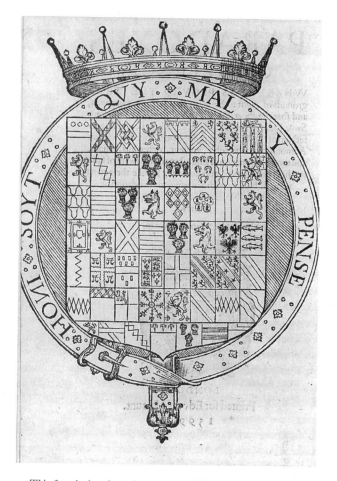

FIGURE 21 *This frontispiece from George Silver,* The Paradoxes of Defense *(1599), depicts the heraldic devices of the knights belonging to the Order of the Garter. Such devices would be worn on tabards, or shirts, worn over chain-mail armor and displayed on battle standards. Combining the devices into one shield and surrounding them with the motto of the Garter Knights, "Shamed be anyone who thinks evil of it," suggest a brotherhood of honor.*

1992 Royal Shakespeare Company production turns Shrewsbury's battle into a spectacle that heightens its ceremonial theatricality. The back wall of the stage rises to reveal a line of timpanists and massed spectators: above them, waves of silken heraldic banners cast shadows against the wall while, downstage, Hal and Hotspur lock swords against a luminous tableau that celebrates and mystifies chivalric history. Not unlike the 1590s Accession Day pageants, Noble's staging reads as a nostalgic attempt to recreate, for a 1990s audience, the romantic spirit of an irretrievable past.

War

Even for the nobles who performed in Elizabeth's spectacles, however, war remained the supreme arena for winning honor and lasting fame (see Vale). Although *Henry IV, Part 1* reflects this view of war as a testing ground for nobility, it remains silent about warfare's material conditions: the probable if fictional statistic that only three of Falstaff's 150 men survive Shrewsbury's battle is as close as the play comes to suggesting a military "history from below." Even the chronicler John Harding, who fought with the Percies at Shrewsbury, offers no detailed description: like other historians, he is primarily interested in ensuring the Percies' reputations and in summarizing outcomes. However, *The Beauchamp Pageant,* a manuscript celebrating the life of Richard Beauchamp, the Earl of Warwick, contains two drawings of Shrewsbury events. One tableau, showing Henry IV knighting Warwick on the battlefield, resembles the final stage pictures of nineteenth- and early-twentieth-century productions of the play, in which massed nobles surround the King and his sons in a display of heroic martial valor (see Figure 22, p. 328). Another drawing, however, comes closer to recording "history from below." The King's forces (on the left) meet those of the Percies (on the right), and Hotspur, the Percy crescent visible on his helmet, falls backward, his breast pierced with an arrow. Here, the artist arranges groups of archers in chain mail, a cavalry charge, and a brutal hand-to-hand combat in a small space, as though capturing a cross-section of the battle for posterity (see Figure 23, p. 329).

Orson Welles's film *Chimes at Midnight* (1965–66) turns the battle into a rhythmically sustained cinematic set piece. Constructed through a carefully orchestrated montage, it begins in slow, chivalric splendor with a cavalry charge that gradually escalates: lances flash through the air, riders get thrown, horses fall belly up, toward the camera. As the focus shifts to foot soldiers engaged in hand-to-hand combat, rapid intercutting produces the illusion of a blow received and one returned (Jorgens; Lyons; Andrew;

McMillin). Enhanced by a realistic soundtrack that captures men shouting and groaning, swords clashing, arrows in flight, and horses whinnying, the spectacle winds down to slow-motion shots of bodies writhing in the mud, forcefully undermining any notions, Elizabethan or modern, of war's supposed glory. Acknowledging its near-legendary status in cinematic history, Kenneth Branagh's film of *Henry V* (1989) reprises Welles's battle, even to borrowing the anthem that counterpoints its horrors.

If these films tap twentieth-century spectators' cultural memory of two world wars, evidence of Shrewsbury's more local early modern significance appears in the map of Shropshire from John Speed's *Theatre of the Empire of Great Britain* (1611/1612), where a tiny, rather schematic drawing in the lower righthand corner records it (see Figure 24, pp. 330–31). Just as Speed's map detaches Shrewsbury's battle from *national* history to make it part of the county's history, other features, such as the arms of Shropshire's prominent earls and the inset bird's-eye view of Shrewsbury, direct attention from the monarch's authority toward that of the county and the city, considered to be the capital of Wales. Designed to accompany his *History of Great Britain*, which, by chronicling the reigns of kings, invited loyalty to England's Crown, Speed's *Theatre* demonstrates another, equally compelling, loyalty — that to the land itself, its shires, cities, villages, and towns (Helgerson 116–17, 132, 145). Read together, Speed's two texts point to the continuing gap between the Crown's absolute dominion and the insistently local claims of the nobility.

These competing loyalties also determined how armies were formed and organized, both in the period to which *Henry IV, Part 1* alludes and in the late-sixteenth-century conditions the play evokes. Even in the late Middle Ages, the feudal system through which gentry and tenants-in-chief assembled, at either the king's behest or that of a noble lord, was being replaced with a form of recruitment called commissions of array, in which appointed commissioners assembled men and retained "the best and most able," who were joined by volunteers from within the realm as well as from abroad. But from the third quarter of the fourteenth century onward, armies were formed by recruiting men under contracts called indentures of war that depended on neofeudal baronial loyalties (Contamine 150–52). In all probability, similar documents set out the terms for amassing the forces that fought Shrewsbury's *historical* battle. Shakespeare's Shrewsbury, however, is embedded in the more complex and conflicting conditions of sixteenth-century history.

The form of military organization Queen Elizabeth inherited was largely medieval in character. Variants of the indenture system existed well into the sixteenth century, and there was no standing army. The Crown depended on the nobility to stockpile stores of arms in each city and village, in manor

FIGURE 22 *This drawing from* The Beauchamp Pageants *(c. 1485–90), a manuscript celebrating the life of Richard Beauchamp, the Earl of Warwick (1389–1439), shows King Henry IV investing the Earl with the Order of the Garter following the Battle of Shrewsbury, 1403.*

houses, town armories, or churches, often under the direction of a local sheriff; men were recruited by means of musters, as the Crown directed. Two 1558 statutes formalized these measures through what amounted to a form of taxation. One divided the nation into ten income groups, spelling out particular requirements for each; the other imposed fines and prison terms on those who failed to attend musters, accepted bribes, or discharged recruits unlawfully (4 and 5 Philip and Mary, repr. in Hughes and Larkin; Cruickshank, *Elizabeth's Army*).

Despite the statutory basis of military obligations, however, it was difficult to distinguish among the rival claims of neofeudal fealties, common law obligations, commissions of array and musters, and royal control over mili-

FIGURE 23 *Representing the Battle of Shrewsbury, this drawing from* The Beauchamp Pageants *(c. 1485–90) is one of the few surviving visual records of the combat. The original caption reads, "Here shows how at the battle of Shrewsbury between King Henry the Fourth and Sir Henry Percy, Earl Richard [of Warwick], there being on the King's party, full notably and manly behaved himself to his great laud and worship. In which battle was slain the said Sir Henry Percy and many other with him. And on the King's party there was slain in the King's coat armor chief of other, the Earl of Stafford, Earl Richard's Aunt's son with many others in great number, on whose souls God have mercy, Amen."*

tary affairs. Even with the development in the 1570s of trained militia bands led by appointed lord-lieutenants, the government's campaign to arm the nation to more modern standards floundered, largely because the Crown was unable to pay for a military establishment (Boynton 91–96). Yet England desperately needed a stable military force, especially during the late 1580s and the 1590s, when an almost total mobilization for defense occurred.

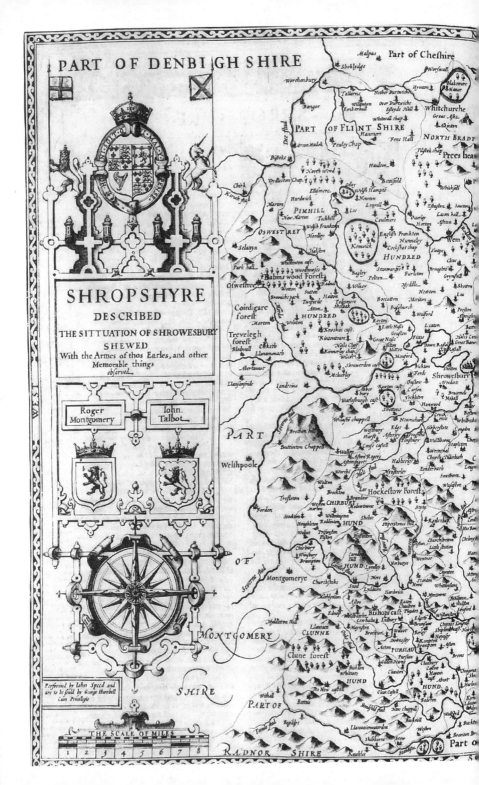

PART OF DENBIGHSHIRE

Part of Cheshire

PART OF FLINT SHIRE

SHROPSHYRE
DESCRIBED

THE SITTUATION OF SHROWESBURY
SHEWED

With the Armes of thos Earles, and other
Memorable things *observed*

Roger
Montgomery

Iohn
Talbot

Performed by Iohn Speed and
are to be fould by George Humbell
Cum Privilegio

THE SCALE OF MILES

1 2 3 4 5 6 7 8

PART

OF

MONTGOMERY

SHIRE

Welshpoole

Montgomerye

RADNOR SHIRE

Part of

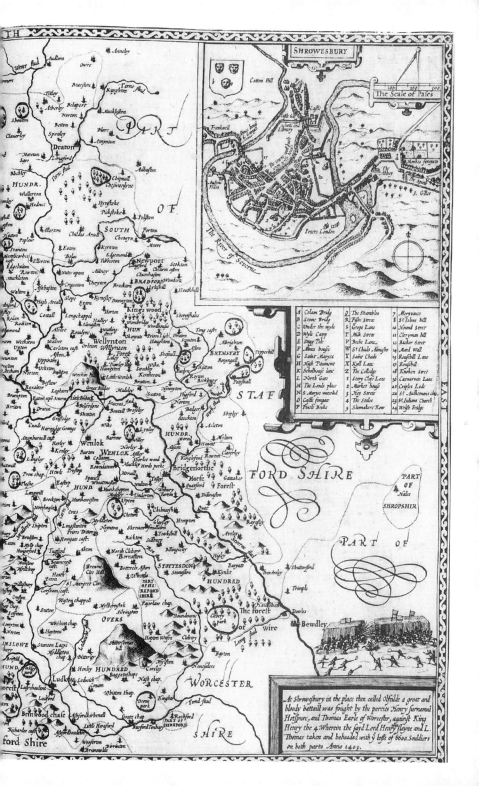

At Shrowsbury in the place then called Olsfilde a great and bloody batteill was fought by the percies Henry surnamd Hotspure, and Thomas Earle of Worcester, against King Henry the 4. Wherein the sayd Lord Henry slayne and L. Thomas taken and beheaded with ÿ losse of 6600. Souldiers on both parts Anno 1403.

Even after the threat posed by the Spanish Armada had been eliminated in 1588, the fear remained that Spain would take over the Netherlands as well as the French ports on which England depended, particularly for the wool trade. The country's borders were far from secure: English troops were constantly engaged in campaigns on behalf of the French Protestants in France and the Dutch insurgents in the Low Countries as well as against the Irish in Ireland. Moreover, expeditions to the New World, with its promise of fame, fortune, and empire, lured many able soldiers away from domestic or Continental service. Such mobilization had a tremendous impact on the national economy: by the early 1590s, the costs of training a man reached £150 a day, and shifting this responsibility onto the counties strained the resources of nobility, clergy, and civil magistrates alike. Levying men for military service became so difficult that troops were often recruited either by opening the jails and forcing prisoners to serve (Falstaff's soldiers who "march wide betwixt the legs, as if they had gyves on" [4.2.30–31] belong to this group) or by means of the press-gang, in which officers would close the church doors and impress every man in the congregation (Fortescue 122).

One response to these conditions was the publication, particularly during the latter half of the sixteenth century, of an astonishing profusion of military treatises. On the one hand, these texts indicate a renewed interest in military *history* and in documenting the "arts" and "stratagems" of war and the traits of an ideal soldiery. On that basis alone, the knowledge they made available had considerable cultural value, particularly at a time of national military crisis. On the other hand, such treatises spoke to what some perceived as the diminished virility of the age — in Samuel Daniel's politic words, a time "wherein began a greater improvement of the Sovereignty, and more came to be effected by wit than by the sword" (*The Collection of the History of England*, "Epistle Dedicatory," 77). Especially for those nobles who saw their status diminished by subjection to a female ruler, such accounts kept alive the desire for a martial culture independent of the Queen's symbolic forms of chivalric worship, one that focused on an exclusively masculine arena of warfare and violence.

◄ FIGURE 24 (overleaf) *This map of Shropshire from John Speed's* Theatre of the Empire of Great Britain *(1611/1612), which contains an inset drawing of Shrewsbury's battle, suggests its historical significance. The caption reads, "At Shrewsbury in the place then called Oldfield a great and bloody battle was fought by the Percies, Henry surnamed Hotspur, and Thomas, Earl of Worcester, against King Henry the 4. Wherein the said Lord Henry was slain and Lord Thomas taken and beheaded with the loss of 6,600 Soldiers on both parts, Year 1403."*

Although the great majority of English military treatises were printed between 1590 and 1600, translations of classical and Continental works such as Machiavelli's *Dell' Arte della Guerra*, which emphasized moral, spiritual, and paternal qualities of leaders that aligned with the chivalric ideals of knighthood, preceded and influenced them. In *An Arithmetical Military Treatise, Named Stratioticos* (1579) Leonard Digges writes that a good general must be "Religious, Temperate, Sober, Wise, Valiant, Liberal, Courteous, Eloquent, of good Fame, and Reputation" — traits that later became codified in Sir William Segar's *Honor Civil and Military* (1602). But Digges also opens a new vogue in military analysis by calling for leaders who are "learned in Histories, and in those Sciences and Arts that may enable him of himself, without direction from others, readily to conceive and judge of Military actions" (305–6). His emphasis on humanist learning was not unique: in *A Right Excellent and Pleasant Dialogue Between Mercury and an English Soldier* (1574), Barnaby Rich had argued that soldiers could be learned men. What was innovative was Digges's insistence that men could fashion themselves as *professional* soldiers in command of a *scientific* body of knowledge. Like the lawyers and merchants gaining preeminence in England in the period, they pursued an *occupation*, and their learning, as much as their field experience, made them valuable assets to the state. That honor itself was being refashioned as a professional pursuit in a burgeoning marketplace economy gave considerable support to a warrior culture as something necessary to the times.

Perhaps the greatest change from the knightly general to the military professional appears in William Garrard's *The Art of War* (1591) and Matthew Sutcliffe's *Right Practice, Proceedings, and Laws of Arms* (1593). Although Sutcliffe adheres to the knightly paradigm by insisting that a general's first requirement is religious faith, both he and Garrard not only agree that leaders must have knowledge of "any stratagem of war" but, by making hierarchical distinctions, they emphasize the importance of particular officers. In 1570, Roger Ascham wrote: "England hath at this time, many worthy Captains and good soldiers, which be in deed, so honest of behavior, so comely of conditions, so mild of manners, as they may be examples of good order, to a good sort of others which never came in war" (*Schoolmaster* 54). But by 1587, Barnaby Rich's *Pathway to Military Practice* implied that the reality falls short of this ideal, for both captains and soldiers. Captains were not only incompetent but also corrupt, their crimes ranging from petty thievery to mass murder. They were cited for immorality, cowardice, absenteeism, disgraceful negligence of men and provisions, disregard for the slightest degree of military discipline, and ignorance of training procedures and tactics. Thomas Nashe placed them among others who "do wholly bestow themselves upon pleasure, and that pleasure they divide . . . either into gaming, following of harlots, drinking, or seeing a Play" (*Pierce Pennilesse* [1592], 88).

Given these contexts, it becomes all too easy to read Falstaff as embodying the corrupt late-sixteenth-century military commander — a guise even more apparent in *Henry IV, Part 2*'s recruiting scene (3.2), which dramatizes the abuses mentioned in military conduct books. But it is also important to recognize that Falstaff voices the claims of a silenced, unrepresented majority, a "commodity of warm slaves" (4.2.13–14) so disreputable that he is ashamed to march through Coventry with them. For such soldiers, as for Falstaff, defining honor in terms of deeds or reputation, chivalric combat, or the conventions of medieval romance is a sentimental extravagance. If England's emergent nation-state and its "noble knights" depended on such values, Falstaff represents a faction that calls that order sharply into question. His is a dissident position at least as potentially powerful as that embraced by the Hotspur of the North or by the courtier-soldier Edmund Spenser called "the flower of chivalry," the Earl of Essex.

Manuals of Honor:
The Ideal and the Practice

The documents in this section convey how chivalric codes of honor were modified and accommodated to the profound sociopolitical changes of the late sixteenth century and how such codes were adopted for military practice. They offer competing perspectives, ranging from that of Sir William Segar, who records the codes governing honorable combat, both in the field and in knightly tournament, to those of Matthew Sutcliffe and Barnaby Rich, professional soldiers who describe ideal military protocol as well as disciplinary measures pertaining to captains and soldiers. Finally, selections from George Silver's treatise, which, like Sutcliffe's, was dedicated to the Earl of Essex, offer advice on the advantages of particular weapons.

As Queen Elizabeth's Garter King at Arms, her chief herald, Segar was the official custodian of a body of knowledge, and his book represents an anthology or archaeology of heraldic arts and chivalric ideals and practices. Written when coats of arms were a mercantile commodity, Segar's book does not predicate knighthood on noble lineage or blood but, like Castiglione's *Courtier* (available to English readers since Thomas Hoby's 1561 translation), represents a courtesy manual of martial virtues that outlines a corporate chivalric code to which princes, knights, and gentlemen are subject. Throughout, he stresses both the need to unite "Laws and Arms" and the intimate connection between personal and collective honor. Although he believes that individual pride and prowess are essential to maintaining name and reputation and that noble deeds confer immortality on the doer, Segar considers one's obligation to lineage, family, and kinship the deepest commitment of all.

Of the three selections from Segar's works, two concern knightly ideals. Whereas "Of Knighthood" lists qualifications reminiscent of medieval knighthood, "The Office and Duty of Every Knight and Gentleman" illustrates how notions that once served feudal fellowships of faith and honor such as the Arthurian Round Table had been renegotiated into a prescriptive code of "good behavior" or manners, the forerunner of bourgeois values. The order of these "honor commandments" is one sign of Segar's attempt to remodel the precepts of feudal loyalty to a country governed by one central authority and to combine two spheres of action, that of the soldier and that of the courtier, the "valiant captain" and the "wise counselor." The third selection, "Of Cowardice," comes from a section listing infractions of specifically *martial* honor: although Segar condemns cowardice above all other transgressions, he notes elsewhere that all instances are to be individually interpreted.

Reading the selections from Segar's code against Barnaby Rich's humanistically inclined descriptions of a captain and a private soldier as well as Matthew Sutcliffe's laws concerning religion, moral matters, and the duties of captains and soldiers reveals how Segar's ideals were translated into practice. Ordinances similar to Sutcliffe's were read out to all officers and soldiers when they took up military service; all were held to such regulations even if they were not present during the reading-out. Since the majority of troops came into the army under a civilian overlord, it was presumed that the duty owed to him would continue in the field, and although it was well understood that a common soldier must obey orders unquestioningly, Sutcliffe spells out even tighter controls over captains and soldiers alike (see Cruickshank, *Army Royal, Elizabeth's Army*). Whereas Rich's observations on contemporary conditions and abuses lead him to evoke Greek ideals and to argue for disciplined obedience, Sutcliffe (who glosses each of his laws with examples from Greek and Roman antiquity) writes what amounts to an appeal for military reform. That he, as well as others, saw the Earl of Essex as embodying the hopes and expectations of national heroism is one sign of how the chivalric image of the courtier-soldier presided over attempts to refashion late-sixteenth-century military culture.

→ SIR WILLIAM SEGAR

From Honor Military and Civil   *1602*

OF KNIGHTHOOD

[A knight] must be of good constitution and convenient strength to endure travel in Actions appertaining to soldiers. [H]e should be well favored of face and comely. He should be of bold aspect, rather inclined to severity than softness. He should be sober, and discreet, not inclined to vain delights or effeminate pleasures; obedient; vigilant and patient; faithful and loyal; constant and resolute; he should be charitable, because wars are not taken in hand for the destruction of Countries, and towns, but the defense of laws and people. Lastly, he should be fortunate, since Fortune is the Lady of Arms, and showeth her power in nothing more than in the adventures of war.

THE OFFICE AND DUTY OF EVERY KNIGHT AND GENTLEMAN

First it behooveth him to fear God, and with all his power to maintain and defend the Christian faith.

To be charitable, and comfort those that are afflicted.

To serve faithfully, and defend his Prince and country courageously.

To forgive the follies and offenses of other men, and sincerely embrace the love of friends.

To esteem truth, and without respect maintain it.

To avoid sloth and superfluous ease.

To spend the time in honest and virtuous actions.

To reverence Magistrates and converse with persons of honor.

To eschew riot and detest intemperance.

To frequent the war, and use military exercises.

To eschew dishonest pleasures, and endeavor to do good unto others.

To accommodate himself to the humor of honest company, and be no wrangler.

To shun the conversation of perverse persons, and behave himself modestly.

Sir William Segar, *Honor Military and Civil* (London, 1602), 49–50, Proem to bk. 2; 60, bk. 2, ch. 7; 16, bk. 1, ch. 13.

To be sober and discreet, no boaster of his own acts, nor speaker of himself.

To desire no excessive riches, and patiently endure worldly calamities.

To undertake enterprises just, and defend the right of others.

To support the oppressed, and help widows and Orphans.

To love God, and be loyal to his Prince.

To prefer honor before worldly wealth, and be both in word and deed just and faithful.

OF COWARDICE

It seemeth that all Military Offenses may be comprised in three, *viz.* Cowardice, Treason, and Disobedience: Yet we will speak more particularly Touching the first. Easily may it be conceived, that Cowardice is the cause and occasion of many other transgressions, for who so is irresolute, or apt to entertain a fear, is also soon persuaded to save himself with dishonor. By Cowardice soldiers do forsake their ranks: and sometimes abandon their Ensign: which faults the Romans punished with death. It was long since by an Edict commanded in *France,* that whosoever did forsake his colors, or the rank wherein he was placed, should receive punishment by passing the pikes. Another kind of cowardice is to feign sickness.

→ MATTHEW SUTCLIFFE

From The Right Practice, Proceedings, and Laws of Arms
1593

CHAPTER XXI

Wherein a form of Military laws requisite to be published and observed of our English soldiers and others employed in public service of their country, is prescribed.
The first part of it containeth laws concerning religion and moral matters.

1. Every Morning at the relieving of the watch, and every Evening at the setting of the watch, all Captains, Soldiers & others, both in camp and gar-

Matthew Sutcliffe, *The Right Practice, Proceedings, and Laws of Arms described out of the doings of the most valiant and expert captains, and confirmed by both ancient, and modern examples and precedents* (London, 1593), 304–5, 316–19.

rison, either in some special place to be appointed, or in their *corps de garde,* or those that watch, in their guard, the rest in some other place, shall assemble to hear prayers, and other exercises of Religion.

2. No enterprise shall be taken in hand, but the companies that are to execute the same shall first commend themselves to God, and pray to him to grant them good success.

3. Every Sunday the whole company at hours appointed shall meet to serve God, so much as the necessities of wars will permit. And for this cause a convenient number of Ministers are to be entertained, and such as abuse them to be severely punished.

4. Notorious swearers and blasphemers shall be punished according to the quality of their offense, yea with death, if their faults be heinous.

5. All abuses of God's word and holy Name in cursing, banning, charming and whatsoever other unlawful practice, shall be punished by imprisonment of the offenders, and death also, if the crime be heinous, and the example scandalous.

6. Many offenses against God and man do spring of dicing, carding, and other such unlawful games. Therefore let all dice, and cards, and such like instruments of abuse be taken away as much as may be, and let such gamesters be admonished, and if they do not so leave, and reform themselves, let them be imprisoned.

7. Common women, let them be whipped out of the camp and garrison, and such soldiers and others as use their company, let them be imprisoned. Officers that give bad examples of such matters, let them lose their places. Suspicious women, let them be banished [from] the camp or garrison.

8. For that God is greatly offended with drunkenness, and the abuses that come of it, and forasmuch also as camps and garrisons are thereby much disordered, and many good men suffer for the abuse of such lewd drunkards: therefore such are to be imprisoned and fed with bread and water, so long as the quality of their offense shall deserve.

[Sutcliffe annotates and interprets each law, offering examples from the Greeks and the Romans as well as from the military laws of Spain and from England's foreign campaigns.]

Containing laws concerning the duties of Captains and soldiers yet more particularly.

1. All Captains, soldiers, and others shall yield their obedience to the lawful commandments of their superiors. Neither shall any lift his weapon

against his commander, correcting him, or others, for their offenses orderly,[1] upon pain of death.

2. No Captain nor officer of a company shall depart the Camp or garrison without license, nor shall lodge or absent himself from his company in time of service, or when the enemy is ready to charge, upon pain of losing his place. Except those always, that have lawful excuses of sickness, or hurts, and have appointed sufficient deputies in their place.

3. All soldiers that wilfully absent themselves without lawful cause from their colors, or company, that goeth to charge, or resist the enemy, deserve death.

4. No Captain nor officer shall defraud the soldier or other person of his pay, that is committed to his hands to be delivered unto him, upon pain of loss of his place.

5. No Captain nor other shall prefer, or subscribe to a false muster roll, or fraudulently give in more, or other names, than he hath presently in his company, upon pain of imprisonment, and loss of his place.

6. No captain, lieutenant, sergeant, nor other that ought to be armed shall come into the field without their ordinary arms, upon pain of two armors to be deducted out of their pay, the one to their own use, the other to some other of the company that wanteth.[2]

7. No soldier nor other shall go into service without the word, and some other mark to be known by,[3] from the enemy, especially in night service, upon pain of imprisonment.

8. No captain, officer, nor other private gentleman in pay shall entertain any other's soldier, or servant, without consent, or lawful dismissal from his former captain or master, upon pain of loss of a month's pay. Neither shall any soldier or servant depart from his captain or master without lawful cause, upon pain of imprisonment, and returning again of soldiers to their captains, of servants to their masters.[4]

9. Captains and officers of companies shall watch and ward with their colors and companies,[5] upon pain of loss of a month's pay.

10. No man shall march with the baggage but the companies appointed; neither shall any march out of his array, or straggle abroad, or go on pilfering when he should march, watch, or serve, upon pain of imprisonment.

---

[1] **offenses orderly:** against established orders.   [2] **wanteth:** a law designed to prevent abuses whereby officers went into battle unarmed, leaving fighting to common soldiers.   [3] **word . . . known by:** password; badge of cognizance.   [4] **returning . . . masters:** and of being returned to his rightful captain or master.   [5] **watch . . . companies:** remain on guard under the banner, or ensign, of their company.

Such are also by bastonates[6] to be corrected by their officers, if they be taken in the manner.

11. No companies shall go on foraging, or make any enterprise against the enemy, upon private motion, without the knowledge and direction of their general commanders.

12. No soldier shall sell, or pawn, or lend, or lose, or give, or cast away, or play, or otherwise make away his horse, or arms, or weapons, or furniture wherewith he is appointed to serve: nor shall suffer his horse by his default to decay, or his arms to rust, or go to spoil upon pain of imprisonment, and infamy both to him that offendeth, and to his abettors, and aiders.

13. No private captain shall give Passport[7] to his soldier that is able to serve, upon pain of loss of his place; neither shall any soldier in time of service depart without Passport, upon pain of death.

14. No soldier nor other being, once placed in array either in marching or fighting, shall depart thence, without lawful cause. Whosoever either to run to spoil,[8] or to fly away, doth abandon his ensign or standing where he is ranged to serve,[9] shall suffer death.

15. No soldier nor others shall use any shouting or crying, or without cause discharge a piece[10] in marching, or embattling, or lying in ambush, upon pain of bastonates presently to be inflicted by the officers upon the offenders taken in the manner, [and] of imprisonment afterward.

16. No man shall give an alarm unto the army marching, or lodging without just cause, and that in quiet sort, nor shall any tumultuously run nor cry upon an alarm taken, upon such penalty, as the circumstance of the offense shall require.

17. He that by negligence or gross ignorance killeth his fellow with his piece, or other weapon, let him die the death.

18. No man shall challenge another,[11] or defy him in camp or garrison, nor accept the challenge, upon pain of imprisonment, and disarming before his company. Neither shall any offer an injury to his fellow to provoke him to fight, nor shall others privately revenge it, upon pain of imprisonment.

19. All brawls, and quarrels betwixt fellows, are to be punished severely. Whatsoever therefore he is that in camp or garrison killeth any man in any sudden brawl or challenge, except he be thereto forced for his own defense, or striketh his fellow being placed in array ready to fight, let him suffer death for it.

---

[6] **bastonates:** bastinados: by cudgeling or beating with a stick or truncheon.   [7] **Passport:** discharge.   [8] **run to spoil:** attempt to pillage.   [9] **ranged to serve:** positioned in rank, as in a battle.   [10] **piece:** firearm.   [11] **challenge another:** to a private duel or quarrel.

20. No soldier nor other shall fraudulently or thievishly take any thing from any man's person, or their lodging, house, or cabin, upon pain of death.

21. When any company of soldiers shall be lodged in any village, or pass through it, or by any dwelling house, or other belonging to our friends, they shall not hurt, nor injure the people in their persons nor goods, upon pain of death, or other grievous punishment according to the quality of their offense.

22. No man shall burn any corn, hay, or forage, or destroy any provision, or house, barn, or cornmill, or other building that may serve for the use of the army, upon pain of death.

23. All murders, perjuries, forgeries, forcing of women, or maidens, cosinages,[12] or other disorders, whereby the army may any way receive disgrace or hurt, although not comprised in these laws, shall be punished by such penalties, as the civil laws, or else common laws of England enjoin in such cases.

24. No soldier nor other shall be mustered, or answer in two companies, or answer to two names in one company, nor shall any victualler, or other that is no soldier, pass in musters for a soldier, upon pain of death.

25. No soldier that hath victuals delivered unto him for certain days, shall spoil or spend the same in less time than is appointed, upon pain of imprisonment.

[Sutcliffe annotates these laws as well, again using a range of examples, together with copious marginal notations in Latin and Greek.]

---

[12] **cosinages:** trickery; thievery.

→ **BARNABY RICH**

From A Pathway to Military Practice   *1587*

Of a Captain

The place of a Captain is not lightly to be considered of. Upon his skill and knowledge consisteth the safety or loss of many men's lives, but especially service standing now as it doth most commonly in skirmishes, where the

---

Barnaby Rich, *A Pathway to Military Practice. Containing offices, Law, Discipline and orders to be observed in an Army, with sundry Stratagems very beneficial for young Gentlemen, or any other that is desirous to have knowledge in Martial exercises* (London, 1587), F4v–G1r, G3r–G4r.

Captain most ordinarily is not helped but with the advantage of his own experience.

In the old time many years ago, when armies many times used to appoint the field, where their whole forces were brought to encounter, the weakness of a Captain might the better be borne withal, when there were so many superior officers to direct him; and yet in those days they used circumspection in nothing more than in choosing of their Captains. But service standing as it doth at this instant over [what] it was then, we ought to have three times more regard than they had, and yet we use ten times less than they did. And I wonder how so many insufficient men dare oppose themselves to undertake a matter of so great importance, whose inexperience, besides (by circumstance) that it concerneth the loss of a country, so in it consisteth the hazard of many men's lives. If it were no more but his own, the matter were the less, for he may value of that as himself shall seem good. But remorse of conscience should touch him to consider of his Countrymen, when his want of knowledge shall sometime breed too much rashness, and sometime again too little courage. A Captain that might be thought worthy should as well have knowledge how to govern, as experience how to train, wherein he is to use great diligence, instructing them in their order of array, the use of their weapons, teaching them to know the sounds of Drums.[1]

He must in no wise be injurious to the soldier for his pay, but as carefully he must use diligence to get it, so as cheerfully he must pay every man his due. He that neglecteth this, neglecteth his own credit and reputation — nay, more: his honesty. Neither is it fit he should go unpunished, that barreth or diminisheth a soldier of his pay. A Captain should be loving and comfortable to his company, and as he is to correct and punish them for their faults, so he is to commend and encourage them in their well doings. Some consideration a Captain should have for the carriage of convenient necessaries for his soldiers, when they go to the field, yet no more than must needs be had. He should have some store of Hatchets to cut boughs to make their Cabins, for want of which they break many Swords. To conclude, a Captain that can carefully consider of his Soldiers' necessities, and lovingly provide to furnish their wants, shall have both unfeigned love, and dutiful obedience of his Soldiers, without the which, he is not only assured to lose his credit, but many times in more peril of his own company than of the enemy.

---

[1] **sounds of Drums:** signals whereby soldiers are commanded what they ought to do.

[Rich describes the duties of the surgeon, the clerk of the band (who keeps accounts) and the corporal and his Lanceprezado, or deputy, in charge of instructing soldiers in the use and maintenance of weapons.]

OF A PRIVATE SOLDIER

In the choice of a Soldier, his manners and conditions [are] first to be respected, otherwise you may make choice of an instrument of many mischiefs. The composition and ability of his body is then to be considered, in the like manner his sufficiency for years.

In England when service happeneth, we disburden the prisons of Thieves, we rob the Taverns and Alehouses of Tosspots and Ruffians, we scour both Town and Country of Rogues and vagabonds. And is not a Captain that is furnished with such a company like to do great service, and to keep them in good discipline? In other Countries where they use the service of malefactors, they admit them not for soldiers, but they send them to their Galleys and to other places of like slavery. And those Captains that hath made trial of such Soldiers would gladly be rid of his charge to be eased of his trouble.

The first thing therefore that is to be respected in a Soldier is the honesty of his mind, which being linked with religion, there is no doubt but that Soldier will be brought both to the fear of God, to the obedience of his Captain, and to the observance of discipline. The *Romans* who for their martial observation were most renowned, the rather to keep Soldiers under awe and discipline, they adjoined to their own laws and ordinances the authority of God, and used with great ceremony to make them swear to keep the disciplines of war. The *Grecians* in like manner, their soldiers being armed and brought to the Church, received this oath:

I will not do any thing unworthy the sacred and holy wars, neither will I abandon or forsake my band & Captain to whom I am appointed. I will fight for the right of the Church and safety of the State. I will not make my Country to be in worse case than it is, but I will make it better than I found it. And I will ever frame myself reverently to obey those laws also that the State shall hereafter by common assent make or set down, that if anyone shall change the laws or not obey them, I will not suffer him to my power, much less will I allow in so doing, but I will be a sure defender of right as well by myself alone, as when I am with others, and I will ever more honor the religion of my Country. To these my sayings I call the Gods to witness.

[Claiming that this, and similar oaths, were administered in antiquity, Rich links the disciplines of war to perfect obedience, citing examples from the Bible as well as from classical times.]

→ GEORGE SILVER

From The Paradoxes of Defense   *1599*

OF THE VANTAGES AND SUFFICIENCY OF THE SHORT SWORD FIGHT IN BATTLE

The short Sword, and Sword and Dagger, are perfect good weapons, and especially in service of the Prince. What a brave weapon is a short sharp light Sword: to carry, to draw, to be nimble withal, to strike, to cut, to thrust both strong and quick. And what a goodly defense is a strong single hilt when men are clustering and hurling together, especially where variety of weapons be, in their motions to defend the hand, head, face, and bodies from blows that shall be given sometimes with Swords, sometimes with two-handed Swords, battle-Axe, Halberds, or black Bills.[1] And sometimes men shall be so near together that they shall have no space scarce to use the blades of their Swords below their waists. Then their hilts (their hands being aloft) defendeth from the blows their hands, arms, heads, faces and bodies: then they lay on, having the use of blows and Gripes, by force of their arms with their hilts, strong blows at the head, face, arms, bodies, and shoulders. And many times, in hurling together, scope is given to turn down their points, with violent thrusts at their faces and bodies, by reason of the shortness of their blades, to the mighty annoyance, discomfort, and great destruction of their enemies. One valiant man with a Sword in his hand will do better service than ten *Italians,* or Italianated with the Rapiers.[2]

---

[1] **Halberds, or black Bills:** heavy axes; these were a combination of spear and battle-ax consisting of a sharp-edged blade ending in a point and a spearhead mounted on a five- to seven-foot-long handle; a concave ax with a spike at the back, its shaft ending in a spearhead.
[2] **Italianated with the Rapiers:** references to combat with rapiers—long, pointed, two-edged swords introduced from Italy; ideal for thrusting because of their length.

George Silver, *The Paradoxes of Defense. Wherein is Proved the True grounds of Fight to be in the short ancient weapons, and that the short Sword hath advantage of the long Sword or long Rapier. And the weakness and imperfection of the Rapier-fights displayed. Together with an Admonition to the noble, ancient, victorious, valiant, and most brave nation of Englishmen, to beware of false teachers of Defense, and how they forsake their own natural fights: with a brief commendation of the noble science or exercising of Arms* (London, 1599), F1r–F3r.

FIGURE 25 *This drawing from George Silver's* The Paradoxes of Defense *(1599) demonstrates how to judge the perfect ("just") length for a sword in relation to one's own stature. With sword and dagger drawn, the soldier takes up a stance, straightens his dagger arm, and draws his sword back "as far as conveniently [he] can" without opening the elbow joint of the sword arm. The idea is to allow maximum movement of both weapons, both in offensive and defensive timing, and to assure perfect balance of the body.*

That all manner of double weapons, or weapons to be used with both hands, have advantage against the single Rapier or single Sword, there is no question to be made.

That the Sword and Buckler Hath the Vantage Against the Sword and Dagger

The Dagger is an imperfect ward,[3] although borne out straight to make the Space narrow,[4] whereby by a little moving of the hand, [it] may be sufficient to save both sides of the head, or to break the thrust from the face or body. Yet for lack of the circumference, his hand will lie too high or too low, or too

---

[3] **ward:** means of guarding oneself. [4] **make the Space narrow:** to narrow the area in which the body is vulnerable to blows.

weak, to defend both blow and thrust. If he lie straight with narrow space, which is best to break the thrust, then he lieth too weak, and too low to defend his head from a strong blow. If he lie high, that is strong to defend his head, but then his space will be too wide to break the thrust from his body. The Dagger serveth well at length to put by[5] a thrust, and at the half Sword to cross the Sword blade,[6] to drive out the Agent, and put him in danger of his life, and safely in any of these two actions to defend himself. But the Buckler,[7] by reason of his circumference and weight, being well carried, defendeth safely in all times and places, whether it be at the point, half Sword, the head, body, and face, from all manner of blows and thrusts whatsoever. Yet I have heard many hold opinion that the Sword and Dagger hath advantage of the Sword and Buckler at the Close,[8] by reason of the length and point of the Dagger; and at the point of the Sword, they can better see to ward than with a Buckler. But I never knew any that won the Close with the Dagger upon the Sword and Buckler, but did with himself out again. For distance[9] being broken, judgment faileth, for lack of time to judge, and the eye is deceived by the swift motion of the hand; and for lack of true Space[10] with the dagger hand, which cannot be otherwise, for lack of the circumference to defend both blow and thrust, it is impossible for lack of true Space in just time, the agent having gotten the true place, to defend one thrust or blow of an hundred. And it is most certain, whosoever closeth with Sword and Dagger against the Sword and Buckler is in great danger to be slain. Likewise at the point within distance, if he stand to defend both blow and thrust with his Dagger, for lack of true space and distance, [even] if he had the best eye of any man and could see perfectly which way the thrust or blow cometh, and when it cometh, as it is not to be denied but he may, yet his space being too large, it helpeth him nothing, because one man's hand being as swift as another man's hand, both being within distance, he that striketh or thrusteth, hurteth the warder. The reason is this: the Agent being in the first motion, although in his offense,[11] [has] further to go than the warder to defend, yet the warder's space being too large, the blow or thrust will be performed home before the warder can come to the true place to defend himself. And although the warder do perfectly see the blow or thrust coming, so shall he see his own ward so far from the true place of his defense, that although he do at that instant time plainly see the blow or thrust coming, it

---

[5] **put by:** parry. [6] **to cross the Sword blade:** to have the dagger and sword crossing one another; an offensive as well as a defensive maneuver. [7] **Buckler:** a small round shield, used primarily to hold off an adversary's blows. [8] **at the Close:** in close fight. [9] **distance:** distance between combatants. [10] **true Space:** enough space for a combatant to maneuver. [11] **offense:** initial position of attack.

shall be impossible for him to recover the true place of his ward;[12] 'til he be wounded. But let the warder with the dagger say that it is not true which I have said, for as he hath eyes to behold the blow or thrust coming, so hath he as good time to defend himself. Herein he shall find himself deceived too. This is the reason: the hand is the swiftest motion, the foot is the slowest; without distance[13] the hand is tied to the motion of the feet, whereby the time of the hand is made as slow as the foot, because thereby we redeem every time lost upon his coming by the slow motion of the foot, & have time thereby to judge when & how he can perform any action whatsoever, and so have we the time of the hand to the time of the feet. Now is the hand in his own course more swifter than the foot or eye. Therefore, within distance[14] the eye is deceived, & judgment is lost. And that is another cause that the warder with the dagger, although he have perfect eyes, is still within distance deceived. For proof that the hand is more swifter than the eye, & thereby deceiveth the eyes: let two stand within distance, & let one of them stand still to defend himself, & let the other flourish and false[15] with his hand, and he shall continually with the swift motions of his hand deceive the eyes of him that standeth watching to defend himself, & shall continually strike him in diverse places with his hand. Again, take this for an example, that the eyes by swift motions are deceived: turn a turn-wheel swift, & you shall not be able to discern with your best eyes how many spokes be in the wheel — no, nor whether there be any spokes at all, or whereof the wheel is made — and yet you see when the wheel standeth still there is a large distance between every spoke. He that will not believe that the swift motion of the hand in fight will deceive the eye, shall stare abroad with his eyes, & feel himself soundly hurt, before he shall perfectly see how to defend himself. So those that trust to their sight, the excellency of a good eye, their great cunning, & perfect wards of the daggers, that they can better see to ward than with a buckler, shall never be deceived. And when they be wounded, they say the Agent was a little too quick for them. Sometimes they say they bare their dagger a little too low. Sometimes they are thrust under the dagger: then they say [that] they bare it a little too high. Sometimes, a thrust being strongly made, they being soundly paid therewith, [they] say they were a little too slow; & sometimes they be soundly paid with a thrust, & they think they were a little too quick. So they that practice or think to be cunning in the dagger ward, are all the days of their lives learning, and are never taught.

---

[12] **true place of his ward:** proper position for defense.   [13] **without distance:** without appropriate distance between combatants.   [14] **within distance:** in close fight.   [15] **false:** feint; pretend to attack.

THAT THE SWORD AND BUCKLER HATH THE VANTAGE AGAINST THE SWORD AND TARGET

The Sword & Target[16] together hath but two fights; that is, the variable fight, & the close fight. For the close fight, the number of his feet are too many to take against any man of skill having the Sword & buckler; & for the variable fight, although not so many in number, yet too many to win the place with his foot to strike or thrust home. The sword & buckler-man can out of his variable, open & gardant[17] fight, come bravely off & on, false and double, strike & thrust home, & make a true cross upon every occasion at his pleasure: if the Sword & Target man will fly to his gardant fight, the breadth of his Target will not suffer it; if to his open fight, then hath the Sword & Buckler man in effect the Sword and Buckler to the single, for in that fight by reason of the breadth, the target can do little good or none at all.

---

[16] **Target:** light shield.   [17] **gardant:** on guard; facing the assailant.

CHAPTER 6

The Oldcastle Controversy:
"What's in a Name?"

✦

Before they were performed or published, all sixteenth-century plays had to be licensed by the Crown's Office of the Revels, and even after such approval, objections to a particular play could cause trouble for its author. Although all of Shakespeare's plays were subject to political censorship, *Henry IV, Part 1* represents an unusual instance in which scholars, drawing on contemporary evidence, can document how and, probably, why the play was censored and explore the consequences of such regulation. These circumstances, however, are also part of a much broader inquiry that extends beyond Shakespeare's play into the sixteenth-century traditions and countertraditions surrounding a controversial fifteenth-century historical figure and moves forward to include late-twentieth-century debates about cultural history, the activity of authorship, and the editing of early modern plays.

The story of *Henry IV, Part 1*'s brush with the censors can be quickly summarized. The character called "Falstaff" was originally called "Oldcastle," a name given to one of Prince Hal's companions in the anonymous *Famous Victories of Henry the Fifth* (1583–88), Shakespeare's dramatic source for the play (see Chapter 4, "The 'Education' of a Prince"). That name, however, also identified a historical Sir John Oldcastle, a captain and Lollard leader who fought for Henry IV in France and Wales and was martyred for his Protestant beliefs during Henry V's reign. Shortly after Shakespeare's play was first performed in 1596–97, the descendants of Oldcastle's widow, Sir William Brooke and his son Henry, the seventh and eighth Lords Cobham, objected to what they saw as a defamation of their ancestral name. And since Sir William was the Lord Chamberlain, with oversight responsibilities for the Master of the Revels, the officer charged with licensing plays, their objections carried considerable weight. Given such sensitivity in high places, Shakespeare changed Oldcastle's name in *Henry IV, Part 1* to "Falstaff" before the play was printed. The text, however, retains traces of "Oldcastle," among which Prince Hal's reference to Falstaff as "my old lad of the castle" (1.2.34) is perhaps the most obvious. But although Oldcastle's name did not appear in print, it was apparently retained in court and private performances — another form of publication — and audiences certainly continued to identify Oldcastle with Falstaff.

Even after the elder Lord Cobham's death, gossip and satirical barbs kept the connection alive, and its controversial impact extended to two other plays. In *The Merry Wives of Windsor* (1597), Master Ford's alias, "Brook," was changed to "Broom," apparently to satisfy Henry Brooke's continuing displeasure at the misuse of his name. And *Henry IV, Part 2* (1600), which had also originally alluded to Oldcastle, concludes its Epilogue with a public disclaimer: "Oldcastle died martyr, and this is not the man" (Ep. 30). Clearly Burbage's company, the Chamberlain's Men, had made a political and social error in transforming Oldcastle into a figure of vice and so blotting the reputation of the powerful Brooke family. In 1600, a rival company, Philip Henslowe's Lord Admiral's Men, capitalized on that error with their own play, *The First Part of the True and Honorable History of the Life of Sir John Oldcastle,* one of a series of "Elect Nation" plays dramatizing the lives of Protestant heroes (Gurr, *Playgoing* 148). Yet even though this play stages a revisionary history, Oldcastle and Falstaff continued to be thought of as interchangeable well into the seventeenth century (Taylor 85–86, 90–91).

Told in this way, the story resembles a libel suit, fed by a powerful family's paranoia about the ridicule of a revered ancestor. But Sir John Oldcastle was a popular figure in Elizabethan England, one whose history was so ambiguous that it could be told and retold with different ideological emphases throughout the sixteenth century. In contemporary accounts, Oldcastle becomes a cultural icon who epitomizes conflicting values (Patterson, *Reading* 130). For some, like John Bale and John Foxe, he was a victimized religious martyr; for others, such as the chronicler John Stow, he was a devious, schismatic heretic and traitor who betrayed his friend and King, Henry V. For Elizabethan puritans who claimed Wycliff and his followers as the origin of their movement, his Lollard sympathies made him a proto-Puritan; for puritan opponents, he was a perverse, subversive sectarian.

All accounts agree about a particular sequence of events and relationships;

how they were interpreted is another matter. Sir John Oldcastle, the High Sheriff of Herefordshire, became Lord Cobham by his second marriage in 1408 to Joan Cobham, a wealthy heiress. Before that, he had gained his military reputation in the border wars (Corbin and Sedge 3); the title page of Bale's account of his martyrdom, picturing him with sword and shield, calls him a "most valiant warrior" (see Figure 26). Hall, Foxe, and Holinshed all record that he was at one time "highly in [Henry V's] favor." When the Archbishop of Canterbury first called him to account for his Lollard beliefs, Henry met privately with him and "lovingly admonished him to reconcile himself to God and his laws" (Hall 48). Oldcastle's Lollardry, derived from John Wycliff's teachings, which stressed private devotions independent of episcopal surveillance, represented an instance of a contested relation between the individual — and in particular, the individual as a *reader* — and the state-supported church. Wycliff's followers were accused of harboring unlicensed preachers on their own estates and of possessing heretical devotional books — that is, books in *English*, the reformers' language of choice, not Latin, the official language of the church. Tied up with literacy and with the spread of print culture, Lollardry was a popular movement that drew support from practitioners of the literate trades: fullers, weavers, dyers, tailors, scriveners, and parchment makers (McFarlane, *Lancastrian Kings* 191–92). Moreover, the specific beliefs and practices the Lollards found decadent or unnecessary — priestly hierarchy, celibacy, transubstantiation, auricular confession, pilgrimages, and the worship of images — struck deep at the doctrines of the established church. The Lollards also opposed war and capital punishment, attacked the "unnecessary arts" of goldsmiths and weapons makers, and called for the disendowment of temporalities, the worldly possessions of the church.

The issue of disendowment, coupled with the Lollards' desire to reestablish the church on the original foundations of pure, primitive Christianity, provoked an alarmist response from the bishops that was heightened by a January 1414 gathering of a Lollard "army" of craftsmen led by Sir Roger Acton in St. Giles Field, just outside London's city gates, where Oldcastle may or may not have been present. According to official reports, a picked band of rebels, disguised as mummers, planned to capture the royal family at Eltham, where Henry V held his Christmas court. The objectives attributed to the Lollards were "wholly to annul the royal estate as well as the estate and office of prelates and religious orders in England, and to kill the king, his brothers, . . . the prelates and other magnates of the kingdom, and to turn men of religion . . . to secular occupations: totally to despoil cathedrals and other churches and religious houses of their relics and other ecclesiastical goods, and to level them completely to the ground" (quoted in Aston 25). Furthermore, none other than Sir John Oldcastle was to be appointed regent.

A Brefe Chronycle concernynge the
Examinacyon and death of the blessed
martyr of Christ syr Johan Oldeca-
stell the lorde Cobham/collected to-
gyther by Johan Bale.

Syr.Iohan.Oldecastel.the.worthy

suffred.death.at.London.Anno.1418.

lorde.Cobham. and. moste.valyaunt.

Warryoure.of.Iesus.Christ.

In the latter tyme shall manye be
chosen / proued / and puryfyed by fyre/
yet shall the vngodly lyue wyckedly styll
and haue no vnderstandynge. Dan.12.

From the bishops' point of view, both the realm and the church were endangered: Acton and his "rebels" were executed, and Oldcastle went into hiding. According to some chronicle accounts, he was implicated in a later assassination attempt on Henry V put forward by the Earl of Cambridge, Lord Scrope of Masham, and Sir Thomas Grey on behalf of Cambridge's claim to the throne. Shakespeare's *Henry V* (1.3) dramatizes the plot, but neither Oldcastle nor Falstaff is part of it. Reportedly, Henry desired to pardon Oldcastle before leaving for France in 1415, but Oldcastle remained undiscovered until December 1417, when he was apprehended at Powis, taken to London, and carted from the Tower to St. Giles Field, where, as depicted in Foxe's *Acts and Monuments* (1563), he was hung in chains and burned and his ashes thrown into the Thames.

As represented in official documents, the Lollards' fifteenth-century history suggested to late-sixteenth-century readers a failed, popular proto-Reformation. It is not difficult to see how that history might be appropriated to serve either the state-supported Anglican faith or that of Elizabethan puritan reformers. But what relation do these controversies have to Shakespeare's Oldcastle/Falstaff? How does the figure of the valiant captain become the cowardly lion who pales at the sight of Blunt's death? How does the Christian martyr turn into a gluttonous tavern "king" who moralizes, swears, threatens repentence, and apes puritan idiom? What happens to the alternate tradition depicting Oldcastle as a warlike heretic who represents a serious threat to the King's person and the state? Some critics argue that Shakespeare blundered or that he simply borrowed Oldcastle's name from *Famous Victories* with no knowledge of its political consequences (see Chapter 4, "The 'Education' of a Prince"); others maintain that he deliberately satirized the Elizabethan Cobhams. As yet, scholars have failed to discover any clear motive behind what appeared, at the time, to be personal parody. There is no ready solution to these puzzling questions, and the Oldcastle matter continues to invite scholarly speculation. Curiously enough, a figure who once stood at the center of contested relations between church and state and whose historical memory was a matter for sixteenth-century religious and cultural debates has become the focus of twentieth-century struggles over textual meanings and contexts. Books, print culture, and interpretation link these areas together: in Oldcastle's case, questions of reading have always been at issue.

With Oldcastle's history in mind, particular moments in *Henry IV, Part 1* stand out in bold relief. Recalling that Oldcastle may have turned traitor once

FIGURE 26 *Sir John Oldcastle, portrayed as a Christian Protestant knight, from the title page of John Bale's* Brief Chronicle Concerning ... Sir John Oldcastle *(1544).*

Henry V was crowned gives Sir John's "Was it for me to kill the heir apparent? Should I turn upon the true prince?" added resonance (2.4.214–15). In the play-within-the-play (2.4), Sir John's two portraits — his self-description as "a virtuous man . . . with virtue in his looks" and Hal's characterization of him as "a devil," "reverend vice," and "villainous abominable misleader of youth" — resemble the opposing sixteenth-century conceptions of Oldcastle. A line such as Hal's "Away, good Ned. Falstaff sweats to death" (2.2.88) and his later insult — "that roasted Manningtree ox with the pudding in his belly" (2.4.360–61) — take on a grisly particularity when read through Oldcastle's martyrdom; and the conclusion of Hal's Shrewsbury epitaph over his "old" friend's body, "Emboweled will I see thee by and by" (5.4.109), alludes to a traitor's fate. Moreover, the fat knight rises from the dead, apparently much like Oldcastle, who allegedly told Sir Thomas Erpingham, just before his execution, that he would "rise from death to life again, the third day." And just as Protestant accounts of Oldcastle's life report that he acknowledged the sins of his wanton youth and vowed to "live cleanly," so does Shakespeare's Sir John promise, at the play's end, to "live cleanly as a nobleman should do" (5.4.155).

These and other instances certainly suggest that Oldcastle's name and historical identity appear to figure in the text. One scholar, Alice Lyle Scoufos, explores such topical parallels to argue that Shakespeare is writing typological satire (88–111). More recently, Kristen Poole reads Oldcastle/Falstaff within the context of Elizabethan polemical religious discourse. She maintains that *Henry IV, Part 1*'s portrait of the Lollard Oldcastle was not "a daring, radical, or innovative departure from the stereotypical image of the puritan" but, instead, was perfectly attuned to the antipuritan literature of the age, especially the anti-Marprelate tracts, as well as burlesque stagings of the Marprelate controversy (1588–90), which often depicted puritans "as grotesque individuals living in carnivalesque communities" (54–55). Such contexts are especially compelling in attempting to reconstruct a late-sixteenth-century reception history for the play.

Given the lack of written evidence, such a history must always be conjectural: it is difficult to know precisely the range and nature of spectators' responses. Whatever those may have been, the relations between actors and their audiences at that historical moment would determine such responses. Moreover, late-sixteenth-century spectators would also have recognized, in Shakespeare's Sir John, a host of purely theatrical ancestors. Scholars identify him with the Plautean tradition of the *miles gloriosus*, or braggart cowardly knight, as in *Thersites* (1537), and with the Vice figure of morality dramas such as *Liberality and Prodigality* (1567?) or *Cambyses* (1569), a play to which Sir John alludes (see Humphreys, Bullough). Indeed, he not only represents an amalgam of familiar character types, but he also absorbs the guises of figures from emblem literature, biblical stories, and the saturnalian revels associated with the Lord of Misrule, as well as that of the wise fool in Erasmus's *Praise of Folly* (see Bevington 31–34).

Another, even more local, possibility connects his figure to the celebrated clown Richard Tarleton, who probably played Derick and Oldcastle in *Famous Victories*. Tarleton's routines often satirized Puritans as well as Catholics, and his spendthrift habits, whoring, and patronage of a particular tavern associate him with Shakespeare's Sir John (see Bryant). Even more significantly, the particular style of comic performance associated with Will Kempe, the Lord Chamberlain's Men's most accomplished comic actor, who played Sir John (see Figure 27), could serve to heighten religious and political topicality and, simultaneously, to deflect its threats through the licensed voice of the clown (see Wiles, Weimann). Although present-day spectators are certainly familiar with the ways in which mass culture constructs its representations on the back of an actor's previous roles as well as around his public persona, the theatrical spaces, playing styles, and conditions of reception have changed considerably. Because we can only pretend to refashion ourselves within an early modern cultural imaginary, the contexts of anti-Puritan parody or satire that enlivened *Henry IV, Part 1* in the late sixteenth century remain distant concerns for late-twentieth-century theatrical practitioners as well as for their audiences.

Certainly by the mid-seventeenth century, audiences knew Oldcastle as Falstaff. The frontispiece to *The Wits, or Sport upon Sport* (1662), a collection of theatrical extracts designed to illustrate the "Variety of Humors of Several Nations," pictures him, together with Mistress Quickly (the hostess), as the most prominent "drolls." Dressed in fashionable Restoration costume, he wears a sword and holds an outsized goblet, the signature of his appetite for drink (see Figure 28). Having taken on the manners of the time, he has already moved away from his guise as Oldcastle to become Shakespeare's most famous comic creation. Falstaff's quick wit, virtuoso skills of self-presentation, and wholehearted embrace of life have been trademarks of his role through the ensuing centuries, and three readily available twentieth-century film- and video-texts explore a range of interpretive possibilities that intersect, in revealing ways, with recent critical reconfigurations of *Henry IV, Part 1*, especially those committed to studying its representation of power.

In the 1979 BBC television production, Anthony Quayle reinvents the Falstaff he played in 1951 at the Shakespeare Memorial Theatre to Richard Burton's Hal. Taking full advantage of the medium, he speaks directly to the camera; like the news analyst's talking head, he seems about to enter the viewer's private space. Although Quayle's engaging presence and highly verbal performance interrupt an otherwise solemn review of "Shakespeare-

FIGURE 27 (above) *Will Kempe, the actor who played Falstaff/Oldcastle in the first performances of* Henry IV, Part I. *This title page of* Kempe's Nine Days' Wonder *(1600) depicts Kempe dancing his way from London to Norwich in a famous "progress," not unlike those taken by the Queen.*

FIGURE 28 (right) *This frontispiece from* The Wits, or Sport upon Sport *(1662) shows how the figures of Falstaff and Mistress Quickly appeared on the Restoration stage. The text consists of a medley of theatrical extracts illustrating "humors," including several by Shakespeare. The collection is attributed to Francis Kirkman.*

history" according to Tillyard, Orson Welles's *Chimes at Midnight* (1965–66), conceived as a myth of the loss of Eden with Falstaff at its center, turns the conventional royal narrative upside down. Welles's Falstaff, a melancholy nostalgic figure (see Figure 29), is seldom off camera, and the film, which repeatedly anticipates his rejection at the end of *Henry IV, Part 2*, at times eulogizes his figure even as it presents an incisive critique of "official" history (see Crowl, Andrew). Michael Bogdanov's English Shakespeare Company production (1987) undermines a chilling, Machiavellian Hal by raiding Welles's film for a revised ending in which John Woodvine's likeably self-insistent Falstaff presents Hotspur's corpse to Henry IV, demanding his due reward and humiliating Hal in front of his father (see McMillin; Hodgdon, *End*).

From Quayle's somewhat conventional jolly humanist to Welles's nearly

tragic figure to Woodvine's historical opportunist (see Figure 30), these Falstaffs embody a tendency to reclaim Falstaff's *history*, if not Oldcastle's ghostly presence. However distinctive their interpretations, these as well as other recent stagings rely on all the authoritative editions that print "Falstaff" as the name of Prince Hal's companion. The one exception, or challenge, to past editorial practice came with the decision of Oxford editors Stanley Wells and Gary Taylor to restore Oldcastle's name to their 1986 edition. Arguing that the change recuperates Shakespeare's "original intention," Taylor claims that retaining "Falstaff" simply bows to the familiar and perpetuates traditions of performance and criticism based on that name. "Falstaff," he writes, "fictionalizes, depoliticizes, secularizes and . . . trivializes the play's most memorable character. It robs the play of that tension created by the distance between two available interpretations of one of its central figures" (95). Other scholars, however, maintain that it is not the role of an editor to "retrospectively save a writer from the censor" (Taylor 85). Ignoring the censors' presence, they argue, not only idealizes the activity of authorship but removes the historical and cultural conditions in which *Henry IV, Part 1* was performed and published (Goldberg, "Commodity"; Kastan, "Killed").

By substituting "Oldcastle" for "Falstaff," readers can easily test the consequences of the reading proposed by the Oxford editors in 1986. And if, as scholars have convincingly argued, Elizabethan spectators were aware of Falstaff's "real" identity as Oldcastle, then part of the pleasure of experiencing the play was in reading the clandestine identity hidden behind the name (Poole 52fn). In one way or another, it would seem, pleasure has always been Falstaff's trademark. However troubling to the critical community, the Oxford editors' decision to turn the sixteenth-century *performance* reading of "Oldcastle" into print has produced a "new" *written* text grounded in theatrical practice, one that validates that practice as a form of publishing. And by regenerating old debates, it has also produced a new historical imaginary for the play, one that has invited critics to rethink its textual and cultural history.

Although it has been part of critical tradition to view Falstaff's an-

---

FIGURES 29 AND 30 *Two faces of Falstaff. Figure 29 (top) features Orson Welles as Falstaff from* Chimes at Midnight *(1965–66). In this film, low-angle shots repeatedly emphasize Falstaff's girth, depicting him as a carnivalesque figure of riot and plenty. This image captures the "old white-bearded Satan" defending himself to Hal-playing-Henry IV in the tavern playlet (2.4). Figure 30 (bottom) shows John Woodvine as Falstaff from the English Shakespeare Company production* The Henrys *(1987). Here Falstaff concocts a hangover cure of six eggs and the residue from a number of bottles, an inventive piece of stage business that capitalizes on the character's resourcefulness and penchant for drink.*

tecedents as more dramatic than historical and to play up an opposition between *Henry IV, Part 1*'s historical and unhistorical characters or persons, the
selections that follow offer ways of seeing Oldcastle/Falstaff not simply as an
autonomous, purely theatrical figure quite independent of historical determination but as a mediation of real historical forces (Holderness 109). The narratives and counternarratives reproduced here open up that issue. Selections
from John Foxe's *Acts and Monuments* seek to revise the "official" accounts
written by Polydore Vergil, Thomas Walsingham, and Richard Grafton and
to absolve Oldcastle of treason; those from Holinshed's *Chronicles* attempt to
mediate among available sources and negotiate a position that invites post-
Reformation readers to view Oldcastle's history in relation to other events.
Selected scenes from *Sir John Oldcastle*, by Michael Drayton, Richard Hathaway, Anthony Munday, and Robert Wilson, offer a representation of Oldcastle quite at odds with that in Shakespeare's play. Though in very different
ways, both plays dramatize the history of a period in which Protestantism
appeared as the revolutionary force it would become in the 1640s, as Puritanism went to war against King Charles I (Holderness 111). In their respec-
tive plays, both Falstaff and Oldcastle represent composite characters who
echo both past and future struggles. Strikingly, both view themselves as *individuals* — a term that never appears in Shakespeare's plays and that comes
into usage only after the Interregnum, the period between Charles I's execution (1649) and the restoration of monarchy under Charles II (1660), during
which Oliver Cromwell headed a revolutionary government (see Stallybrass). Certainly either Falstaff's Rabelaisian ego or Oldcastle's insistence
that conscience defines both "the person" and his beliefs appear to be omens
of a change that would, at least for a time, enable Englishmen to think of
themselves not as the King's subjects but as citizens of a commonwealth.

→ JOHN FOXE

From Acts and Monuments   *1563*

The Martyrdom of Sir John Oldcastle

Like the Protestant bishop John Bale, whose *Brief Chronicle Concerning the Examination and Death of the Blessed Martyr of Christ Sir John Oldcastle the Lord
Cobham* (1544) recounts Oldcastle's history, John Foxe recognized that Henry
VIII's Reformation meant revising historiographical practice. Writing under
royal patronage, fifteenth-century chroniclers had produced accounts support-
ive of the established Roman Catholic Church; but the "new" Protestantism required transforming Oldcastle and other Lollards from villains to heroes, from

FIGURE 31 *This woodcut from a later edition of John Foxe's* Acts and Monuments *(1583) depicts Sir John Oldcastle's martyrdom.*

subversive ideologues to proto-Protestant martyrs. In contrast to Hall and Holinshed's state or protonational histories, Foxe produced a church history grounded on an idea and on ideology: his aim was to create a new conception of the church. Available for reading in churches together with the Bible and the Homilies, his book had the status of hagiography, or saints' lives, for sixteenth-century Protestant apologists (Gurr, *Playgoing* 148). To compete with the Roman Catholic practice of observing saints' days, Foxe attempted to establish a Protestant calendar of saints, setting aside specific days devoted to his "new" saints' memories, celebrating their faith and their martyrdom (see Figure 31).

Foxe imports Bale's account of Oldcastle's history wholesale, adding his own "opinions." Punctuated with polemic against the bishops' attempt to repress the spread of the Gospel by "misnamed Lollards," his account also attacks previous historians. In a later edition (1583), he calls them "spider-catchers" who "heap up a dunghill of dirty dialogues, containing nothing in them but malicious railing, virulent slanders, manifest untruths, opprobrious contumelies, & stinking blasphemies, able almost to corrupt & infect the air." Thomas Arundel, the Archbishop of Canterbury, is his primary target; by contrast, he avoids canceling out

Henry V's heroic legend. Rather than accusing either the state or the King's person, Foxe represents Henry as sympathetic toward Oldcastle but bound, as the head of a state religion, by the clergy's insistence on Roman Catholic dogma. Casting Arundel as Caiaphas, the high priest who presided at the trial that condemned Jesus, Foxe exposes the clergy as acting falsely in the King's name. Although he never calls for a separation between secular and ecclesiastical authorities — an argument both unthinkable and treasonous at the time — Foxe's account of Oldcastle's history certainly points in that direction by stressing the monolithic power of the church and the clergy's duplicity in misleading both the King and the general public.

The following selections concern the initial accusations brought against Oldcastle that led to his interviews with the King, his confession of belief, his examination (the first occasion on which a Lollard knight was made to answer for his opinions before an ecclesiastical judge), and his martyrdom. Although Foxe's account differs markedly from that of Holinshed, who attempts to distance his position from either Catholic or Protestant orthodoxies, Foxe anticipates Holinshed's strategy of including official documents. Yet the order in which he compiles these documents structures his argument, allowing his own voice to control the debate. Nonetheless, others' voices compete for attention: Oldcastle's meeting with Henry V, for instance, is partially dramatized; and the "transcript" of his examination records a number of voices. Moreover, Oldcastle's confession, in which he acknowledges commiting five of the seven deadly sins (pride, wrath, gluttony, covetousness, and lechery), not only links him to Falstaff as an archetype of moral chaos but expresses contradictory attitudes toward religious doctrine that recall Sir John's. Also, Mistress Quickly's account of Falstaff's death in *Henry V* (2.3) seems to recall Foxe's monument to Oldcastle. In his deathbed mutterings he mentions the "Whore of Babylon," and, although Falstaff does not ascend to heaven in a chariot, he is taken up into "Arthur's bosom," a (more or less) true knight of an ancient proto-Protestant order.

From *Acts and Monuments*

THE HISTORY OF THE MOST VALIANT AND WORTHY MARTYR OF CHRIST SIR JOHN OLDCASTLE KNIGHT, LORD COBHAM, WITH THE WHOLE PROCESS OF HIS EXAMINATION, DEATH AND MARTYRDOM, FOR THE TRUE PROTECTION OF CHRIST'S GOSPEL

[In 1413, Thomas Arundel, the Archbishop of Canterbury, "so fierce as ever was Pharaoh, Antiochus, Herod, or Caiaphas," called a "universal Synod of all the papistical clergy of England" to counter the "most godly enterprise" of John Wycliff's disciples.]

As these high prelates, with their Pharisees and Scribes, were thus gathered in this pestilent council against the Lord and his word, first there resorted unto them the twelve inquisitors of heresies (whom they had appointed at Oxford the year afore, to search out heretics with all Wycliff's books) and they brought two hundred and sixty-six faithful conclusions, which they had collected as heresies [out] of the said books. [Foxe names the inquisitors and condemns them as "subtle sorcerers" who, in order to "stop the mouths of the common people," claimed that they met under the pretence of unifying and reforming the Church of England.]

After a certain communication they concluded among themselves, that it was not possible for them to make whole Christ's coat without seam (meaning thereby their patched Popish synagogue), unless certain great men were brought out of the way, which seemed to be the chief maintainers of the said disciples of Wycliff. Among whom the most noble knight, Sir John Oldcastle, the Lord Cobham, was complained of by the proctors, yea, rather betrayers of Christ in his faithful members, to be the chief principal. Him they accused, first, for a mighty maintainer of suspected preacher[s] in the dioceses of London, Rochester, and Hereford, contrary to the minds of their ordinaries.[1] Not only they affirmed him to have sent thither the said preachers, but also to have assisted them there by force of arms, notwithstanding their Synodal constitution made afore to the contrary. Last of all, they accused him, that he was far otherwise in belief of the Sacrament of the altar, of penance, of pilgrimage, of Image worshipping, and of the ecclesiastical power, than the holy church of Rome had taught many years before.

---

[1] **contrary . . . ordinaries:** those whose preaching countered the prescribed service of the Mass.

John Foxe, *Acts and Monuments of these latter and perilous days, touching matters of the Church, wherein are comprehended and described the great persecutions & horrible troubles, that have been wrought and practiced by the Romish Prelates, Specially in this realm of England and Scotland, from the year of our Lord a thousand unto the time now present* (London, 1563), 261–81.

In the end, it was concluded among them, that, without any further delay, process should [be cited] out against him, as against a most pernicious heretic.

Some of that fellowship which were of more crafty experience than the other, would in no case have that matter so rashly handled but thought this way much better. Considering the said Lord Cobham was a man of great birth, and in favor at that time with the King, their counsel was to know first the King's mind, to save all things upright. This counsel was well accepted, and thereupon the Archbishop Thomas Arundel, with his other bishops and a great part of the Clergy, went straightways unto the King, as then remaining at Kensington, and there laid forth most grievous complaints against the said Lord Cobham, to his great infamy and blemish, being a man most Godly. The King gently heard those blood thirsty raveners, & far otherwise than became his princely dignity, he instantly desired them that in respect of his noble stock and knighthood, they should yet favorably deal with him. And that they would, if it were possible, without all rigor or extreme handling, reduce him again to the church's unity. He promised them also that in case they were not contented to take some deliberation, his self would seriously common the matter with him.

Anon after, the King sent for the said Lord Cobham. And as he was come, he called him secretly, admonishing him betwixt him and him, to submit himself to his mother the holy church, and as an obedient child, to acknowledge himself culpable. Unto whom the Christian knight made this answer: "You, most worthy prince," saith he, "I am always prompt and willing to obey forasmuch as I know you a Christian king, and the appointed minister of God, bearing the sword to the punishment of ill doers and for safeguard of them that be virtuous. Unto you, next my eternal God, owe I my whole obedience and submit me thereunto, as I have done ever, all that I have, either of fortune or nature, ready at all times to fulfil whatsoever ye shall in the Lord command me. But as touching the Pope & his spiritualty, truly I owe them neither suit nor service, forsomuch as I know him, by the scriptures, to be the great Antichrist, the son of perdition, the open adversary of God, and the abomination standing in the holy place." When the King had heard this, with such like sentences more, he would talk no longer with him, but left him so utterly.

And as the Archbishop resorted again unto him for an answer, he gave him his full authority to cite him, examine him, and punish him, according to the devilish decrees which they call the laws of holy church. Then the said Archbishop, by the counsel of his other bishops and clergy, appointed to call before him Sir John Oldcastle, the Lord Cobham, and to cause him personally to appear to answer to such suspect articles as they should lay against him. [Arundel sends his chief Summoner to Oldcastle, with a "very sharp citation"; but Oldcastle, suspecting misuse of the King's word, refuses to consent to "these most devilish practices of the priests." The Archbishop has citations set upon the gates of Rochester cathedral, charging Oldcastle to appear before him on 11 September 1413. Followers of Oldcastle take down the letters, and when new ones are put up, they are also "rent down and utterly consumed."]

Then, forsomuch as he did not appear at the day appointed at Leeds (where as he sat in consistory, as cruel as ever was Caiaphas, with his court of hypocrites about him), he judged him, denounced him, and condemned him, of most deep contumacy. After that, when he had been falsely informed by his hired spies, and other glozing glaverers,[2] that the said Lord Cobham had laughed him to scorn, disdained all his doings, maintained his old opinions, condemned the church's power, the dignity of a bishop, and the order of priesthood (for of all these was he then accused), in his moody madness, without just proof, did he openly excommunicate him. Yet was he not with all this fierce tyranny qualified but commanded him to be cited afresh, to appear afore him the Saturday before the feast of Saint Matthew the Apostle, with these cruel threatenings added thereunto. That if he did not obey at the day, he would more extremely handle him. And to make himself more strong towards the performance thereof, he compelled the lay power, by most terrible menacings of curses and interdictions, to assist him against that seditious apostate, schismatic, that heretic, the troubler of the public peace, that enemy of the Realm, and great adversary of all holy church; for all these hateful names did he give him.

This most constant servant of the Lord and worthy knight, Sir John Oldcastle, the Lord Cobham, beholding the unpeaceable fury of Antichrist thus kindled against him, perceiving himself also compassed on every side with deadly dangers, he took paper and pen in hand, and so wrote a Christian confession or reckoning of his faith (which followeth hereafter) and both signed and sealed it with his own hand, wherein he also answereth to the four chiefest articles that the Archbishop laid against him. That done, he took the copy with him, and went therewith to the King, trusting to find mercy and favor at his hand. None other was that confession of his, than the common belief or sum of the church's faith, called the Apostles' Creed, of all Christian men then used. As thus.

---

[2] **glozing glaverers:** specious deceivers.

THE CHRISTIAN BELIEF OF THE LORD COBHAM

[After reciting the Apostles' Creed, Cobham affirms his belief in the Trinity, in Jesus Christ as the head of the church, and in the sacraments; he also sets out the duties of priests, knights, and commons.]

Finally, this is my faith also, that God will ask no more of a Christian believer in this life, but only to obey the precepts of that most blessed law. If any Prelates of the Church require more, or else any other kind of obedience, than this to be used, he condemneth Christ, exalting himself above God, and so becometh an open Antichrist. All the premises I believe particularly, and generally all that God hath left in his holy scripture, that I should believe. Instantly desiring you, my liege Lord and most worthy King, that this confession of mine may be justly examined by the most godly wise and learned men of your realm. And if it be found in all points agreeing to the verity, then let it be so allowed, and I, thereupon, holden for none other than a true Christian. If it be proved otherwise, then let it be utterly condemned: provided always, that I be taught a better belief by the word of God; and I shall most reverently at all times obey thereunto.

This brief confession of his faith the Lord Cobham wrote (as is mentioned afore) and so took it with him to the court, offering it with all meekness unto the King, to read it over. The King would in no case receive it, but commanded it to be delivered unto them that should be his judges. Then desired he, in the King's presence, that a hundred knights and esquires might be suffered to come in upon his purgation, which he knew would clear him of all heresies. Moreover he offered himself, after the law of arms, to fight for life or death with any man living, Christian or Heathen, in the quarrel of his faith, the King and the lords of his council excepted. Finally, with all gentleness, he protested before all that were present, that he would refuse no manner of correction that should after the laws of God be ministered unto him; but that he would at all times, with all meekness, obey it. Notwithstanding all this, the King suffered him to be summoned personally in his own privy chamber. Then said the Lord Cobham to the King, that he had appealed from the Archbishop to the Pope of Rome, and therefore he ought, he said, in no case to be his judge. And having his appeal there at hand ready written, he showed it with all reverence to the King. Wherewith the King was then much more displeased than afore, and said angrily to him, that he should not pursue his appeal; but rather he should tarry in hold, till such time as it were of the Pope allowed. And then, would he or nild he, the Archbishop should be his judge. Thus was there nothing allowed that the good Lord Cobham had lawfully afore required. But, for so much as he would not be sworn in all things to submit himself to the church, and so to take what penance the Archbishop would enjoin him, he was arrested again at the King's commandment, and so led forth to the Tower of London, to keep his day (so was it then spoken) that the Archbishop had appointed him afore in the King's chamber.

[In the first examination of Oldcastle (23 September 1413), Archbishop Arundel offers him absolution, but he "showed as though he had given no ear, having his mind otherwise occupied, & so desired no absolution"; instead, he replies to the accusations by repeating his confession of belief, touching on the sacraments, penance, images, and pilgrimage. Questioning him further, the Archbishop warns him that in failing to respond directly to the accusations against him, he can be openly proclaimed as a heretic. Saying, "Do as ye shall think best, for I am at a point," Oldcastle refers the clergy to his "bill," a general statement of belief that carefully avoids the Bishop's specific charges. Foxe gives "The Determination of the Archbishop and Clergy," followed by Oldcastle's second examination: the excerpts following concern specific points of doctrine.]

The Latter Examination of the Lord Cobham

"My Lord Cobham," saith this doctor [John Kemp], "we must briefly know your mind concerning these four points here following. The first of them is this." And then he read upon the bill: "The faith and determination of holy church touching the blessed Sacrament of the altar is this. That after the sacramental words be once spoken by a priest in his Mass, the material bread, that was before bread, is turned into Christ's very body, and the material wine is turned into Christ's blood. And so there remaineth in the Sacrament of the altar from thenceforth no material bread nor material wine, which were there before the sacramental words were spoken. Sir, believe you not this?"

The Lord Cobham said, "This is not my belief. But my faith is, as I said to you afore, that in the worshipful Sacrament of the altar is very Christ's body in the form of bread."

Then said the Archbishop, "Sir John, ye must say otherwise."

The Lord Cobham said, "Nay, that I shall not, if God be upon my side (as I trust he is) but that there is Christ's body in form of bread, as the common belief is." Then read the doctor again:

"The second point is this. Holy church hath determined that every Christian man, living here bodily upon the earth, ought to be shriven to a priest ordained by the church, if he may come to him. Sir, what say you to this?"

The Lord Cobham answered and said, "A diseased or sore wounded man had need to have a sure wise surgeon and a true, knowing both the ground and the danger of the same. Most necessary were it, therefore, to be first shriven unto God, which only knoweth our diseases and can help us. I deny not in this the going to a priest, if he be a man of good life and learning, for the laws of God are to be required of the priest which is godly learned. But if he be an idiot or a man of vicious living that is my curate, I ought rather to flee from him than to seek unto him. For sooner might I catch ill of him that is nought, than any goodness towards my soul's health."

Then read the doctor again:

"The third point is this. Christ ordained St. Peter the Apostle to be his vicar here in earth, whose see is the church of Rome. And he granted that the same power which he gave unto Peter should succeed unto all Peter's successors, which we call now Popes of Rome, by whose special power, in churches particular, he ordained Prelates and Archbishops, Parsons, curates, and other degrees more, unto whom Christian men ought to obey after the laws of the church of Rome. This is the determination of holy Church. Sir, believe ye not this?"

To this he answered and said, "He that followeth Peter most nigh in pure living, is next unto him in succession. But your Lordly order esteemeth not greatly the lowly behavior of poor Peter, whatsoever he prate of him. Neither care ye greatly for the humble manners of them that succeeded him till the time of Silvester, which for the more part were martyrs, as I told you afore. Ye can let all their good conditions go by you, and not hurt yourselves with them at all. All the world knoweth this well enough by you, and yet ye can make boast of Peter."

With that, one of the other doctors asked him: "Then what do you say of the Pope?"

The Lord Cobham answered, "As I said before, he and you together make whole the great Antichrist. Of whom he is the great head; you Bishops, Priests, Prelates, and Monks, are the body, and the begging Friars are the tail, for they cover the filthiness of you both, with their subtle sophistry. Neither will I in conscience obey any of you all, till I see you, with Peter, follow Christ in conversation."

Then read the doctor again:

"The fourth point is this. Holy church hath determined that it is meritorious to a Christian man to go on Pilgrimage to holy places. And there specially to worship holy relics and images of saints, Apostles, Martyrs, confessors, and all other saints besides approved by the church of Rome. Sir, what say ye to this?"

Whereunto he answered, "I owe them no service by any commandment of God, & therefore I mind not to seek them for your covetousness. It were best ye swept them fair from cobwebs and dust, and so laid them up for catching of scathe. Or else to bury them fair in the ground, as ye do other aged people which are God's images. It is a wonderful thing that saints, now being dead, should become so covetous and needy, and thereupon so bitterly beg, which all their life time hated all covetousness and begging. But this I say unto you, and I would all the world should mark it. That with your Shrines and Idols, your feigned absolutions and pardons, ye draw unto you the substance, wealth, and chief pleasures of all Christian Realms."

"Why sir" (said one of the clerks), "will ye not worship good images?"

"What worship should I give unto them?" said the Lord Cobham.

Then said Friar [Thomas] Palmer unto him, "Sir, will ye worship the cross of Christ, that he died upon?"

"Where is it?" said the Lord Cobham.

The friar said, "I put you the case, Sir, that it were here, even now before you."

The Lord Cobham answered, "This is a great wise man, to put me an earnest question of a thing, and yet he himself knoweth not where the thing itself is. Yet once again I ask you, What worship I should do unto it?"

A clerk said unto him, "Such worship as Paul speaketh of, and that is this. God forbid that I should joy, but only in the cross of Jesus Christ."

Then said the Lord Cobham, and spread his arms abroad, "This is a very cross, yea, and so much better than your cross of wood, in that it was created of God. Yet will not I seek to have it worshipped."

Then said the Bishop of London, "Sir, yet wot well that he died on a material cross."

The Lord Cobham said, "Yea, and I wot also, that our salvation came not in by that material cross, but alone by Him which died thereupon. And well I wot, that holy St. Paul rejoiced in none other cross, but in Christ's passion and death only, and in his own sufferings of like persecution with Him, for the selfsame verity that he had suffered for afore."

Another clerk yet asked him, "Will ye then do no honor to the holy cross?"

He answered him, "Yes, if he were mine own, I would lay him up honestly, and see unto him that he should take no more scathes abroad nor be robbed of his goods, as he is nowadays."

Then said the Archbishop unto him, "Sir John, ye have spoken here many wonderful words to the slanderous rebuke of the whole spiritualty, giving a great ill example unto the common sort here, to have us in the more disdain. Much time have we spent here about you, and all in vain, so far as I can see. Well, we must be now at this short point with you, for the day passeth away. Ye must either submit yourself to the ordinance of holy church, or else throw yourself (no remedy) into most deep danger. See to it in time, for else anon it will be else too late."

The Lord Cobham said, "I know not to what purpose I should otherwise submit me. Much more have you offended me, than ever I offended you, in thus troubling me before this multitude."

Then said the Archbishop unto him, "We once again require you to remember yourself well, & to have none other manner [of] opinion in these matters, than the universal faith and belief of the holy church of Rome is. And so, like an obedient child, return again to the unity of your mother. See to it, I say, in time, for yet ye may have remedy, whereas anon it will be too late."

The Lord Cobham said expressly before them all, "I will none otherwise believe in these points than I have told you here afore. Do with me what you will."

Finally, then the Archbishop said, "Well, then I see none other, but we must needs do the law; we must proceed forth to the sentence definitive, and both judge ye and condemn ye for an heretic."

And with that the Archbishop stood up and read there a bill of his condemnation, all the clergy and laity vailing their bonnets.[3]

[Foxe gives "The Definitive Sentence of his Condemnation"; the text of a letter written by Cobham's friends in his defense, and the clergy's reply, "An Abjuration counterfeited of the Bishops" (which Cobham never saw). After sentencing, Cobham was returned to prison, where, after a time, he "escaped out of the Tower of London in the night, and so fled into Wales, whereas he continued more than four years after."]

The Latter Imprisoning and Death of the Lord Cobham

[Lord Powis, at whose castle in Wales Cobham sought refuge, betrays him; Cobham is taken again to the Tower and again condemned of heresy and treason.]

And, upon the day appointed, he was brought out of the Tower with his arms bound behind him, having a very cheerful countenance. Then was he laid upon a hurdle, as though he had been a most heinous traitor to the crown, and so drawn forth into St. Giles's Field, where as they had set up a new pair of Gallows. As he was coming to the place of execution, and was

---

[3] **vailing their bonnets:** removing their hats as a sign of submission to the law and as a sign of Cobham's condemnation.

taken from the hurdle, he fell down devoutly upon his knees, desiring Almighty God to forgive his enemies. Then stood he up and beheld the multitude, exhorting them in most godly manner to follow the laws of God written in the Scriptures, and in any wise to beware of such teachers as they see contrary to Christ in their conversation and living, with many other special counsels. Then was he hanged up there by the middle in chains of iron, and so consumed alive in the fire, praising the name of God so long as his life lasted. In the end, he commended his soul into the hands of God, and so departed hence most Christianly, his body resolved into ashes.

And this was done in the year of our Lord 1418, which was the fifth year of the reign of King Henry the fifth, the people there present showing great dolor. How the priests that time fared, blasphemed, and accused, requiring the people not to pray for him, but to judge him damned in hell for that he departed not in the obedience of their Pope, it were too long to write.

This terrible kind of death, with gallows, chains, and fire, appeareth not very precious in the eyes of men that be carnal, no more than did the death of Christ, when he was hanged up among thieves. The righteous seemeth to die (saith the wise man) in the sight of them which are unwise, and their end is taken for very destruction. Ungodly souls thinketh their lives very madness, and their passage hence without all honor, but though they suffer pain before men, saith he, yet is their expectation full of immortality. They are accounted for the children of God, and have their portion among the saints. As gold in the furnace doth God try his elect, and as a most pleasant burnt offering receiveth he them to rest.

The more hard the passage be, the more glorious shall they appear in the latter resurrection. Not that the afflictions of this life are worthy of such a glory, but that it is God's heavenly pleasure so to reward them. Never are the judgments and ways of men like unto the judgments and ways of God, but contrary evermore, unless they be taught of him. In the latter time (saith the Lord unto Daniel) shall many be chosen, proved, and purified by fire, yet shall the ungodly live wicked still, and have no understanding that is of faith. By an angel from heaven was John earnestly commanded to write: that blessed are the dead which hence departed in the Lord. Right dear (saith David) in the sight of God is the death of his true servants. Thus resteth this valiant Christian knight, Sir John Oldcastle, under the altar of **GOD,** which is Jesus Christ, among that godly company which in the kingdom of patience, suffered great tribulation with the Death of their bodies for His faithful word and testimony, abiding there with them, He fulfilling of their whole number, and the full restoration of His elect. The which He grant in effect at this time appointed, which is one God eternal. Amen.

[Foxe includes two other documents: Thomas Arundel's "Epistle . . . to the Bishop of London" and "The catholic faith and confession of the Lord Cobham." Summarizing, Foxe repeats his account of Cobham's martyrdom.]

This is not to be forgotten, which is reported by many, that he should say: that he should die here in earth after the sort and manner of Elijah; the which, whether it sprang of the common people without cause, or that it was foreshowed by him, I think it not without good consideration, or that it sprang not without some gift of prophecy, the end of the matter doth sufficiently prove. For, like as when Elijah should leave this mortal life, he was carried by a fiery chariot into immortality; even so the order of this man's death, not being much unlike, followed the figure of his departure. For he, first of all, being lifted up upon the gallows, as into a chariot and encompassed round about with flaming fire; what other thing, I pray you, did this most holy martyr of Christ represent, than only a figure of a certain Elijah, flying up into heaven. The which went up into heaven by a fiery chariot.

→ RAPHAEL HOLINSHED

From The Chronicles of England, Scotland, and Ireland 1587

Sir John Oldcastle

Unlike Foxe, who lifts Oldcastle's history free of contemporary events, Holinshed embeds his account within a larger narrative that encompasses the first five years of Henry V's reign (1413–1417) and interweaves foreign and domestic affairs. Within this widened view, the Oldcastle matter appears in the context of Henry V's legendary history: an aggressive military foreign policy and, at home, a strong alignment between church and state in the interest of national unity. Sixteenth- and early-seventeenth-century readers and spectators knew the foreign policy best: dramatized in Shakespeare's *Henry V* (1600), it was also the subject of popular ballad literature. The same is true for the late twentieth century, where that heroic history has been sustained in popular cultural memory by Laurence Olivier's and Kenneth Branagh's 1944 and 1989 films. The Oldcastle story, however, points to the other side of Henry's legend: his strategic alliance with the church and his acceptance (following Henry IV's statute instituting punishment for heresy) of religious persecution as a principle of rule. Offering evidence of a continuing religious controversy that marked Henry's reign, Oldcastle's history is an unstable component of that legend (Patterson, *Reading* 131–32). It was also especially pertinent to late-sixteenth-century conditions, where a similarly antagonistic relation between church and sect, between center and margins, was being played out in the struggle between state religion and Puritan reformers. And for Holinshed, the Oldcastle matter not only becomes part of his own interest, as a post-Reformation historian, in the prehistory of that movement but also points to the instability of "history" itself.

Before Holinshed, writers in the Protestant tradition such as John Bale and John Foxe had attacked previous historians, and modern historians have raised similar questions about the trustworthiness of sources (see Aston; Wylie). Among those cited by Holinshed, Thomas Walsingham was a monk and, consequently, an enemy of Lollardry, and Titus Livius's *Vita Henrici Quinti* (translated anonymously into English as *The First English Life of Henry V* [1513]) was written under the patronage of Humphrey, Duke of Gloucester, Henry's younger brother. As the story passed to the next generation of chroniclers, Vergil and Fabian produced accounts that applied its lessons to the reign of Henry VIII. All of these writers, as well as John Stow, embraced "interested" or "official" positions: for them, Oldcastle becomes "a demon whose appearance at the beginning of [Henry V's] reign has to be exorcised before the miracle of Agincourt can take place" (Patterson, *Reading* 133). Hall seems to concur, for he gives only brief attention to Oldcastle's rebellion before turning to his primary emphasis, Henry's "Victorious Acts" in France. But, although he leaves Oldcastle's history unfinished, his succinct account of the rebellion not only lacks the hostility of his predecessors' but defers judgment "to men indifferent." "For surely," he writes, "all conjectures be not true, nor all writings are not the Gospel, & therefore because I was neither a witness of the fact, nor present at the deed, I overpass that matter and begin another" (49).

Holinshed not only relies on Hall's account but extends the questions he raises about historical verifiability and diversity of opinion. His careful attributions, both in marginal notations and in his text, can be read as one sign of Holinshed's inability to produce a definitive version of "what really happened." Among these citations, the parenthetical "as Thomas Walsingham confesseth" is especially telling, given the Lollards' denial of the church's position on auricular confession. Although he repeats the story of the armed rising, Holinshed never explicitly states that such a "rebellion" did occur; and by placing Oldcastle in Wales, "where he remained for a season," he leaves considerable uncertainty as to whether Oldcastle actually headed those assembled at Ficket's Field. Clearly mistrusting Walsingham's report of 50,000 "servants, prentices, and citizens confederate with them," he downplays such rumors of widespread *popular* rebellion by distinguishing, in a marginal note, between "the common fame" and "search[ing] out an exquisite truth." Like Hall, he evades the issues that Protestant historians had called into question: whether Oldcastle's followers were guilty as charged and whether they were traitors and/or heretics. Instead of acknowledging such historians overtly, Holinshed concludes his commentary on the January 1414 rising by referring his readers to "others" who "have so largely treated thereof." Elizabethan readers would have little doubt that one of these was John Foxe, who suggested that Acton and the "rebels" were simply members of a private congregation, not an armed band of traitors (Patterson, *Reading* 150). As with his account of Henry IV's

Northern rebellion, Holinshed invites readers to be their own historians (see Chapter 1, "Historiography and the Uses of History"). In the case of Oldcastle, however, he even more cautiously withholds judgment; passing on a legacy of doubts, he attempts to set all religious "affections" aside.

When recording the rest of Oldcastle's history, Holinshed is equally circumspect about what he includes and what he omits. Following out his theme of how "books" are central to this narrative, he repeats Walsingham's story of the defaced books discovered "in a husbandman's house" near St. Albans by the abbot's servants after Oldcastle himself had narrowly escaped. But where Walsingham rails against the blasphemies committed against the Blessed Virgin Mary ("which on account of horror he refrains from describing"), Holinshed marks his own presence, and his sense of historical change, by substituting "as then was thought due our lady" for Walsingham's overt Catholic sympathies (Patterson, *Reading* 151). Finally, Holinshed embeds his unusually spare account of Oldcastle's 1417 arrest and execution within another narrative, that of Henry V's siege of Faleis. Ignoring any suggestion that Oldcastle had been involved in treacherous dealings with the Scots earlier in the same year, Holinshed also omits Walsingham's story that Oldcastle had, at his execution, promised his own resurrection in three days in order to ensure "peace for his sect" (*Historia anglia* 2: 326, 328). Whether or not he "actually" made such a promise, it does mark the vitality of Oldcastle's own legend of resistance and nonconformity (Patterson, *Reading* 152). And placed as it is, surrounded by the details of the King's successful military campaign and of levying more monies to "furnish [his] great charges," Oldcastle's death emerges as a domestic incident that interrupts the trajectory of Henry's own legend.

From *The Chronicles of England, Scotland, and Ireland*

Also in this first yéere of this kings reigne, sir John Oldcastell, which by his wife was called lord Cobham, a valiant capteine and a hardie gentleman, was accused to the archbishop of Canturburie of certeine points of heresie, who knowing him to be highlie in the kings favour, declared to his highnesse the whole accusation. The king first having compassion of the noble man, required the prelats, that if he were a straied shéepe, rather by gentlenes than by rigor to reduce him to the fold. And after

Raphael Holinshed, *The Chronicles of England, Scotland, and Ireland* (London, 1587; rpt. London 1808), 62–64, 91–94.

this, he himselfe sent for him, and right earnestlie exhorted him, and lovinglie admonished him to reconcile himselfe to God and to his lawes. The lord Cobham not onelie thanked him for his most favorable clemencie, but also declared first to him by mouth, and afterwards by writing, the foundation of his faith, and the ground of his beliefe, affirming his grace to be his supreme head and competent judge, and none other person, offering an hundred knights and esquiers to come to his purgation, or else to fight in open lists in defence of his just cause.

The king understanding and persuaded by his councell, that by order of the lawes of his realme, such accusations touching matters of faith ought to be tried by his spiritual prelats, sent him to the Tower of London, there to abide the determination of the clergie, according to the statutes in that case provided, after which time a solemne sessión was appointed in the cathedrall church of saint Paule, upon the thrée and twentith day of September, and an other the five and twentith daie of the same moneth, in the hall of the Blacke friers at London, in which places the said lord was examined, apposed, and fullie heard, and in conclusion by the archbishop of Canturburie denounced an heretike, & remitted againe to the Tower of London, from which place, either by helpe of fréends, or favour of kéepers, he privilie escaped and came into Wales, where he remained for a season.

After this, the king kéeping his Christmasse at his manor of Eltham, was advertised, that sir Roger Acton knight a man of great wit and possessions, John Browne esquire, John Beverlie priest, and a great number of other were assembled in armour against the king, his brethren, the clergie and realme. These newes came to the king, on the twelfth daie in Christmasse, whereupon understanding that they were in a place called Ficket field beside London, on the backe side of saint Giles, he streight got him to his palace at Westminster, in as secret wise as he might, and there calling to him certeine bands of armed men, he repaired into saint Giles fields, néere to the said place (where he understood they should fullie méet about midnight) and so handled the matter, that he tooke some, and slue some, even as stood with his pleasure. The

Sir John Oldcastell escaped out of the Tower.

Titus Livius

1414

Hall.
A commotion raised by sir Roger Acton and others.

Titus Livius.

The rebels surprised.

capteins of them afore mentioned, being apprehended, were brought to the kings presence, and to him declared the causes of their commotion & rising, accusing a great number of their complices.

Thom. Walsin.

The king used one policie, which much served to the discomfiting of the adversaries (as Thom. Walsingham saith) which was this: he gave order, that all the gates of London should be streictlie kept and garded, so as none should come in or out, but such as were knowen to go to the king. Hereby came it to passe, that the chiefest succour appointed to come to the capteins of the rebels, was by that meanes cut off where otherwise suerlie (had it not beene thus prevented and staied) there had issued foorth of London to have joined with them, to the number (as it was thought) of fiftie thousand persons, one and other, servants, prentises, and citizens, confederate with them that were thus assembled in Ficket field. Diverse also that came from sundrie parts of the realme, hasting towards the place, to be there at their appointed time, chanced to light among the kings men, who being taken and demanded whither they went with such spéed, answered, they came to meet with their capteine the lord Cobham.

By this excessive number it may appeare, that *Walsingham* reporteth this matter according to the cōmon fame, and not as one that searched out an exquisite truth.

But whether he came thither at all, or made shift for himselfe to get awaie, it dooth not appeare; for he could not be heard of that time (as Thomas Walsingham confesseth) although the king by proclamation promised a thousand marks to him that could bring him foorth, with great liberties to the cities or townes that would discover where he was. By this it maie appeare, how greatlie he was beloved, that there could not one be found, that for so great a reward would bring him to light. Among other that were taken was one William Murlie, who dwelt in Dunstable, a man of great wealth, and by his occupation a brewer, an earnest mainteiner of the lord Cobhams opinions, and (as the brute[1] ran) in hope to be highlie advanced by him if their purposed devise had taken place, apparant by this; that he had two horsses trapped with guilt harnesse led after him, and in his bosome a paire of gilt spurs (as it was déemed) prepared for himselfe to

William Murlie.

---

[1] **brute**: bruit; rumor.

weare, looking to be made knight by the lord Cobhams hands at that present time. But when he saw how their purpose quailed, he withdrew into the citie with great feare to hide himselfe; howbeit he was perceived, taken, and finallie executed among others.

To conclude, so manie persons hereupon were apprehended, that all the prisons in and about London were full, the chiefe of them were condemned by the cleargie of heresie and atteinted of high treason in the Guildhall of London, and adjudged for that offense to be drawen and hanged, and for heresie to be consumed with fire, gallowes and all, which judgement was executed the same moneth, on the said sir Roger Acton, and eight and twentie others.

Sir Roger Acton & his complices condemned of treason and heresie.

Some saie, that the occasion of their death was onelie for the conveieng of the lord Cobham out of prison. Others write, that it was both for treason and heresie, and so it appeareth by the record. Certeine affirme, that it was for feined causes surmized by the spiritualtie, more upon displeasure than truth, and that they were assembled to heare their preacher (the foresaid Beverlie) in that place there, out of the waie from resort of people, sith[2] they might not come togither openlie about any such matter, without danger to be apprehended; as the manner is, and hath beene ever of the persecuted flocke, when they are prohibited publikelie the exercise of their religion. But howsoever the matter went with these men, apprehended they were, and diverse of them executed (as before ye have heard) whether for rebellion or heresie, or for both (as the forme of the indictment importeth) I néed not to spend manie words, sith others have so largelie treated thereof; and therefore I refer those that wish to be more fullie satisfied herein unto their reports.

[During Lent, French ambassadors from the Dauphin bring Henry V a token of tennis balls (as in *Henry V* 1.2). The death of Thomas Arundel, Archbishop of Canterbury. Henry Percy, Hotspur's son, is restored to the lands and earldom of Northumberland. Henry V's campaigns in France. The Scots invade England.]

---

[2] **sith:** since.

The same time, the lord Cobham, sir John Oldcastell, whilest he shifted from place to place to escape the hands of them, who he knew would be glad to laie hold on him, had conveied himselfe in secret wise into an husbandmans house, not farre from S. Albons, within the precinct of a lordship belonging to the abbat of that towne. The abbats servants getting knowledge hereof, came thither by night, but they missed their purpose, for he was gone; but they caught diverse of his men, whome they caried streict to prison. The lord Cobham herewith was sore dismaied, for that some of them that were taken were such as he trusted most, being of counsell in all his devises. In the same place, were found books written in English, and some of those books in times past had beene trimlie gilt, limned,[3] and beautified with images, the heads whereof had béene scraped off, and in the Letanie they had boltted[4] foorth the name of our ladie, and of other saints, till they came to the verse Parce nobis Dommine.[5] Diverse writings were found there also, in derogation of such honor as then was thought due our ladie. The abbat of saint Albons sent the booke so disfigured with scrapings & blottings out, with other such writings as there were found, unto the king; who sent the booke againe to the archbishop, to shew the same in his sermons at Paules crosse in London, to the end that the citizens and other people of the realme might understand the purposes of those that then were called Lollards, to bring them further in discredit with the people.

Sir John Old-castell.

The servants of the abbat of S. Albons go about to catch the lord Cobham.

[Henry V's siege of Faleis during the winter of 1418.]

The Frenchmen notwithstanding this siege, valiantlie defended their wals, and sometimes made issues foorth, but small to their gaine: and still the Englishmen with their guns and great ordinance made batterie to the wals and bulworks. The winter season was verie cold, with sharpe frost, & hard weather; but the Englishmen made such shift for provision of all things necessarie to serve their turns, that they were sufficientlie provided, both

Thom. Wals.

---

[3] **limned:** drawn; illuminated. [4] **boltted:** blotted. [5] **Parce nobis Dommine:** Spare us, Lord.

against hunger and cold: so that in the end, the Frenchmen perceiving they could not long indure against them,
offered to talke, and agréed to give over the towne, if no
rescue came by a certeine daie appointed. About the same
season was sir John Oldcastell, lord Cobham taken, in the
countrie of Powes land, in the borders of Wales, within a
lordship belonging to the lord Powes, not without danger
and hurts of some that were at the taking of him: for they
could not take him, till he was wounded himselfe.

*Sir John Old-
castell taken.*

At the same time, the states of the realme were assembled at London, for the levieng of monie, to furnish the
kings great charges, which he was at about the maintenance of his wars in France: it was therefore determined,
that the said sir John Oldcastell should be brought, and
put to his triall, yer the assemblie brake up. The lord
Powes therefore was sent to fetch him, who brought him
to London in a litter, wounded as he was: herewith, being
first laid fast in the Tower, shortlie after he was brought
before the duke of Bedford, regent of the realme, and the
other estates, where in the end he was condemned; and
finallie was drawen from the Tower unto saint Giles field,
and there hanged in a chaine by the middle, and after
consumed with fire, the gallowes and all.

*Sir John Old-
castell executed.*

→ **MICHAEL DRAYTON, RICHARD HATHAWAY,
ANTHONY MUNDAY, AND ROBERT WILSON**

From The True and Honorable History of the Life of Sir John Oldcastle

1600

Oldcastle offers a serious and positive treatment of Puritanism that clearly counters Shakespeare's parodic portrayal of Falstaff's anti-Puritan sentiments, a response that seeks to reconstitute the historical Oldcastle's memory along the
lines set out by Foxe and, later, by Holinshed's carefully mediated account.
Promising "fair truth," not "forged invention," the play's prologue announces: "It
is no pampered glutton we present, / Nor aged counsellor to youthful sins; / But
one whose virtues shone above the rest, / A valiant martyr and a virtuous peer"

Michael Drayton, Richard Hathaway, Anthony Munday, and Robert Wilson, *The First Part of
the True and honorable history, of the life of Sir John Oldcastle, the good Lord Cobham. As it hath been
lately acted by the right honorable the Earl of Nottingham, Lord High Admiral of England, his servants* (London, 1600), D2v–D4v, F2r–G1v.

(ll.6–9). Some scholars think that the play may reflect the beliefs of Lord Howard of Effingham, the patron of the Lord Admiral's Men; others even surmise that it may have been commissioned by the Brooke family (Gurr, *Playing* 148). Whatever the case, only the first part survives, and its narrative traces the most controversial events in Oldcastle's history — the clergy's accusations against him, his relation to Henry V, the supposed rebellion, and his part in the Earl of Cambridge's plot to assassinate the King. Just as *Famous Victories* provides a dramatic ground plan for *Henry IV* and *Henry V,* the structure of events and details of character and language in those plays all reappear, though considerably transformed, in *Oldcastle.* The play moves between state and ecclesiastical proceedings, preparations for conspiracy and "rebellion," and scenes of tavern and provincial life to include a wide variety of locales and roles — aristocrats, Welsh tenants, Lancashire carriers, and Dunstable maltmen. Drayton and his collaborators revise historical sequence freely to suit their own agenda, which attempts to place Oldcastle's views within acceptable late-sixteenth-century orthodoxies and apart from those of more radical Puritan fundamentalists.

Matters of politics and religion were not dealt with lightly on the early modern stage: criticizing the politics or conduct of the sovereign and commenting on religious controversy could prevent a play from being licensed. Nonetheless, existing statutes were somewhat arbitrarily enforced; certainly stage plays glanced at Catholics and Puritans alike. *Oldcastle,* however, exhibits considerable policy in representing Oldcastle's Lollard beliefs as well as the beliefs of the King and the clergy. Rather than casting Thomas Arundel, the Archbishop of Canterbury, as Oldcastle's persecutor, that role falls to the Bishop of Rochester, a rabid heresy-hunter whose extremist views gain him little support, even from the King. In a complementary move, the play whitewashes Oldcastle completely. Not only does he comply with his sovereign's middle-of-the-road Anglican views on religion, but his forgiving attitude toward his persecutors, his fortitude, and his devotion to his wife mark him with exemplary *private* virtues that identify him with widely held, entirely acceptable Puritan values. By adhering to these values, *Oldcastle* offers an instance of how the early-fifteenth-century proto-Reformation "worked in the cultural memory to authorize the not entirely submissive or state-approved Protestantism of the end of the sixteenth century" (Patterson, *Reading* 152–53).

Rehabilitating Oldcastle's Protestant belief, however, addresses only one strand of his history. In order to vindicate him further, the play disperses the subversive potential attached to his qualities as militant and traitor among other characters. Capitalizing on the ambiguities noted by historians, the play revises historical chronology to acquit Oldcastle of both counts. Distancing *Oldcastle's* hero from Shakespeare's Falstaffian reveler, however, is a slightly trickier proposition. To be sure, Oldcastle's first appearance easily reworks Falstaff's military reputation by showing the charitable landowner giving alms to a group of Shrewsbury veterans — those Falstaff had condemned to "the town's end, to beg during life" (5. 3. 36). But in order to disassociate Oldcastle even more securely from Falstaff, the play creates another Sir John — a thieving priest who takes on the fat knight's avarice and, by keeping a concubine named Doll, absorbs his lechery as well. Like the brewer Murley, who joins Acton's rising in order to please his wife with a newly bought knighthood, Doll's desires, which focus on buying status and nobility, set her apart from Lady Cobham's wifely devotion and her wish for a peaceful, removed life. And just as issues of religious controversy are disarmed by *Oldcastle*'s focus on conscience as central to all belief, any hints of aristocratic disaffection are displaced into a lively fantasia of Shakespeare's *Henry* plays that risks tipping Drayton's play back into the comic saturnalia from which it tries to escape.

At its close, *Oldcastle* glances at the whole question of Oldcastle's previous misrepresentations by sending up representation itself in a whirlwind of comic disguisings. In a St. Albans tavern where nearly all the characters come to rest, inhabit the same rooms, and exchange apparel, Oldcastle and his Lady escape, only to be falsely accused of murdering Sir Richard Lee's son, lately returned from the Earl of Essex's Irish campaign. Sir John, however, identifies the real murderer, a thieving Irishman named MacChane, who is condemned to hang; set free, the Oldcastles go into hiding at Lord Powis's castle in Wales. In this somewhat strained topical resolution of religious and political loyalties, any taint attached to Oldcastle becomes displaced onto MacChane. Ireland and the Irish, not Protestantism, represent the "true" late-sixteenth-century threat to national security.

The scenes reproduced here convey some sense of how the play reconceives Oldcastle, renegotiates his chronicle and religious histories, and interweaves signs of Falstaff's theatrical history. Scene 6, Oldcastle's private interview with Henry and the first turning point in the play's dramatization of his fluctuating fortunes, represents the pull between personal conscience and the demands of loyalty to the state that weaves throughout the play. Scenes 10 and 11 displace Oldcastle's rebellion, which is never staged, into an encounter between the disguised King Henry and Sir John that not only recalls *Henry IV, Part 1*'s Gads Hill robbery and Falstaff's inflated account of his assailants (1.1; 2.2) but also draws on events Shakespeare dramatizes in *Henry V* (4.1). When, the night before Agincourt's battle, the disguised King Henry V walks among his men, he first encounters Pistol, who challenges him; later, as Henry (still in disguise) attempts to convince three soldiers (Bates, Court, and Williams) that the King's war is just, he exchanges gloves with the refractory Williams, vowing to meet him in combat once the battle is over. Like *Henry V*'s glove exchange, the halved angel in *Oldcastle* tests a subject's loyalty to his King.

From *The True and Honorable History of the Life of Sir John Oldcastle*

[Scene 1: A violent quarrel opens the play: not based on historical sources, it resembles the opening of Shakespeare's *Romeo and Juliet* (1594–95). The Sheriff of Hereford brings rumors of Oldcastle's "conspiracy" to a judge, who proclaims him innocent of faction against the King and the realm. Scene 11:

The Bishop of Rochester complains about Lord Cobham and his followers to
Suffolk, who informs the King; Henry, refusing to believe that Cobham is a
traitor, agrees to "school him privately," much to Suffolk's displeasure. Scene
III: Lord Cobham gives money to beggars. Scene IV: Harpoole makes the
Archbishop's Summoner literally eat his words. Scene V: Acton, Bourne, Bev-
erley, and Murley — Cobham's followers — agree to meet at Ficket's Field.]

[SCENE VI]

Enter K. Harry, Suffolk, Butler, and Oldcastle kneeling to the King.

HARRY:
    'Tis not enough, Lord Cobham, to submit;
    You must forsake your gross opinion.
    The Bishops find themselves much injured,
    And though for some good service you have done,
    We for our part are pleas'd to pardon you,   5
    Yet they will not so soon be satisfied.

COBHAM:
    My gracious Lord, unto your Majesty,
    Next unto my God, I owe my life,
    And what is mine, either by nature's gift,
    Or fortune's bounty, all is at your service;   10
    But for obedience to the Pope of Rome,
    I owe him none, nor shall his shaveling° priests
    That are in England, alter my belief.
    If out of holy Scripture they can prove,
    That I am in an error, I will yield,   15
    And gladly take instruction at their hands.
    But otherwise, I do beseech your grace,
    My conscience may not be encroach'd upon.

HARRY:
    We would be loath to press° our subjects' bodies,
    Much less their souls, the dear redeemed part,   20
    Of him that is the ruler of us all.
    Yet let me counsel ye, that might command,
    Do not presume to tempt them with ill words,
    Nor suffer any meetings to be had
    Within your house, but to the uttermost,   25
    Disperse the flocks of this new gathering sect.

---

12. **shaveling:** contemptuous term for a tonsured ecclesiastic.   19. **press:** oppress; possibly
with the sense of torturing as well.

COBHAM:

My liege, if any breathe that dares come forth,
And say, my life in any of these points
Deserves th'attainder° of ignoble thoughts,
Here stand I, craving no remorse at all,
But even the utmost rigor may be shown.   30

HARRY:

Let it suffice we know your loyalty.
What have you there?

COBHAM:

A deed of clemency,
Your Highness, pardon for Lord Powis' life,   35
Which I did beg, and you, my noble Lord,
Of gracious favor did vouchsafe to grant.

HARRY:

But it is not signed with our hand.

COBHAM:

Not yet, my Liege.   *One ready with pen and ink.*

HARRY:

The fact, you say, was done,   40
Not of prepensed° malice, but by chance?

COBHAM:

Upon mine honor so, no otherwise.

HARRY:

There is his pardon; bid him make amends,   *Writes.*
And cleanse his soul to God for his offense.
What we remit, is but the body's scourge.   *Enter Bishop [of Rochester].* 45
How now, Lord Bishop?

BISHOP:

Justice, dread Sovereign.
As thou art King, so grant I may have justice.

HARRY:

What means this exclamation, let us know?

BISHOP:

Ah my good Lord, the state's abus'd,   50
And our decrees most shamefully profan'd.

HARRY:

How, or by whom?

---

29. **th'attainder:** the accusation.   41. **prepensed:** premeditated.

BISHOP:
> Even by this heretic,
> This Jew, this Traitor to your majesty.

COBHAM:
> Prelate, thou liest, even in thy greasy maw,°   55
> Or whosoever twits me with the name,
> Of either traitor, or of heretic.

HARRY:
> Forbear, I say, and Bishop, show the cause
> From whence this late abuse hath been deriv'd.

BISHOP:
> Thus, mighty King, by general consent,   60
> A messenger was sent to cite this Lord,
> To make appearance in the consistory,°
> And coming to his house, a ruffian slave,
> One of his daily followers, met the man,
> Who, knowing him to be a parator,°   65
> Assaults him first, and after in contempt
> Of us, and our proceedings, makes him eat
> The written process, parchment, seal and all:
> Whereby his master neither was brought forth,
> Nor we but scorn'd for our authority.   70

HARRY:
> When was this done?

BISHOP:
> At six a clock this morning.

HARRY:
> And when came you to court?

COBHAM:
> Last night, my Lord.

HARRY:
> By this it seems he is not guilty of it,   75
> And you have done him wrong t'accuse him so.

BISHOP:
> But it was done, my lord, by his appointment,
> Or else his man durst ne'er have been so bold.

HARRY:
> Or else you durst be bold, to interrupt,

---

55. **maw:** throat; gullet. 62. **consistory:** the diocesan court. 65. **parator:** apparitor; an officer of an ecclesiastic court.

And fill our ears with frivolous complaints.   80
Is this the duty you do bear to us?
Was't not sufficient we did pass our word
To send for him, but you misdoubting it,
Or which is worse, intending to forestall
Our regal power, must likewise summon him?   85
This savors of Ambition, not of zeal,
And rather proves you malice his estate
Than any way that he offends the law.
Go to, we like it not, and he your officer,
That was employed so much amiss herein,   90
Had his desert for being insolent.   *Enter Huntington.*
So, Cobham, when you please, you may depart.

COBHAM:
I humbly bid farewell unto my liege.   *Exit.*

HARRY:
Farewell. What's the news by Huntington?

HUNTINGTON:
Sir Roger Acton, and a crew, my Lord,   95
Of bold seditious rebels, are in Arms,
Intending reformation of Religion.
And with their Army they intend to pitch,
In Ficket Field, unless they be repuls'd.

HARRY:
So near our presence? Dare they be so bold?   100
And will proud war, and eager thirst of blood,
Whom we had thought to entertain far off,
Press forth upon us in our native bounds?
Must we be forc'd to handsel° our sharp blades
In England here, which we prepar'd for France?   105
Well, a God's name be it. What's their number, say,
Or who's the chief commander of this rout?

HUNTINGTON:
Their number is not known, as yet (my Lord)
But 'tis reported Sir John Oldcastle
Is the chief man, on whom they do depend.   110

HARRY:
How, the Lord Cobham?

---

104. **handsel:** test; try for the first time.

HUNTINGTON:
Yes, my gracious Lord.

BISHOP:
I could have told your majesty as much
Before he went, but that I saw your Grace
Was too much blinded by his flattery.   115

SUFFOLK:
Send post, my Lord, to fetch him back again.

BUTLER:
Traitor unto his country, how he smooth'd,°
And seemed as innocent as Truth itself.

HARRY:
I cannot think it yet he would be false,
But if he be, no matter, let him go,   120
We'll meet both him and them unto their woe.

BISHOP:
This falls out well, and at the last I hope
To see this heretic die in a rope.   *Exeunt.*

[Scene VII: Cambridge, Scrope, and Grey lay out Cambridge's claim to the throne and their plot with King Charles of France against Henry V. Though appearing to sign the others' compact, Oldcastle vows in an aside to discover the plot to the King, reassures his wife and Lord and Lady Powis, and leaves for court. Scene VIII: The brewer Murley, anticipating a knighthood, prepares his men for the rising, which is never staged. Scene IX: Doll solicits Sir John of Wrotham for money. As Scene X, continued here, begins, Henry V orders forces to meet the rebels and disguises himself.]

KING:
It's time, I think, to look unto rebellion,
When Acton doth expect unto his aid,
No less than fifty thousand Londoners.
Well, I'll to Westminster in this disguise,
To hear what news is stirring in these brawls.   5

Enter Sir John.

SIR JOHN: Stand, true man, says a thief!
KING: Stand, thief, says a true man. How if a thief?
SIR JOHN: Stand thief, too.

---

117. **smooth'd:** flattered; glossed over faults.

KING: Then, thief or true man, I see I must stand. I see, howsoever the world wags, the trade of thieving yet will never down. What art thou? 10

SIR JOHN: A good fellow.

KING: So am I too; I see thou dost know me.

SIR JOHN: If thou be a good fellow, play the good fellow's part: deliver thy purse without more ado.

KING: I have no money. 15

SIR JOHN: I must make you find some before we part. If you have no money you shall have ware° — as many sound dry blows as your skin can carry.

KING: Is that the plain truth?

SIR JOHN: Sirra, no more ado. Come, come, give me the money you have. 20 Dispatch, I cannot stand all day.

KING: Well, if thou wilt needs have it: there 'tis. Just [is] the proverb: one thief robs another. Where the devil are all my old thieves that were wont to keep this walk? Falstaff, the villain, is so fat, he cannot get on's horse, but methinks Poins and Peto should be stirring hereabouts. 25

SIR JOHN: How much is there on't, of thy word?

KING:

A hundred pounds in Angels,° on my word,
The time has been I would have done as much
For thee, if thou hadst passed this way, as I have now.

SIR JOHN: Sirra, what art thou? Thou seem'st a gentleman. 30

KING: I am no less; yet a poor one now, for thou hast all my money.

SIR JOHN: From whence cam'st thou?

KING: From the court at Eltham.

SIR JOHN: Art thou one of the King's servants?

KING: Yes, that I am, and one of his chamber. 35

SIR JOHN: I am glad thou art no worse, thou mayst the better spare thy money.

And thinks't thou thou mights't get a poor thief his pardon if he should have need?

KING: Yes, that I can. 40

SIR JOHN: Wilt thou do so much for me, when I shall have occasion?

KING: Yes, faith, will I, so it be for no murder.

SIR JOHN: Nay, I am a pitiful thief; all the hurt I do a man, I take but his purse. I'll kill no man.

---

17. **ware:** literally, goods; here, however, just deserts.   27. **Angels:** gold coins with the device of the archangel Michael and the dragon, worth one-third to one-half of a pound.

KING: Then of my word, I'll do it.   45

SIR JOHN: Give me thy hand of the same.

KING: There 'tis.

SIR JOHN: Methinks the King should be good to thieves, because he has been a thief himself, though I think now he be turned true man.

KING: Faith, I have heard indeed he has had an ill name that way in his   50 youth. But how cans't thou tell he has been a thief?

SIR JOHN:

How? because he once robb'd me before I fell to the trade myself; when that foul villainous guts, that led him to all that roguery, was in's company there, that Falstaff.

KING (*aside*): Well, if he did rob thee then, thou art but even with him now,   55 I'll be sworn. Thou knowest not the King now, I think, if thou sawest him?

SIR JOHN: Not I, i'faith.

KING (*aside*): So it should seem.

SIR JOHN: Well, if old King Henry had liv'd, this King that is now, had made thieving the best trade in England.   60

KING: Why so?

SIR JOHN: Because he was the chief warden of our company. It's pity that ere he should have been a King, he was so brave a thief. But Sirra, wilt remember my pardon if need be?

KING: Yes, faith will I.   65

SIR JOHN: Wilt thou? Well then, because thou shalt go safe — for thou mayest hap (being so early) be met with again, before thou come to Southwark — if any man when he should bid thee good morrow, bid thee stand, say thou but "Sir John," and he will let thee pass.

KING: Is that the word? Well then, let me alone.   70

SIR JOHN: Nay, Sirra, because I think indeed I shall have some occasion to use thee, & as thou comest oft this way, I may light on thee another time not knowing thee, here, I'll break this Angel. Take thou half of it; this is a token betwixt thee and me.

KING: God have mercy, farewell.   75

SIR JOHN: O my fine golden slaves, here's for thee, wench. I'faith now, Doll, we will revel in our bever,° this is a tithe pig° of my vicarage. God have mercy, neighbor Shooter's hill, you paid your tithe honestly. Well, I hear there is a company of rebels up against the King, got together in Ficket field near Holborn, and as it is thought here in Kent, the King will   80 be there tonight in's own person, Well, I'll to the King's camp, and it shall

---

77. **bever:** between-meals drink; also, bower.   **tithe pig:** a pig taken as a tithe, or tax; the tenth part of a person's goods.

go hard, but if there be any doings, I'll make some good boot amongst
them.   *Exit.*

[SCENE XI]

[Henry V, Suffolk, and Huntington, all in disguise as common soldiers,
gamble and dice. Sir John joins the play and loses everything to the King,
except for the broken angel.]

SIR JOHN:
  All's gone but that.
HUNTINGTON:
  What, half a broken angel?
SIR JOHN:
  Why sir, 'tis gold.
HARRY:
  Yea, and I'll cover it.
SIR JOHN:
  The devil do ye good on't. I am blind; ye have blown me up.°   5
HARRY:
  Nay, tarry, priest, ye shall not leave us yet;
  Do not these pieces fit each other well?
SIR JOHN:
  What if they do?
HARRY:
  Thereby begins a tale:
  There was a thief, in face much like Sir John,   10
  But 'twas not he — that thief was all in green —
  Met me last day on Black Heath, near the park,
  With him a woman. I was all alone,
  And weaponless; my boy had all my tools,
  And was before providing me a boat.   15
  Short tale to make: Sir John — the thief I mean —
  Took a just hundredth pound in gold from me.
  I storm'd at it, and swore to be reveng'd,
  If ere we met. He, like a lusty thief,
  Brake with his teeth this Angel just in two,   20
  To be a token at our meeting next,
  Provided I should charge no Officer

---

5. **blown me up:** he is either deceived or broke; ruined.

To apprehend him, but at weapon's point
Recover that, and what he had beside.
Well met, Sir John, betake ye to your tools   25
By torch light, for, master parson, you are he
That had my gold.

SIR JOHN: Zounds,° I won't in play, in fair square play, of the keeper of
Eltham park, and that I will maintain with this poor whinyard.° Be you
two honest men to stand and look upon's, and let's alone, and take nei-   30
ther part.

HARRY:
Agreed. I charge ye do not budge a foot.
Sir John, have at ye.

SIR JOHN:
Soldier, 'ware your sconce.°

*Here as they are ready to strike, enter Butler and draws his weapon and steps betwixt
them.*

BUTLER:
Hold, villains, hold! My Lords, what do ye mean,   35
To see a traitor draw against the King?

SIR JOHN:
The King! God's will, I am in a proper pickle.

HARRY:
Butler, what news? Why dost thou trouble us?

BUTLER:
Please it your Highness, it is break of day.
And as I scouted near to Islington,   40
The gray-ey'd morning gave me glimmering
Of armed men coming down Highgate hill,
Who by their course are coasting hitherward.

HARRY:
Let us withdraw, my Lords. Prepare our troops
To charge the rebels if there be such cause.   45
For this lewd priest, this devilish hypocrite,
That is a thief, a gamester, and what not,
Let him be hang'd up for example sake.

SIR JOHN: Not so, my gracious sovereign. I confess I am a frail man, flesh
and blood as other are: but set my imperfections aside, by this light ye   50

---

28. **Zounds:** by his (Christ's) wounds; an oath.   29. **whinyard:** a short-sword.   34. **'ware
your sconce:** watch your head.

have not a taller man, nor a truer subject to the Crown and State, than
Sir John of Wrotham.

HARRY: Will a true subject rob his King?

SIR JOHN: Alas, 'twas ignorance and want, my gracious liege.

HARRY:
'Twas want of grace. Why, you should be as salt   55
To season others with good document;°
Your lives as lamps to give the people light,
As shepherds, not as wolves to spoil the flock.
Go hang him, Butler.

BUTLER:
Didst thou not rob me?   60

SIR JOHN: I must confess I saw some of your gold. But my dread Lord, I
am in no humor for death; therefore save my life. God will that sinners
live! Do not you cause me die. Once in their lives the best may go astray,
and if the world say true, yourself (my liege) have been a thief.

HARRY:
I confess I have,   65
But I repent and have reclaim'd myself.

SIR JOHN:
So will I do if you will give me time.

HARRY:
Wilt thou? My lords, will you be his sureties?

HUNTINGTON:
That when he robs again, he shall be hang'd.

SIR JOHN:
I ask no more.   70

HARRY:
And we will grant thee that.
Live and repent, and prove an honest man,
Which when I hear, and safe return from France,
I'll give thee living. Til when, take thy gold,
But spend it better than at cards or wine,   75
For better virtues fit that coat of thine.

SIR JOHN:
Vivat Rex & currat lex!° My liege, if ye have cause of battle, ye shall see
Sir John of Wrotham bestir himself in your quarrel.   *Exeunt.*

---

56. **document:** instruction.   77. *Vivat Rex & currat lex:* May the King live and the law
continue.

Bibliography

><

Primary Sources

Alley, Hugh. "A Caveatt for the Citty of London, OR a forewarninge of offences against penall Lawes." London 1598. Folger Ms V. a. 318. facs, rpt. as *Hugh Alley's Caveat: The Markets of London in 1598*. Ed. Ian Archer, Caroline Barron, and Vanessa Harding. London: London Topographical Society Publication No. 137, 1988.

Anonymous. *The Famous Victories of Henry V.* [1583–88]. T. Creede, 1598.

Ascham, Roger. *The Scholemaster, or plaine and perfite way of teachyng children the Latin tong.* J. Daye, 1570 (STC 832).

Bacon, Sir Francis. *The Essayes or Counsels, Civill and Morall.* Ed. Michael Kiernan. Cambridge: Harvard UP, 1985.

Baldwin, William [comp.]. *A Myrroure for Magistrates.* T. Marshe, 1559 (STC 1247).

Bale, John. *Dramatic Writings of John Bale, Bishop of Ossary.* Guildford: Traylen, 1966.

Beard, Thomas. *The Theatre of God's Judgements: or, a Collection of Histories.* A. Islip, 1597 (STC 1659).

Bodin, J. *The Six Bookes of a Commonweale.* [1606] Trans. Richard Knolles. Ed. Kenneth Douglas McRae. Cambridge: Harvard UP, 1962.

Bowen, Ivor, ed. *The Statutes of Wales.* London: T. Fisher Unwin, 1908.

The Brut, or The Chronicles of England. Part II. Ed. Friedrich W. D. Brie. Early English Text Society, 1908. New York: Kraus, 1971.

Bullough, Geoffrey. *Narrative and Dramatic Sources of Shakespeare.* Vol. 4. London: Routledge, 1962.

Camden, William. *Annales.* Trans. as *The True and Royal History of Elizabeth, Queen of England.* Ed. W. T. MacCaffrey. Chicago: U of Chicago P, 1970.

Camden, William. *Britain, or a Chorographicall description of England, Scotland and Ireland.* Trans. P. Holand, imp. G. Bishop [and] J. Norton, 1610 (STC 4509).

Castiglione, Baldassare. *The Courtyer.* [1528] Done into Englyshe by T. Hoby. W. Seres, 1561 (STC 4778).

Chambers, E. K. *The Elizabethan Stage.* 4 vols. Oxford: Clarendon, 1923.

Daniel, Samuel. *Collected Works in Verse and Prose.* Ed. Alexander B. Grosart. London: Russell and Russell, 1963.

———. *Collection of the Historie of England.* N. Okes for the author, 1618 (STC 6248).

———. *The First Foure Bookes of the Civile Wares.* P. Short for S. Waterson, 1595 (STC 6244).

Dekker, Thomas. *Lanthorne and Candle-Light, or the Second part of the Belman.* For J. Busbie, 1608 (STC 6485).

———. *O per se O, or a new cryer of Lanthorne and Candlelight.* For J. Busbie, 1612 (STC 6487).

Digges, Leonard. *An Arithmeticall Militare treatise, named Stratioticos.* H. Bynneman, 1579 (STC 6848).

Digges, Thomas. *Foure Paradoxes, or politque discourses, all newly published.* H. Lownes for C. Knight, 1604 (STC 6872).

Dod, John, and Robert Cleaver. *A Godly Forme of Household Government, to be practised of all Christian Householders.* T. Crede for T. Man, 1621 (STC 5384a).

Drayton, Michael, et al. *The True and Honourable History of the Life of Sir John Oldcastle, The Good Lord Cobham.* S[ims] for T. Pavier, 1600 (STC 18795).

Edelen, George, ed. *The Description of England: The Classic Contemporary Account of Tudor Social Life.* 1968. New York: Dover, 1994.

Elyot, Sir Thomas. *The Boke named the Governour.* T. Bertheleti, 1531 (STC 7635).

Erasmus, Desiderius. *De Civilitate morun [sic] puerilium: A Lytell Booke of Good Maners for Chyldren: into the Englysshe tonge by R. Whytyngton.* W. de Worde. 1532 (STC 10467).

———. *The Education of a Christian Prince.* Ed. and trans. Lester K. Born. New York: Columbia UP, 1936.

Foxe, John. *Actes and Monuments.* J. Day, 1563 (STC 11222).

Garrard, William. *The Arte of Warre.* For R. Warde, 1591 (STC 11625).

Gosson, Stephen. *Plays confuted in Five Actions.* For T. Gosson, 1582 (STC 12095).

——. *The Schoole of Abuse, conteining a pleasaunt invective against poets, pipers, plaiers, jesters, and such like caterpillers of a commonwealth.* For T. Woodcocke, 1579 (STC 12097).

Greene, Robert. *The Second Part of Conny-Catching.* J. Wolfe for W. Wright, 1591 (STC 12281).

Halle, Edward. *The Union of the Two Noble and Illustre Families of Lancaster and York.* . . . 1548 rev. ed. London: J. Johnson, 1809.

Hardyng, John. *The Chronicle of J. Hardyng from the firste begynnyng of Englande.* Ex. off. R. Graftoni, 1543 (STC 12767).

Harman, Thomas. *A Caveat or warening for Common Cursetors.* W. Gryffth, 1567 (STC 12787).

Hayward, John. *The First Part of the Life and Raigne of King Henrie IIII.* J. Woolfe, 1599 (STC 12995).

Heywood, Thomas. *An Apology for Actors.* N. Okes, 1612 (STC 13309).

Holinshed, Raphael. *The Chronicles of England, Scotland, and Ireland.* At the expenses of J. Harison, G. Bishop, R. Newberie, H. Denham and J. Woodcocke, 1587 rev. ed. London: J. Jonson, 1807 (v. 1), 1808 (v. 3).

An Homilie Agaynst Disobedience and Wylful Rebellion. R. Jugge and J. Carwood, 1571 (STC 13679).

Hughes, Charles, ed. *Shakespeare's Europe: A Survey of the Condition of Europe at the End of the Sixteenth Century.* [1903] 2nd ed. New York: Benjamin Blom, 1967.

Hughes, Paul L., and James F. Larkin, eds. *Tudor Royal Proclamations.* 3 vols. New Haven: Yale UP, 1969.

Hurault, M. Jacques. *Politicke, Moral and Martial Discourses.* Trans. Arthur Golding. A. Islip, 1595 (STC 14000).

Kemp, William. *Kemps Nine Daies Wonder, performed in a daunce from London to Norwich.* E. A[llde] for N. Ling, 1600 (STC 14923).

Kingsford, C. L., ed. *The First English Life of Henry V.* Oxford: Clarendon, 1911.

[Machiavelli, Niccolò]. *Nicholas Machiavel's Prince.* Tr. E. D[acres]. R. Bishop for W. Hils, sold by D. Pakeman, 1640 (STC 17168).

Nashe, Thomas. *Pierce Penilesse his Supplication to the Diuell.* [J. Charlewood for] R. Jhones, 1592 (STC 18371).

Nichols, John. *The Progresses and Public Processions of Queen Elizabeth.* 3 vols. London, 1823. New York: Burt Franklin, 1966.

Peele, George. *Polyhymnia, Describing The Honourable Triumph at Tilt.* [1590]. *Works of George Peele.* Ed. A. H. Bullen. Port Washington: Kennikat, 1966.

Ponet, John. *A Short Treatise of Politike Power, and of the true Obedience which subjectes owe to kynges and other civile Governours, with an Exhortacion to all true naturall Englishe men, compyled by D. I. P. B. R. W.* 1556 (STC 20178).

Rich, Barnaby. *A Pathway to military practise.* J. Charlewood for R. Walley, 1587 (STC 20995).

——. *A Right Excellent and Pleasant Dialogue, betwene Mercury and an English Souldier.* 1574 (STC 20998).

Segar, Sir William. *Booke of Honour and Armes.* T. Orwin for R. Jhones, 1590 (STC 22163).

——. *Honour, Military and Civil.* R. Barker, 1602 (STC 22164).

Sidney, Sir Philip. *Defense of Poesy.* Ed. Lewis Soens. Lincoln: U of Nebraska P, 1970.

Silver, George. *The Paradoxes of Defence, wherein is proved the true grounds of fight to be in the short ancient weapons.* [R. Field] for E. Blount, 1599 (STC 22554).

Smith, Thomas. *The Complete Souldier, containing the Whole art of Gunnery.* 2nd ed. H. L[ownes] for R. Dawlman, 1628 (STC 22856).

Speed, John. *The Counties of Britain: A Tudor Atlas by John Speed.* Ed. Nigel Nicolson. London: Pavilion, 1988.

——. *The Historie of Great Britaine.* W. Hall and J. Beale, for J. Sudbury and G. Humble, 1611 (STC 23045).

——. *Theatre of the Empire of Great Britaine, presenting an exact Geography of England, Scotland, Ireland, etc.* W. Hall and J. Beale, for J. Sudbury and G. Humble, 1611 (STC 23041).

Starkey, Thomas. *A Dialogue between Reginald Pole and Thomas Lupset.* [1553–56].

Stow, John. *The Annales of England, from the First Inhabitation untill 1592.* R. Newbery, 1592 (STC 23334).

——. *A Summarie of Englyshe Chronicles.* Ed. T. Marshe, 1565 (STC 23319).

——. *Survay of London.* J. Windet, 1603 (STC 23343).

Stubbes, Phillip. *The Anatomie of Abuses: Contayning a Discoveries, or brief Summarie of such Notable Vices and Imperfections, as now raigne in many Christian Countreyes of the Worlde; but (especiallie) in a verie famous Ilande called Ailgna.* R. Jones, 1583 (STC 23376).

Swetnam, Joseph. *The Araignment of lewde, idle, froward, and unconstant women: Or the vanitie of them, choose you whether.* [Tho. Tel-troth, pseudonym.] E. Allde for T. Archer, 1615 (STC 23533).

Tarlton, Richard. *Tarltons Jests: drawne into these three parts.* J. H[aviland] for A. Crooke, 1638 (STC 23684).

Thirsk, Joan, and J. P. Cooper, eds. *Seventeenth-Century Economic Documents.* Oxford: Clarendon, 1972.

Tyndale, William. *The Obedience of a Christian Man.* 1550 (STC 24452).

Vives, Juan Luis. *A very Frutefull and Pleasant Boke called the Instruction of a Christen Woman.* Turned into Englysshe by R. Hyrde. In the house of T. Berthelet, 1529 (STC 24856).

Walsingham, Sir Thomas. *De republica Anglorum. The Maner of Governement of England.* H. Midleton for G. Seton, 1581 (STC 22857).

Warner, William. *Albion's England.* G. Robinson for T. Cadman, 1586 (STC 25079).

Watson, Foster, ed. *Vives and the Renascence Education of Women.* New York: Longmans, 1912.

Secondary Sources

Agnew, Jean-Christophe. *Worlds Apart: The Market and the Theatre in Anglo-American Thought.* Cambridge: Cambridge UP, 1986.

Amussen, Susan Dwyer. *An Ordered Society: Gender and Class in Early Modern England*. New York: Columbia UP, 1993.

Andrew, Dudley. *Film in the Aura of Art*. Princeton: Princeton UP, 1984.

Archer, Ian. "The Nostalgia of John Stow." *The Theatrical City: Culture, Theatre and Politics in London 1576–1649*. Ed. David L. Smith et al. Cambridge UP, 1995, 17–34.

———. *The Pursuit of Stability: Social Relations in Elizabethan London*. Cambridge: Cambridge UP, 1991.

Aston, Margaret. *Lollards and Reformers: Images and Literacy in Late Medieval Religion*. London: Hambledon, 1984.

Axton, Marie. *The Queen's Two Bodies: Drama and the Elizabethan Succession*. London: Royal Historical Society, 1977.

Barber, C. L. *Shakespeare's Festive Comedy: A Study of Dramatic Form and Its Relation to Social Custom*. Princeton: Princeton UP, 1959.

Barber, C. L., and Richard Wheeler. *The Whole Journey: Shakespeare's Power of Development*. Berkeley: U of California P, 1986.

Barker, Felix, and Peter Jackson. *London: 2000 Years of a City and Its People*. London: Cassell, 1974.

Barroll, Leeds. "A New History for Shakespeare and His Time." *Shakespeare Quarterly* 39 (1988): 441–64.

Beier, A. L., and Roger Finlay, eds. *London 1500–1700: The Making of the Metropolis*. London: Longman, 1986.

Belsey, Catherine. *The Subject of Tragedy: Identity and Difference in Renaissance Drama*. London: Methuen, 1985.

Bentley, G. E. *The Profession of Dramatist in Shakespeare's Time, 1590–1642*. Princeton: Princeton UP, 1971.

Bevington, David, ed. *Henry IV, Part 1*. Oxford: Clarendon, 1987.

———. *Tudor Drama and Politics: A Critical Approach to Topical Meaning*. Cambridge: Harvard UP, 1968.

Bogdanov, Michael, and Michael Pennington. *The English Shakespeare Company: The Story of "The Wars of the Roses" 1986–1989*. London: Nick Hern, 1990.

Boose, Lynda E. "Scolding Brides and Bridling Scolds: Taming the Woman's Unruly Member." *Shakespeare Quarterly* 42.2 (1991): 179–213.

Boynton, Lindsay. *The Elizabethan Militia 1558–1638*. London: Routledge, 1967.

Bray, Alan. *Homosexuality in Renaissance England*. London: Gay Men's, 1982.

Bristol, Michael. *Carnival and Theater: Plebian Culture and the Structure of Authority in Renaissance England*. London: Methuen, 1985.

Bruster, Douglas. *Drama and the Market in the Age of Shakespeare*. Cambridge: Cambridge UP, 1992.

Bryant, J. A. "Shakespeare's Falstaff and the Mantle of Dick Tarlton." *Studies in Philology* 51 (1954): 149–62.

Burke, Peter. *Popular Culture in Early Modern Europe*. New York: New York UP, 1978.

Bushnell, Rebecca W. *Tragedies of Tyrants: Political Thought and Theater in the English Renaissance.* Ithaca: Cornell UP, 1990.

Campbell, Lily B. *Shakespeare's Histories: Mirrors of Elizabethan Policy.* San Marino: Huntington Library, 1958.

Canny, Nicholas P. *The Elizabethan Conquest of Ireland: A Pattern Established, 1565–76.* Hassocks: Harvester, 1976.

Cartelli, Thomas. *Marlowe, Shakespeare, and the Economy of Theatrical Experience.* Philadelphia: U of Pennsylvania P, 1991.

de Certeau, Michel. *The Writing of History.* Trans. Tom Conley. New York: Columbia UP, 1988.

Clark, Peter. *The English Alehouse: A Social History 1200–1830.* London: Longman, 1983.

Cohen, Walter. *Drama of a Nation: Public Theater in Renaissance England and Spain.* Ithaca: Cornell UP, 1985.

Contamine, Philippe. *War in the Middle Ages.* Oxford: Blackwell, 1984.

Cook, Ann J. *The Privileged Playgoers of Shakespeare's London, 1576–1642.* Princeton: Princeton UP, 1981.

Corbin, Peter, and Douglas Sedge, eds. *The Oldcastle Controversy.* Manchester: Manchester UP, 1991.

Cressy, David. *Education in Tudor and Stuart England.* New York: St. Martin's, 1975.

Crowl, Samuel. "The Long Good-Bye: Welles and Falstaff." *Shakespeare Quarterly* 31 (1980): 369–80.

Cruickshank, C. G. *Army Royal: Henry VIII's Invasion of France. 1513.* Oxford: Clarendon, 1969.

———. *Elizabeth's Army.* Oxford: Clarendon, 1966.

Dolan, Frances E. *Dangerous Familiars: Representations of Domestic Crime in England 1550–1700.* Ithaca: Cornell UP, 1994.

Dollimore, Jonathan, and Alan Sinfield, eds. *Political Shakespeare: New Essays in Cultural Materialism.* Manchester: Manchester UP, 1985.

Empson, William. *Some Versions of Pastoral.* Norfolk: New Directions, 1950.

Ferguson, Arthur B. *The Chivalric Tradition in Renaissance England.* London: Associated UP, 1986.

Findlay, Heather. "Renaissance Pederasty and Pedagogy: The Case of Shakespeare's Falstaff." *Yale Journal of Criticism* 3 (1989): 229–38.

Fortescue, J. W. "The Army: Military Service and Equipment." *Shakespeare's England: An Account of the Life and Manners of His Age.* Vol. 1. Oxford: Clarendon, 1917. 112–26.

Fumerton, Patricia. "Not Home: Alehouses, Vagrancy, and Broadside Ballads." Papers from Folger "Material London ca. 1600" conference, April 1995. Ed. Lena Cowen Orlin. (Forthcoming.)

Goldberg, Jonathan. "The Commodity of Names: 'Falstaff' and 'Oldcastle' in 1 *Henry IV." Reconfiguring the Renaissance: Essays in Critical Materialism.* Ed. Jonathan Crew. London: Associated UP, 1992. 76–88.

——, ed. *Queering the Renaissance.* Durham: Duke UP, 1994.

——. *Sodometries: Renaissance Texts, Modern Sexualities.* Stanford: Stanford UP, 1992.

Gowing, Laura. "Gender and the Language of Insult in Early Modern London." *History Workshop* 35 (1993): 1–21.

——. "Language, Power, and the Law: Women's Slander Litigation in Early Modern London." *Women, Crime and the Courts in Early Modern England.* Ed. Jennifer Kermode and Garthine Walker. Chapel Hill: U of North Carolina P, 1994.

Greenblatt, Stephen. *Renaissance Self-Fashioning from More to Shakespeare.* Chicago: U of Chicago P, 1980.

——. "Invisible Bullets." *Shakespearean Negotiations: The Circulation of Social Energy in Renaissance England.* U of California P, 1988. 21–65.

Gurr, Andrew. "The Authority of the Globe and the Fortune." Papers from Folger "Material London ca. 1600" conference, April 1995. Ed. Lena Cowen Orlin. (Forthcoming.)

——. *Playgoing in Shakespeare's London.* Cambridge: Cambridge UP, 1987.

——. *The Shakespearean Stage 1574–1642.* 3rd ed. Cambridge: Cambridge UP, 1994.

Hawkins, Sherman H. "*Henry IV*: The Structural Problem Revisited." *Shakespeare Quarterly* 33 (1982): 278–301.

Helgerson, Richard. *Forms of Nationhood: The Elizabethan Writing of England.* Chicago: U of Chicago P, 1992.

Henderson, Katherine Usher, and Barbara F. McManus. *Half Humankind: Contexts and Texts of the Controversy about Women in England, 1540–1640.* Urbana: U of Illinois P, 1985.

Highley, Christopher. "Wales, Ireland, and *1 Henry IV*." *Renaissance Drama* ns 21 (1990): 91–114.

Hodgdon, Barbara. *The End Crowns All: Closure and Contradiction in Shakespeare's History.* Princeton: Princeton UP, 1991.

——, ed. *Henry IV, Part 2.* Shakespeare in Performance Series. Manchester: Manchester UP, 1993.

Holderness, Graham. *Shakespeare's History.* New York: St. Martin's, 1985.

Howard, Jean E. "The New Historicism in Renaissance Studies." *English Literary Renaissance* 16 (1986): 13–43.

——. *The Stage and Social Struggle in Early Modern England.* London: Routledge, 1994.

Hudson, Winthrop S. *John Ponet (1516?–1556), Advocate of Limited Monarchy.* Chicago: U of Chicago P, 1942.

Humphreys, A. R., ed. *King Henry IV, Part 1.* 1960. London: Methuen, 1978.

Hutson, Lorna. *The Usurer's Daughter: Male Friendship and Fictions of Women in Sixteenth-Century England.* London: Routledge, 1994.

James, Mervyn. *Society, Politics and Culture: Studies in Early Modern England.* Cambridge: Cambridge UP, 1986.

Jorgens, Jack. *Shakespeare on Film*. Bloomington: U of Indiana P, 1977.
Jorgenson, Paul A. *Shakespeare's Military World*. Berkeley: U of California P, 1956.
Kantorowicz, Ernst. *The King's Two Bodies: A Study in Mediaeval Political Theology*. Princeton: Princeton UP, 1957.
Kastan, David Scott. " 'Killed with Hard Opinions': Oldcastle, Falstaff, and the Reformed Text of *1 Henry IV*." *Textual Formations and Reformations*. Ed. Thomas L. Berger and Laurie McGuire. (Forthcoming.)
———. " 'Proud Majesty Made a Subject': Shakespeare and the Spectacle of Rule." *Shakespeare Quarterly* 37 (1986): 459–75.
———. *Shakespeare and the Shapes of Time*. Hanover: UP of New England, 1982.
Keen, Maurice. *Chivalry*. New Haven: Yale UP, 1984.
Kelly, H. A. *Divine Providence in the England of Shakespeare's Histories*. Cambridge: Harvard UP, 1970.
Kelly, Joan. *Women, History, and Theory: The Essays of Joan Kelly*. Chicago: U of Chicago P, 1986.
Kelso, Ruth. *Doctrine for the Lady of the Renaissance*. Urbana: U of Illinois P, 1956.
Kermode, Jenny, and Catherine Walker, eds. *Women, Crime and the Courts in Early Modern England*. Chapel Hill: U of North Carolina P, 1994.
Laroque, François. *Shakespeare's Festive World: Elizabethan Seasonal Entertainment and the Professional Stage*. Cambridge: Cambridge UP, 1991.
Laslett, Peter. *The World We Have Lost*. New York: Scribner, 1973.
Lyons, Bridget Gellert, ed. *Chimes at Midnight*. New Brunswick: Rutgers UP, 1988.
Manley, Lawrence. *Literature and Culture in Early Modern London*. Cambridge: Cambridge UP, 1995.
———. "Of Sites and Rites." *The Theatrical City: Culture, Theatre and Politics in London, 1576–1649*. Ed. David L. Smith, Richard Strier, and David Bevington. Cambridge: Cambridge UP, 1995. 35–54.
Marcus, Leah. *Puzzling Shakespeare: Local Reading and Its Discontents*. Berkeley: U of California P, 1988.
McCoy, Richard C. *The Rites of Knighthood: The Literature and Politics of Elizabethan Chivalry*. Berkeley: U of California P, 1989.
McDonald, Russ. *The Bedford Companion to Shakespeare*. Boston: Bedford–St. Martin's, 1996.
McFarlane, K. B. *Lancastrian Kings and Lollard Knights*. Oxford: Clarendon, 1972.
———. *The Origins of Religious Dissent in England*. New York: Collier, 1966. Rpt. of *John Wycliffe and the Beginnings of English Nonconformity*. 1952.
McMillin, Scott, ed. *Henry IV, Part 1*. Shakespeare in Performance Series. Manchester: Manchester UP, 1991.
Melchiori, Giorgio. "Reconstructing the *Ur-Henry IV*." *Essays in Honour of Kristian Smidt*. Ed. Peter Bilton et al. Oslo: Oslo UP, 1986. 59–77.
Montrose, Louis. *The Purpose of Playing: Shakespeare and the Cultural Politics of the Elizabethan Theatre*. Chicago: U of Chicago P, 1996.

Morgan, Prys. "From a Death to a View: The Hunt for the Welsh Past in the Romantic Period." *The Invention of Tradition.* Ed. Eric Hobsbawm and Terence Ranger. Cambridge: Cambridge UP, 1983. 43–100.

Morgann, Maurice. *Shakespearean Criticism.* Ed. Daniel A. Fineman. Oxford: Clarendon, 1972.

Mullaney, Steven. *The Place of the Stage: License, Play, and Power in Renaissance England.* Chicago: U of Chicago P, 1988.

Palmer, William. "Gender, Violence, and Rebellion in Tudor and Early Stuart Ireland." *Sixteenth Century Journal* 23.4 (1992): 699–712.

Patterson, Annabel. *Censorship and Interpretation: The Conditions of Writing and Reading in Early Modern England.* Madison: U of Wisconsin P, 1984.

——. *Reading Holinshed's Chronicles.* Chicago: U of Chicago P, 1994.

Pocock, J. G. A. *The Machiavellian Moment: Florentine Political Thought and the Atlantic Republican Tradition.* Princeton: Princeton UP, 1975.

Poole, Kristen. "Saints Alive! Falstaff, Martin Marprelate, and the Staging of Puritanism." *Shakespeare Quarterly* 46.1 (1995): 47–75.

Powell, Chilton Latham. *English Domestic Relations 1487–1653: A Study of Matrimony and Family Life in Theory and Practice as Revealed by the Literature, Law, and History of the Period.* New York: Columbia UP, 1917.

Prockter, Adrian, and Robert Taylor, comps. *The A to Z of Elizabethan London.* London: Harry Margary and Guildhall Library, 1979.

Purkiss, Diane. "Material Girls: The Seventeenth-Century Woman Debate." *Women, Texts and Histories 1575–1760.* Ed. Clare Brant and Diane Purkiss. London: Routledge, 1992.

Rackin, Phyllis. "Foreign Country: The Place of Women and Sexuality in Shakespeare's Historical World." *Enclosure Acts: Sexuality, Property, and Culture in Early Modern England.* Ed. Richard Burt and John Michael Archer. Ithaca: Cornell UP, 1994. 68–95.

——. *Stages of History: Shakespeare's English Chronicles.* Ithaca: Cornell UP, 1990.

Rappaport, Steve. *Worlds within Worlds: Structures of Life in Sixteenth-Century London.* Cambridge: Cambridge UP, 1989.

Reay, Barry, ed. *Popular Culture in Seventeenth-Century England.* New York: St. Martin's, 1985.

Reese, M. M. *The Cease of Majesty.* New York: St. Martin's, 1961.

Ribner, Irving. *The English History Play in the Age of Shakespeare.* Princeton: Princeton UP, 1957.

Rowse, A. L. *The Expansion of Elizabethan England.* London: Macmillan, 1955.

Scoufos, Alice Lyle. *Shakespeare's Typological Satire: A Study of the Falstaff-Oldcastle Problem.* Athens: Ohio UP, 1979.

Sharpe, J. A. *Crime in Early Modern England 1550–1750.* Cambridge: Cambridge UP, 1984.

Shuger, Debora K. *Habits of Thought in the English Renaissance: Religion, Politics, and the Dominant Culture.* Berkeley: U of California P, 1990.

Siegel, Paul N. "Shakespeare and the Neo-Chivalric Cult of Honour." *Shakespeare in His Time and Ours.* Notre Dame: U of Notre Dame P, 1968. 122–62.

Simon, Joan. *Education and Society in Tudor England.* Cambridge: Cambridge UP, 1967.

Sinfield, Alan. *Faultlines: Cultural Materialism and the Politics of Dissident Reading.* Berkeley: U of California P, 1992.

Skinner, Quentin. *The Foundations of Modern Political Thought.* Cambridge: Cambridge UP, 1978.

Smith, Lacey Baldwin. *Treason in Tudor England: Politics and Paranoia.* Princeton: Princeton UP, 1986.

Stallybrass, Peter. "Shakespeare, the Individual, and the Text." *Cultural Studies.* Ed. Lawrence Grossberg, Cary Nelson, and Paula Treichler. New York: Routledge, 1992. 593–610.

Stallybrass, Peter, and Allon White. *The Politics and Poetics of Transgression.* Ithaca: Cornell UP, 1986.

Strier, Richard. "Faithful Servants: Shakespeare's Praise of Disobedience." *The Historical Renaissance: New Essays on Tudor and Stuart Literature and Culture.* Ed. Heather Dubrow and Richard Strier. Chicago: U of Chicago P, 1988. 104–33.

Strong, Roy. *The Cult of Elizabeth: Elizabethan Portraiture and Pageantry.* Berkeley: U of California P, 1977.

Taubin, Amy. "Objects of Desire." *Sight and Sound* ns 1.9 (1992): 8–13.

Taylor, Gary. "The Fortunes of Falstaff." *Shakespeare Survey* 38 (1985): 95–100.

Tennenhouse, Leonard. *Power on Display.* London: Methuen, 1986.

Tillyard, E. M. W. *The Elizabethan World Picture.* London: Chatto, 1943.

———. *Shakespeare's History Plays.* 1944. New York: Macmillan, 1947.

Traub, Valerie. *Desire and Anxiety: Circulations of Sexuality in Shakespearean Drama.* London: Routledge, 1992. 50–70.

Underdown, David. *Revel, Riot and Rebellion: Popular Politics and Culture in England 1603–1660.* Oxford: Clarendon, 1985.

Vale, Malcolm. *War and Chivalry: Warfare and Aristocratic Culture in England, France and Burgundy at the End of the Middle Ages.* Athens: Ohio UP, 1981.

Watt, Tessa. *Cheap Print and Popular Piety, 1550–1640.* Cambridge: Cambridge UP, 1991.

Webb, Henry J. "Elizabethan Soldiers: A Study in the Ideal and the Real." *The Western Humanities Review* 4.1 (1949–50): 19–33 and 4.2 (1950): 141–54.

Weimann, Robert. *Shakespeare and the Popular Tradition.* Baltimore: Johns Hopkins UP, 1978.

Weinstein, Rosemary. *Tudor London.* London: Museum of London, 1994.

Wells, Stanley, and Gary Taylor, eds. *William Shakespeare: The Complete Works.* Oxford: Clarendon, 1986.

Wikander, Matthew H. *The Play of Truth and State: Historical Drama from Shakespeare to Brecht.* Baltimore: Johns Hopkins UP, 1986.

Wiles, David. *Shakespeare's Clown: Actor and Text in the Elizabethan Playhouse.* Cambridge: Cambridge UP, 1987.

Williams, Glanmor. *Religion, Language and Nationality in Wales.* Cardiff: U of Wales P, 1979.

Willson, Robert F., Jr. "Recontextualizing Shakespeare on Film: *My Own Private Idaho.*" *Shakespeare Bulletin* 10.3 (1992): 34–37.

Wilson, John Dover. *The Fortunes of Falstaff.* Cambridge: Cambridge UP, 1943.

Woolf, D. R. *The Idea of History in Early Stuart England: Erudition, Ideology, and "The Light of Truth" from the Accession of James I to the Civil War.* Toronto: U of Toronto P, 1990.

Wrightson, Keith. *English Society, 1580–1680.* New Brunswick: Associated UP, 1982.

Wylie, J. H. *The Reign of Henry V.* 3 vols. Cambridge: Cambridge UP, 1914.

Yates, Frances A. *Astrea; The Imperial Theme in the Sixteenth Century.* London: Routledge, 1975.

ACKNOWLEDGMENTS

The First Part of King Henry the Fourth from *The Complete Works of Shakespeare*. Ed. David Bevington. 4th ed. Copyright © 1992 by HarperCollins, Inc. Reprinted by permission of HarperCollins, Inc.
Figure 1. Title page of *Henry IV, Part I*, 1598 (Trinity classmark Capell R. 20 [4]). By permission of the Master and Fellows of Trinity College, Cambridge.

CHAPTER 1
Figure 3. Facsimile of the title page of Hall's *The Union of Two Noble and Illustre Families of Lancastre and York*, 1548 edition, STC 12721. By permission of the Folger Shakespeare Library.
Figure 4. Facsimile of the first page of Hall's *The Union of Two Noble and Illustre Families of Lancastre and York*, 1548 edition, STC 12721. By permission of the Folger Shakespeare Library.
Figure 5. Illustration of Owen Glendower in Battle from *Beauchamp Pageants*. By permission of the British Library. Cott. Jul E IV Art. 6 folio 3v.

CHAPTER 3
Figure 6. Map of Kingdom of England from *Theatre of the Empire of Great Britain* by John Speed. STC 23041.2. By permission of the Folger Shakespeare Library.
Figure 7. Map of Middlesex from *Theatre of the Empire of Great Britain* by John Speed. STC 23041.2. By permission of the British Library.
Figure 8. "Agas" Map of London showing Eastcheap/Candlewick Street District. Reprinted with permission of Guildhall Library, Corporation of London.
Figure 9. Hugh Alley, *A Caveat for the City of London, Eastcheap Market*. Ms V.a.318. By permission of the Folger Shakespeare Library.
Figure 10. "The Lawes of Drinking" (1617). By permission of the British Library. Manuscript No. C40620.
Figure 11. "'Tis Merrie when Gossips meete." STC 21410.2. By permission of the Folger Shakespeare Library.
Figure 12. Tavern Scene from the English Shakespeare Company's *The Henrys*. Photograph by Laurence Burns.
Figure 13. Falstaff, Mistress Quickly, and Doll Tearsheet from Orson Welles's *Chimes at Midnight*. Museum of Modern Art/Film Stills Archive.
Figure 14. Mother Louse: an old-style aleshousekeeper" (c. 1650). By permission of the British Library. Prints and Drawings Acc. No. 48/9.11/483 in c.x.12.
Figure 15. Frontspiece from *The English Gentlewoman*. STC 3565. By permission of the Folger Shakespeare Library.
Welsh passages in *Henry IV, Part I* (3.1.190–227) from The Royal Shakespeare Company's 1964 production, prompt copy. Shakespeare Centre Library, Stratford-upon-Avon.

CHAPTER 4
Figure 16. *Catechism*, 1573, STC 18711. By permission of the Folger Shakespeare Library.
Figure 17. Henry IV and Hal from Orson Welles's *Chimes at Midnight*. Museum of Modern Art/Film Stills Archive.

CHAPTER 5

Figure 18. "Tilt with Lances." College of Arms, London, MS. M. 6, f. 56.

Figure 19. "Tilt with Arms." College of Arms, London, MS. M. 6, f. 62.

Figure 20. Portrait of Essex. By courtesy of the National Portrait Gallery, London.

Figure 21. "Coats of Arms of Garter Knights" from *Paradoxes of Defence* by George Silver (1599). STC 22554. By permission of the Folger Shakespeare Library.

Figure 22. Knighting at Shrewsbury from *Beauchamp Pageants*. By permission of the British Library. Cott. Jul. E IV Art. 6 f4v 1781.

Figure 23. Battle scene at Shrewsbury from *Beauchamp Pageants*. By permission of the British Library. Cott. Jul. E IV f4 8452449.

Figure 24. Map of Shropshire from *Theatre of the Empire of Great Britain* by John Speed. STC 23041.2. By permission of the British Library.

Figure 25. "Woodcut showing sword lengths" from *Paradoxes of Defence* by George Silver (1599). STC 22554. By permission of the Folger Shakespeare Library.

CHAPTER 6

Figure 26. Illustration of Sir John Oldcastle from *Brief Chronicle Concerning . . . Sir John Oldcastle* by John Bale (1544). STC 1276. By permission of the Folger Shakespeare Library.

Figure 27. *Kemps nine daies wonder* (1600). PN 2598 K6 1876. By permission of the Folger Shakespeare Library.

Figure 28. Frontispiece from *The Wits, I* (1662). W3218. By permission of the Folger Shakespeare Library.

Figure 29. Orson Welles as Falstaff in *Chimes at Midnight*. Museum of Modern Art/Film Stills Archive.

Figure 30. John Woodvine as Falstaff in the English Shakespeare Company's *The Henrys*. Photograph by Laurence Burns.

Figure 31. Illustration of Oldcastle's Martyrdom ("Burning of Lord Cobham") from *Acts and Monuments* by John Foxe, p. 542. STC 11222. By permission of the Folger Shakespeare Library.

Index

⇥⇤